THE
SCOTTISH
LAW
DIRECTORY

FEES
SUPPLEMENT
2009

 LexisNexis®

Members of the LexisNexis Group worldwide

United Kingdom	LexisNexis Butterworths, a Division of Reed Elsevier (UK) Ltd, Halsbury House, 35 Chancery Lane, London, WC2A 1EL and Robert Stevenson House, 1–3 Baxter's Place, Leith Walk, Edinburgh EH1 3AF
Argentina	LexisNexis Argentina, BUENOS AIRES
Australia	LexisNexis Butterworths, CHATSWOOD, New South Wales
Austria	LexisNexis Verlag ARD Orac GmbH & Co KG, VIENNA
Canada	LexisNexis Butterworths, MARKHAM, Ontario
Chile	LexisNexis Chile Ltda, SANTIAGO DE CHILE
Czech Republic	Nakladatelství Orac sro, PRAGUE
France	Editions du Juris-Classeur SA, PARIS
Hong Kong	LexisNexis Butterworths, HONG KONG
Hungary	HVG-Orac, BUDAPEST
India	LexisNexis Butterworths, NEW DELHI
Ireland	Butterworths (Ireland) Ltd, DUBLIN
Italy	Giuffrè Editore, MILAN
Malaysia	Malayan Law Journal Sdn Bhd, KUALA LUMPUR
New Zealand	LexisNexis Butterworths, WELLINGTON
Poland	Wydawnictwo Prawnicze LexisNexis, WARSAW
Singapore	LexisNexis Butterworths, SINGAPORE
South Africa	Butterworths SA, DURBAN
Switzerland	Stämpfli Verlag AG, BERNE
USA	LexisNexis, DAYTON, Ohio

© Reed Elsevier (UK) Ltd 2009

Published by LexisNexis Butterworths

A CIP Catalogue record for this book is available from the British Library.

ISBN for the complete set of volumes 9781 405 742 559

Typeset by Columns Design Ltd, Reading, Berkshire, England
Printed and bound by Polestar Wheaton's Ltd

Visit LexisNexis Butterworths at www.lexisnexis.co.uk

CONTENTS

Note: All fees are up to date to 30th June 2009

COST OF TIME

An Explanation of the Cost of Time

Prepared by the Remuneration Committee of the Law Society of Scotland

© THE LAW SOCIETY OF SCOTLAND — 1992, 2004

DEFINITIONS

Fee-earners Fee-earners are those members of staff in an office who perform legal work directly attributable and chargeable to specific clients as opposed to staff members such as typists, receptionists, clerks and juniors who perform general work which cannot be charged directly to any specific client and whose cost is recovered as a general overhead.

Notional salary In order to calculate the basic cost of time for each fee-earner, it is necessary to assign to each profit-sharing partner a 'notional salary'. This is not the anticipated income of the partner, but represents a reasonable level of professional remuneration before full account is taken of such factors as responsibility, commercial risk, pension provision, and interest on capital. The level of notional salary is a matter of judgment and may depend upon the age, experience, and ability of each partner.

Chargeable hours Chargeable hours are the hours in the year worked during normal working hours during which the fee-earner is actually and directly engaged on work for clients for which a charge will be made.

Hourly cost rate The hourly cost rate is the amount per chargeable hour which each fee-earner requires to earn in the course of undertaking work for clients in order to meet the firm's overheads and salaries (including notional salaries of profit-sharing partners).

Base factor The base factor is the cost of the time spent on a particular piece of business for a client. It is calculated from the hourly cost rates for the fee-earners involved.

Supplementary factor The supplementary factor is a supplement or weighting added in appropriate circumstances to the time cost of a piece of legal work in order to produce a fair and reasonable fee for such work after taking into account all the circumstances affecting it.

INTRODUCTION

In 1982 the Law Society of Scotland published the booklet *Time Costing and Time Recording*. This was intended for members and their firms as a particularly relevant guide to assist in the determination of the level of fees to be charged in order to enable the solicitor to meet his overheads and earn a reasonable rate of return for work which he does. In 1988 a revised edition of the time-costing section of the original booklet was produced under the title *The Cost of Time*.

The principles underlying the cost of time calculations remain valid and, in today's increasingly competitive conditions, of vital importance for realistic financial management. The Council considers that it is *essential* for each firm to be aware of the true cost of running its business. The Remuneration Committee has produced this updated edition of *The Cost of Time* to incorporate revised figures which more accurately reflect current financial conditions.

For any firm a key element in the calculation of its cost of time is the determination of the average number of *chargeable* hours worked per annum by each fee-earner. In order that realistic fees may be charged, it is also necessary to record the chargeable time spent by each fee-earner on each individual transaction. These requirements mean that some reasonably accurate form of time recording must be adopted. For the purpose of time costing, however, it is important to note that such a form of time recording need *not* be a complicated or costly procedure. There are various methods of time recording but these are not the subject of this article.

Time costing as management tool

Time costing and time recording are management tools by which a firm discovers on the basis of properly identified numbers of working hours the rates at which its fee-earners require to generate income to cover the firm's overheads and remunerate its staff and partners at actual or notional salary levels. Time costing identifies in terms of hourly cost rates the fees which fee-earners require to produce to meet such overheads and salaries. Time costs are obtained by applying a formula based on the known and estimated current costs of running the practice, assumed notional salaries for profit-sharing partners and an assumed number of chargeable hours during which each fee-earner performs legal work directly chargeable to clients.

The levels of notional salary and the number of chargeable hours which fee-earning staff can work each year are matters of judgment and experience but the concepts themselves are essential ingredients of the formula. Each year for its Cost of Time Survey the Council fixes notional salaries. (See the definitions above.)

By making the notional salaries for profit-sharing partners the same for all firms, it is possible to compare the costs of carrying out legal work in firms of vastly dissimilar compositions and activity and to establish average cost rates for the whole country. Chargeable hours are the hours in the year worked during normal working hours in which the fee-earner is actually and directly engaged on work for clients and which he would expect an auditor to allow as a charge in an account to a client. Such hours worked should not be confused with time spent on office administration, committee work, work for charitable or youth organisations, being on holiday, ill, and so on. By using these assumptions (notional salary and chargeable hours) along with the actual costs of an individual firm, an average rate per hour each fee-earner is obtained which, if charged to clients, would enable that firm to meet its overheads and pay its salary bills including the notional salaries of profit-sharing partners. It is recognised that in practice actual rates for individual hours will vary about the average. By applying the formula to the information as to their costs given by all firms, the average cost per hour for Scottish solicitors may be calculated.

Ability to compare costs

On the administration level, individual firms, by comparing their costs per hour against the hourly costs of other firms in the Scottish legal profession, can ascertain whether or not their operations are being performed economically and efficiently. If a firm's hourly cost for fee-earners is above the average, then it may be that changes require to be made in that firm to improve its efficiency and productivity. It may be that the firm is simply operating in a high-cost area where rents, rates and salaries are themselves above average, but, in any case, it is only healthy and sensible for a firm to know how it compares with others so that it may make positive decisions about its future and how it wishes to conduct and charge for its business.

Time recording

Time recording combined with carefully calculated hourly cost rates is essential to firms which wish to know the cost of performing certain work within their operation or the cost of running various departments in their office, the efficiency of those performing the work and how the fee income produced by such persons or departments compares with the operating cost. Moreover, the public expects the profession to be scientific about pricing its services and to be able to give sound answers when asked to justify its fees. If a solicitor develops a system which disciplines him into making a daily or weekly return of the time he has spent on clients' work, he becomes progressively less likely to omit an entry and more likely to charge properly at the completion of the work.

An efficient time-recording system will assist in arriving at a more accurate judgment of the number of chargeable hours. Experience of time recording suggests that the number of chargeable hours which can be worked in a full year *within normal working hours* varies between 700 and 1,200. This may seem surprisingly low but is based on the experience of those who have used such a system for a prolonged period.

Profitability and efficient charging

Time costing and recording show which areas are unprofitable, which areas are neglected and which areas are being charged promptly and properly. Solicitors are in business and must constantly consider how they can increase productivity so as to maintain earnings in the face of ever-increasing costs. The solicitor should be asking and should be able to answer such questions as — Is the right work being done by the right people? What are the different cost rates for the fee-earners doing the same job? Are too many simple jobs being done by partners at unnecessary expense? Are some people in the office overloaded and some not fully stretched? Are some taking much longer than others on the same type of work and, if so, why? What is the extent of the loss being made in certain areas of work within the office and why? Are there jobs which a solicitor can no longer economically undertake to do? If so, what are they? Are fee notes being prepared and sent out on the completion of the work, and if not, why not? Are the proper fees being charged? These are all questions of importance which require to be asked and answered. They will be answered by paying attention to time, by recording it carefully, and by analysing the information obtained with these management objectives in mind.

Time costing and fee charging

It is most important for the solicitor to keep clear in his mind the distinction between a cost rate, which can be ascertained from the method set out below, and the charge rate to be used when deciding on the fee for a piece of work. Applying the method enables the solicitor to calculate with considerable accuracy the average cost rate which each fee-earner must achieve to ensure that overheads, staff salaries and notional salaries for partners are covered. Inevitably, however, the hourly charge rate implicit in the fees actually rendered for various pieces of business will vary widely from the cost rate. For example, a fee-earner engaged in legal aid work will be limited in what he may charge by the legal aid tables even though that may represent a charge rate lower than the cost rate. In general business it will always be appropriate to consider in addition to time spent on a transaction the other aspects, such as the value, and this may bring out a fee substantially higher than the cost rate. For whatever reason, fees in some circumstances may not be charged or recovered in respect of time spent on a piece of business. What the firm must endeavour to ensure is that each fee-earner produces by way of fees at least the sum found by multiplying that fee-earner's chargeable hours by his hourly cost rate. If a fee-earner fails to achieve that target then the firm's net income will suffer. If, overall, the fee-earners fail to reach the target then the partners will not receive their notional salaries. Equally any fee-earner who exceeds his target figure will tend to increase the firm's profits and if the firm's overall target is exceeded then the profit-sharing partners will receive more than the notional salaries allotted to them.

In the modern situation, both competitive and regulated, no solicitor has complete control over what he can charge. Quite apart from the limitations imposed by the court tables, every client is entitled to have any fee taxed by an auditor unless there is a written fee-charging agreement between solicitor and client. In considering the fee to charge, the solicitor will always wish to have regard to the guidelines now incorporated into the *Table of Fees for General Business* as approved by the Council of the Law Society of Scotland. The solicitor will also require to have regard to market forces. However, the information obtained from a proper analysis of cost rates will permit the solicitor to assess whether a particular fee for a particular piece of business would in fact be profitable. The firm will naturally seek to devote as much of its fee-earners' time as possible to work where the charge rate implicit in a properly charged fee exceeds the cost rate of the fee-earner concerned. It will also wish as far as possible to exclude business where the fee which can be charged represents a charge rate lower than the fee-earner's cost rate.

Without the information about costs rates derived from the method set out below, the solicitor may have difficulty in assessing the fee which should be charged for any particular item of work. He will be unable to answer the key question — If I carry out this work at that fee, will that increase or reduce the profitability of my firm?

THE TIME COST METHOD

The objective

The method aims to determine hourly cost rates for each individual fee-earner or category of fee-earner by (1) estimating the total income which a firm must receive in the current year to recover its costs including the notional salaries of profit-sharing partners and (2) requiring each fee-earner to generate an appropriate part of this income.

Ascertaining firm's total costs

To the estimated total direct expenses of running the firm for the current year a hypothetical figure is added which represents the total amount of the notional salaries credited to each profit-sharing partner. To such estimated total expenditure are added further allowances to cover the cost of pension provision, interest on working capital and the effect of inflation.

The precise figures to be used for notional salaries are a matter of judgment. Each year the Remuneration Committee of the Law Society of Scotland, having regard to relevant earnings indices, identifies two notional salaries, which it considers reflect reasonable levels of remuneration for junior and senior profit-sharing partners respectively before full account is taken of such factors as responsibility, commercial risk, pension provision, and interest on capital.

The calculation of hourly cost rates should be recognised as an important basic tool for the financial management of a practice. By making realistic estimates of all components of the expense of running a practice, the total income necessary to meet this cost can be determined. Furthermore, by allocating to each fee-earner a share of the total overheads and by considering appropriate categories of fee-earners, it is possible to identify the profitability or otherwise of certain areas of work.

Compiling total-cost information

Certain necessary information should be extracted from the latest accounts of the firm. Other information relating to the current year, possibly including estimated values, is also needed. Ideally information should be assembled immediately after staff salaries for the current year have been decided. If this is not practicable, the calculations should include an appropriate allowance for estimated salary increases.

I Actual costs from firm's last set of accounts

From the *latest accounts* the following figures are required:

(1) The total actual expenses of the firm including any allowance for depreciation but excluding notional salaries.

(2) The specific amounts included in the figures of total actual expenses for —

  (a) staff salaries, pensions, employer's pension contributions and employer's National Insurance contributions for *all* employed members of staff including *salaried* partners and consultants,

  (b) rent of office premises, and

  (c) special provisions (i.e., any unusual item which will not be repeated in the current year).

(3) The amounts shown in the year-end balance sheet for —

  (a) the total of partners' balances, and

  (b) the gross value of office premises (if any).

II Current year actual figures or future estimates

For the *current year* the following values are required:

(1) The total amount (in respect of all employed members of staff including salaried partners and consultants) which will be paid by the firm as staff salaries, pensions, employer's pension contributions and employer's National Insurance contributions. If no further salary reviews will take place in the current year this will be a known figure. Otherwise an estimated value, which makes allowance for any anticipated salary increases should be used.

(2) The current *market rent* of the premises. If no rent is paid or if the actual rent is significantly below the market rent, estimate the market rent as accurately as possible.

(3) The annual salary in the current year for each *individual* employed fee-earner. If further salary reviews are to be made, this may require to be an estimated figure.

(4) For fee-earners who are employed part-time calculate the appropriate fraction of time spent by them on work compared to a full-time fee-earner. For example, two-fifths may be the appropriate fraction for a fee-earner who is employed two days per week.

III Summary

The total actual expenses of the firm from the latest accounts therefore emerge as follows:

(1) staff salaries, pensions, employer's pension contributions and employer's National Insurance contributions,

(2) rent,

(3) special provisions, and

(4) all other expenses.

Estimate of effect of inflation

In determining the 'all other expenses' component, allowance must be made for the effect of inflation. One possible approach would be to use an estimated percentage increase in an appropriate price index from the middle of the last accounting year to the middle of the current year. While it has been common in the past to use the Retail Price Index, recent experience suggests that the costs of running a legal firm may change at a different rate from the items included in the RPI, so that RPI inflation may provide only a rough estimate of the necessary allowance. Once a realistic percentage increase has been identified, the amount of all other expenses for the last accounting year should be increased by this percentage to estimate all other expenses for the current year.

Notional salaries, pension provisions and interest on capital

It is necessary to decide on the appropriate notional salaries and pension provisions for profit-sharing partners and to identify an appropriate figure for interest on the working capital of the firm. Each firm must use its own judgment as to the level or levels of notional salaries. In the following example, figures of £55,000, £55,000 and £50,000 have been selected for illustrative purposes; two partners are regarded as being senior and the other junior. A reasonable figure to cover the cost of pension provisions is $17\frac{1}{2}\%$ of the total notional salaries each year. An appropriate figure for interest on working capital can be obtained by applying the current base rate of one of the clearing banks to the total balances of the partners' accounts reduced by the deduction from such balances of the balance sheet value of any office premises (since this is already covered by estimating a realistic commercial rent for the premises).

Total current costs of firm

Thus the *total costs* of the firm for the current year can be calculated by adding:

(1) salaries, pensions, employer's pension contributions and employer's National Insurance contributions in respect of all employed members of staff including salaried partners and consultants (see II(1) above),

(2) rent of office premises (see II(2) above),

(3) special provisions (if any),

(4) total notional salaries for profit-sharing partners,

(5) pension provisions for profit-sharing partners,

(6) interest on working capital, and

(7) all other office expenses (see III(4) above as adjusted for inflation allowance).

Once these total costs for the current year have been identified a share of the costs must be allocated to each fee-earner in the firm and the appropriate number of chargeable hours for each fee-earner decided before hourly cost rates can be calculated.

Allocation of total current costs among fee-earners

Each fee-earner can be assigned directly his salary or notional salary, but there is no uniquely correct method of allocating between the different fee-earners the balance of total costs not expended on fee-earners' salaries. In practice, an acceptable method is to allocate one-half of this balance in proportion to salary and one-half on a per capita basis. The allocation of the total costs in this way is used in the following illustrative example.

The corresponding hourly cost rates on two alternative methods of allocating the balance of total costs, (i) all in proportion to fee-earners' salaries and none per capita, and (ii) all on a per capita basis and none in proportion to salary, are also shown in an Appendix.

Chargeable hours and hourly cost rates

If accurate time records are kept, the number of chargeable hours per annum for any one fee-earner will be known for the previous year and this can be used as an estimate of his number of chargeable hours for the current year. For each fee-earner his hourly cost rate is obtained by dividing his share of the total costs by his number of chargeable hours. If accurate time records are not kept, as accurate an estimate as possible of the annual number of chargeable hours for each fee-earner will require to be made.

Since the accuracy of estimating numbers of chargeable hours is of crucial significance to the determination of hourly cost rates, all firms are strongly urged to adopt time-recording methods (which need *not* be complex in nature) so that accurate financial information relating to their businesses is available.

If each fee-earner earns fees at his appropriate hourly rate for the total number of chargeable hours allocated to him, then after meeting all other expenses the amount available for distribution among the profit- sharing partners will be exactly sufficient to provide them with their notional salaries, pension provisions and interest on working capital.

Example of time cost method

A firm has seven fee-earners as follows:

profit-sharing partners	:	A, B and C
salaried partner	:	D
qualified assistant	:	E
unqualified assistant	:	F
trainee	:	G

The unqualified assistant is employed on a part-time basis, working mornings only. All the other fee-earners work full-time.

The firm's financial year ends on 31st December. The accounts for the last year have just become available and this calculation is being made in early March of the current year.

Following the procedure described above, the following figures from the *latest accounts* are extracted:

I   (1)   Total expenses of firm: £440,000

      (2)   (a)   Amount included in (1) for staff salaries and pensions and employer's pension and National Insurance contributions for all employed members of staff (including the *salaried* partner): £225,000

            (b)   Amount included in (1) for rent: £6,000 (this rental figure is significantly below a market rent for the premises. See II(2) below)

            (c)   Amount included in (1) for special provisions: NIL

      (3)   (a)   Total partners' balances: £180,000

            (b)   Balance sheet value of office premises: £30,000.

II   For the *current year* the following values apply:

      (1)   Total amount payable as staff salaries and pensions and employer's pension and National Insurance contributions for all employed members of staff (including the *salaried* partner): £240,000 (a review of salaries will be made at 30th June and this value allows for an estimated increase of £15,000 on the figure of £225,000 shown in the latest accounts)

      (2)   Rent (i.e., realistic market rent for premises): £20,000

      (3)   Annual salaries of employed fee-earners:

          D   :   £36,000

          E   :   £27,000

          F   :   £ 9,000 (part-time employee)

          G   :   £12,000

          (These values are estimated total salaries in the current year, after allowance is made for likely salary increases).

      (4)   Fraction for part-time fee-earner F: 0.5 (mornings only).

Allowance for inflationary growth in combined 'other expenses'

Current retail price inflation is between 2% and 3% per annum. The recent experience of the firm suggests, however, that its costs are increasing at a somewhat greater rate than the RPI. For purposes of this illustration it is considered that 3% is a reasonable estimate for the increase in 'other expenses'.

Special provisions for current year

These should cover any extraordinary items of a non-recurring nature. For this example no special provision is envisaged in the current year.

Chargeable hours per annum for fee-earners

A	:	1,000
B	:	1,000
C	:	1,000
D	:	1,000
E	:	1,200
F	:	600 (part-time employee)
G	:	800

Notional salaries for profit-sharing partners

A	:	£ 55,000
B	:	£ 55,000
C	:	£ 50,000
Total	:	£160,000

(*Note:* These values are purely illustrative. A and B are senior partners and so have higher notional salaries than C who is a junior partner.)

Calculation of hourly cost rates for fee-earners

From the above figures hourly cost rates for the current year can be calculated. First, the total current costs of the firm must be estimated. Thereafter, the overheads (i.e., estimated total costs less notional salaries for profit-sharing partners and actual salaries for other fee-earners) must be allocated between individual fee-earners and hourly cost rates obtained. The detailed calculations are illustrated below together with explanatory notes. It will be seen that individual hourly cost rates are identified in column (8) in the schedule below.

Estimated total current costs of firm

(1) Staff salaries and National Insurance contributions	£240,000
(2) Rent	£ 20,000
(3) Special provisions	NIL
(4) Notional salaries for profit-sharing partners	£160,000
(5) Pension provisions for profit-sharing partners	
(see note (*a*) below)	£ 28,000
(6) Interest on working capital — 4%	
of £180,000 – £30,000 (see note (*b*) below)	£ 6,000
(7) Other expenses (see calculation (*c*) below)	£215,270
Estimated total costs for current year	669,270

Notes

(a) Pension provision is taken as $17\frac{1}{2}\%$ of total notional salaries (i.e., $17\frac{1}{2}\%$ of 160,000).

(b) The working capital is obtained as the total amount of the partners' balance less the balance sheet value of the office premises, i.e., in this example, £180,000–£30,000 = £150,000. It is assumed that the base interest rate of the firm's bank is 4% per annum.

(c) Other expenses'

Total expenses (per latest accounts)		£440,000
Deduct amounts included in above for		
(i) Staff salaries, employers' N.I. (etc.)	£225,000	
(ii) Rent	£6,000	
(iii) Special provisions	NIL	
		£231,000
Total 'other expenses' (for latest year)		£209,000
Add increase for inflation 3%		
(see note (*d*) below)		£ 6,270
Estimated 'other expenses' for current year		£215,270

(d) As described above, for this example 3% is considered to be a realistic increase for inflation

Individual schedule for hourly cost rates

'Basic calculation', apportioning 50% of non-salary overheads per capita and 50% per salary.

Fee-earner	Fraction of full-time	Actual or notional salary (note (a))	Balance of estimated total costs		Share of total costs (3)+(4)+(5) (note (d))	Chargeable hours per annum	Hourly cost rate (6)÷(7)
			Proportion per capita (note (b))	Proportion per salary (note (c))			
(1)	(2)	(3)	(4)	(5)	(6)	(7)	(8)
A	1	£55,000	£32,713	£47,930	£135,643	1,000	£135.64
B	1	55,000	32,713	47,930	135,643	1,000	135.64
C	1	50,000	32,713	43,573	126,286	1,000	126.29
D	1	36,000	32,713	31,373	100,086	1,000	100.09
E	1	27,000	32,713	23,529	83,242	1,200	69.37
F	0.5	9,000	16,357	7,843	33,200	600	55.33
G	1	12,000	32,713	10,457	55,170	800	68.96
Total	6.5	£244,000	£212,635	£212,635	£669,270		

Two-tier system of hourly cost rates

By adding together the items in column (6) in respect of fee-earners A, B, C, D and E and dividing this by the total of the corresponding items in column (7) there is obtained an overall hourly cost rate for all qualified solicitors in the firm of $\frac{£580,900}{5,200} = £111.71$. Applying the same procedure to the items in column (6) and column (7) in respect of fee-earners F and G provides an overall cost rate for all unqualified fee-earners of $\frac{£88,370}{1,400} = £63.12$.

Notes

(a) For each fee-earner this is his current annual salary (or notional salary).

(b) The estimated total costs for the current year are £669,270 (as calculated on p. 7) and the total fee-earners' salaries for the current year are £244,000 (the total value of column (3)). The balance of the total costs is thus £669,270 – £244,000 = £425,270. One-half of this balance is £212,635 and this figure should be the total of both column (4) and column (5). The values to be given in column (4) (i.e., the 'per capita' allocation of one-half of the balance of the total costs) are proportional to the values in column (2) and total £212,635. Since the total of column (2) is 6.5, therefore in column (4) a full-time fee-earner is allocated an amount £212,635 ÷ 6.5 = £32,713 and a part-time fee-earner is allocated the appropriate fraction (in this case, one-half) of this amount. (To avoid rounding errors the part-time fee earner is allocated £16,357.)

(c) The values to be given in column (5) are proportional to the values in column (3) and total £212,635. Since the total of column (3) is £244,000, each fee-earner is thus allocated his salary multiplied by $\frac{£212,635}{244,000}$, i.e., 0.87145 times his salary. Thus 0.87145 x £55,000 = £47,930 etc. Minor adjustments of no significance are made to avoid rounding errors.

(d) Columns (4) and (5) are completed as described in (b) and (c) above. For each fee-earner column (6) is obtained by adding columns (3), (4) and (5).

A check that columns (4) and (5) have been completed correctly is provided by the fact that the total of column (6) equals the estimated total costs (i.e., £669,270).

Calculation of the zero-income hourly cost rate for profit-sharing partners

The estimated total costs for the current year (£669,270) include £160,000 for the notional salaries and £28,000 for pension provision for the profit-sharing partners. (See page 7 above.) When these two items, which together amount to £188,000, are deducted from the total costs the balance, which may be called the 'basic costs' for the year, is obtained as £481,270. This is the amount of fee-income which the firm will require simply to meet its current overheads (including a realistic rental for its premises) and to provide the profit-sharing partners with interest on their working capital. If each of the employed fee-earners (D, E, F and G) generates fee income at his hourly rate for the assumed number of chargeable hours, the employed fee- earners will generate total fee income of £271,698 (i.e. £100,086 + £83,242 + £33,200 +£55,170, as shown in column (6) of the table on page 8). This total falls short of the basic costs by an amount £209,572 (i.e. £481,270 – £271,698). This means that £209,572 is the amount of fee income which the profit-sharing partners must themselves generate simply to cover the balance of the overheads of the firm and to provide themselves with interest on their working capital – without, however, receiving any remuneration themselves.

The profit-sharing partners have between them a total of 3,000 chargeable hours per annum. Accordingly, the zero-income hourly cost rate for the profit-sharing partners is $\frac{£209,572}{3,000}$ i.e. £69.86.

Adjustment for administrative duties of one particular profit-sharing partner

Within the organisation of a legal firm one profit-sharing partner may, on a continuing basis, be recognised as devoting a significant fraction of his time to administrative duties with a consequential reduction in his available chargeable hours. To allow for this, an estimate is made of the fraction and this fraction of his notional salary is transferred from his direct salary costs to the overheads of the firm and shared out among all fee-earners on the basis adopted for distributing overheads. The remainder of his notional salary is attributed directly to him. His chargeable hours are reduced by the estimated fraction.

If, in the illustrative example above, partner A devoted 20% of his time to administration, his notional salary of £55,000 would be regarded as £44,000 (80%) directly attributable to him and £11,000 (20%) as additional overheads to be shared among all fee-earners. His chargeable hours would be reduced to 800 (80% of 1,000). The resulting calculation, on the basis that the balance of the estimated total costs is distributed half per capita and half per salary is shown below. For fee-earner A the entry in column (2) is now 0.8 and the entry in column (3) is £44,000. The total of column (2) becomes 6.3 and the total of column (3) becomes £233,000. The estimated total costs are £669,270 (as before). The balance of the estimated total costs is therefore £436,270. One-half of this figure is £218,135 and this amount should be the total of both column (4) and column (5).

The resulting hourly cost rates are shown in column (8). It will be noted that the hourly rates for partners A and B are still equal but that all hourly cost rates have been increased by the necessary inclusion of the additional £11,000 as overheads. On the basis of a two-tier system of cost rates, the hourly rates for qualified solicitors and for unqualified fee-earners are:

Solicitors (ABCDE) $\frac{£576,674}{5,000}$ = £115.33;

Unqualified fee-earners (FG) $\frac{£92,596}{1,400}$ = £66.14.

In this case the zero-income hourly cost rate for the profit-sharing partners is readily calculated to be £70.52.

Adjusted individual schedule for hourly cost rates

Alternative calculation allowing for additional administrative duties of one profit-sharing partner.

Fee-earner	Fraction of full-time	Actual or notional salary	Balance of estimated total costs		Share of total costs (3)+(4)+(5)	Chargeable hours per annum	Hourly cost rate (6)÷(7)
			Proportion per capita	Proportion per salary			
(1)	(2)	(3)	(4)	(5)	(6)	(7)	(8)
A	0.8	£44,000	£27,700	£41,193	£112,893	800	£141.12
B	1	55,000	34,625	51,491	141,116	1,000	141.12
C	1	50,000	34,625	46,810	131,435	1,000	131.43
D	1	36,000	34,625	33,703	104,328	1,000	104.33
E	1	27,000	34,624	25,278	86,902	1,200	72.42
F	0.5	9,000	17,312	8,426	34,738	600	57.90
G	1	12,000	34,624	11,234	57,858	800	72.32
Total	6.3	£233,000	£218,135	£218,135	£669,270		

Appendix

Allocation of the balance of the estimated total costs on alternative bases

As has been remarked on page 5, although each fee-earner can be assigned directly his salary (or notional salary) there is no uniquely correct way of allocating the balance of the estimated total costs among the fee-earners. In the illustrative example above one-half of this balance was allocated in proportion to salary and one-half on a per capita basis. This is generally considered to be an acceptable method.

In certain circumstances, however, it may be considered appropriate to apportion the balance of costs on an alternative basis. For example, a firm may wish to reduce (or increase) the differential in its cost rates across the range of fee-earners. A reduction in the spread of cost rates can be obtained by allocating the *entire* balance of the estimated total cost on a per capita basis. Conversely, the range of the cost rates will be increased, if the entire balance is allocated in proportion to salary.

The important point is the following. Whatever the basis of allocation of the balance of the total estimated costs, provided that the resulting cost rates are used consistently (for each fee-earner or for groups of fee- earners) and that each fee-earner works the assumed number of chargeable hours during which he generates fee income at his hourly rate, the income of the firm will be sufficient to provide the profit-sharing partners with their notional salaries, pension provision, and interest on capital.

In relation to the illustrative example previously discussed, revised calculation of the hourly cost rates on alternative bases are given below.

(a) Allocation of entire balance of estimated total costs per capita

As before, the balance of the estimated total cost is £425,270 (i.e., £669,270 – £244,000) (see note (*b*) on p. 8). This figure must now be the total of column (4) (see tabe on p. 11). Column (5) is left blank, since there is no allocation in proportion to salary. Since there are 6.5 fee-earners, each full-time fee-earner is allocated an amount £425,270 ÷ 6.5 = £65,426. The part-time fee-earner is allocated an appropriate fraction (in this case one-half) of this amount. In fact, to avoid rounding errors, one of the full-time fee-earners is allocated £65,427, but this is of no practical significance. For each fee-earner the appropriate value is entered in column (4) of the table below.

For each fee-earner columns (1), (2), (3) and (7) are the same as in the previous calculation. Column (4) is determined in the manner just described. Again a check on the calculations is provided by the fact that the total of column (6) is £669,270 (i.e., the estimated total costs).

The resulting hourly cost rates are given in column (8). It should be noted that the rates range from £69.52 (for the unqualified assistant F) to £120.43 (for the profit-sharing partners A and B). This range of cost rates should be compared with the range £55.33 to £135.64 obtained in the original calculation (p. 8).

On the basis of a two-tier system, the resulting hourly cost rates for qualified solicitors and for unqualified fee-earners are:

Solicitors (ABCDE) $\dfrac{£550,131}{5,200}$ = £105.79;

Unqualified fee-earners (FG) $\dfrac{£119,139}{1,400}$ = £85.10.

These rates should be compared with the values £111.71 and £63.12 previously obtained (see p. 8).

Individual schedule for hourly cost rates (alternative basis (a))

Alternative calculation: allocating *all* non-salary overheads *per capita*.

Fee-earner	Fraction of full-time	Actual or notional salary	Balance of estimated total costs		Share of total costs	Chargeable hours per annum	Hourly cost rate
			Proportion per capita	Proportion per salary	(3)+(4)+(5)		(6)÷(7)
(1)	(2)	(3)	(4)	(5)	(6)	(7)	(8)
A	1	£55,000	£65,426	—	£120,426	1,000	£120.43
B	1	55,000	65,426	—	120,426	1,000	120.43
C	1	50,000	65,427	—	115,427	1,000	115.43
D	1	36,000	65,426	—	101,426	1,000	101.43
E	1	27,000	65,426	—	92,426	1,200	77.02
F	0.5	9,000	32,713	—	41,713	600	69.52
G	1	9,000	65,426	—	77,426	800	96.78
Total	6.5	£244,000	£425,270	—	£669,270		

(b) Allocation of entire balance of estimated total costs in proportion to salary

The balance of the estimated total costs (i.e., £425,270) must now be the total of column (5) (see table on p. 12). Column (4) is left blank, since there is no allocation on a per capita basis. The entries in column (5) are proportional to those in column (3). Since the total of column (3) is £244,000, in column (5) each fee-earner is therefore

allocated his salary multiplied by $\dfrac{£425,270}{244,000}$ i.e., 1.74291 times his salary. Thus 1.74291 x £55,000 = £95,860 etc. (see column (5)). Minor adjustments, of no practical significance, are made to avoid rounding errors.

The remaining columns are completed as before and, again, a check is provided by the fact that the total of column (6) is £669,270 (i.e., the estimated total costs).

The range of the resulting cost rates should be noted. The hourly rates range from £41.14 (for the trainee and unqualified assistant) to £150.86 (for the profit-sharing partners A and B). On the basis of a two-tier system, the hourly cost rates for qualified solicitors and for unqualified fee-earners are:

Solicitors (ABCDE) $\dfrac{£611,669}{5,200}$ = £117.63;

Unqualified fee-earners (FG) $\dfrac{£57,601}{1,400}$ = £41.14.

Individual schedule for hourly cost rates (alternative basis (*b*))

Alternative calculation: allocating *all* non-salary overheads *per salary*.

Fee-earner	Fraction of full-time	Actual or notional salary	Balance of estimated total costs		Share of total costs (3)+(4)+(5)	Chargeable hours per annum	Hourly cost rate (6)÷(7)
			Proportion per capita	Proportion per salary			
(1)	(2)	(3)	(4)	(5)	(6)	(7)	(8)
A	1	£55,000	—	£95,860	£150,860	1,000	£150.86
B	1	55,000	—	95,860	150,860	1,000	150.86
C	1	50,000	—	87,145	137,145	1,000	137.14
D	1	36,000	—	62,745	98,745	1,000	98.74
E	1	27,000	—	47,059	74,059	1,200	61.72
F	0.5	9,000	—	15,686	24,686	600	41.14
G	1	12,000	—	20,915	32,915	800	41.14
Total	6.5	£244,000	—	£425,270	£669,270		

CONCLUSION

This article demonstrates to the profession the means of discovering the time cost of fee-earners within a solicitor's practice and emphasises the importance of time recording within that context. It tries to show how any practice using the time cost method can ascertain its own cost rates and thereby improve its efficiency and profitability by redeploying its resources and either abandoning or reorganising those activities which are losing money or not providing a satisfactory return. Application of the method to the firm's affairs will show the cost of running various departments within the office and will enable the firm to analyse these costs and thus combat inefficiency by redistributing the work, eradicating duplication and ending waste. It will provide scope for improvement within the office, highlight the practice's strengths and weaknesses and show the effectiveness or otherwise of the fee-earners within the organisation. It will enable firms to compare productivity within departments and may allow comparison with other firms of like size and similar business, both locally and nationally. It will clearly establish areas of profit and loss and point the direction in which the firm should be proceeding. It will make solicitors think commercially as well as professionally. It will provide a skill for the solicitor which it is very much in his interest to acquire.

A simple, straightforward system of charging fees, which is easily applied and readily understood, is a worthy objective. It is hoped that this article will assist the profession in achieving this objective.

COST OF TIME SURVEY

The outcome of the 2005 survey into the cost of time revealed that the hourly cost for running all solicitors' practices was £119.39.

Capital Adequacy

The Society Issues Guidance

These guidance notes are reprinted, with kind permission of the Law Society of Scotland, from the *Journal of the Law Society of Scotland*, September 1997.

WHY ISSUE GUIDANCE?

Following a period of consultation and discussion the Guarantee Fund Committee Working Party has recommended the production of guidance notes on the subject of capital adequacy in legal practices. The guidance notes are thought to be a valuable and confidential method of allowing solicitors to measure their own firm's financial standing. The problem of not having any standard to apply to the firm's balance sheet and profitability means that each firm is forced to make a personal decision about its level of reserves. This healthy independence has drawbacks in dealing with banks and other financial institutions because there are no opportunities for solicitors to make comparisons with other equivalent businesses.

The Society is increasingly aware of market pressures and tighter lending policies which combine to cause problems to practices where these questions have never been faced before. The guidance notes are intended to help the independent firm to check on its financial health. Help and advice are also available if the standard is not being met by the practice by telephoning 0131–226 7411 and asking for Leslie Cumming or one of his team.

The guidance notes are intended to help solicitors assess their financial position by fixing realistic values in areas where business optimism can traditionally overrule prudence. It is recognised that many solicitors have adopted conservative accounting policies in dealing with debtors and work in progress. If the test check produces a negative or poor balance sheet result because of these accounting policies—for example, cash- based accounts or nominal work in progress values—it is recommended that a realistic value be included in the adjusted figures to produce the most accurate result.

The trend of the business measured consistently and regularly can be a powerful management tool. In addition to testing earlier years' accounts, the ratios can be done quarterly or half-yearly to measure the rate of improvement or decline. The more regularly this check is carried out the better judgment can be made on the state of the practice's financial health.

BASIC STANDARDS

The standard measures are intended to look at balance sheet ratios and profitability. The results of the tests should be considered in three stages, action being taken or advice being sought depending on the results of your own firm's calculations.

1. Is the practice solvent?

If the method of calculating the value of your balance sheet as set out in Schedule 1 (p. 14) is applied to your firm's balance sheet, does the result show a negative value? If the answer is yes, some advice is required on how to deal with the situation. The position is serious and must not be ignored.

2. Are the capital reserves inadequate?

The standard measures should be applied to the balance sheet figures. If the firm is solvent but the partners' capital does not achieve 20% of the value of total assets, some action needs to be taken to strengthen the position. Again, advice should be sought if the remedial action to be taken is not obvious.

3. Profitability

The net profit before tax should be at least 20% of income.

If equity partners charge salaries to the profit and loss account these should be added to the profit.

If the results of the calculations do not achieve the 20% level on both balance sheet and profitability calculations the practice is considered to be in a marginal position. If this is the case, action must be taken to improve the ratios without delay. Again, advice should be sought if the remedial action is not obvious.

BENCHMARK TESTS

The two key tests are as follows.

1. Partnership solvency test/capital adequacy test

$$\frac{\text{Total partners' capital reserves}}{\text{Total gross partnership assets}} \times \frac{100}{1} = X\%$$

Where X% is less than 0% the partnership is deemed to be insolvent and advice must be sought at once. Where X% is a positive figure, this measures the extent of capital cover in the practice. A target of over 20% is thought to be prudent.

2. Profitability of the practice

$$\frac{\text{Total annual profits before tax}}{\text{Total annual income}} \times \frac{100}{1} = Y\%$$

where Y% is targeted to be more than 20%.

The higher the assets and profitability ratios are, the stronger the firm's position is. Results in the 0% to 20% range are a cause for concern and indicate a lack of financial stability. Well-run partnerships may be targeting annual profit ratios in excess of 30%.

Strong balance sheets will include a 50% partnership funding of working capital and at least a 30% stake in any properties owned by the partnership.

It will be helpful to check the equivalent figures in the previous two years to measure whether the position is stable, improving or declining. Any strong reduction in performance, even in a strong set of accounts, should be treated as an early warning.

If you are unable to meet the basic minimum standards as set out above you must take advice from another experienced solicitor, accountant or the Society. The smaller the ratios, the more urgent is the need for advice. Firms with losses or negative capital reserves must act at once.

SCHEDULE I

Benchmark tests—definitions and calculations

Step 1—Valuing assets

—Fixed assets. Using written-down values per your balance sheet is generally acceptable and will include properties, office equipment and cars.

—Goodwill. This asset is ignored for the purposes of the test.

—Work in progress. This must be prudently valued. Any estimate of work in progress must be capable of being confirmed by reference to time records or files and should not exceed three months' average fee income (excluding any element of profit).

—Debtors. The value must exclude any bad or doubtful debts. The total for this asset must be linked to the annual fee income. The test value should be the lesser of the actual total or three months' fee income.

—Cash. Actual value on deposits.

—Listed investments. Cost or market value. If the market value is the lesser figure this should be used.

The total assets value which has resulted from these calculations is used for the balance sheet ratio calculation.

Step 2—Calculating liabilities

This will include any bank overdrafts, loans or business mortgages or personal loans by third parties to the partnership or the sole practitioner in his or her business.

Also to be included are creditors of the business, hire-purchase liabilities on the firm's assets and income tax and VAT liabilities on the profit and income figures included in the accounts.

Step 3—Adjusted balance sheet partnership reserves

The partnership capital reserves which form the balancing figure to the revised balance calculations will reflect the balance sheet adjustments for the value of any assets which require to be written down or excluded as set out under Step 1 above. The gross balance sheet value of assets, including current assets and the net partnership capital figures devised from the adjusted balance sheet, are used in the calculation of the balance sheet ratios required under the benchmark tests 1 and 2. The resulting figure is used for the balance sheet ratio calculation.

Step 4—Calculating the ratio

The revised capital reserves figures (Step 3) should be divided by the adjusted gross assets (Step 1) and expressed as a percentage.

Step 5—Total income and net profit

The figures for total income should be as per the annual accounts and may include fees, commissions, interest earned or other income generated by the practice.

The balancing figure on the revised balance sheet is the partnership capital reserves. This will need to be reduced to allow for the reduction or writing off of any assets required under Step 1.

The figure of annual profit after all overheads and operating charges including finance and depreciation charges but before tax and partners' drawings is used for this calculation.

Step 6—Profitability in the practice

The calculation of the annual figure of profitability as a percentage is done by using the values set out in Step 5.

SCHEDULE II

Sample calculations—Example I

(a) Balance sheet adjustments

	Actual £	Test £
Goodwill	100,000	Nil
Property at valuation	120,000	120,000
Other fixed assets	60,000	60,000
	280,000	180,000
Current assets		
WIP	140,000	43,000
Debtors	45,000	45,000
Client account surplus (net)	1,000	1,000
	186,000	89,000
Total assets	466,000	269,000
Liabilities		
Trade creditors	15,000	15,000
Bank overdraft	50,000	50,000
Term loan	100,000	100,000
Total liabilities	165,000	165,000
Partners' capital	301,000	104,000
	466,000	269,000
Comparative ratios		
—capital/assets	65%	39%

Sample calculations—Example II

(a) Balance sheet adjustments

	Actual £	Test £
Goodwill	100,000	Nil
Fixed assets	60,000	60,000
	160,000	60,000
Current assets		
WIP	140,000	43,000
Debtors	45,000	45,000
Client account surplus (net)	1,000	1,000
	186,000	89,000
Total assets	346,000	149,000
Liabilities		
Trade creditors	25,000	25,000
Bank overdraft	100,000	100,000
Total liabilities	125,000	125,000
Partners' capital	221,000	24,000
	346,000	149,000
Comparative ratios		
—capital/assets	64%	16%

Example I (cont.)

(b) Profit and loss statement

	Actual	Actual
	£	£
Income—fees		280,000
—commissions		20,000
		300,000
Expenses		
Salaries	160,000	
Office expenses	30,000	
Car expenses	15,000	
Professional fees	7,500	
Miscellaneous	12,000	
Interest	6,000	
Depreciation	15,000	245,500
Net profit before tax		54,500
Profit ratio		18%

(c) Benchmark ratios

Balance sheet

$$\frac{\text{Capital}}{\text{Total assets}} \times \frac{100}{1} = X\%$$

$$\frac{£104,000}{£269,000} \times \frac{100}{1} = 38.7\%$$

Profitability

$$\frac{\text{Net profit}}{\text{Income}} \times \frac{100}{1} = Y\%$$

$$\frac{£54,500}{£300,000} \times \frac{100}{1} = 18.2\%$$

Note: The strong balance sheet is being threatened by a weak profit position. If this three-partner firm cannot live on the profits, a slow decline in the balance sheet position will result in a problem.

Example II (cont.)

(b) Profit and loss statement

	Actual	Actual
	£	£
Income—fees		280,000
—commissions		20,000
		300,000
Expenses		
Salaries	160,000	
Office expenses	42,000	
Car expenses	15,000	
Professional fees	7,500	
Miscellaneous	12,000	
Interest	5,000	
Depreciation	15,000	256,500
Net profit		43,500
Profit ratio		14.5%

(c) Benchmark ratios

Balance sheet

$$\frac{£24,000}{£149,000} \times \frac{100}{1} = 16.1\%$$

Profitability

$$\frac{£43,500}{£300,000} \times \frac{100}{1} = 14.5\%$$

Note: Balance sheet. The strong position shown per the actual balance sheet is undermined by the lack of property assets and by the high goodwill and work in progress figures.

Note: Profit and loss statement. Below-average results. The problems have to be addressed before they get worse. Profits must be improved and the balance sheet strengthened. There is very little leeway.

Sample calculation—Example III

(a) Balance sheet adjustments

	Actual	Test
	£	£
Goodwill	50,000	Nil
Fixed assets	15,000	15,000
	65,000	15,000
Current assets		
WIP	25,000	13,000
Debtors	15,000	15,000
Client account surplus (net)	1,000	1,000
	41,000	29,000
	106,000	44,000
Liabilities		
Trade creditors	10,000	10,000
Bank overdraft	35,000	35,000
	45,000	45,000
Partners' capital	61,000	(1,000)
	106,000	44,000
Comparative ratios		
capital/assets	58%	Negative

Note: The reduction in asset value has produced a negative capital value—insolvency on this benchmark test.

(b) Profit and loss statement

	£
Total income	85,000
Total expenses	
(not set out in detail)	65,000
Net profit	20,000

(c) Benchmark ratios

Balance sheet
  insolvent   Take advice on the position

Profitability

$$\frac{£20,000}{£85,000} \times \frac{100}{1} = 23.5\%$$

Note: This sole practitioner's profitability is acceptable but modest. How can the weak balance sheet be improved? Action to reduce borrowings and improve profit should be taken now.

All three examples show an original profit and capital reserve position which ranges from adequate to strong. Once the tests are applied inherent weaknesses in the figures become apparent. Complacency is dangerous in any of these circumstances.

SOLICITORS' FEES

Solicitors (Scotland) Act 1980 (c 46)

[Section 61A was inserted in the Solicitors (Scotland) Act 1980 (c 46) by s 36(3) of the Law Reform (Miscellaneous Provisions) (Scotland) Act 1990 (c 40) and took effect on 4th July 1992 (SI 1992 No 1599).]

Solicitors' fees

61A.—(1) Subject to the provisions of this section, and without prejudice to—

(a) section 32(1)(i) of the Sheriff Courts (Scotland) Act 1971; or

(b) section 5(h) of the Court of Session Act 1988,

where a solicitor and his client have reached an agreement in writing as to the solicitor's fees in respect of any work done or to be done by him for his client it shall not be competent, in any litigation arising out of any dispute as to the amount due to be paid under any such agreement, for the court to remit the solicitor's account for taxation.

(2) Subsection (1) is without prejudice to the court's power to remit a solicitor's account for taxation in a case where there has been no written agreement as to the fees to be charged.

(3) A solicitor and his client may agree, in relation to a litigation undertaken on a speculative basis, that, in the event of the litigation being successful, the solicitor's fee shall be increased by such a percentage as may, subject to subsection (4), be agreed.

(4) The percentage increase which may be agreed under subsection (3) shall not exceed such limit as the court may, after consultation with the Council, prescribe by act of sederunt.

Solicitors (Scotland) (Client Communication) Practice Rules 2005

Rules dated 24th March 2005, made by the Council of the Law Society of Scotland under section 34(1) of the Solicitors (Scotland) Act 1980 and approved by the Lord President of the Court of Session in terms of section 34(3) of the said Act.

Citation and Commencement

1. (1) These Rules may be cited as the Solicitors (Scotland) (Client Communication) Practice Rules 2005.
   (2) These Rules shall come into operation on 1st August 2005.

Definitions and Interpretation

2. (1) In these Rules, unless the context otherwise requires:–

"**the 1986 Act**" means the Legal Aid (Scotland) Act 1986;
"**the Act**" means the Solicitors (Scotland) Act 1980;
"**advice and assistance**" means advice and assistance as defined in section 6(1) of the 1986 Act to which Part II of the 1986 Act applies;
"**civil legal aid**" has the meaning given to it in section 13(2) of the 1986 Act;
"**client**" means a person who instructs a solicitor or to whom a solicitor tenders for business;
"**the Council**" means the Council of the Society;
"**legal aid**" has the meaning given to it in section 41 of the 1986 Act;
"**the Society**" means the Law Society of Scotland;
"**solicitor**" means a solicitor holding a practising certificate under the Act and includes a firm of solicitors and an incorporated practice; and
"**special urgency work**" has the meaning given to it in Regulation 18 of the Civil Legal Aid (Scotland) Regulations 2002.

(2) The Interpretation Act 1978 applies to the interpretation of these Rules as it applies to the interpretation of an Act of Parliament.

(3) The headings to these Rules do not form part of these Rules.

Provision of Information

3. A solicitor shall when tendering for business or at the earliest practical opportunity   upon   receiving instructions to undertake any work on behalf of a client, provide the following information to the client in writing:

   (a)   details of the work to be carried out on behalf of the client;

   (b)   save where the client is being provided with legal aid or advice and assistance, details of either–

      (i) an estimate of the total fee to be charged for the work, including VAT and outlays which may be incurred in the course of the work; or

      (ii) the basis upon which a fee will be charged for the work, including VAT and outlays which may be incurred in the course of the work;

   (c)   if the client is being provided with advice and assistance or legal aid–

      (i) where advice and assistance is being provided, details of the level of contribution required from the client, and

      (ii) where civil legal aid, special urgency work or advice and assistance is being provided, an indication of the factors which may affect any contribution which may be required from the client or any payment which may be required from property recovered or preserved;

   (d)   the identity of the person or persons who will principally carry out the work on behalf of the client; and

   (e)   the identity of the person whom the client should contact if the client becomes concerned in any way with the manner in which the work is being carried out.

Exceptions

4. (1) Where a client regularly instructs a solicitor in the same type of work, he need not be provided with the information set out in rule 3 in relation to a new instruction to do that type of work, provided that he has previously been supplied with that information in relation to a previous instruction to do that type of work and is informed of any differences between that information and the information which, if this paragraph (1) did not apply, would have been required to be provided to him in terms of rule 3.

(2) Where there is no practical opportunity for a solicitor to provide the   information set out in rule 3 to a client before the conclusion of the relevant work for that client then that information need not be provided to that client.

(3) Where a client is a child under the age of 12 years then the information set out in rule 3 need not be provided to that client.

Waiver

5. The Council shall have the power to waive any of the provisions of these Rules either generally or in any particular circumstances or case, provided that such waiver may be made subject to such conditions as the Council may in its discretion determine.

Professional Misconduct

6. Breach of these Rules may be treated as professional misconduct for the purposes of Part IV of the Act (Complaints and Disciplinary Proceedings).

Repeals

7. The Solicitors (Scotland) (Client Communication) (Residential Conveyancing) Practice Rules 2003 are hereby revoked.

Guidance Notes on the Solicitors (Scotland) (Client Communication) Practice Rules 2005

The above Practice Rules will come into force on 1st August 2005. They have been made under Section 34 of the Solicitors (Scotland) Act 1980. The Rules have been approved by the Lord President. They require solicitors to provide information in writing to clients about certain specific matters namely

(a) Details of the work to be done;

(b) An estimate of the total fee including VAT and outlays or the basis upon which the fee will be charged, including VAT and outlays;

(c) Details of any contribution towards Legal Advice & Assistance or Legal Aid and details of the effect of preservation or recovery of any property if relevant;

(d) Who will do the work;

(e) Who the client(s) should contact if they wish to express concern about the manner in which the work is being carried out.

With certain exceptions (see below) this information must be provided at the earliest practicable opportunity upon receiving instructions. It does not have to be contained in a single letter to comply with the Rule, but unless there is a particular reason why it cannot be done in a single letter, there is a risk of omitting certain of the information if it is done in different stages.

If a firm is tendering for new business, either from an established client or a new client, the information can be given when tendering. If it is, and the tender is accepted, there is no need to repeat the information subsequently.

It is quite in order to give the client more information than is necessary to comply with the Rule, but the Rule sets out the minimum requirement.

Exceptions

There are only 3 automatic exceptions to the Rule:

First where a client regularly instructs a solicitor in the same type of work, the information does not have to be provided repeatedly but it will have to be provided on at least the first occasion, and it will have to be updated if there is a change in the information previously provided. Client means any person who instructs a solicitor, which includes lenders as well as individual purchasers or borrowers. If the fee for the lenders work is included in the fee to be charged to the individual purchaser or borrower, that is all that need be said about fees in the information given to the lender.

The second exception is where there is no practical opportunity for the information to be provided before the conclusion of the work. That means where the work is completed at a single meeting. For example a client who may be about to go on holiday and wishes to make a will may have instructions implemented immediately and sign the will at the first meeting. It will not be necessary for solicitors receiving instructions on an agency basis to provide information to the principle solicitor acting, although it is prudent to have an agreed basis of charging for agency work.

The third exception is children under the age of 12. If the client is the child's parent or guardian (for example in a personal injury case) the information will still need to be provided.

Fees

With the withdrawal of the Society's Table of Fees, it will not be appropriate to refer to fees recommended by the Society. If, for example in executries, the file is to be feed by an external fee charger such as an Auditor or Law Accountant, the basis on which the external fee charger will be asked to fee up the file needs to be stated to the client needs to be included. If hourly rates are reviewed during the course of the work, the clients will need to be told about any increase or there is a risk that firms will be unable to charge the higher rate.

As well as the hourly rate any commission which will be charged on capital transactions or on the sale of a house would need to be included. In any matter where the account is being rendered on a detailed basis, the charges for letters, drafting papers, etc will need to be expressed as well as the hourly rate. They can be in a separate schedule referred to in the basic letter.

In terms of Section 61A of the Solicitors (Scotland) Act 1980, where a solicitor and client enter into a written fee charging agreement it is not competent for the Court to refer any dispute in the matter to the Auditor for taxation. Where an hourly rate is specified, and that is accepted in writing, the client would still be entitled to seek a taxation, but would not be able to challenge the agreed hourly rate at such a taxation.

It should be made clear at the outset whether the fee quoted is the fee to be charged or only an estimate. If it is not stated as an estimate and the client accepts it in writing, that could be regarded as a written fee charging agreement under Section 61A of the 1980 Act. If a client has been given an estimate, they should be advised in writing when it becomes known that the cost of work will materially exceed such an estimate. It is good practice to advise the client when the limit of the original estimate is being approached.

Information should be clear, and terms with which the client may not be familiar such as "outlays" may need to be briefly explained. If a payment to account is required, that should be clearly stated, as well as the consequences of failing to pay it on time. For example in a Court matter if the client is advised that failure to make a payment to account will lead to the solicitor withdrawing from acting, there is unlikely to be a professional difficulty about withdrawing from acting in compliance with that. However if the consequence is not stated, and the proof is approaching, solicitors could be vulnerable to a complaint if they withdraw at a late stage to the potential prejudice of the client.

If the clients costs are to be paid by a third party such as a Trade Union or Legal Expenses Insurer, specific details of the basis of charging do not need to be set out when writing to the individual client but any part of the fee which that client may be asked to pay should be included— such as a success fee in a speculative action.

While it is not strictly necessary to comply with the Practice Rule, it is also strongly recommended that any potential liability for other people's costs should be explained. This would include a tenant's liability to meet a landlord's fees as well as the potential liability for expenses in a Court action.

Executries and Trusts

In executries where the only executors are solicitors in the firm, the information should be provided to the residuary beneficiaries, as they will be meeting the fees out of there shares of the residue. In other executries the information should be provided to the non solicitor executors.

Legal Aid

It is not necessary to comply with the Rule for solicitors to explain the Statutory payment Scheme to Legal Aid clients in relation to Legal Advice & Assistance or Legal Aid. Solicitors may wish to forward copies of leaflets provided by SLAB to clients in receipt of Advice & Assistance or Legal Aid. If solicitors do wish to communicate detailed advice to clients about Advice & Assistance or Legal Aid, including for example the clients requirement to report changes in circumstances, that is optional and may be done in a separate letter.

Waivers

The Rules give the Council power to grant a waiver which may be subject to conditions. In practice this power will be delegated to the Professional Practice Committee, which meets monthly except in August. A specific reason should be given for seeking the waiver, and the request is likely to be continued for such information if it is not provided initially.

Failing to Comply with the Rules

The Rules state in terms that a breach may be treated as professional misconduct. For the avoidance of doubt, an occasional failure to send the information required, or sending information which does not fully comply with the Rule, is likely to be dealt with in the first instance as a matter for professional practice guidance. However regular failure to provide the information required may lead to a formal complaint about the solicitor's conduct, which may be categorised as professional misconduct.

Practice Guideline: Form of Accounts and Taxation

1. Accounts – preparation and presentation

(a)   The form in which a solicitor presents an account is a matter for the solicitor's personal preference but if the person liable to pay requires details, the solicitor must give a narrative or summary sufficient to indicate the nature and the extent of the work done. If a breakdown is requested the solicitor should give such information as can readily be derived from the records, such as the total recorded time spent, the number and length of meetings, the number of letters and of telephone calls. No charge may be made for preparing the note of fee or for the provision of such information. However if having been given such information the party paying insists on a fully itemised account, the cost of preparing that may be charged to them.

(b)   If the paying party is still dissatisfied the solicitor must inform them of the availability of taxation by an auditor and the procedure. If the payer requests a taxation without a fully itemised account, the solicitor may have such an account prepared at his own expense. That full account may be submitted for taxation even if it is for a greater amount than the original note of fee.

(c)   A solicitor may submit the file to an auditor of court or a law accountant for assessment of the fee, but it is stressed that a unilateral reference of this kind does not constitute a taxation. Such assessment of a fee must never be represented as a taxation or as having any official status. The fee for such a reference is not chargeable to the party paying unless that has been included in the terms of business intimated to the client at the outset. If the note of fee is disputed, the solicitor must advise of the right to taxation as above, although the fee note should be taxed by a different auditor from the one who prepared it.

2. Taxation

(a) Remit

The essence of taxation is that it proceeds upon either a remit by the court or a joint reference by both the solicitor and the party paying, including non-contentious cases in (c) below.

(b) Disputed accounts

When the party paying, whether client or third party, requires that the solicitor's account be taxed, the solicitor cannot refuse to concur in the reference unless the solicitor and client have entered into a written fee charging agreement in which the actual fee has been agreed, as opposed to the basis on which the fee is to be charged. The solicitor must forthwith submit the file and all relevant information including a note of fee or detailed account to the auditor. It is for the auditor to determine the procedure to be followed. In normal cases this will be a diet of taxation which should be intimated to the client by the solicitor. Evidence of: such intimation, which may be by ordinary first class post, may be required if the client does not appear at the diet. If either of the parties wishes to make written submissions, the auditor will ensure that each party is fully aware of the other's representations.

(c) Non-contentious cases

Taxation is necessary by law and in practice in certain circumstances. The accounts of a solicitor acting for:

an administrator of a company under the Insolvency Acts;

a liquidator appointed by the court;

a creditors' voluntary liquidator;

a trustee in bankruptcy;

a judicial factor;

curators of all kinds must be taxed.

A solicitor who acts:

as an administrator of a client's funds under a power of attorney where the granter is incapable;

in a representative capacity, e.g. a sole executor should have a fee note prepared or taxed by an auditor of court. A certificate by an auditor is appropriate in these cases.

A solicitor who is a co-executor with an unqualified person must not make a unilateral reference to the auditor for taxation. Such a reference needs the concurrence of the other executor. The auditor may require intimation of the taxation to any other party with an interest in the residue of the estate.

(d) Style of remit

A formal remit may be in the following form:

(place) (date). I, AB as Executor of the late CD and we, Messrs E & F, Solicitors to the Executor, hereby request the Auditor of the (Sheriff Court of /Court of Session) to tax the remuneration due and payable to the Solicitors for their whole work and responsibility in connection with (matter).

Signed: AB, E & F

This, however, is not essential; all the auditor requires is to be satisfied that the client is concurring in the request for taxation and accepting that it will be binding. It is often in practice a matter of agreement reached at an early meeting between solicitor and client. Any reasonable record of such an agreement having been reached will be sufficient for the auditor.

3. Expenses of taxation

The auditor will usually charge a fee for the taxation. It may be 3% or 4% of the amount of the account after taxation and may attract VAT. Any award of expenses of the taxation - not only the auditor's fee but also the time and expenses of parties attending - is wholly within the discretion of the auditor. If the matter is settled within the seven days preceding the diet of taxation the auditor may still charge a proportion of his fee, not exceeding 50%, at his discretion.

Solicitor and Client Accounts in the Sheriff Court

Act of Sederunt (Solicitor and Client Accounts in the Sheriff Court) 1992

(SI 1992 No 1434)

Remit of solicitor's account for taxation

2.—(1) Subject to section 61A(1) of the Solicitors (Scotland) Act 1980, the sheriff may remit the account of a solicitor to his client to the Auditor of Court for taxation.

(2) Where a remit is made under sub-paragraph (1)—

(a) the solicitor shall, within 21 days, lodge with the Auditor the account, which shall be in such form as shall enable the Auditor readily to establish the nature and extent of the work done to which the account relates and shall detail the outlays incurred by the solicitor, together with such supporting material as is necessary to vouch the items on the account;

(b) the Auditor shall assign a diet of taxation not earlier than fourteen days from the date he receives the account and intimate that diet forthwith to the solicitor;

(c) the solicitor shall then, forthwith, send by first class recorded delivery post a copy of the account lodged to the client (if such a copy has not already been sent to the client) and give notice in terms of Form A in the Schedule to this Act of Sederunt, of the date, time and place of the taxation to the client;

(d) the Auditor shall report his decision to the court and shall forthwith send a copy of his report to the solicitor and to the client; and

(e) the solicitor or the client may, provided that he or his representative has attended at the diet of taxation, lodge a note of reasoned objections to the report within seven days from the date of the report, and the sheriff shall dispose of such objections in a summary manner, with or without answers.

Taxation of litigation account

3.—(1) Where the Auditor taxes the account of a solicitor to his client in respect of the conduct of a litigation on behalf of the client, he—

(a) shall allow a sum in respect of such work and outlays as have been reasonably incurred;

(b) shall allow in respect of each item of work and outlay such sum as may be fair and reasonable having regard to all the circumstances of the case;

(c) shall, in determining whether a sum charged in respect of an item of work is fair and reasonable, take into account—

(i) the complexity of the litigation and the number, difficulty or novelty of the questions raised;

(ii) the skill, labour, specialised knowledge and responsibility involved;

(iii) the time spent on the item of work and on the litigation as a whole;

(iv) the number and importance of any documents or other papers prepared or perused without regard to length;

(v) the place where and the circumstances (including the degree of expedition required) in which the solicitor's work or any part of it has been done;

(vi) the amount or value of any money or property involved in the litigation; and

(vii) the importance of the litigation or its subject matter to the client;

(d) shall presume (unless the contrary is demonstrated to his satisfaction) that—

(i) an item of work or outlay was reasonably incurred if it was incurred with the express or implied approval of the client;

(ii) the fee charged in respect of an item of work or outlay was reasonable if the amount of the fee or the outlay was expressly or impliedly approved by the client; and

(iii) an item of work or outlay was not reasonably incurred, or that the fee charged in respect of an item of work or outlay was not reasonable if the item of work, outlay or fee charged, was unusual in the circumstances of the case, unless the solicitor informed the client prior to carrying out the item of work or incurring the outlay that it might not be allowed (or that the fee charged might not be allowed in full) in a taxation in judicial proceedings between party and party; and

(e) may disallow any item of work or outlay which is not vouched to his satisfaction.

SCHEDULE   Paragraph 2(2)(c)

Notice to Client Intimating Diet of Taxation of Solicitors' Account

FORM A

To: (*name and address*)

Date: (*date of posting*)

(*Name of solicitors*), Applicant v. [CD]. Respondent.

Case Number:

1.   We enclose a copy of the solicitors' account in respect of which we seek payment.

2.   The sheriff has remitted the account to the Auditor of Court for taxation (assessment).

3.   The taxation hearing will take place at (*place*) Sheriff Court (*address*), in (*location*) on (*date and time*).

4.   If you wish to object to any part of the account you must appear or be represented at the taxation hearing.

5.   You will lose any right to object to the account if you do not appear or are not represented at the taxation hearing.

(*signed*)

Solicitors [for Pursuers]

(*address*)

IF YOU ARE UNCERTAIN ABOUT THE EFFECT OF THIS NOTICE CONSULT A SOLICITOR

Table of Fees of Solicitors in the Court of Session

Act of Sederunt (Rules of the Court of Session) 1994

(SI 1994 No 1443)

[Chapter 42 is printed as amended by:

Act of Sederunt (Rules of the Court of Session 1994 Amendment No 2) (Fees of Solicitors) 1995 (SI 1995 No 1396);

Act of Sederunt (Rules of the Court of Session Amendment No 1) (Fees of Solicitors) 1996 (SI 1996 No 237);

Act of Sederunt (Rules of the Court of Session Amendment No 3) (Miscellaneous) 1996 (SI 1996 No 1756);

Act of Sederunt (Rules of the Court of Session Amendment) (Miscellaneous) 1998 (SI 1998 No 890);

Act of Sederunt (Rules of the Court of Session Amendment No 3) (Fees of Solicitors) 1998 (SI 1998 No 2674);

Act of Sederunt (Rules of the Court of Session Amendment No 7) (Miscellaneous) 1999 (SSI 1999 No 109) which came into force on 29th October 1999;

Act of Sederunt (Rules of the Court of Session Amendment No 4) (Miscellaneous) 2001 (SSI 2001 No 305) which came into force on 18th September 2001;

Act of Sederunt (Rules of the Court of Session Amendment No 5) (Fees of Solicitors) 2001 (SSI 2001 No 441) which came into force on 1st January 2002;

Act of Sederunt (Rules of the Court of Session Amendment) (Fees of Solicitors, Shorthand Writers and Witnesses) 2002 (SSI 2002 No 301) which came into force on 1st July 2002;

Act of Sederunt (Rules of the Court of Session Amendment) (Fees of Solicitors) 2003 (SSI 2003 No 194) which came into force on 1st April 2003;

Act of Sederunt (Rules of the Court of Session Amendment No 3) (Fees of Solicitors) 2004 (SSI 2004 No 151) which came into force on 4th May 2004;

Act of Sederunt (Rules of the Court of Session Amendment No 4) (Fees of Solicitors) 2006 (SSI 2006 No 294) which came into force on 15th July 2006;

Act of Sederunt (Rules of the Court of Session Amendment) (Fees of Solicitors) 2008 (SSI 2008 No 39) which came into force on 15th February 2008.]

CHAPTER 42

TAXATION OF ACCOUNTS AND FEES OF SOLICITORS

PART I — TAXATION OF ACCOUNTS

Remit to the Auditor

42.1.—(1) Where expenses are found due to a party in any cause, the court shall —

(a) pronounce an interlocutor finding that party entitled to expenses and, subject to rule 42.6(1) (modification of expenses awarded against assisted persons), remitting to the Auditor for taxation; and

(b) without prejudice to rule 42.4 (objections to report of the Auditor), unless satisfied that there is special cause shown for not doing so, pronounce an interlocutor decerning against the party found liable in expenses as taxed by the Auditor.

(2) Any party found entitled to expenses shall —

(a) lodge an account of expenses in process not later than four months after the final interlocutor in which a finding in respect of expenses is made or within such further period as the court may allow on special cause shown;

(aa) if he has failed to comply with sub-paragraph (a), lodge such account at any time with leave of the court but subject to such conditions (if any) as the court thinks fit to impose; and

(b) give written intimation of the lodging of the account, and send a copy of it, to the party found liable to pay those expenses.

(3) Rule 4.6(1) (intimation of steps of process) shall not apply to the lodging of an account of expenses.

Diet of taxation

42.2.—(1) On receipt of the process of the cause, the Auditor shall —
- (a) fix a diet for taxation; and
- (b) intimate the diet to —
  - (i) the party found entitled to expenses; and
  - (ii) the party found liable in expenses.

(2) At the diet of taxation, the party found entitled to expenses shall make available to the Auditor all vouchers, documents, drafts or copies of documents sought by the Auditor and relevant to the taxation.

Report of taxation

42.3.—(1) The Auditor shall —
- (a) prepare a report of the taxation of the account of expenses, stating the amount of expenses as taxed;
- (b) transmit the process of the cause and the report to the appropriate department of the Office of Court; and
- (c) on the day on which he transmits the process, intimate that fact and the date of his report to each party to whom he intimated the diet of taxation.

(2) The party found entitled to expenses shall, within 7 days after the date of the report prepared under paragraph (1), exhibit the taxed account, or send a copy of it, to the party found liable to pay the expenses.

Objections to report of the Auditor

42.4.—(1) Any party to a cause who has appeared or been represented at the diet of taxation may state any objection to the report of the Auditor by lodging in process a note of objection within 14 days after the date of the report.

(2) A party lodging a note of objection shall —
- (a) intimate a copy of the note to any other party who appeared or was represented at the diet of taxation and to the Auditor;
- (b) apply by motion for an order —
  - (i) allowing the note to be received; and
  - (ii) ordaining the Auditor to state by minute, within 14 days after intimation under sub-paragraph (c), the reasons for his decision in relation to the items to which objection is taken in the note; and
- (c) intimate forthwith to the Auditor a copy of the interlocutor pronounced on a motion under sub-paragraph (b).

(3) After the minute of the Auditor has been lodged in process, the party who lodged the note of objection shall, in consultation with any other party wishing to be heard, arrange with the Keeper of the Rolls for a diet of hearing before the appropriate court.

(4) At the hearing on the note of objection, the court may —
- (a) sustain or repel any objection in the note or remit the account of expenses to the Auditor for further consideration; and
- (b) find any party liable in the expenses of the procedure on the note.

(5) In the event of an objection being sustained, the court shall ordain the Auditor to amend his report to give effect to the decision of the court.

Modification or disallowance of expenses

42.5.—(1) —In any cause where the court finds a party entitled to expenses, the court may direct that expenses shall be subject to such modification as the court thinks fit.

(2) Where it appears to the Auditor that a party found entitled to expenses —
- (a) was unsuccessful, or
- (b) incurred expenses through his own fault,

in respect of a matter which would otherwise be included in those expenses, the Auditor may disallow the expenses in respect of that matter in whole or in part.

Modification of expenses awarded against assisted persons

42.6.—(1) In a cause in which the court finds an assisted person liable in expenses, the court may, on the motion of any party to the cause, instead of remitting the account of expenses of the party in whose favour the finding is made to the Auditor for taxation, determine to what extent the liability of the assisted person for such expenses shall be modified under —

    (a)   section 2(6)(e) of the Legal Aid (Scotland) Act 1967; or

    (b)   section 18(2) of the Legal Aid (Scotland) Act 1986.

(2) Where a remit is made to the Auditor for taxation in a cause in which an assisted person is found liable in expenses, an application for modification under a statutory provision mentioned in paragraph (1) may be made by motion within 14 days after the date of the report of the Auditor made under rule 42.3 (report of taxation).

Taxation of solicitors' own accounts

42.7.—(1) Subject to section 61A(1) of the Solicitors (Scotland) Act 1980, the court may remit to the Auditor the account of a solicitor to his client —

    (a)   where the account is for work done in relation to a cause in the Court of Session, on the motion of the solicitor or the client; or

    (b)   in an action in which the solicitor or his representative sues the client for payment of the account.

(2) A motion under paragraph (1)(a) may be enrolled notwithstanding that final decree in the cause has been extracted.

(3) The account referred to in paragraph (1) shall —

    (a)   be in such form as will enable the Auditor to establish the nature and extent of the work done to which the account relates;

    (b)   detail the outlays incurred by the solicitor; and

    (c)   be accompanied by such supporting material as is necessary to vouch the items in the account.

(4) The Auditor shall —

    (a)   fix a diet of taxation not earlier than 14 days after the date on which he receives the account; and

    (b)   intimate the diet to the solicitor.

(5) On receipt of intimation of the diet of taxation from the Auditor, the solicitor shall forthwith send to his client by registered post or the first class recorded delivery service —

    (a)   a copy of the account to be taxed;

    (b)   a copy of the interlocutor remitting the account; and

    (c)   a notice in Form 42.7 of the date, time and place of the diet of taxation.

(6) In taxing an account remitted to him under paragraph (1), the Auditor —

    (a)   shall allow a sum in respect of such work and outlays as have been reasonably incurred;

    (b)   shall allow, in respect of each item of work and outlay, such sum as may be fair and reasonable having regard to all the circumstances of the case;

    (c)   shall, in determining whether a sum charged in respect of an item of work is fair and reasonable, take into account any of the following factors:–

        (i)   the complexity of the cause and the number, difficulty or novelty of the questions raised;

        (ii)   the skill, labour, and specialised knowledge and responsibility required, of the solicitor;(iii) the time spent on the item of work and on the cause as a whole;

        (iv)   the number and importance of any documents prepared or perused.

        (v)   the place and circumstances (including the degree of expedition required) in which the work of the solicitor or any part of it has been done;

        (vi)   the importance of the cause or the subject-matter of it to the client;

        (vii)   the amount or value of money or property involved in the cause; and

        (viii) any informal agreement relating to fees;

    (d)   shall presume (unless the contrary is demonstrated to his satisfaction) that —

(i) an item of work or outlay was reasonably incurred if it was incurred with the express or implied approval of the client;

(ii) the fee charged in respect of an item of work or outlay was reasonable if the amount of the fee or the outlay was expressly or impliedly approved by the client; and

(iii) an item of work or outlay was not reasonably incurred, or that the fee charged in respect of an item of work or outlay was not reasonable if the item of work, outlay or fee charged, was unusual in the circumstances of the case, unless the solicitor informed the client before carrying out the item of work or incurring the outlay that it might not be allowed (or that the fee charged might not be allowed in full) in a taxation in a cause between party and party; and

(e) may disallow any item of work or outlay which is not vouched to his satisfaction.

(7) The Auditor shall —

(a) prepare a report of the taxation of the account remitted to him under paragraph (1);

(b) transmit his report to the appropriate department of the Office of Court; and

(c) send a copy of his report to the solicitor and the client.

(8) The solicitor or his client may, where he or a representative attended the diet of taxation, state any objection to the report of the Auditor; and rule 42.4 (objections to report of the Auditor) shall apply to such objection as it applies to an objection under that rule.

Part II — Fees of Solicitors

Application and interpretation of this Part

42.8.—(1) This Part applies to fees of solicitors in a cause other than fees —

(a) provided for by regulations made by the Secretary of State under section 14A of the Legal Aid (Scotland) Act 1967; or

(b) for which the Secretary of State may make regulations under section 33 of the Legal Aid (Scotland) Act 1986.

(2) In this Part, "the Table of Fees" means the Table of Fees in rule 42.16.

Form of account of expenses

42.9.—An account of expenses presented to the Auditor in accordance with an order of the court shall set out in chronological order all items in respect of which fees are claimed.

Basis of charging

42.10.—(1) Only such expenses as are reasonable for conducting the cause in a proper manner shall be allowed.

(2) Where the work can properly be performed by a solicitor local to the party, the Auditor in taxing an account shall allow such expenses as would have been incurred if the work had been done by the nearest local solicitor, including reasonable fees for instructing and corresponding with him, unless the Auditor is satisfied that it was in the interests of the client that the solicitor in charge of the cause should attend personally.

(3) Subject to paragraph (4), a solicitor may charge an account either on the basis of Chapter I or on the basis of Chapter III of the Table of Fees, but he may not charge partly on one basis and partly on the other.

(4) Where the inclusive fees set out in Chapter III of the Table of Fees are not conveniently applicable or do not properly cover the work involved, an account may be charged on the basis of Chapter I of that Table.

(5) The Auditor may increase or reduce an inclusive fee in Chapter III of the Table of Fees in appropriate circumstances whether or not those circumstances fall under Part IX of that Chapter.

42.11.—[Rule 42.11 revoked by SI 1998 No. 2674.]

Value added tax

42.12.—(1) Where work done by a solicitor constitutes a supply of services in respect of which value added tax is chargeable by him, there may be added to the amount of fees an amount equal to the amount of value added tax chargeable.

(2) An account of expenses or a minute of election to charge the inclusive fee in paragraph 1 of Chapter III of the Table of Fees shall contain a statement as to whether or not the party entitled to the expenses is registered for the purposes of value added tax.

Charges for witnesses

42.13.—(1) Charges for the attendance at a proof or jury trial of a witness —

    (a) present but not called to give evidence, or

    (b) who is held as concurring with another witness who has been called, may be allowed if a party has, at any time before the diet of taxation, enrolled a motion for the name of that witness to be noted in the minute of proceedings in the cause.

(2) Subject to paragraph (3), where it was responsible in any cause to employ a skilled person to make investigations or to report for any purpose, any charges for such investigations and report and for any attendence at any proof or jury trial shall be allowed in addition to the ordinary witness fee of such person at such rate as the Auditor shall determine is fair and reasonable.

(2A) Subject to paragraph (3)(a) in the case of a skilled witness and paragraph (3)(b) in the case of a professional witness, in any cause in which evidence has been given by affidavit, charges shall be allowed to the deponent in terms of paragraph (2) of this rule or of paragraph (2)(a)(iii) of Chapter II of the Table of Fees as the case may be.

(3) The Auditor may make no determination under paragraph (2) or (2A) unless the court has, on granting a motion made for the purpose, before or at the time at which it awarded expenses or on a motion enrolled at any time thereafter but before the diet of taxation —

    (a) certified that the witness was a skilled witness; and

    (aa) certified that it was reasonable to employ that person to make investigations or to report; and

    (b) recorded the name of that witness in the interlocutor pronounced by the court.

(4) Where a motion under paragraph (3) is enrolled after the court has awarded expenses, the expenses of the motion shall be borne by the party enrolling it.

Additional fee

42.14.—(1) An application for the allowance of an additional fee shall be made by motion to the court.

(2) The court may, on such an application to it —

    (a) determine the application itself; or

    (b) remit the application to the Auditor for him to determine whether an additional fee should be allowed.

(3) In determining whether to allow an additional fee under paragraph (2), the court or the Auditor, as the case may be, shall take into account any of the following factors:–

    (a) the complexity of the cause and the number, difficulty or novelty of the questions raised;

    (b) the skill, time and labour, and specialised knowledge required, of the solicitor or the exceptional urgency of the steps taken by him;

    (c) the number or importance of any documents prepared or perused;

    (d) the place and circumstances of the cause or in which the work of the solicitor in preparation for, and conduct of, the cause has been carried out;

    (e) the importance of the cause or the subject-matter of it to the client;

    (f) the amount or value of money or property involved in the cause;

    (g) the steps taken with a view to settling the cause, limiting the matters in dispute or limiting the scope of any hearing.

(4) In fixing an additional fee, the Auditor shall take into account any of the factors mentioned in paragraph (3).

Fees of a reporter

42.15. Subject to any other provision in these Rules, any order of the court or agreement between a party and his solicitor, where any matter in a cause is remitted by the court, at its own instance or on the motion of a party, to a reporter or other person to report to the court —

    (a) the solicitors for the parties shall be personally liable, in the first instance, to the reporter or other person for his fee and outlays unless the court otherwise orders; and

    (b) where —

        (i) the court makes the remit at its own instance, the party ordained by the court, or

        (ii) the court makes the remit on the motion of a party, that party, shall be liable to the reporter or other person for his fee and outlays.

Table of fees

42.16.—(1) —The Table of Fees shall regulate the fees of a solicitor charged in an account in any cause between party and party.

(2) In the Table of Fees, "sheet" means a page of 250 or more words or numbers.

(3) The Table of Fees is as follows.

TABLE OF FEES

CHAPTER I — TABLE OF DETAILED CHARGES

[Chapter I is printed as amended by:

Act of Sederunt (Rules of the Court of Session 1994 Amendment No 2) (Fees of Solicitors) 1995 (SI 1995 No 1396) which came into force on 22nd June 1995;

Act of Sederunt (Rules of the Court of Session Amendment No 1) (Fees of Solicitors) 1996 (SI 1996 No 237) which came into force on 1st April 1996;

Act of Sederunt (Rules of the Court of Session 1994 Amendment No 3) (Fees of Solicitors) 1998 (SI 1998 No 2674) which came into force on 1st December 1998;

Act of Sederunt (Rules of the Court of Session Amendment No 8) (Fees of Solicitors) 1999 (SSI 1999 No 166) which came into force on 1st January 2000;

Act of Sederunt (Rules of the Court of Session Amendment No 8) (Fees of Solicitors) 2000 (SSI 2000 No 450) which came into force on 1st January 2001;

Act of Sederunt (Rules of the Court of Session Amendment No 5) (Fees of Solicitors) 2001 (SSI 2001 No 441) which came into force on 1st January 2002;

Act of Sederunt (Rules of the Court of Session Amendment) (Fees of Solicitors, Shorthand Writers and Witnesses) 2002 (SSI 2002 No 301) which came into force on 1st July 2002;

Act of Sederunt (Rules of the Court of Session Amendment) (Fees of Solicitors) 2003 (SSI 2003 No 194) which came into force on 1st April 2003;

Act of Sederunt (Rules of the Court of Session Amendment No 3) (Fees of Solicitors) 2004 (SSI 2004 No 151) which came into force on 4th May 2004;

Act of Sederunt (Rules of the Court of Session Amendment No 2) (Fees of Solicitors) 2005 (SSI 2005 No 147) which came into force on 25th April 2005;

Act of Sederunt (Rules of the Court of Session Amendment No 4) (Fees of Solicitors) 2006 (SSI 2006 No 294) which came into force on 1st July 2006;

Act of Sederunt (Rules of the Court of Session Amendment No 2) (Fees of Solicitors) 2007 (SSI 2007 No 86) which came into force on 1st April 2007;

Act of Sederunt (Rules of the Court of Session Amendment) (Fees of Solicitors) 2008 (SSI 2008 No 39) which came into force on 1st April 2008;

Act of Sederunt (Rules of the Court of Session Amendment No 2) (Fees of Solicitors) 2009 (SSI 2009 No 82) which came into force on 27th April 2009.]

1. Framing documents   £

    (a)   Framing precognitions and other papers (but not including affidavits), per sheet 17.95

    (b)   Framing formal documents such as inventories and title pages etc., per sheet 7.45

    (c)   Framing affidavits, per sheet 26.45

    (d)   Framing accounts of expenses, per sheet 17.25

Note: Where a skilled witness prepares his own precognition or report, the solicitor shall be allowed half drawing fees for perusing it (whether or not in the course of doing so he revises or adjusts it).

2. Copying

For the copying of papers by whatever means —

    (a)   where a copy is required to be lodged, or sent, in pursuance of any of rules 4.7, 22.1 and 22.3, such charge as the Auditor may from time to time determine (and he may make different provision for different classes of case); and

    (b)   in any other case, if the Auditor determines (either or both) that —

        (i)   the copying had to be done in circumstances which were in some way exceptional;

        (ii) the papers which required to be copied were unusually numerous having regard to the nature of the cause,

such charge, if any, as the Auditor considers reasonable (but a charge based on time expended by any person in copying shall not be allowed).

Notes

1. Where a dermination is required under sub-paragraph (b), the purpose of copying, the number of copies made and the charge claimed shall be shown in the account.

2. Copying done other than in the place of business of the solicitor shall be shown as an outlay.

		£
3. Revising		
Papers drawn by counsel, open and closed records, etc., for each five sheets or part of a sheet		7.45

4. Citation of parties, witnesses, havers and instructions to messenger-at-arms

(a)	Each party	17.95
(b)	Each witness or haver	17.95
(c)	Instructing messenger-at-arms including examining, execution and settling fee	17.95

5. Time charge

(a)	Preparation for proof, jury trial or any other hearing at court, per quarter hour or such other sum as in the opinion of the Auditor is justified	35.50
(b)	Attendance at meetings, proof, jury trial or any other hearing at court including waiting time, or consultation with counsel, per quarter hour or such other sum as in the opinion of the Auditor is justified	35.50
(c)	Perusal of documents per quarter hour or such other sum as in the opinion of the Auditor is justified	35.50
(d)	Allowance for time of clerk, one-half of the above	
(e)	Attendance at Office of Court —	
	(i) for making up and lodging process	17.95
	(ii) for lodging all first steps of process	17.95
	(iii) for performance of formal work (other than work under head (ii))	7.45

Notes

1. Time necessarily occupied in travelling is to be regarded as if occupied on business. Reasonable travelling and maintenance expenses are to be allowed in addition.

2. In the event of a party in a proof or jury trial being represented by one counsel only, allowance may be made to the solicitor should the case warrant it, for the attendance of a clerk at one-half the rate chargeable for the attendance of the solicitor.

6. Correspondence

(a)	Letters including instruction to counsel (whether sent by hand, post, telex or facsimile . transmission), each page of 125 words	17.95
(b)	Formal letters	3.70
(c)	Telephone calls (except under sub-paragraph (d))	7.45
(d)	Telephone calls (lengthy), to be charged at attendance rate.	

Note: In relation to sub-paragraph (d), whether a telephone call is "lengthy" will be determined by the Auditor.

CHAPTER II — WITNESSES' FEES

[Chapter II is printed as amended by:

Act of Sederunt (Rules of the Court of Session Amendment) (Witnesses' Fees) 1999 (SI 1999 No 187) which came into force on 1st March 1999;

Act of Sederunt (Rules of the Court of Session Amendment) (Fees of Solicitors, Shorthand Writers and Witnesses) 2002 (SI 2002 No 301) which came into force on 1st July 2002;

Act of Sederunt (Rules of the Court of Session Amendment No 2) (Fees of Solicitors) 2005 (SSI 2005 No 147) which came into force on 25th April 2005;

Act of Sederunt (Rules of the Court of Session Amendment) (Miscellaneous) 2007 (SSI 2007 No 7) which came into force on 29th January 2007.]

1. Skilled persons

Where it was reasonable to employ a skilled person to make investigation or to report for any purpose, any charges for such investigations and report and for any attendance at any proof or jury trial shall be allowed at a rate which the Auditor of Court shall determine is fair and reasonable.

2. Witnesses

A person who is cited to give evidence and in consequence incurs financial loss shall be allowed reimbursement, being such reasonable sum as the Auditor may determine to have been reasonably and necessarily incurred by the witness, but not exceeding £400 per day.

3. Travelling allowance

In respect of any witness there shall be allowed a travelling allowance, being such sum as the Auditor may determine to have been reasonably and necessarily incurred by the witness in the travelling from and to the witnesses' residence or place of business and the Court.

4. Subsistence allowance

In respect of any witness there shall be allowed a subsistence allowance, being such sum as the Auditor may determine to have been reasonably incurred by the witness for the extra cost of subsistence during the witnesses' absence from the witnesses' home or place of business for the purpose of giving evidence, and where the witness reasonably requires to stay overnight, for the reasonable cost of board and lodging.

5. Value Added Tax

Where any witness is a taxable person in terms of the Value Added Tax Act 1983, the amount of value added tax may be added by the witness to the witnesses' note of fee, and may be paid to the witness by the Solicitor.

6. Receipts and vouchers

Receipts and detailed vouchers for all payments claimed in respect of a witness shall be produced to the party found liable in expenses, prior to the taxation of the Account of Expenses, and to the Auditor, if the Auditor requires.

7. Account of fees of witnesses

The fees charged for any witness shall be stated in the Account of Expenses in a lump sum and the details of the charges shall be entered in a separate schedule appended to the Account as follows:

Name and designation	Where from	Days charged	Rate per day	Travelling and subsistence allowance	Total	Taxed off

CHAPTER III

[Chapter III is printed as amended by:

Act of Sederunt (Rules of the Court of Session 1994 Amendment No 2) (Fees of Solicitors) 1995 (SI 1995 No 1396) which came into force on 22nd June 1995;

Act of Sederunt (Rules of the Court of Session Amendment No 1) (Fees of Solicitors) 1996 (SI 1996 No 237) which came into force on 1st April 1996;

Act of Sederunt (Rules of the Court of Session Amendment No 3) (Fees of Solicitors) 1998 (SI 1998 No 2674) which came into force on 1st December 1998;

Act of Sederunt (Rules of the Court of Session Amendment No 8) (Fees of Solicitors) 1999 (SSI 1999 No 166) which came into force on 1st January 2000;

Act of Sederunt (Rules of the Court of Session Amendment No 8) (Fees of Solicitors) 2000 (SSI 2000 No 450) which came into force on 1st January 2001;

Act of Sederunt (Rules of the Court of Session Amendment No 5) (Fees of Solicitors) 2001 (SSI 2001 No 441) which came into force on 1st January 2002;

Act of Sederunt (Rules of the Court of Session Amendment) (Fees of Solicitors, Shorthand Writers and Witnesses) 2002 (SSI 2002 No 301) which came into force on 1st July 2002;

Act of Sederunt (Rules of the Court of Session Amendment) (Fees of Solicitors) 2003 (SSI 2003 No 194) which came into force on 1st April 2003;

Act of Sederunt (Rules of the Court of Session Amendment No 3) (Fees of Solicitors) 2004 (SSI 2004 No 151) which came into force on 4th May 2004;

Act of Sederunt (Rules of the Court of Session Amendment No 2) (Fees of Solicitors) 2005 (SSI 2005 No 147) which came into force on 25th April 2005;

Act of Sederunt (Rules of the Court of Session Amendment No 4) (Fees of Solicitors) 2005 (SSI 2006 No 294) which came into force on 1st July 2006;

Act of Sederunt (Rules of the Court of Session Amendment No 2) (Fees of Solicitors) 2007 (SSI 2007 No 86) which came into force on 1st April 2007;

Act of Sederunt (Rules of the Court of Session Amendment) (Fees of Solicitors) 2008 (SSI 2008 No 39) which came into force on 1st April 2008;

Act of Sederunt (Rules of the Court of Session Amendment No 2) (Fees of Solicitors) 2009 (SSI 2009 No 82) which came into force on 27th April 2009.]

PART I — UNDEFENDED CAUSES

(other than consistorial actions)

1. Inclusive fee

In all undefended causes where no proof is led, the pursuer's solicitor may at his option elect to charge an inclusive fee to cover all work from taking instructions up to and including obtaining extract decree. The option shall be exercised by the solicitor for the pursuer endorsing a minute of election to the above effect on the principal summons or petition before decree is taken.

		£
(a)	All work up to and obtaining extract decree	321.35
(b)	Outlays to an amount not exceeding £407.70 (exclusive of value added tax) shall also be allowed.	

PART II — UNDEFENDED CONSISTORIAL ACTIONS

(other than by affidavit procedure in Part III of this Chapter)

1. All work (other than precognitions) up to and including the calling of the summons in court   451.20
Note: Precognitions to be charged as in paragraph 5 of Part V of this Chapter of this Table.

2. Incidental procedure

Fixing diet, enrolling action, preparing for proof, citing witnesses, etc	258.10

3. Amendment

(a)	Where summons amended, re-service is not ordered and motion is not starred	66.25
(b)	Where summons amended, re-service is not ordered and motion is starred	95.60
(c)	Where summons amended and re-service is ordered	118.85

4. Commission to take evidence on interrogatories

(a)	All work up to and including lodging of completed interrogatories, but excluding attendance at execution of commission	116.10
(b)	Attendance at execution of commission (if required), per quarter hour	35.50
(c)	In addition a fee per sheet for completed interrogatories, including all copies, of	19.85

5. Commission to take evidence on open commission £

    (a) All work up to and including lodging of report of commission, but excluding attendance at execution of commission 107.25

    (b) Attendance at execution of commission, per quarter hour 35.50

6. Other matters

Where applicable, charges under paragraphs 6, 7, 10, 14, 16 and 21 of Part V of this Chapter of this Table.

7. Proof and completion fee

All work to and including sending extract decree, but excluding account of expenses 321.35

8. Accounts

Framing and lodging account and attending taxation 99.00

PART III — UNDEFENDED CONSISTORIAL ACTIONS

(affidavit procedure)

1.—(1) This paragraph applies to any undefended action of divorce or separation where —

    (a) the facts set out in section 1(2)(a) (adultery) or 1(2)(b) (unreasonable behaviour) of the Divorce (Scotland) Act 1976 ("the 1976 Act") are relied on;

    (b) there are no conclusions relating to any ancillary matters; and

    (c) the pursuer seeks to prove those facts by means of affidavits.

(2) The solicitor for the pursuer may, in respect of the work specified in column 1 of Table A below, charge the inclusive fee specified in respect of that work in column 2 of that Table.

(3) Where the pursuer has been represented in respect of work specified in column 1 of Table A below by an Edinburgh solicitor and a solicitor outside Edinburgh, the Auditor may, where he is satisfied that it was appropriate for the pursuer to be so represented, allow the inclusive fee specified in column 3 instead of the inclusive fee specified in column 2 of that Table.

TABLE A

Column 1 *Work done*	Column 2 *Inclusive fee* £	Column 3 *Discretionary inclusive fee Edinburgh solicitor and solicitor outside Edinburgh* £
1. All work to and including calling of the summons	708.90	809.60
2. All work from calling to and including swearing affidavits	504.10	612.00
3. All work from swearing affidavits to and including sending extract decree	154.65	227.15
4. All work to and including sending extract decree	1367.65	1649.25

2.—(1) This paragraph applies to any undefended action of divorce or separation where —

    (a) the facts set out in section 1(2)(c) (desertion), 1(2)(d) (two years' non-cohabitation and consent) or 1(2)(e) (five years' non-cohabitation) of the 1976 Act are relied on;

(b) there are no conclusions relating to any ancillary matters; and

(c) the pursuer seeks to prove those facts by affidavit.

(2) The solicitor for the pursuer may, in respect of the work specified in column 1 of Table B below, charge the inclusive fee specified in respect of that work in column 2 of that Table.

(3) Where the pursuer has been represented in respect of work specified in column 1 of Table B below by an Edinburgh solicitor and a solicitor outside Edinburgh, the Auditor may, where he is satisfied that it was appropriate for the pursuer to be so represented, allow the inclusive fee specified in respect of that work in column 3 instead of the inclusive fee specified in column 2 of that Table.

TABLE B

Column 1 Work done	Column 2 Inclusive fee £	Column 3 Discretionary inclusive fee Edinburgh solicitor and solicitor outside Edinburgh £
1. All work to and including calling of the summons	583.30	683.90
2. All work from calling to and including swearing affidavits	280.55	356.35
3. All work from swearing affidavits to and including sending extract decree	154.65	227.15
4. All work to and including sending extract decree	1018.40	1267.15

3. If —

(a) the solicitor for the pursuer charges an inclusive fee under either paragraph 1 or 2 of this Part, and

(b) the action to which the charge relates includes a conclusion relating to an ancillary matter, in addition to that fee he may charge in respect of the work specified in column 1 of Table C below the inclusive fee specified in respect of that work in column 2 of that Table.

TABLE C

Column 1 Work done	Column 2 Discretionary inclusive fee Edinburgh solicitor and solicitor outside Edinburgh
1. All work to and including calling of the summons	132.40
2. All work from calling to and including swearing affidavits	148.65
3. All work under items 1 and 2	280.75

PART IV — OUTER HOUSE PETITIONS

1. **Unopposed petition**   £

(a) All work including precognitions and all copyings, up to and obtaining extract decree   668.70

(b) Where the party has been represented by an Edinburgh solicitor and a solicitor outside Edinburgh, the Auditor may, where he is satisfied that it was necessary for the party to be so represented, allow a fee of 926.40

(c) Outlays including duplicating charges to be allowed in addition.

2. Opposed petition £

   (a) All work (other than precognitions) up to and including lodging petition, obtaining and executing warrant for service 492.90

   (b) Outlays including duplicating charges to be allowed in addition.

   (c) Where applicable, charges under paragraphs 1A, 2, 3 and 5 to 21 of Part V of this Chapter of this table

3. Reports in opposed petitions

   (a) For each report by the Accountant of Court 75.10

   (b) For any other report, as under paragraph 6 of Part V of this Chapter of this Table.

4. Obtaining bond of caution 76.55

PART V — DEFENDED ACTIONS

1. Instruction £

   (a) All work (apart from precognitions) from commencement until lodgment of open record 683.85

   (b) Instructing re-service where necessary 73.75

   (c) If counterclaim lodged, additional fee for each party 143.85

1A. Work before action commences

All work which the Auditor is satisfied has reasonably been undertaken in contemplation of, or preparatory to, the commencement of proceedings   438.20

or such other sum as in the opinion of the Auditor is justified.

2. Record

   (a) All work in connection with adjustment and closing of record including subsequent work in connection with By Order Adjustment Roll 727.15

   (b) All work as above, so far as applicable, where cause settled or disposed of before record closed 449.80

   (c) If consultation held before record closed, additional fees may be allowed as follows —

      (i) arranging consultation 73.75

      (ii) attendance at consultation, per quarter hour 38.85

   (d) Additional fee to sub-paragraph (a) or (b), (to include necessary amendments) to the pursuer and existing defender, to be allowed for each pursuer, defender or third party brought in before the record is closed, each of 215.80

   (e) If an additional pursuer, defender or third party is brought in after the record is closed, an additional fee shall be allowed to the existing pursuer and the existing defender or defenders, each of 320.30

2A. Notes of Argument

   (a) Instructing, perusing and lodging first Note of Arguments (either party) 142.65

   (b) Perusing opponent's Note of Arguments 77.65

   (c) Instructing, perusing and lodging any further Note of Arguments (either party) 77.65

3. Procedure Roll or hearing

   (a) Preparing for hearing including all work, incidental work and instruction of counsel ... 143.85

   (b) Attendance fee, per quarter hour 38.85

   (c) Advising and work incidental to it 107.65

4. Adjustment of issues and counter-issues

   (a) All work in connection with and incidental to the lodging of an issue, and adjustment and approval of it 136.70

   (b) If one counter-issue, additional fee to pursuer of 38.85

£

  (c) Where more than one counter-issue, an additional fee to pursuer for each additional counter-issue 19.50

  (d) All work in connection with lodging of counter-issue and adjustment and approval of it 136.70

  (e) Fee to defender or third party for considering issue where no counter-issue lodged 38.85

  (f) Fee to defender or third party for considering each additional counter-issue 19.50

5. Precognitions

Taking and drawing precognitions, per sheet 72.35

Note: Where a skilled witness prepares his own precognition or report, the solicitor shall be allowed, for perusing it (whether or not in the course of doing so he revises or adjusts it), half of the taking and drawing fee per sheet.

6. Reports obtained under order of court excluding Auditor's report

  (a) All work incidental to it 155.00

  (b) Additional fee for perusal of report, per quarter hour 21.60
       or such other sum as in the opinion of the Auditor is justified.

7. Specification of documents

  (a) Instructing counsel, revising and lodging and all incidental procedure to obtain a diligence up to and including obtaining interlocutor 143.90

  (b) Fee to opponent 69.90

  (ba) Arranging commission to recover documents, citing havers, instructing commissioner and shorthand writer and preparation for commission 135.80

  (bb) Attendance at execution of commission, per quarter hour, of 69.90

  (c) Fee to opponent 38.85

  (d) If alternative procedure adopted, a fee per person on whom order served, of 57.60

  (e) Fee for perusal of documents recovered under a specification of documents (or by informal means) where not otherwise provided for in the Table of Fees, per quarter hour 38.85

8. Commission to take evidence on interrogatories

  (a) Applying for commission to cover all work up to and including lodging report of commission with completed interrogatories and cross-interrogatories 268.05

  (b) Fee to opponent if cross-interrogatories lodged 234.05

  (c) Fee to opponent if no cross-interrogatories lodged 86.40

  (d) In addition to above, fee per sheet to each party for completed interrogatories or cross-interrogatories, including all copies, of 21.60

9. Commission to take evidence on open commissions

  (a) Applying for commission up to and including lodging report of commission, but excluding sub-paragraph (c) 320.30

  (b) Fee to opponent 143.85

  (c) Fee for attendance at execution of commission, per quarter hour, o 38.85

10. Miscellaneous motions and minutes where not otherwise covered by this Part

  (a) Where attendance of counsel and/or solicitor not required 38.85

  (b) Where attendance of counsel and/or solicitor required inclusive of instruction of counsel, not exceeding half hour 107.65

  (c) Thereafter attendance fee, per additional quarter hour 38.90

  (d) Instructing counsel for a minute (other than a minute ordered by the court), revising and lodging as a separate step in process including any necessary action 107.65

  (e) Perusing a minute of admission or abandonment 38.85

11. Incidental Procedure (not chargeable prior to approval of issue or allowance of proof)

Fixing diet, obtaining note on the line of evidence, etc., borrowing and returning process, lodging productions, considering opponent's productions, and all other work prior to the consultation on the sufficiency of evidence 407.00

12. Amendment of record
£

(a) Amendment of conclusions only, fee to proposer 107.65

(b) Amendment of conclusions only, fee to opponent 38.85

(c) Amendment of pleadings after record closed, where no answers to the amendment are lodged, fee to proposer 158.20

(d) In same circumstances, fee to opponent 72.65

(e) Amendment of pleadings after record closed, where answers are lodged, fee for proposer and each party lodging answers 368.50

(f) Fee for adjustment of minute and answers, where applicable, to be allowed in addition to each party, of 205.00

13. Preparation for proof or jury trial (to include fixing consultation on the sufficiency of evidence, fee-funding precept, citing witnesses, all work checking and writing up process and preparing for proof or jury trial)

(a) If action settled before proof or jury trial, or lasts only one day, to include, where applicable, instruction of counsel 989.45

(b) For each day or part of day after the first, including instruction of counsel 88.15

(c) Preparing for adjourned diets and all work incidental to it as in sub-paragraph (a), if adjourned for more than five days 108.35

(d) If consultation held before proof or jury trial, attendance at it, per quarter hour 38.85

14. Copying

For the copying of papers by whatever means —

(a) where a copy is required to be lodged, or sent, in pursuance of any of rules 4.7, 22.1 and 22.3, such charge as the Auditor may from time to time determine (and he may make different provision for different classes of case); and

(b) in any other case, if the Auditor determines (either or both) that —

(i) the copying had to be done in circumstances which were in some way exceptional;

(ii) the papers which required to be copied were unusually numerous having regard to the nature of the cause,

such charge, if any, as the Auditor considers reasonable (but a charge based on time expended by any person in copying shall not be allowed).

Notes

1. Where a dermination is required under sub-paragraph (b), the purpose of copying, the number of copies made and the charge claimed shall be shown in the account.

2. Copying done other than in the place of business of the solicitor shall be shown as an outlay.

15. Settlement

(a) Settlement by tender

(i) Lodging or considering first tender 215.80

(ii) Lodging or considering each further tender 143.85

(iii) If tender accepted, an additional fee to each accepting party 143.85

(b) Extrajudicial settlement — advising on, negotiating and agreeing extrajudicial settlement (not based on judicial tender) to include preparation and lodging of joint minute 359.90

(c) The Auditor may allow a fee in respect of work undertaken with a view to settlement (whether or not settlement is in fact agreed), including offering settlement, of 611.85

(d) If consultation held to consider tender, extra judicial settlement (not based on judicial tender) or with a view to settlement (whether or not settlement is in fact agreed) attendance at it, per quarter hour 38.85

16. Hearing limitation fee

To include all work undertaken with a view to limiting the matters in dispute or limiting the scope of any hearing, and including exchanging documents, precognitions and expert reports, agreeing any fact, statement or document, and preparing and lodging any joint minute 764.95

17. Proof or jury trial   £

Attendance fee, per quarter hour 38.85

18. Accounts

(a) To include framing, adjusting and lodging account 232.95

(b) To include considering Notes of Objections, and generally preparing for taxation 232.95

(c) Attendance at taxation, per quarter hour 38.85

19. Ordering and obtaining extract   57.60

20. Final procedure

(a) If case goes to proof or jury trial, or is settled within 14 days before the diet of proof or jury trial, to include all work to close of cause so far as not otherwise provided for 291.60

(b) In any other case 88.15

PART VA — Defended Personal Injuries Actions Commenced on or after
1 April 2003

1. Precognitions/Expert Reports/Factual Reports   £

(a) Taking and drawing precognitions, per sheet 72.25

(b) Perusal fee for consideration of Reports (whether or not in the course of doing so he revises or adjusts it), half thereof, per sheet 36.15

2. Pre-Litigation Fee

All work which the Auditor is satisfied has reasonably been undertaken in contemplation of, or preparatory to the commencement of proceedings particularly to include communications between parties in relation to areas of medical/quantum/discussion re settlement or such other sum as in the opinion of the Auditor is justified 437.35

3. Instruction

(a) To cover all work (except as otherwise specially provided for in this Chapter) from commencement to the lodging of Defences 682.50

(b) Specification of Documents per Form 43.2–B 95.85

(ba) Fees to opponent for considering Specification of Documents 68.70

(c) In the event of the Summons being drafted without the assistance of Counsel or a Solicitor-Advocate such further fee will be allowed as the Auditor considers appropriate 232.60

(d) Instructing re-service where necessary 73.65

(e) If counterclaim lodged, additional fee for each party to include Answers 232.60

(f) Arranging commission to recover documents, citing havers, instructing Commission and shorthand writer and preparation for commission 129.95

(g) Attendance at execution of commission, to include travelling, per quarter hour of 38.85

(h) If alternative procedure adopted, a fee per person on whom order served of 57.45

(i) Fee for perusal of documents recovered under a specification of Documents (or by informal means) where not otherwise provided for in the Table of Fees, per quarter hour 38.85

4. Record

(a) All work in connection with adjustment and closing of record 725.60

(b) All work as above, so far as applicable, where cause settled or disposed of before record closed 448.95

(c) If consultation held before record closed, additional fees may be allowed as follows:

     (i) arranging consultation 73.65

     (ii) attendance at consultation, to include travelling, per quarter hour 38.85

(d) Additional fee to sub-paragraph (a) or (b) (to include necessary Amendments) to the pursuer and existing defender, to be allowed for each pursuer, defender or third party brought in before the record is closed, each of 215.30

£

(e) If an additional pursuer, defender or third party is brought in after the record is closed, an additional fee shall be allowed to the existing pursuer and the existing defender or defenders, each of 319.75

4A. Notes of Argument

(a) Instructing, perusing and lodging first Note of Arguments where ordained by the Court (either party) 142.65

(b) Perusing opponent's Note of Arguments 77.65

(c) Instructing, perusing and lodging any further Note of Arguments where ordained by the Court (either party) 77.65

5. Valuation of claim

(a) Fee to cover Note on Quantum/Valuation of Claim 465.20

(b) Opponent's fee for inspection of Valuation of Claim 232.60

(c) Inspection of documents, per quarter hour 38.85

6. Adjustment of issues and counter-issues

(a) All work in connection with and incidental to the lodging of an issue, and adjustment and approval of it 136.45

(b) If one counter-issue, additional fee to pursuer of 38.85

7. By Order Roll/Variation of timetable order/Adjustment on Final Decree/Interim Payment of Damages

(a) Fee to cover preparing and instruction of Counsel, to include attendance not exceeding half an hour 107.35

(b) Thereafter attendance fee, per additional quarter hour 38.85

(c) In the event of a separate Advising/Opinion and all work incidental thereto 107.35

8. Reports obtained under order of court excluding Auditor's Report

(a) All work incidental to it 154.50

(b) Additional fee for perusal of report, per quarter hour or such other sum as in the opinion of the Auditor is justified 21.60

9. Incidental Procedure (not chargeable prior to approval of issue or allowance of proof)

Noting diet, obtaining note on the line of evidence, etc, borrowing and returning process, and all other work prior to consultation on the sufficiency of evidence 406.05

10. Specification of documents (if further Specification considered necessary)

(a) Instructing counsel, revising and lodging and all incidental procedure to obtain a diligence up to and including obtaining interlocutor 143.65

(b) Fee to opponent 69.75

(c) Arranging commission to recover documents, citing havers, instructing commissioner and shorthand writer and preparations for commission 129.95

(ca) Fee to opponent 69.90

(d) Attendance at execution of commission, per quarter hour, of 38.85

(e) If alternative procedure adopted, a fee per person on whom order served, of 57.45

(f) Fee for perusal of documents recovered under a specification of documents (or by informal means) where not otherwise provided for in the Table of Fees, per quarter hour 38.85

11. Commission to take evidence on interrogatories

(a) Applying for commission to cover all work up to and including lodging report of commission with completed interrogatories and cross-interrogatories 291.00

(b) Fee to opponent if cross-interrogatories lodged 233.55

(c) Fee to opponent if no cross-interrogatories lodged 87.05

(d) In addition to above, fee per sheet to each party for completed interrogatories or cross-interrogatories, including all copies, of 21.60

12. Commission to take evidence on open commission £

  (a) Applying for commission up to and including lodging report of commission, but excluding sub-pargraph (c) 319.75

  (b) Fee to opponent 143.65

  (c) Fee for attendance at execution of commission, to include travelling, per quarter hour, of 38.85

13. Miscellaneous motions and minutes where not otherwise covered by this Part

  (a) Where attendance of counsel and/or solicitor not required 38.85

  (b) Where attendance of counsel and/or solicitor required inclusive of instruction of counsel, not exceeding half hour 110.60

  (c) Thereafter attendance fee, per quarter hour 38.85

  (d) Instructing counsel for a minute/note on further procedure (if applicable), revising and lodging as a separate step in process including any necessary action 107.35

  (e) Perusing a minute of admission or abandonment/note ordered by Court/notice of grounds 38.85

14. Amendment of record

  (a) Amendment of conclusions only, fee to proposer 107.35

  (b) Amendment of conclusions only, fee to opponent 38.85

  (c) Amendment of pleadings after record closed, where no answers to the amendment are lodged, fee to proposer 157.90

  (d) In same circumstances, fee to opponent 72.55

  (e) Amendment of pleadings after record closed, where answers are lodged, fee for proposer and each party lodging answers 367.60

  (f) Fee for adjustment of minute and answers, where applicable, to be allowed in addition to each party, of 204.60

15. Copying

For the copying of papers by whatever means —

  (a) Where a copy is required to be lodged, or sent, in pursuance of any Rules 4.7, 22.1 and 22.3, such charge as the Auditor may from time to time determine (and he may make different provision for different classes of case); and

  (b) In any other case, if the Auditor determines (either or both) that —

    (i) the copying had to be done in circumstances which were in some way exceptional;

    (ii) the papers which required to be copied were unusually numerous having regard to the nature of the cause, such charge, if any, as the Auditor considers reasonable (but a charge based on time expended by any person in copying shall not be allowed).

Notes:

  1. Where a determination is required under sub-paragraph (b), the purpose of copying, the number of copies made and the charge claimed shall be shown in the account.

  2. Copying done other than in the place of business of the solicitor shall be shown as an outlay.

16. Preparation for proof or jury trial

(to include fixing consultation on the sufficiency of evidence, fee-funding precept, citing witnesses, all work checking and writing up process and preparing for proof or jury trial)

  (a) If action settled before proof or jury trial, or lasts only one day, to include where applicable, instruction of counsel 987.40

  (b) For each day or part of day after the first, including instruction of counsel 87.95

  (c) Preparing for adjourned diets and all work incidental to it as in sub-paragraph (a), if adjourned for more than five days 179.75

  (d) If consultation held before proof or jury trial, attendance at it, per quarter hour 38.85

17. Pre-trial meeting

  (a) Fee arranging pre-trial meeting (each occasion) 73.65

  (b) Fee preparing for pre-trial meeting 387.65

£

(c) Fee attending pre-trial meeting, per quarter hour 38.85

(d) Joint Minute of pre-trial meeting —

    (i) in respect of Section 1 only 119.75

    (ii) in respect of Sections 1 and 2 only 239.40

    (iii) in respect of Sections 1 and 3 only 278.20

    (iv) in respect of Sections 1, 2 and 3 only 359.15

18. Hearing limitation fee

For any work undertaken to limit matters in dispute not otherwise provided for — subject to details being provided 310.30

19. Settlement

(a) Settlement by tender —

    (i) Lodging or considering first tender 215.40

    (ii) Lodging or considering each further tender 143.65

    (iii) If tender accepted, an additional fee to each accepting party 143.65

(b) Extrajudicial settlement — advising on, negotiating and agreeing extrajudicial settlement (not based on judicial tender or joint minute) to include preparation and lodging of joint minute 359.15

(c) The Auditor may allow a fee in respect of work undertaken with a view to settlement (whether or not settlement is in fact agreed), including offering settlement, of 610.40

(d) If consultation held to consider tender, extrajudicial settlement (not based on judicial tender) or with a view to settlement (whether or not settlement is in fact agreed), attendance at it, per quarter hour 38.85

20. Proof or jury trial

Attendance fee, per quarter hour 38.85

21. Accounts

(a) Preparation of judicial account, to include production of vouchers and adjustment of expenses 310.30

(b) Perusal of points of objections, per quarter hour 25.85

(c) Attendance at taxation, per quarter hour 25.85

22. Ordering and obtaining extract 57.45

23. Final procedure

(a) If case goes to proof or jury trial, or is settled within 14 days before the diet of proof or jury trial, to include all work to close of cause so far as not otherwise provided for 291.00

(b) In any other case 87.60

PART VI — INNER HOUSE BUSINESS

1. Reclaiming motions £

(a) Fee for appellant for all work up to interlocutor sending cause to roll 215.80

(b) Fee for respondent 107.65

(c) Additional fee for each party for preparing or revising every 50 pages of Appendix 90.25

2. Appeals from inferior courts

(a) Fee for appellant 260.75

(b) Fee for respondent 129.25

(c) Additional fee for each party for preparing or revising every 50 pages of Appendix 88.15

3. Summar Roll

(a) Preparing for discussion and instructing counsel 215.85

(b) Attendance fee, per quarter hour 38.85

4. Other matters £

Where applicable, charges under Part V of this Chapter of this Table.

5. Special cases, Inner House petitions and appeals other than under paragraph 2 of this Part

According to circumstances of the case.

6. Obtaining bond of caution 88.15

PART VII — ADMIRALTY AND COMMERCIAL CAUSES, MERCANTILE SEQUESTRATIONS AND APPLICATIONS FOR SUMMARY TRIAL UNDER SECTION 26 OF THE ACT OF 1988 AND CAUSES REMITTED FROM THE SHERIFF COURT

Charges under this Part shall be based on this Table according to the circumstances.

PART VIII — SOLICITORS EXERCISING RIGHTS OF AUDIENCE UNDER SECTION 25 OF THE SOLICITORS (SCOTLAND) ACT 1980

1. The Auditor shall allow to a solicitor who exercises a right of audience by virtue of section 25A of the Solicitors (Scotland) Act 1980 such fee for each item of work done by the solicitor in the exercise of such right as he would allow to counsel for an equivalent item of work.

2. Where a solicitor exercises a right of audience by virtue of section 25A of the Solicitors (Scotland) Act 1980, and is assisted by another solicitor or a clerk, the Auditor may also allow attendance fees in accordance with Parts IV and V of this Chapter of this Table.

PART IX — GENERAL

The Auditor shall have the power to apportion the foregoing fees in this chapter between parties' solicitors in appropriate circumstances or to modify them in the case of a solicitor acting for more than one party in the same cause or in the case of the same solicitor acting in more than one cause arising out of the same circumstances or in the event of a cause being settled or disposed of at a stage when the work covered by an inclusive fee has not been completed.

CHAPTER IV — TRANSCRIPTS OF EVIDENCE ETC.

[Chapter IV is printed as amended by:

Act of Sederunt (Rules of the Court of Session 1994 Amendment) (Shorthand Writers' Fees) 1995 (SI 1995 No 1023) which came into force on 1st May 1995;

Act of Sederunt (Rules of the Court of Session Amendment No 2) (Fees of Shorthand Writers) 1996 (SI 1996 No 754) which came into force on 1st May 1996;

Act of Sederunt (Rules of the Court of Session Amendment No 5) (Transcripts of Evidence and Attendance Fees for Shorthand Writers etc.) 1997 (SI 1997 No 1260) which came into force on 1st May 1997;

Act of Sederunt (Rules of the Court of Session Amendment No 2) (Fees of Shorthand Writers) 1998 (SI 1996 No 993) which came into force on 1st May 1998;

Act of Sederunt (Rules of the Court of Session Amendment No 2) (Fees of Shorthand Writers) 1999 (SI 1999 No 615) which came into force on 1st May 1999;

Act of Sederunt (Rules of the Court of Session Amendment No 2) (Fees of Shorthand Writers) 2000 (SSI 2000 No 143) which came into force on 1st June 2000;

Act of Sederunt (Rules of the Court of Session Amendment No 2) (Fees of Shorthand Writers) 2001 (SSI 2000 No 135) which came into force on 1st May 2001;

Act of Sederunt (Rules of the Court of Session Amendment) (Fees of Solicitors, Shorthand Writers and Witnesses) 2002 (SSI 2002 No 301) which came into force on 1st July 2002;

Act of Sederunt (Rules of the Court of Session Amendment No 4) (Fees of Shorthand Writers) 2003 (SSI 2003 No 247) which came into force on 1st June 2003;

Act of Sederunt (Rules of the Court of Session Amendment No 2) (Fees of Shorthand Writers) 2004 (SSI 2004 No 150) which came into force on 4th May 2004;

Act of Sederunt (Rules of the Court of Session Amendment No 3) (Fees of Shorthand Writers) 2005 (SSI 2005 No 148) which came into force on 25th April 2005;

Act of Sederunt (Rules of the Court of Session Amendment No 2) (Fees of Shorthand Writers) 2006 (SSI 2006 No 87) which came into force on 1st May 2006;

Act of Sederunt (Rules of the Court of Session Amendment No 3) (Fees of Shorthand Writers) 2007 (SSI 2007 No 234) which came into force on 1st May 2007;

Act of Sederunt (Rules of the Court of Session Amendment No 2) (Fees of Shorthand Writers) 2008 (SSI 2008 No 120) which came into force on 5th May 2008;

Act of Sederunt (Rules of the Court of Session Amendment No 4) (Fees of Shorthand Writers) 2009 (SSI 2009 No 105) which came into force on 4th March 2009.]

1. Attendance of shorthand writer

Attendance by shorthand writer at proof, jury trial or commission, per hour, with a minimum fee of £151.39 per day 37.87

2. Notes of evidence: extension by shorthand writer or transcriber

(a) Except where these are transcribed daily, per sheet 6.20

(b) Where these are transcribed daily, per shee 7.59

(c) Where notes of evidence have been directed to be supplied for the use of the court, copies may be made available to parties, payable to the shorthand writer or transcriber by the solicitor for the parties obtaining the copies, per sheet 0.50

Notes

1. Transcripts of evidence will be made only on directions from the court, and the cost of them in defended causes will, in the first instance, be payable by the solicitors for the parties in equal proportions. The daily transcripts of evidence shall be made only if all compearing parties consent. When an undefended cause is continued, or where for other reasons the court considers it necessary that transcripts be made for the use of the court and so directs, the cost will be borne by the solicitor for the pursuer in the first instance. In any cause where transcripts have not been made, but are required for a reclaiming motion, the solicitor for the reclaimer may request that they be made; and when they are thus available they will be lodged in court, the cost of transcription being payable in the first instance by the solicitor for the reclaimer.

2. In any cause where the court, on a motion enrolled for the purpose, certifies that there is reasonable ground for reclaiming and that the reclaimer is unable, for financial reasons, to meet the cost of the necessary transcription from which copies for the use of the Inner House are made, the cost of such transcription will be paid out of public funds.

PART III — FEES IN SPECULATIVE CAUSES

Fees of solicitors in speculative causes

42.17.—(1) Where —

(a) any work is undertaken by a solicitor in the conduct of a cause for a client,

(b) the solicitor and client agree that the solicitor shall be entitled to a fee for the work only if the client is successful in the cause, and

(c) the agreement is that the fee of the solicitor for all work in connection with the cause is to be based on an account prepared as between party and party,

the solicitor and client may agree that the fees element in that account shall be increased by a figure not exceeding 100 per cent.

(2) The client of the solicitor shall be deemed to be successful in the cause where —

(a) the cause has been concluded by a decree which, on the merits, is to any extent in his favour;

(b) the client has accepted a sum of money in settlement of the cause; or

(c) the client has entered into a settlement of any other kind by which his claim in the cause has been resolved to any extent in his favour.

(3) In paragraph (1), "the fees element" means all the fees in the account of expenses of the solicitor —

(a) for which any other party in the cause other than the client of the solicitor has been found liable as taxed or agreed between party and party;

(b) before the deduction of any award of expenses against the client; and

(c) excluding the sums payable to the solicitor in respect of —

(i) any fees payable for copying documents and the proportion of any session fee in the Table of Fees and posts and incidental expenses under rule 42.11;

(ii) any additional fee allowed under rule 42.14 to cover the responsibility undertaken by the solicitor in the conduct of the cause; and

(iii) any charges by the solicitor for his outlays.

Table of Fees of Solicitors in the Sheriff Court

Act of Sederunt (Fees of Solicitors in the Sheriff Court) (Amendment and further provisions) 1993 (SI 1993 No 3080)

[This Schedule is printed as amended by:

Act of Sederunt (Fees of Solicitors in the Sheriff Court) (Amendment) 1998 (SI 1998 No 2675) which came into force on 1st December 1998;

Act of Sederunt (Fees of Solicitors in the Sheriff Court) (Amendment) 2002 (SSI 2002 No 235) which came into force on 10th June 2002;

Act of Sederunt (Fees of Solicitors in the Sheriff Court) (Amendment No 2) 2002 (SSI 2002 No 274) which came into force on 1st July 2002;

Act of Sederunt (Fees of Solicitors in the Sheriff Court) (Amendment No 4) 2002 (SSI 2002 No 568) which came into force on 1st January 2003;

Act of Sederunt (Fees of Solicitors and Witnesses in the Sheriff Court) (Amendment) 2004 (SSI 2004 No 152) which came into force on 4th May 2004;

Act of Sederunt (Fees of Solicitors in the Sheriff Court) (Amendment) 2008 (SSI 2008 No 40) which came into force on 1st April 2008;

Act of Sederunt (Fees of Solicitors in the Sheriff Court) (Amendment No. 2) 2008 (SSI 2008 No 72) which came into force on 31st March 2008.]

SCHEDULE

GENERAL REGULATIONS

1.   The Tables of Fees in this Schedule shall regulate the taxation of accounts between party and party; and shall be subject to the aftermentioned powers of the court to increase or modify such fees.

2.   The pursuer's solicitor's account shall be taxed by reference to the sum decerned for unless the court otherwise directs.

3.   Where an action has been brought under summary cause procedure, only expenses under Chapter IV of the Table of Fees shall be allowed unless the court otherwise directs.

4.   Fees for work done in terms of the Social Work (Scotland) Act 1968 and summary applications shall be chargeable under Chapter III of the Table of Fees.

5.   The court shall have the following discretionary powers in relation to the Table of Fees:

(a)   In any case the court may direct that expenses shall be subject to modification.

(b)   The court may, on a motion on or after the date of any interlocutor disposing of expenses, pronounce a further interlocutor regarding those expenses allowing a percentage increase in the fees authorised by the Table of Fees to cover the responsibility undertaken by the solicitor in the conduct of the cause. In fixing the amount of the percentage increase the following factors shall be taken into account:

(i)   the complexity of the cause and the number, difficulty or novelty of the questions raised;

(ii)   the skill, time and labour and specialised knowledge required, of the solicitor;

(iii)   the number and importance of any documents prepared or perused;

(iv)   the place and circumstances of the cause or in which the work of the solicitor in preparation for, and conduct of, the cause has been carried out;

(v)   the importance of the cause or the subject matter of it to the client;

(vi)   the amount or value of money or property involved in the cause;

(vii)   the steps taken with a view to settling the cause, limiting the matters in dispute or limiting the scope of any hearing.

(c)   Where a party or his solicitor abandons, fails to attend or is not prepared to proceed with any diet of proof, debate, appeal or meeting ordered by the court, the court shall have power to decern against that party for payment of such expenses as it considers reasonable.

6. The expenses to be charged against an opposite party shall be limited to proper expenses of process, subject to this proviso that precognitions, plans, analyses, reports, and the like (so far as relevant and necessary for proof of the matters in the record between the parties), although taken or made before the bringing of an action or the preparation of defences, or before proof is allowed, and although the case may not proceed to trial or proof, may be allowed.

7. Except as otherwise provided in the Table of Fees, a solicitor may charge an account either on the basis of the inclusive fees of Chapters I and II or on the basis of the detailed fees of Chapter III of the Table of Fees, but he may not charge partly on the one basis and partly on the other.

8. In order that the expenses of litigation may be kept within proper and reasonable limits only such expenses shall be allowed in the taxation of accounts as are reasonable for conducting it in a proper manner. It shall be competent to the auditor to disallow all charges for papers, parts of papers or particular procedure or agency which he shall judge irregular or unnecessary.

9. Notwithstanding that a party shall be found entitled to expenses generally yet if on the taxation of the account it appears that there is any particular part of the cause in which such party has proved unsuccessful or that any part of the expenses has been occasioned through his own fault he shall not be allowed the expense of such part of the proceedings.

10. When a remit is made by the court regarding matters in the record between the parties to an accountant, engineer, or other reporter the solicitors shall not, without special agreement, be personally responsible to the reporter for his remuneration, the parties alone being liable therefor.

11. Subject to paragraph 14 of these General Regulations, in all cases, the solicitor's outlays reasonably incurred in the furtherance of the cause shall be allowed.

12. In the taxation of accounts where counsel is employed:

(a) counsel's fees and the fees for instruction of counsel in Chapter II and Chapter III of the Table of Fees are to be allowed only where the court has sanctioned the employment of counsel; and

(b) except on cause shown, fees to counsel and solicitor for only two consultations in the course of the cause are to be allowed.

13. Where work done by a solicitor constitutes a supply of services in respect of which value added tax is chargeable by him, there may be added to the amount of fees an amount equal to the amount of value added tax chargeable.

14. In Chapter IV, of the Table of Fees —

(a) necessary outlays, including fees for witnesses, are allowable in addition to the fees allowable under that Chapter;

(b) in Parts I, II and III, sheriff officers' fees and costs of advertising are allowable as outlays;

(c) in Parts I and II, in respect of paragraph 3 (attendance at court), and in Part III (Defended Actions and Defended Actions: Personal Injury Claims only), in respect of paragraph 5 (attendance at court), no fee is allowable for attendance at a continuation of the first calling, unless specially authorised by the court;

(d) in Part II, in respect of paragraph 7 (precognitions), and in Part III (Defended Actions and Defended Actions: Personal Injury Claims only), in respect of paragraph 6 (precognitions), in a case where a skilled witness prepares his own precognition or report, half of the drawing fee is allowable to the solicitor for perusing it (whether or not in the course of doing so he revises or adjusts it);

(e) in Part II, in respect of paragraph 15, and in Part III (Defended Actions and Defended Actions: Personal Injury Claims only), in respect of paragraph 19 (appeals), no fees shall be allowed in respect of accounts of expenses when the hearing on the claim for expenses takes place immediately on the sheriff or sheriff principal announcing his decision;

(f) except in personal injury claims falling within paragraph I (actions of a value from £1,000 to £2,500) of the following table all fees chargeable under that Chapter in respect of the actions mentioned in the left-hand column of the following table shall unless the sheriff, on a motion in that behalf, otherwise directs, be reduced by the amount of the percentage specified opposite those actions in the right-hand column of the following table:

TABLE

Actions	Percentage reduction
1. of a value* from £1,000 to £2,500	25%
2. of a value* of less than £1,000	50%

* "value" in relation to any action in which a counterclaim has been lodged, is the total of the sums craved in the writ and the sum claimed in the counterclaim.

   (g) in Part I, in respect of paragraph 1 (instruction fees), in relation to actions for reparation there are allowable such additional fees for precognitions and reports as are necessary to permit the framing of the writ and necessary outlays in connection therewith; and

   (h) in Part II, the fee allowable in respect of paragraph 14 (supplementary note of defence) is a fixed fee allowable only when a supplementary note of defence is ordered by the court.

TABLE OF FEES

[This Table of Fees is printed as amended by:

Act of Sederunt (Fees of Solicitors in the Sheriff Court) (Amendment) 1994 (SI 1994 No 1142) which came into force on 24th May 1994;

Act of Sederunt (Fees of Solicitors in the Sheriff Court) (Amendment) 1995 (SI 1995 No 1395) which came into force on 22nd June 1995;

Act of Sederunt (Fees of Solicitors in the Sheriff Court) (Amendment) 1996 (SI 1996 No 236) which came into force on 1st April 1996;

Act of Sederunt (Fees of Solicitors in the Sheriff Court) (Amendment) 1998 (SI 1998 No 2675) which came into force on 1st December 1998;

Act of Sederunt (Fees of Solicitors in the Sheriff Court) (Amendment) 1999 (SSI 1999 No 149) which came into force on 1st January 2000;

Act of Sederunt (Fees of Solicitors in the Sheriff Court) (Amendment) 2000 (SSI 2000 No 420) which came into force on 1st January 2001;

Act of Sederunt (Fees of Solicitors in the Sheriff Court) (Amendment) 2001 (SSI 2001 No 438) which came into force on 1st January 2002;

Act of Sederunt (Fees of Solicitors in the Sheriff Court) (Amendment) 2002 (SSI 2002 No 235) which came into force on 10th June 2002;

Act of Sederunt (Fees of Solicitors in the Sheriff Court) (Amendment No 4) 2002 (SSI 2002 No 568) which came into force on 1st January 2002;

Act of Sederunt (Fees of Solicitors in the Sheriff Court) (Amendment) 2003 (SSI 2003 No 162) which came into force on 1st April 2003;

Act of Sederunt (Fees of Solicitors and Witnesses in the Sheriff Court) (Amendment) 2004 (SSI 2004 No 152) which came into force on 4th May 2004;

Act of Sederunt (Fees of Solicitors and Witnesses in the Sheriff Court) (Amendment No 2) 2004 (SSI 2004 No 196) which came into force on 3rd May 2004;

Act of Sederunt (Fees of Solicitors and Witnesses in the Sheriff Court) (Amendment) 2005 (SSI 2005 No 149) which came into force on 25th April 2005;

Act of Sederunt (Fees of Solicitors in the Sheriff Court) (Amendment) 2006 (SSI 2006 No 295) which came into force on 1st July 2006;

Act of Sederunt (Fees of Solicitors in the Sheriff Court) (Amendment) 2007 (SSI 2007 No 87) which came into force on 1st April 2007;

Act of Sederunt (Fees of Solicitors in the Sheriff Court) (Amendment) 2008 (SSI 2008 No 40) which came into force on 1st April 2008;

Act of Sederunt (Fees of Solicitors in the Sheriff Court) (Amendment) 2009 (SSI 2009 No 81) which came into force on 27th April 2009.]

CHAPTER I

PART I. — UNDEFENDED ACTIONS (OTHER THAN ACTIONS OF DIVORCE OR SEPARATION AND ALIMENT (AFFIDAVIT PROCEDURE))

£

1. *Actions (other than those specified in paragraph 2 of this Chapter) in which decree is granted without proof —*

    (a) Inclusive fee to cover all work from taking instructions up to and including obtaining extract decree 265.30

    (b) In cases where settlement is effected after service of a writ but before the expiry of the induciae 212.10

    (bb) In cases where a court appearance is necessary because of a time to pay direction an additional fee of 59.45

    (c) If the pursuer's solicitor elects to charge this inclusive fee he shall endorse a minute to that effect on the initial writ before ordering extract of decree. Outlays such as court fees shall be chargeable in addition and taxation shall be unnecessary

2. *Actions of separation and aliment, adherence and aliment and custody and aliment where proof (other than by way of affidavit evidence) takes place —*

    (a) Inclusive fee to cover all work from taking instructions up to and including obtaining extract decree 927.00

    (b) If the pursuer's solicitor elects to charge this inclusive fee he shall endorse a minute to that effect on the initial writ after the close of the proof and before extract of the decree is ordered; and when the option is so exercised decree for expenses shall be granted against the defender for said sum together with the court fee, any shorthand writer's fee actually charged as provided by Act of Sederunt and also any other necessary outlays without the necessity for taxation.

3. Petition for appointment or discharge of a curator bonis —

    (a) Inclusive fee to cover all work enquiring into estate and taking instructions up to and including obtaining extract decree 827.65

    (b) (i) If the solicitor elects to charge the inclusive fee and to recover only the normal outlays as set out in head (ii) of this sub-paragraph, he shall endorse on the petition before ordering extract of the decree a minute setting out the said fee and the outlays. Taxation of charges so specified shall not be necessary.

        (ii) The normal outlays referred to in head (i) of this sub-paragraph are: reasonable fees for medical reports; court dues for deliverance; sheriff officers' fees for service; advertising costs incurred; and value-added tax chargeable on solicitors' fees.

PART II. — UNDEFENDED ACTIONS OF DIVORCE AND OF SEPARATION AND ALIMENT (AFFIDAVIT PROCEDURE)

1. In any undefended action of divorce or separation and aliment where —

    (a) the facts set out in section 1(2)(b) (unreasonable behaviour) of the Divorce (Scotland) Act 1976 ("the 1976 Act") are relied on;

    (b) there is no crave relating to any ancillary matters; and

    (c) the pursuer seeks to prove those facts by means of affidavits,

the pursuer's solicitor may, in respect of the work specified in column 1 of Table A, charge the inclusive fee specified in respect of that work in column 2 of that Table.

TABLE A

Column 1 *Work done*	Column 2 *Inclusive fee* £
1. All work to and including the period of notice	652.05
2. All work from the period of notice to and including swearing affidavits	463.30
3. All work from swearing affidavits to and including sending extract decree	142.65
4. All work to and including sending extract decree	1260.15
Add process fee	of 10%

2. In any undefended action of divorce or separation and aliment where —

    (a)   the facts set out in sections 1(2)(a) (adultery), 1(2)(c) (desertion), 1(2)(d) (two years' non-cohabitation and consent) and 1(2)(e) (five years' non-cohabitation) of the 1976 Act are relied on;

    (b)   there is no crave relating to any ancillary matters; and

    (c)   the pursuer seeks to prove those facts by means of affidavits,

the pursuer's solicitor may, in respect of work specified in column 1 of Table B, charge the inclusive fee specified in respect of that work in column 2 of that Table.

TABLE B

Column 1 *Work done*	Column 2 *Inclusive fee* £
1. All work to and including the period of notice	536.55
2. All work from the period of notice to and including swearing affidavits	258.20
3. All work from swearing affidavits to and including sending extract decree	142.65
4. All work to and including sending extract decree	938.40
Add process fee	of 10%

3. If —

    (a)   the pursuer's solicitor charges an inclusive fee under either paragraph 1 or paragraph 2 of this Part; and

    (b)   the action to which the charge relates includes a crave relating to an ancillary matter,

in addition to that fee he may charge, in respect of the work specified in column 1 of Table C, the inclusive fee specified in respect of that work in column 2 of that Table.

TABLE C

Column 1 *Work done*	Column 2 *Inclusive fee* £
1. All work to and including the period of notice	258.20
2. All work from the period of notice to and including swearing affidavits	151.10
4. All work under items 1 and 2	410.15
Add process fee	of 10%

4. If the pursuer's solicitor elects to charge an inclusive fee under this Part he shall endorse a minute to that effect on the initial writ before extract of the decree is ordered; and when the option is so exercised decree for expenses shall be granted against the defender for said sum together with necessary outlays; and taxation shall be unnecessary.

CHAPTER II

[Part I was revoked by Act of Sederunt (Fees of Solicitors in the Sheriff Court) (Amendment) 2000 (SSI 2000 No 420) with effect from 1st January 2001.]

PART II. — DEFENDED ORDINARY ACTIONS, COMMERCIAL ACTIONS AND FAMILY ACTIONS COMMENCED ON OR AFTER 1ST JANUARY 1994

£

1A. *Work before action commences – Ordinary Action and Family Action* — To cover all work which the Auditor is satisfied has reasonably been undertaken in contemplation of, or preparatory to, the commencement of proceedings 403.00

or such lesser sum as in the opinion of the Auditor is justified.

1B. Work before action commences – Commercial Action – To cover all work which the Auditor is satisfied has reasonably been undertaken in contemplation of, or preparatory to, the commencement of proceedings in a commercial action or such other sum as in the opinion of the Auditor is justified 588.85

1. *Instruction —*

    (a) To cover all work (except as otherwise specially provided for in this Chapter) from commencement to the lodging of defences including copyings 728.60

    (b) Where separate statement of facts and counterclaim and answers lodged, additional fee of 242.85

2. *Precognitions* — Taking and drawing — per sheet 66.50

    Note: Where a skilled witness prepares his own precognition or report, the solicitor shall be allowed half of above drawing fee for perusing it (whether or not in the course of doing so he revises or adjusts it).

3. *Productions —*

    (a) For lodging productions — each inventory 79.55

    (b) For considering opponent's productions — each inventory 39.55

4. *Adjustment* — To cover all work (except as otherwise specially provided for in this Chapter) in connection with the adjustment of the record including making up and lodging certified copy record —

    (a) Agent for any party 331.85

    (b) If action settled before expiry of adjustment period, each original party's agent 198.90

    (c) If additional defender brought in before Options Hearing, additional fee to each original party's agent 79.55

    (d) If additional defender brought in after Options Hearing, additional fee to each original party's agent 106.10

5. *Affidavits* — To framing affidavits, per sheet 26.45

6. *Options Hearing or Child Welfare Hearing* — To include preparation for and conduct of (each of) an Options Hearing or a Child Welfare Hearing and noting interlocutor —

    (a) Where initial hearing does not exceed one half hour 265.30

    (b) Where initial hearing exceeds one half hour — for every extra quarter hour 39.55

    (c) where hearing continued, for each continued hearing that does not exceed one half hour. 132.85

    (d) where continued hearing exceeds one half hour — for every extra quarter hour 39.55

    (e) for lodging and intimating or for considering note of the basis of preliminary plea — for each note lodged 66.50

7. *Additional Procedure* — for all work subsequent to Options Hearing including preparation for and attendance at procedural hearing —

where hearing does not exceed one half hour 263.80

for every extra quarter hour 39.55

7A. *Case Management Conference – Commercial Action —*

    (a) to include preparation for and all work incidental thereto prior to the first case management conference 212.10

£

(b) to include preparation and all work incidental thereto prior to each subsequent conference 106.10

(c) for every quarter hour engaged at conference.. 39.55

(d) waiting time – per quarter hour.. 35.50

Note: Where case management conference takes place by way of telephone or other remote means the foregoing charges shall apply.

7B. *Note of Arguments – Commercial Action –*

(a) fee for lodging and intimating or for considering first Note of Arguments 185.95

(b) for each Note lodged thereafter.. 66.50

8. *Debate (other than on evidence) –*

(a) Where counsel not employed

(i) To include preparation for and all work in connection with any hearing or debate other than on evidence 285.45

(ii) For every quarter hour engaged 39.55

(b) Where counsel employed, fee to solicitor appearing with counsel – per quarter hour 35.50

(c) Waiting time – per quarter hour 35.50

9. *Interim Interdict Hearings and other Interim Hearings —*

(a) Preparation for each hearing — each party... 132.55

(b) Fee to conduct hearing — per quarter hour 39.55

(c) If counsel employed, fee to attend hearing — per quarter hour 35.50

(d) Waiting time — per quarter hour 35.50

10. *Reports obtained under order of court —*

(a) Fee for all work incidental thereto 146.05

(b) Additional fee per sheet of report (maximum £62.80) 18.60

11. *Commissions to take evidence —*

(a) On interrogatories —

(i) Fee to solicitor applying for commission to include drawing, intimating and lodging motion, drawing and lodging interrogatories, instructing commissioner and all incidental work (except as otherwise specially provided for in this Chapter) but excluding attendance at execution of commission 397.95

(ii) Fee to opposing solicitor if cross-interrogatories prepared and lodged 265.30

(iii) If no cross-interrogatories lodged 79.55

(b) Open Commissions —

(i) Fee to solicitor applying for commission to include all work (except as otherwise specially provided for in this Chapter) up to lodging report of commission but excluding attendance thereat.. 265.35

(ii) Fee to opposing solicitor... 132.55

(iii) Fee for attendance at execution of commission — per quarter hour......................... 39.55

(iv) If counsel employed, fee for attendance of solicitor — per quarter hour 35.50

(v) Travelling time — per quarter hour.. 35.50

12. *Specification of documents —*

(a) Fee to cover drawing, intimating and lodging specification and relative motion

(i) Where motion unopposed 145.85

(ii) Where motion opposed — additional fee per quarter hour 35.50

(b) Fee to opposing solicitor —

(i) Where motion not opposed 79.65

(ii) Where motion opposed — additional fee per quarter hour 35.50

£

(c) Fee for citation of havers, preparation for and attendance before commissioner at execution of commission —

    (i) Where attendance before commissioner does not exceed one hour 145.85

    (ii) For each additional quarter hour after the first hour... 39.55

(d) If optional procedure adopted — fee per person upon whom order is served 35.70

(e) Fee for perusal of documents recovered — per quarter hour 35.50

13. *Amendment of record* —

    (a) (i) Fee to cover drawing, intimating and lodging minute of amendment and relative motion.. 132.55

      (ii) Fee for perusal of answers 53.25

      (iii) Fee for any court appearance necessary — per quarter hour 35.50

    (b) (i) Fee to opposing solicitor — for perusing minute of amendment............................ 106.10

      (ii) Fee for preparation of answers... 53.25

      (iii) Fee for any court appearance necessary — per quarter hour 35.50

    (c) Fee for adjustment of minute and answers where applicable to be allowed in addition to each party... 132.55

14. *Motions and minutes* —

    (a) Fee to cover drawing, intimating and lodging any written motion or minute, including a reponing note, and relative attendances at court (except as otherwise specially provided for in this Chapter) —

      (i) Where opposed... 185.95

      (ii) Where unopposed (including for each party a joint minute other than under paragraph 20(b)).. 79.55

    (b) Fee to cover considering opponent's written motion, minute or reponing note, and attendance at court —

      (i) Where opposed... 185.95

      (ii) Where unopposed 79.55

14A.*Withdrawal of solicitors* —

    (a) Fee to cover all work in preparation for any diet (or any diets) fixed under rule 24.2(1) and attendance at first such diet 132.50

    (b) Fee for attendance at each additional such diet, per quarter hour 35.50

14B.*Attendance not otherwise provided for* –

Court attendance not otherwise provided for –

    (a) where hearing does not exceed one half hour.. 79.15

    (b) where hearing exceeds one half hour – for every extra quarter hour 39.55

15. *Hearing limitation* —

Fee to include work (except as otherwise specially provided for in this Chapter) undertaken with a view to limiting the scope of any hearing, and including the exchange of documents, precognitions and expert reports, agreeing any fact, statement or document not in dispute, preparing and intimating any notice to admit or notice of non-admission and preparing and lodging any joint minute, not exceeding 662.40

16. *Procedure preliminary to proof* —

    (a) Fee to cover all work preparing for proof (except as otherwise specially provided for in this Chapter

      (i) If action settled or abandoned not later than 14 days before the diet of proof 424.40

      (ii) In any other case 769.00

    (b) Fee to cover preparing for adjourned diet and all incidental work as in (a) if diet postponed for more than 6 days, for each additional diet... 172.55

    (c) Fee for attendance inspecting opponent's documents — per quarter hour..................... 39.55

			£
17. *Conduct of proof* —			
(a)	Conduct of proof and debate on evidence if taken at close of proof — per quarter hour		39.55
(b)	If counsel employed, fee to solicitor appearing with counsel — per quarter hour		35.50
(c)	Waiting time — per quarter hour		35.50

18. *Debate on evidence* —

(a)	Where debate on evidence not taken at conclusion of proof, preparing for debate		132.55
(b)	Fee for conduct of debate — per quarter hour		39.55
(c)	If counsel employed, fee to solicitor appearing with counsel — per quarter hour		35.50
(d)	Waiting time — per quarter hour		35.50

19. *Appeals* —

(a)   To sheriff principal —

(i)	Fee to cover instructions, marking of appeal or noting that appeal marked, noting diet of hearing thereof and preparation for hearing	397.95
	If counsel employed —	225.75
(ii)	Fee to cover conduct of hearing — per quarter hour	39.55
(iii)	If counsel employed, fee to solicitor appearing with counsel — per quarter hour	35.50
(iv)	Waiting time — per quarter hour	35.50

(b)   To Court of Session —

Fee to cover instructions, marking appeal or noting that appeal marked and instructing Edinburgh correspondents 132.55

20. *Settlements* —

(a)   Judicial tender —

(i)	Fee for preparation and lodging or for consideration of each minute of tender	145.85
(ii)	Fee on acceptance of tender, to include preparation and lodging or consideration of minute of acceptance and attendance at court when decree granted in terms thereof	119.50

(b)   Extra-judicial settlement —

Fee to cover negotiations resulting in settlement, framing or revising joint minute and attendance at court when authority interponed thereto (not to include drawing, intimating and lodging any written motion) 265.20

(c)   Whether or not fees are payable under (a) or (b) above where additional work has been undertaken with a view to effecting settlement, including offering settlement, although settlement is not agreed — not exceeding 265.20

(d)   If consultation held to consider tender, extra judicial settlement (not based on judicial tender) or with a view to settlement (whether or not settlement is in fact agreed), attendance at it, per quarter hour 35.50

21. *Final procedure* —

(a)   Fee to cover settling with witnesses, enquiring for cause at avizandum and noting final interlocutor 198.90

(b)   Fee to cover drawing account of expenses, arranging, intimating and attending diet of taxation and obtaining approval of auditor's report and where necessary, ordering, procuring and examining extract decree or adjusting account with opponent 172.55

22. *Copying*

For the copying of papers by whatever means, if the Auditor determines (either or both) that —

(a)   the copying had to be done in circumstances which were in some way exceptional;

(b)   the papers which required to be copied were unusually numerous having regard to the nature of the case,

such charge, if any, as the Auditor considers reasonable (but a charge based on time expended by any person shall not be allowed).

Notes

1. Where a determination is required under this paragraph, the purpose of copying, the number of copies made and the charge claimed shall be shown in the account.

2. Copying done other than in the place of business of the solicitor shall be shown as an outlay.

23. *Process fee —*

Fee to cover all consultations between solicitor and client during the progress of the cause and all communications, written or oral, passing between them — 10 per cent on total fees and copyings allowed on taxation

24. *Instruction of counsel —*   £

   (a) Fee for instructing counsel to revise pleadings 79.55

   (b) Fee for instructing counsel to attend court 172.55

   (c) Fee for attending consultation with counsel —

       (i)   where total time engaged does not exceed one hour 172.55

       (ii) for each additional quarter hour 35.50

CHAPTER III

CHARGES FOR TIME, DRAWING OF PAPERS, CORRESPONDENCE, ETC

                                                                                                     £

1. Attendance at court conducting trial, proof or formal debate or hearing — per quarter hour 39.20

2. Time occupied in the performance of all other work including attendances with client and others and attendances at court in all circumstances, except as otherwise specially provided

   (a) Solicitor — per quarter hour 35.50

   (b) Allowance for time of clerk — one half of above

Note: Time necessarily occupied in travelling to such to be chargeable at these rates.

3. Drawing all necessary papers (other than affidavits) (the sheets throughout this Chapter to consist of 250 words or numbers) — per sheet 17.95

4. Framing affidavits — per sheet 26.65

5. Revising papers where revisal ordered — for each five sheets 7.45

6. *Copying*

For the copying of papers by whatever means, if the Auditor determines (either or both) that —

   (a) the copying had to be done in circumstances which were in some way exceptional;

   (b) the papers which required to be copied were unusually numerous having regard to the nature of the case,

such charge, if any, as the Auditor considers reasonable (but a charge based on time expended by any person shall not be allowed).

Notes

1. Where a determination is required under this paragraph, the purpose of copying, the number of copies made and the charge claimed shall be shown in the account.

2. Copying done other than in the place of business of the solicitor shall be shown as an outlay.

7. Certifying or signing a document 7.45

8. Perusing any document — per quarter hour 35.50

		£
9.	Lodging in process —	
	Each necessary lodging in or uplifting from process; also for each necessary enquiry for documents due to be lodged	7.45
10.	Borrowing process —	
	Each necessary borrowing of process to include return of same	7.45
11.	Extracts	
	Ordering, procuring and examining extracts, interim or otherwise	35.70
12.	Correspondence, intimations, etc..	
	(a) Formal letters and intimations..	3.40
	(b) Letters other than above — per page of 125 words..	17.95
	(c) Telephone calls except under (d)..	7.45
	(d) Telephone calls (lengthy) to be treated as attendances or long letters.	
13.	Citations	
	Each citation of party or witness including execution thereof....................................	17.95
14.	Instructions to officers	
	(a) Instructing officer to serve, execute or intimate various kinds of writs or diligence including the examination of executions..	7.45
	(b) For each party after the first on whom service or intimation is simultaneously made	7.45
	(c) Agency accepting service of any writ	17.95
	(d) Reporting diligence	17.95
15.	Personal diligence	
	(a) Recording execution of charge...	17.95
	(b) Procuring flat..	17.95
	(c) Instructing apprehension	17.95
	(d) Framing state of debt and attendance at settlement	21.60
16.	Sales	
	(a) Obtaining warrant to sell...	17.95
	(b) Instructing auctioneer or officer to conduct sale..	17.95
	(c) Perusing report of sale...	17.95
	(d) Reporting sale under poindings or sequestrations or any other judicial sales..................	17.95
	(e) Noting approval of roup roll	17.95
	(f) Obtaining warrant to pay...	17.95

CHAPTER IV — SUMMARY CAUSES

PART I — UNDEFENDED ACTIONS

	£
1. To include taking instructions, framing summons and statement of claim, obtaining warrant for service, instructing service as necessary by sheriff officer (where appropriate), attendance endorsing minute for and obtaining decree in absence and extract decree..............................	218.75
2. Service —	
(a) Citation by post wheresoever after the first citation for each party...............................	13.05
(b) Framing and instructing service by advertisement — for each party..............................	38.40
3. Attendance at court...	38.40

PART II — DEFENDED ACTIONS (COMMENCED BEFORE 10TH JUNE 2002)

£

1. Instructions fee, to include taking instructions (including instructions for a counterclaim), framing summons and statement of claim, obtaining warrant for service, instructing service as necessary by sheriff officer (where appropriate), attendance endorsing minute for and obtaining decree in absence and extract decree 174.65

2. Service —

    (a) Citation by post within the United Kingdom, Isle of Man, Channel Islands, or the Republic of Ireland — for each party 14.45

        Citation by post elsewhere — for each party.. 31.85

    (b) Instructing service or reservice by sheriff officer including perusing execution of citation and settling sheriff officer's fee — for each party.. 14.45

    (c) Framing and instructing service by advertisement — for each party............................... 46.10

3. Attendance at court —

    Attendance at any diet except otherwise specially provided. 46.10

4. Preparing for proof, to include all work in connection with proof not otherwise provided for 158.95

5. Fee to cover preparing for adjourned diet and all incidental work if diet for more than six days – for each adjourned diet 76.35

6. (a) Drawing and lodging inventory of productions, lodging the productions specified therein and considering opponent's productions (to be charged only once in each process)... 69.75

    (b) Where only one party lodges productions, opponent's charges for considering same...... 31.95

7. Precognitions —

    (a) Drawing precognitions, including instructions, attendances with witnesses and all relative meetings and correspondence — per witness 69.75

    (b) Where precognitions exceed 2 sheets — for each additional sheet............................... 31.95

8. Motions and minutes —

    Fee to cover drawing, intimating and lodging of any written motion or minute, excluding a minute or motion to recall decree, and relative attendance at court (except as otherwise provided in this Chapter) —

    (a) Where opposed... 94.90

    (b) Where unopposed (including for each party a joint minute or joint motion)................... 58.50

9. Fee to cover considering opponent's written motion or minute excluding minute or motion to recall decree and relative attendance at court —

    (a) Where motion or minute opposed.. 76.35

    (b) Where motion or minute unopposed 46.10

10. Conduct of proof —

    (a) Fee to cover conduct of proof or trial and debate on evidence taken at close of proof — per half hour 46.10

    (b) Waiting time — per half hour 24.05

11. Settlements —

    (a) Judicial tender, fee for consideration of, preparing and lodging of tender...................... 94.90

        (i) Fee for consideration and rejection tenders 69.75

        (ii) Fee on acceptance of tender — to include preparing and lodging, or consideration of minute of acceptance and attendance at court when decree granted in terms thereof.. 69.75

    (b) Extra-judicial settlement — fee to cover negotiations resulting in settlement, framing or revising joint minute and attendance at court when authority interponed thereto............ 158.95

12. Specification of documents —   £

  (a) Fee to cover drawing, intimating and lodging specification of documents and relative motion and attendance at court 79.35

  (b) Inclusive fee to opposing Solicitor.. 71.20

  (c) Fee to citation of havers, preparation for and attendance before commissioner, to each party — for each half hour.. 46.10

  (d) If alternative procedure adopted, a fee per person upon whom order served.................... 31.95

13. Commissions to take evidence —

  (a) Fee to cover drawing, lodging and intimating motion and attendance at court

     (i) Where opposed.. 94.90

     (ii) Where unopposed.. 58.50

  (b) Fee to cover considering such motion and attendance at court

     (i) Where opposed.. 76.35

     (ii) Where unopposed.. 46.10

  (c) Fee to cover instructing commissioner and citing witnesses.. 46.10

  (d) Fee to cover drawing and lodging interrogatories and cross-interrogatories — per sheet.. 31.95

  (e) Attendance before commissioner — per hour 44.40

  (f) Travelling time — per hour.. 31.95

14. Supplementary note of defence (when ordered).. 31.95

15. Appeals

  (a) Fee to cover instructions, marking of appeal or noting that appeal marked, noting of diet of hearing thereof and preparation for hearing 214.45

  (b) Fee to cover conduct of hearing — per half hour.. 46.10

16. Final procedure —

  (a) Fee to cover settling with witnesses, enquiring for cause at avizandum, noting final interlocutor.. 94.90

  (b) Fee to cover drawing account of expenses, arranging, intimating and attending hearing on expenses, and obtaining approval of sheriff clerk's report 94.90

  (c) Fee to cover considering opponents' account of expenses and attendance at hearing on expenses.. 46.10

PART III — DEFENDED ACTIONS (COMMENCED AFTER 10TH JUNE 2002)

          £

1. Work before action commences — to cover all work of a pre-litigation basis, to include discussions/correspondence with opposing party, exchange of documentation, etc (not exceeding 1 hour) 145.85

2. (a) Instruction fee to include taking instructions, framing summons and statement of claim, statement of valuation, obtaining warrant for service, enquiring for and consideration of Response Form (1½ hours).. 218.75

  (b) Where counter claim and answers lodged, additional fee of (1½ hours)............................ 218.75

  (c) If additional defender/third party brought in, additional fee to each original party's agent (1 hour) 145.85

3. Service — ....

  (a) Citation by post within the United Kingdom, Isle of Man, Channel Islands, or the Republic of Ireland — for each party 15.00

       Citation by post elsewhere — for each party.. 33.15

  (b) Instructing service or reservice by sheriff officer including perusing execution of citation and settling sheriff officer's fee — for each party.. 15.00

  (c) Framing and instructing service by advertisement — for each party.............................. 47.95

4. Attendance at first calling —   £

  (a) To include necessary preparation for and conduct of (each of) such hearings and noting interlocutor (1½ hours) 218.75

  (b) Where waiting/hearing exceeds one half hour — for every extra quarter hour 36.55

5. Attendance at court

  Attendance at any diet except as otherwise specially provided — per half hour 36.55

6. Precognitions — taking and drawing — per sheet.. 53.15

  Note: Where a skilled witness prepares his own precognition or report, the solicitor shall be allowed half of above drawing fee for perusing it (whether or not in the course of doing so he revises or adjusts it).

7. Reports obtained under Order of Court —

  (a) All work incidental to it 116.60

  (b) Additional fee for perusal of report, per quarter hour.. 28.50

8. Productions —

  (a) For lodging productions — each inventory 63.45

  (b) For considering opponent's productions — each inventory 31.75

9. Affidavits — to framing affidavits (where ordered) per sheet.. 21.15

10. Motions and minutes — Fee to cover drawing, intimating and lodging of any written motion or minute, excluding a minute or motion to recall decree, and relative attendance at court (except as otherwise provided in this Chapter) —

  (a) Where opposed... 148.40

  (b) Where unopposed — including for each party a joint minute or joint motion (other than under paragraph 14(b)).. 63.45

  (c) Where motion exceeds half hour, additional fee per quarter hour.................................... 28.50

11. Fee to cover conducting opponent's written motion or minute excluding minute or motion to recall decree and relative attendance at court —

  (a) Where motion or minute opposed 148.40

  (b) Where motion or minute unopposed 63.45

  (c) Where motion exceeds half hour, additional fee per quarter hour.................................... 28.50

12. Hearing Limitation —

  Fee to include work done (except as otherwise specially provided for in this Chapter) undertaken with a view to limiting the scope of any hearing, and including the agreement of evidence generally including the exchange of documents, precognitions and expert reports, agreeing any fact, statement or document not in dispute, preparation and lodging of witness list, preparing Schedule of Damages and preparing and lodging joint minute (not exceeding 1 hour).. 145.85

13. Procedure preliminary to proof —

  (a) Fee to cover all work preparing proof (except as otherwise specially provided for in this chapter)

    (i) If action settled or abandoned not later than 7 days before the diet of proof 364.45

    (ii) In any other case 437.35

  (b) Fee to cover preparing for adjourned diet and all incidental work as in (a) if diet postponed for more than 6 days, for each additional diet 137.95

  (c) Fee for attendance inspecting opponent's documents — per quarter hour....................... 31.75

14. Conduct of proof —

  (a) Fee to cover conduct of proof or trial and debate on evidence taken at close of proof — per quarter hour 31.75

  (b) Waiting time — per half hour 28.50

15. Debate on Evidence —   £

   (a) Where debate on evidence not taken at conclusion of proof, preparing for debate 105.95

   (b) Fee for conduct of debate — per quarter hour..   31.75

16. Settlements —

   (a) Judicial tender —

      (i) Fee for preparation and lodging or for consideration of each minute of tender 116.40

      (ii) Fee on acceptance of tender, to include preparation and lodging or consideration of minute of acceptance and attendance at court when decree granted in terms thereof...   95.45

   (b) Extra judicial settlement —

   Fee to cover negotiations resulting in settlement, framing or revising joint minute and attendance at court when authority interponed thereto 211.80

   (c) Whether or not fees are payable under (a) or (b) above where additional work has been undertaken with a view to effecting settlement, including offering settlement, although settlement is not agreed — not exceeding 211.80

17. Specification of documents —

   (a) Fee to cover drawing, intimating and lodging specification and relative motion —

      (i) Where motion unopposed 116.40

      (ii) Where motion opposed — additional fee per quarter hour......................................   28.50

   (b) Fee to opposing solicitor—

      (i) Where motion unopposed 63.45

      (ii) Where motion opposed — additional fee per quarter hour......................................   28.50

   (c) Fee for citation of havers, preparation for and attendance before commissioner at execution of commission —

      (i) Where attendance before commissioner does not exceed one hour.........................   116.40

      (ii) For each additional quarter hour after the first hour..   31.75

   (d) If optional procedure adopted — fee per person upon whom order is served 28.50

   (e) Fee for perusal of documents recovered — per quarter hour 28.50

18. Commissions to take evidence — Open Commissions

   (a) Fee to solicitor applying for commission to include all work (except as otherwise specially provided for in this chapter) up to lodging report of commission but excluding attendance thereat 211.80

   (b) Fee to opposing solicitor 105.95

   (c) Fee for attendance at execution of commission — per quarter hour...............................   31.75

19. Appeals —

   (a) Fee to cover instructions, marking of appeal or noting that appeal marked, noting of diet of hearing thereof, perusing Stated Case, framing Questions in Law and Adjustment thereof, preparation for hearing...   317.90

   (b) Fee to cover conduct of hearing on Adjustments — per quarter hour.............................   31.75

   (c) Conduct of Appeal — per quarter hour..   31.75

20. Final Procedure —

   (a) Fee to cover settling with witnesses and noting final interlocutor 159.10

   (b) Fee to cover drawing of expenses, arranging, intimating and attending diet of taxation and obtaining approval of auditor's report and where necessary, ordering, procuring and examining extract decree or adjusting account with opponent...   137.95

   (c) Fee to cover considering opponent's account of expenses, objections and attendance at hearing on expenses — per quarter hour 28.50

PART III — DEFENDED ACTIONS: PERSONAL INJURY CLAIMS ONLY
(COMMENCED ON OR AFTER 10TH JUNE 2002)

£

1. Work before action commences — to cover all work of a pre-litigation basis, to include discussions/correspondence with opposing party, exchange of documentation, etc (not exceeding 3 hours)... 414.90

2. (a) Instruction fee to include taking instructions, framing summons and statement of claim, statement of valuation, obtaining warrant for service, enquiring for and consideration of Response Form (not exceeding 2 hours)... 437.35

   (b) Where counter claim and answers lodged, additional fee of (not exceeding 1½ hours) 218.75

   (c) If additional defender/third party brought in, additional fee to each original party's agent (not exceeding 1½ hours)... 218.75

3. Service —

   (a) Citation by post within the United Kingdom, Isle of Man, Channel Islands, or the Republic of Ireland — for each party 18.05

       Citation by post elsewhere — for each party... 39.65

   (b) Instructing service or reservice by sheriff officer including perusing execution of citation and settling sheriff officer's fee — for each party 18.05

   (c) Framing and instructing service by advertisement — for each party............................... 47.95

4. Attendance at first calling —

   (a) To include necessary preparation for and conduct of (each of) such hearings and noting interlocutor (2 hours).. 285.20

   (b) Where waiting/hearing exceeds one half hour — for every extra quarter hour 39.55

5. Attendance at court

   Attendance at any diet except as otherwise specially provided — per half hour 79.55

6. Precognitions — taking and drawing — per sheet.. 66.35

   Note: Where a skilled witness prepares his own precognition or report, the solicitor shall be allowed half of above drawing fee for perusing it (whether or not in the course of doing so he revises or adjusts it).

7. Reports obtained under Order of Court —

   (a) All work incidental to it 145.85

   (b) Additional fee for perusal of report, per quarter hour.. 18.50

8. Productions —

   (a) For lodging productions — each inventory 79.55

   (b) For considering opponent's productions — each inventory 39.55

9. Affidavits — to framing affidavits (where ordered) per sheet.. 26.55

10. Motions and minutes — Fee to cover drawing, intimating and lodging of any written motion or minute, excluding a minute or motion to recall decree, and relative attendance at court (except as otherwise provided in this Chapter)

    (a) Where opposed 185.65

    (b) Where unopposed — including for each party a joint minute or joint motion (other than under paragraph 14(b))... 79.55

    (c) Where motion exceeds half hour, additional fee per quarter hour.................................... 39.55

11. Fee to cover considering opponent's written motion or minute excluding minute or motion to recall decree and relative attendance at court —

    (a) Where motion or minute opposed 185.65

    (b) Where motion or minute unopposed 79.55

    (c) Where motion exceeds half hour, additional fee per quarter hour.................................... 39.55

12. Procedure preliminary to proof —   £

    (a)   Fee to cover all work preparing proof — as follows — exchanging of witness list, documents list, skilled witnesses, reports, consideration of defender's schedule of damages, citation of witnesses, general preparation for Proof (except as otherwise specially provided for in this chapter) (not exceeding 3 hours)

        (i)   If action settled or abandoned not later than 7 days before the diet of proof 583.10

        (ii)   In any other case 768.25

    (b)   Fee to cover preparing for adjourned diet and all incidental work as in (a) if diet postponed for more than 6 days, for each additional diet 172.35

13. Hearing Limitation —

    Fee to include work done (except as otherwise specially provided for in this Chapter) undertaken with a view to limiting the scope of any hearing, and including the agreement of evidence generally including the agreement of photographs, sketch plans, documents, precognitions and expert reports, agreeing any fact, statement or documents, agreeing Schedule of Damages and preparing and lodging joint minute of admissions (not exceeding 3 hours) 583.10

14. Conduct of proof —

    (a)   Fee to cover conduct of proof or trial and debate on evidence taken at close of proof — per quarter hour 39.55

    (b)   Waiting time — per half hour 35.60

15. Debate on Evidence —

    (a)   Where debate on evidence not taken at conclusion of proof, preparing for debate 132.55

    (b)   Fee for conduct of debate — per quarter hour.. 39.55

16. Settlements —

    (a)   Judicial tender —

        (i)   Fee for preparation and lodging or for consideration of each minute of tender 145.50

        (ii)   Fee on acceptance of tender, to include preparation and lodging or consideration of minute of acceptance and attendance at court when decree granted in terms thereof... 119.40

    (b)   Extra judicial settlement —

    Fee to cover negotiations resulting in settlement, framing or revising joint minute and attendance at court when authority interponed thereto 264.85

    (c)   Whether or not fees are payable under (a) or (b) above where additional work has been undertaken with a view to effecting settlement, including offering settlement, although settlement is not agreed — not exceeding 198.80

17. Specification of documents —

    (a)   Fee to cover drawing, intimating and lodging specification and relative motion —

        (i)   Where motion unopposed 145.50

        (ii)   Where motion opposed — additional fee per quarter hour 35.60

    (b)   Fee to opposing solicitor—

        (i)   Where motion unopposed 145.50

        (ii)   Where motion opposed — additional fee per quarter hour 35.60

    (c)   Fee for citation of havers, preparation for and attendance before commissioner at execution of commission —

        (i)   Where attendance before commissioner does not exceed one hour 145.50

        (ii)   For each additional quarter hour after the first hour... 39.55

    (d)   If optional procedure adopted — fee per person upon whom order is served 35.60

    (e)   Fee for perusal of documents recovered — per quarter hour 35.60

18. Commissions to take evidence — Open Commissions —   £

   (a) Fee to solicitor applying for commission to include all work (except as otherwise
        specially provided for in this chapter) up to lodging report of commission but excluding
        attendance thereat 264.95

   (b) Fee to opposing solicitor 132.55

   (c) Fee for attendance at execution of commission — per quarter hour.............................. 39.55

19. Appeals —

   (a) Fee to cover instructions, marking of appeal or noting that appeal marked, noting of diet
        of hearing thereof, perusing Stated Case, framing Questions in Law and Adjustment
        thereof, preparation for hearing.. 397.50

   (b) If Counsel employed 225.30

   (c) Fee to cover conduct of hearing on Adjustments —per quarter hour.............................. 39.55

   (d) Conduct of Appeal — per quarter hour.. 39.55

20. Final Procedure —

   (a) Fee to cover settling with witnesses and noting final interlocutor 198.80

   (b) Fee to cover drawing of expenses, arranging, intimating and attending diet of taxation
        and obtaining approval of auditor's report and where necessary, ordering, procuring and
        examining extract decree or adjusting account with opponent... 172.35

   (c) Fee to cover considering opponent's account of expenses and attendance at hearing on
        expenses.. 35.60

21. Instruction of Counsel —

   (a) Fee for instructing counsel to attend court... 172.35

   (b) Fee for attending consultation with counsel —

        (i) Where total time engaged does not exceed 1 hour.. 172.35

        (ii) For each additional quarter hour... 35.60

Note: Excludes Adjustment, Debate, Amendment, Interrogatories, Process Fee.

Act of Sederunt (Fees of Solicitors in Speculative Actions) 1992
(SI 1992 No 1879)

[This Act of Sederunt came into force on 24th August 1992.]

Speculative fee charging agreement

2. (1) Where —

(a) Any work is undertaken by a solicitor in the conduct of litigation for a client; and

(b) the solicitor and the client agree that the solicitor shall be entitled to a fee for the work only if the client is successful in the litigation; and

(c) the agreement is that the solicitor's fee for all work in connection with the litigation is to be based on an account prepared as between party and party,

the solicitor and client may agree that the fees element in that account, as hereinafter defined, shall be increased by a figure not exceeding 100%.

(2) The client shall be deemed to be successful in the litigation where —

(a) the litigation has been concluded by the pronouncing of a decree by the court which, on the merits, is to any extent in his favour;

(b) the client has accepted a sum of money in settlement of his claim in the litigation; or

(c) the client has entered into a settlement of any other kind by which his claim in the litigation has been resolved to any extent in his favour.

(3) The fees element referred to in sub-paragraph (1) above shall, subject to sub-paragraph (4) below, comprise all the fees in the solicitor's account of expenses for which any other party to the litigation has been found liable, taxed as between party and party or agreed, before the deduction of any award of expenses against the client.

(4) The fees element referred to in sub-paragraph (3) shall not include the sums payable to the solicitor in respect of —

(a) any fees payable for copying papers and the proportion of any process fee and posts and incidents exigible thereon;

(b) any discretionary fee allowed under Regulation 5 of the General Regulations set out in the Schedule to the Act of Sederunt (Fees of Solicitors in the Sheriff Court) 1989; and

(c) any charges by the solicitor for his outlays.

Act of Sederunt (Fees of Witnesses and Shorthand Writers in the Sheriff Court) 1992 (SI 1992 No 1878)

SCHEDULE 1

WITNESSES' FEES

[Schedule 1 is substituted by:

Act of Sederunt (Fees of Witnesses and Shorthand Writers in the Sheriff Court) (Amendment) 2000 (SSI 2002 No 280) which came into force on 1st July 2002.

Amended by

Act of Sederunt (Fees of Solicitors and Witnesses in the Sheriff Court) (Amendment) 2004 (SSI 2004 No 152) which came into force on 4th May 2004.]

1. Skilled Persons

Where it is necessary to employ a skilled person to make investigation in order to qualify that person to report and/or give evidence in any action, charges for such investigations and for attendance at any hearing in the action shall be allowed at a rate which the Auditor of court shall determine is fair and reasonable provided that the court grants a motion to that effect not later than the time at which it awards expenses and the witness's name is recorded in the interlocutor.

2. Witnesses

A person who is cited to give evidence and in consequence incurs financial loss shall be allowed reimbursement, being such reasonable sum as the Auditor may determine to have been reasonably and necessarily incurred by the witness, but not exceeding £250 per day.

3. Travelling Allowance

In respect of any witness there shall be allowed a travelling allowance, being such sum as the Auditor may determine to have been reasonably and necessarily incurred by the witness in the travelling from and to the witnesses' residence or place of business and the Court.

4. Subsistence Allowance

In respect of any witness there shall be allowed a subsistence allowance, being such sum as the Auditor may determine to have been reasonably incurred by the witness for the extra cost of subsistence during the witnesses' absence from the witnesses' home or place of business for the purpose of giving evidence, and where the witness reasonably requires to stay overnight, for the reasonable cost of board and lodging.

5. Value Added Tax

Where any witness is a taxable person in terms of the Value Added Tax Act 1983, the amount of value added tax may be added by the witness to the witnesses' note of fee, and may be paid to the witness by the Solicitor.

6. Receipts and Vouchers

Receipts and detailed vouchers for all payments claimed in respect of a witness shall be produced to the party found liable in expenses, prior to the taxation of the Account of Expenses, and to the Auditor, if the Auditor requires.

7. Account of fees of Witnesses

The fees charged for any witness shall be stated in the Account of Expenses in a lump sum and the details of the charges shall be entered in a separate schedule appended to the Account as follows:

Name and designation	Where from	Days charged	Rate per day	Travelling and subsistence allowance	Total	Taxed off

SCHEDULE 2
SHORTHAND WRITERS' FEES

[Schedule 2 is printed as amended by:

Act of Sederunt (Fees of Shorthand Writers in the Sheriff Court) (Amendment) 1995 (SI 1995 No 1024) which came into force on 1st May 1995;

Act of Sederunt (Fees of Shorthand Writers in the Sheriff Court) (Amendment) 1996 (SI 1996 No 767) which came into force on 1st May 1996;

Act of Sederunt (Fees of Shorthand Writers in the Sheriff Court) (Amendment) 1997 (SI 1997 No 1118) which came into force on 1st May 1997;

Act of Sederunt (Fees of Shorthand Writers in the Sheriff Court) (Amendment No 2) 1997 (SI 1997 No 1265) which came into force on 1st May 1997;

Act of Sederunt (Fees of Shorthand Writers in the Sheriff Court) (Amendment) 1998 (SI 1998 No 999) which came into force on 1st May 1998;

Act of Sederunt (Fees of Shorthand Writers in the Sheriff Court) (Amendment) 1999 (SI 1999 No 613) which came into force on 1st May 1999;

Act of Sederunt (Fees of Shorthand Writers in the Sheriff Court) (Amendment) 2000 (SSI 2000 No 145) which came into force on 1st June 2000;

Act of Sederunt (Fees of Shorthand Writers in the Sheriff Court) (Amendment) 2001 (SSI 2001 No 136) which came into force on 1st May 2001;

Act of Sederunt (Fees of Witnesses and Shorthand Writers in the Sheriff Court) (Amendment) 2002 (SSI 2002 No 280) which came into force on 1st July 2002;

Act of Sederunt (Fees of Shorthand Writers in the Sheriff Court) (Amendment) 2003 (SSI 2003 No 246) which came into force on 1st June 2003;

Act of Sederunt (Fees of Shorthand Writers in the Sheriff Court) (Amendment) 2004 (SSI 2004 No 149) which came into force on 4th May 2004;

Act of Sederunt (Fees of Shorthand Writers in the Sheriff Court) (Amendment) 2005 (SSI 2005 No 150) which came into force on 25th April 2004;

Act of Sederunt (Fees of Shorthand Writers in the Sheriff Court) (Amendment) 2006 (SSI 2006 No 86) which came into force on 1st May 2006;

Act of Sederunt (Fees of Shorthand Writers in the Sheriff Court) (Amendment) 2007 (SSI 2007 No 211) which came into force on 1st May 2007;

Act of Sederunt (Fees of Shorthand Writers in the Sheriff Court) (Amendment) 2008 (SSI 2008 No 118) which came into force on 5th May 2008;

Act of Sederunt (Fees of Shorthand Writers in the Sheriff Court) (Amendment) 2009 (SSI 2009 No 103) which came into force on 4th May 2009.]

1. *Attendance*   £

    Attending at proofs or commissions —

    (a) per hour 37.87

    (b) minimum per day 151.39

2. *Cancellation*

    Where intimation of cancellation of attendance is made to the shorthand writer —

    (a) more than 21 days prior to the date of attendance no fee shall be charged;

    (b) 21 days or less prior to, and before 4 pm on the day prior to the date of attendance 75% of the minimum daily fee in paragraph 1(b) shall be charged;

    (c) on or after 4 pm on the day prior to the date of attendance the minimum daily fee in paragraph 1(b) shall be charged.

3. *Subsistence Allowance*

    A shorthand writer shall be allowed a subsistence allowance appropriate to civil servants entitled to class 2 rates.

4. *Transcripts*

    Extending notes of evidence —

    (a) subject to (b) below, per sheet of 250 words 6.20

    (b) overnight, per sheet of 250 words 7.59

5. *Copies*

    Copies of notes of evidence by carbon or any other means —

    per sheet 0.50

Rules as to Retaining Fees for Advocates

I. Special Retainers

1. A special retainer may be given with reference to any particular cause, and may be given in name and on behalf of one party, or of several parties having the same interest in the particular cause.

2. If the cause be not in dependence, the name and designation of the party, or (if more than one) of all the parties for whom the counsel is intended to be retained, should be distinctly specified in the letter of retainer. A retainer for A B and others, in any action between them and C D, or a retainer for A B in any action between him and C D and others, relative to a particular contract, or the like, is a good retainer for A B against C D, but not for or against others unnamed, who, when action is raised, may come to have a common interest with A B or C D as pursuers or defenders. But if the particular process or action is so described in the retainer as to be identified, and the counsel is expressly retained for or against the whole pursuers or defenders in that particular action, it is not necessary to specify all the names.

3. Counsel may be retained by special retainer for a corporation or public company, or for a common trading company, by its company name, without specifying the names of the partners, but this will not operate as a retainer for any individual partner for his separate or individual interest even in the same matter.

4. A special retainer endures for a year, but must be renewed before the expiry of every year, except in the case of a depending process, as explained in next rule.

5. A special retainer gives to the client a right to the services of the counsel retained throughout the whole progress of the cause, without the necessity of annual renewal. But if the counsel retained is not employed in any step of the cause in which, according to ordinary practice, such counsel — junior or senior as the case may be — would be employed, the retainer falls. The professional duty of counsel in matters of confidentiality will preclude his further involvement in the case for any other party.

II. Implied Retainer

1. When a counsel is employed to draw or revise a summons, defences, or other pleading, or is instructed to appear for a party to a cause in court, that is equivalent to a special retainer in the cause for the party by whom he is so employed or instructed.

2. But when a counsel is merely consulted as to the merits of a case, or gives advice, verbal or written, as to the raising or defending of an action intended or threatened, he is not thereby retained in the cause, but may be precluded by reason of confidentiality from acting for another party in the same cause.

III. General Retainers

1. A general retainer secures the services of a counsel for the party in all cases in which he may be engaged as a party on the record.

2. A general retainer may be expressed in general terms, provided the name and designation of the party may be distinctly stated.

3. If a special retainer be offered to a counsel, such instructions or employment in a cause as imply a special retainer, it is the duty of his clerk forthwith to intimate this to the agent of the party for whom he is retained in general, who may then send a special retainer applicable to the particular case, and is in that event entitled to a preference over the prior special retainer, or implied special retainer, on the other side. But if the agent of the party who has given the general retainer fails upon such notice to send a special retainer, it is the duty of the counsel to accept the special retainer, or instructions or employment offered on the other side.

4. A general retainer endures for the lifetime of the client and counsel, subject, however, to this condition, that if the client becomes a party to any action to process after the general retainer is given and does not employ the counsel who holds his general retainer, the retainer falls *eo ipso*, not merely as regards the particular case, but absolutely and to all effects.

5. General retainers are preferable according to their dates. If a counsel holds a general retainer for the pursuer, and also a general retainer for the defender of an action, he will be found to act for that party whose general retainer is earliest in date, provided that party avails himself of his preference by sending a special retainer applicable to the case. If the first special retainer comes from the party whose general retainer is the latest in date, notice must be given to the party having the right of preference, in the manner already explained, and that party must forthwith send his special retainer, otherwise the counsel will be bound to accept the special retainer of the party whose general retainer is latest in date.

12th June 1878

The Dean of Faculty determined that a general retainer binds counsel who accepts it to appear for person sending it in every Court of Law in Scotland, civil or criminal, in which his client is interested, and specially it binds counsel to appear for any client who is indicated before Court of Justiciary.

Only exceptions to rule are — (1) appeals to House of Lords; (2) Courts in which counsel are not expected to attend, eg Police Courts and Licensing Courts of Justices.

2008 Scheme

REVISED 2008 SCHEME
for the
ACCOUNTING FOR AND RECOVERY
OF COUNSEL'S FEES

Issued by the authority of
THE FACULTY OF ADVOCATES

Status of counsel's fees

1.—(1) Except in legal aid cases, or as otherwise provided for, every solicitor who instructs counsel has a professional obligation so far as reasonably practicable to ensure payment of counsel's fees, either as agreed or, failing agreement, as taxed by the Auditor of the Court of Session or the auditor of the appropriate sheriff court, as the case may be, on the basis of agent and client, client paying.

It will be good practice, where there is any room for doubt about the ability of the client to reimburse him for payment of counsel's fees, for the instructing solicitor to take an adequate deposit against costs to be incurred. Payment of counsel's fees shall be made in accordance with the provisions of paragraph 7.

Except as provided hereafter "the instructing solicitor" means the solicitor who instructs counsel. Where, however, the letter of instruction in terms of paragraph 2 (d) includes the name of the correspondent firm in Scotland from whom the instruction originates "the instructing solicitor" in this paragraph and in paragraphs 7(3), 7(7) and 7(8) means the correspondent firm in Scotland from whom the instruction originates.

(2) As standard practice, each item of work will be the subject of a proposed fee as it is undertaken. Where it is intended that payment of fees should be deferred, whether for a particular case or otherwise, agreement to such a process must be concluded with counsel's clerk prior to or at the time of issue of instructions. Where such agreement has been concluded, it will be assumed, provided all relevant letters of instruction note the basis of deferment and unless the counsel's clerk has specifically re-negotiated the matter with the solicitor concerned, that any other counsel whom the solicitor instructs in the same case, including other counsel to whom the instructions are passed on, will accept instructions on the same basis.

(3) A note of proposed fee will normally be issued within 30 days of completion of the item of work concerned. If counsel fails to issue a note of a proposed fee within 30 days of completion of an item of work, the instructing solicitor may make a request in writing to the counsel for a proposed note of fee to be issued in relation to that item. Unless otherwise agreed, if counsel fails without good reason to issue a proposed note of fee within 6 weeks of such a request, the instructing solicitor shall have no obligation to ensure payment thereof. Any dispute regarding the failure by counsel to issue a proposed note of fee and the obligation of the solicitor in that event shall be referred to the Committee referred to in paragraph 9. The Committee shall consider the matter having regard to any representations made by counsel and the solicitor and shall make recommendations to the Dean of Faculty. The decision of the Dean of Faculty shall be final.

(4) Whilst responsibility for meeting counsel's fees in a legally aided case is assumed by the Scottish Legal Aid Board, it remains incumbent upon the instructing solicitor to take reasonable care to comply with his obligations under the legal aid legislation. Where it becomes necessary to instruct counsel before the issue of a legal aid certificate, or after its expiry or suspension, the instructing solicitor must be prepared to accept the obligation so far as reasonably practicable of meeting counsel's fees, or issue instructions on a speculative basis. In each case the letter of instruction must be clear on the point.

Letters of instruction

2. The letter of instruction shall contain the following information:-

    (a) the name of the counsel instructed;

    (b) the name of the case or an identifying description of the matter to which the letter relates; (it is essential that such description should be consistent in succeeding instructions so that case records may be correctly integrated);

    (c) where appropriate, the party for whom counsel is instructed to appear, or whom counsel is instructed to advise or represent;

    (d) where appropriate, the name of the correspondent firm in Scotland from whom the instruction originates;

(e)   any reference which the solicitor wishes Faculty Services Limited to quote on counsel's account;

(f)   the Faculty Services Limited case reference (except in the instance of the first instructions in a case or where the first fee note has yet to be issued);

(g)   where appropriate, the legal aid reference; and

(h)   where fees are to be paid otherwise than when rendered, a note to that effect.

Fee with instructions and retainers

3. If a solicitor wishes to tender a fee with his instructions, he should do so by means of a cheque for the fee together with the appropriate VAT drawn in favour of Faculty Services Limited, or in favour of counsel if counsel is not a subscriber. The same applies to fees sent as retainers. A VAT receipt will then be issued by Faculty Services Limited, or by counsel's clerk where counsel is not a subscriber.

Special arrangements as to fees

4.—(1) Solicitors are at liberty to negotiate in advance with counsel's clerk the fees to be paid in any particular case or matter including speculative cases and deferment of fees. Likewise the basis on which fees are to be settled may be agreed by prior negotiation with counsel's clerk. Where agreement of this kind has been made, and in so doing the right to proceed to taxation has not been expressly reserved, it cannot thereafter be altered or taken to the Auditor for adjudication except by subsequent agreement between counsel and solicitor. It should be noted that the only proper channel of communication regarding counsel's fees is through counsel's clerk or , following the issue of a proposed fee note, through Faculty Services Limited. This does not mean that when a case is marked speculative, the only fees liable to be paid to counsel are those which are judicially recoverable by the solicitor. Counsel can insist on a taxation in any event to protect and preserve his fees.

(2)   Counsel may accept instructions on a speculative basis but are not bound to do so. A solicitor may only instruct counsel to act on a speculative basis in any case where the solicitor is acting on such a basis. (For the avoidance of doubt a speculative case is one where the solicitor is only to be paid a fee if the client is successful in the litigation). If a solicitor wishes to instruct counsel on this basis, he must state the fact explicitly in every letter of instruction in the case. It may not be assumed that because one counsel agrees to accept such instructions another will also agree to do so. During the course of a speculative action counsel shall raise notes of proposed fee in the ordinary way.

N.B. Counsel are not permitted to accept instructions on a contingency basis i.e. that fees will be based on any quantum measurement of the outcome.

Rendering of notes of proposed fees

5.—(1) In normal circumstances, Faculty Services Limited shall send to the instructing solicitor a note of proposed fee in respect of each item of work within a case as it is undertaken.

(2)   In respect of criminal legal aid cases, notes of proposed fee may be sent direct to the Scottish Legal Aid Board; but in that event a copy of the note of proposed fee will be sent to the solicitor endorsed to the effect that the fee note has been rendered direct. Notes of proposed fee rendered under this rule and received prior to the solicitor rendering his own account will be included in the solicitor's account and will be dealt with by the Scottish Legal Aid Board in accordance with the relevant arrangements.

(3)   If the instructing solicitor wishes to question the fee proposed by counsel he should inform Faculty Services Limited in writing as soon as possible and in any event within 6 weeks of the issue of the note of proposed fee. Where the instructing solicitor feels that a particular fee is grossly excessive, he may refer the matter to the Dean of Faculty.

(4)   Where, following notification to Faculty Services Limited as set out in sub-paragraph (3), the appropriate fee cannot be agreed, the Auditor of the Court of Session or the Auditor of the appropriate sheriff court, as the case may be, shall adjudicate as to what is a reasonable fee. Unless otherwise agreed in advance, this will be on an agent and client, client paying basis. In the event that there is at that time a final taxation disposing of expenses on an agent and client basis, such adjudication shall take place as part of that final taxation. Where there is no such taxation there may be a separate taxation if either the solicitor or counsel so wish. Where the amount of counsel's fee on the basis of agent and client is challenged at taxation, counsel or his representative shall be entitled to appear before the Auditor and make representations, and the diet of taxation may, if necessary, be adjourned for this purpose. In general, the expenses incurred in taxing counsel's fees shall form part of the general expenses of taxation, but if the Auditor considers the fee proposed by counsel to be excessive, and if counsel has exercised the right to appear before the Auditor and make representations, the Auditor may, at his discretion, order that such part of the expenses of taxation as are attributable to the intervention of counsel be borne by counsel.

(5) It should be noted that, unless otherwise agreed in advance, counsel's fees are to be paid on an agent and client, client-paying basis and are not restricted to what may be recoverable on a party and party basis. Counsel may accept instructions for pursuers in personal injury actions on the basis that he will only receive such fees as are recovered in judicial expenses but is not bound to do so. If a solicitor wishes to instruct counsel on this basis he must state the fact explicitly in every letter of instruction in the case. It may not be assumed that because one counsel agrees to adopt such instructions another will also agree to do so. If such a request is not specified in any letter of instruction counsel who accepts those instructions will be entitled payment of his fee for the work undertaken in terms of said letter of instruction even if the fee is not ultimately recovered from another party to the action.

Completion

6.—(1) This paragraph refers to cases where payment of fees has been deferred by prior agreement, speculative cases and civil legal aid cases.

(2) "Completion" in this paragraph means practical completion of the litigation up to the point to which it has been agreed that payment of fees should be deferred. The fact of completion shall be notified by the instructing solicitor to Faculty Services Limited as soon as practicable but in any event within one calendar month of that completion. In speculative and legal aid cases, and cases under the deferred guidelines in the Appendix hereto, Faculty Services Limited will make enquiry regarding completion one year after the last note of proposed fee is rendered. If no reply is received within one month, the case will be deemed to be completed. Where counsel has reason to believe that completion has been achieved, he may instruct Faculty Services Limited to initiate the process described at subparagraph (3). If completion has not in fact been achieved, the instructing solicitor should so inform Faculty Services Limited as soon as possible and preferably within 14 days of receipt of the statement.

(3) When completion is notified to Faculty Services Limited by the instructing solicitor, he shall indicate the date of the latest item of work undertaken by counsel. Where such date is more than 30 days prior to the receipt of notification of completion, Faculty Services Limited shall normally issue a statement forthwith. If the date of the latest item of work is less than 30 days prior to receipt of notification, issue of the statement may be deferred for a reasonable period having regard to paragraph 1 (3) hereof to allow Faculty Services Limited to obtain the appropriate information from counsel. In legal aid cases only notification of the fee by Faculty Services Limited will take place within 60 days of the instructing solicitor advising them of completion, failing which the solicitor will be entitled to render his account from the Board and, for the avoidance of any doubt will have no further liability to counsel in relation to any fees not yet rendered (unless recovered from the Board) The statement to be sent to the instructing solicitor shall take the form of a computer printout showing all appropriate details of the case including all fees indicating which items, if any, have been paid and shall be accompanied by all notes of proposed fee not already issued.

Payment of fees

7.—(1) Payment of fees in all cases where counsel is a subscriber should be made to Faculty Services Limited and NOT to counsel. Where counsel is not a subscriber payment should be to counsel and remittance should be to counsel's clerk.

(2) Payment will be expected when the note of proposed fee has been issued or on the issue of a statement in terms of paragraph 6(3) except as otherwise provided or agreed. For the purpose of this scheme the fees shall be regarded as "due" as from this point.

(3) In criminal legal aid cases, the instructing solicitor shall be responsible for furnishing counsel with such documentation as is required by the Scottish Legal Aid Board. It shall be the further responsibility of both the instructing solicitor and counsel to submit his account to the Scottish Legal Aid Board within three calendar months of conclusion of the trial or appeal as the case may be. Where such prompt submission of the solicitor's account cannot be made, Faculty Services Limited should be advised of the delay and the reasons for this in writing within the three month period outlined above. Where such prompt submission of the solicitor's account is made, Faculty Services Limited may be so advised. Otherwise, fees in this category shall be regarded as "due" six months from the conclusion of a criminal case to allow for submission of accounts by the instructing solicitor to the Scottish Legal Aid Board and for processing by the Board.

(4) Fees shall be placed in the "due" category by Faculty Services Limited at the end of the calendar month in which they become "due".

(5) Where fees have remained unpaid in the "due" category for one full calendar month and there has been no advice of good reason for delay in payment or non-payment, Faculty Services Limited shall place the case in the "overdue" category.

(6) Where fees have remained unpaid in the "overdue" category for a full calendar month and there has been no advice of good reason for delay in payment or non-payment, Faculty Services Limited shall intimate to the instructing solicitor an intention to refer the matter to the Committee referred to in paragraph 9.

(7) If the instructing solicitor has a reason for the non-payment of counsel's fees, he shall, within 21 days of receipt of intimation of the intention to refer the matter to the Committee, provide for the use of the Committee a brief report explaining that reason and a proposed timescale for payment or an explanation as to why he believes the proposed fee should be withdrawn. This report shall be considered by the Committee along with any representations from the counsel concerned. Thereafter the Committee shall make a recommendation to the Dean of Faculty as to whether in the Committee's view there is a good reason for non-payment. The recommendation of the Committee shall be intimated to the instructing solicitor.

(8) If no such report is received from the instructing solicitor the matter will be referred by Faculty Services Limited to the Dean of Faculty.

(9) If the Dean of Faculty does not accept there is good reason for non-payment, he shall write to the instructing solicitor, with a copy where appropriate to the senior partner and to the correspondent Edinburgh firm, in the following terms:—

"I am advised by Faculty Services Limited that the fees listed in the attached schedule have been overdue for payment for 3 full calendar months and the Committee and I / I have determined that no good reason has been intimated for non-payment. Under mandate from the Faculty I am obliged to advise you that unless settlement is received within one full calendar month from service of this notice, the name of your firm and its partners will be advertised within the practising membership of Faculty as defaulting in payment of fees, whereafter members will be permitted to accept instructions which come from you only in legal aid cases or if accompanied by payment of the appropriate fee."

(10) At the end of one full calendar month after the notice set out in subparagraph (9) has been served and in the event that the overdue fees in question remain unpaid, the Dean of Faculty, except where there is good reason to the contrary, shall advise practising members of Faculty in the following terms:-

"Non-payment of counsel's fees

Heading (Name of firm)
Heading (Partners)

I am advised by Faculty Services Limited that counsel's fees issued to the above firm remain overdue and unpaid without good reason having been given. Having myself applied for payment to the firm in writing in the terms authorised by the Faculty, and having been informed by Faculty Services Limited that payment has not been received despite my application, I now give notice that instructions which come directly or indirectly from this firm or its partners may be accepted only in legal aid cases or if accompanied by payment of an appropriate fee."

A copy of this notice shall be sent to the firm concerned and, where appropriate, to the correspondent Edinburgh firm.

(11) At the time that the Dean of Faculty advises the Faculty as set out in sub-paragraph (10), he shall also write to the Law Society of Scotland as follows:-

"Non-payment of counsel's fees

Heading (Name of firm)
Heading (Partners)

I have to advise you that the above firm has failed to meet its professional obligation to ensure payment of counsel's fees. The Committee has intimated to me that no good reason has been advanced for such failure [or – Notwithstanding the view of the Committee that a good reason has been advanced for non payment I have concluded that I do not accept there is a good reason for such failure]. Having served due notice of my intention to do so, I have today instructed members of Faculty that instructions which come directly or indirectly from this firm or its partners may be accepted only in legal aid cases or if accompanied by payment of an appropriate fee. Please treat this letter as a formal complaint."

A copy of this letter shall be sent to the firm in question and, where appropriate, to the correspondent Edinburgh firm.

(12) In normal circumstances payment of the fees in question will result in immediate revocation by the Dean of Faculty of his advice to practising members of Faculty in terms of paragraph 7(10), but in exceptional circumstances such revocation may, in the discretion of the Dean of Faculty, be delayed or

otherwise withheld. Notice of the decision of the Dean of Faculty will be sent to the Law Society, to the firm concerned and, where appropriate, to the correspondent Edinburgh firm.

(13) Where a case is legally aided and has been placed in the "due" category in accordance with subparagraph (3), Faculty Services Limited may apply for payment direct to the Scottish Legal Aid Board.

Monitoring outstanding fees

8. At the beginning of each month Faculty Services Limited shall provide to each firm of solicitors a statement in the form of a computer printout (analysed by partner where requested) of all cases where fees of subscribers are regarded as due for payment. The statement will highlight fees that are currently under dispute. There will be no such listing of those cases where by prior agreement payment of fees is deferred and remains deferred. Likewise, uncompleted legal aid cases will not be listed. It is open to a solicitor to seek a full listing of all cases at any time or on a regular basis. Correspondent firms of solicitors will receive a statement of all cases where fees have been issued and remain outstanding

Commitee

9. There will be a Committee comprising 3 members of the Faculty of Advocates appointed by the Dean. The remit of the Committee will be:

    (a)   To consider the Scheme for Accounting for and Recovery of counsel's Fees and make recommendations to the Faculty on amendments thereto.

    (b)   To carry out regular review of the financial limits for payment of counsel's fees in terms of Guidelines 3 and 4 to the Scheme's Appendix and make recommendations on an annual basis.

    (c)   To consider cases where a report is made in terms of paragraph 7(7) in connection with a dispute between the instructing solicitor and Faculty Services Limited as to whether "good reason" exists for non payment of counsel's fees and make recommendations to the Dean of Faculty.

Speculative and civil legal aid cases

10. In speculative cases, and in civil legal aid cases where a solicitor proposes to accept judicial expenses in lieu of a claim against the legal aid fund, before those judicial expenses are agreed or determined the solicitor shall confer with counsel's clerk in order to agree (i) what part of any proposed agreed global sum for judicial expenses represents counsel's fees; (ii) the sums for counsel's fees to be included in any account of judicial expenses to be submitted to the Auditor for taxation.

Non-subscribers

11. Where counsel are not subscribers to Faculty Services Limited this Scheme applies with such modifications as are necessary to take account of that fact: in particular (without prejudice to the generality of this paragraph) all references to Faculty Services Limited (except those in this paragraph and in paragraphs 3 and 7(1), and in the Appendix) shall be read as being references instead to "counsel's clerk".

Scope

12. This Scheme applies to the instruction by solicitors of counsel. For the avoidance of doubt it does not apply to (i) fees rendered by counsel for work done other than in their capacity as advocates (e.g. as a Commissioner, Reporter or Curator) (ii) direct access instructions.

APPENDIX

GUIDELINES TO COUNSEL IN RESPECT OF DEFERMENT OF FEES
UNDER THE NEW SCHEME FOR
THE ACCOUNTING FOR AND RECOVERY OF FEES IN CIVIL CASES

In terms of paragraphs 1(2) and 4(1) of the Scheme, deferment of payment of fees is permitted under an agreement reached by the solicitor with counsel's clerk. In order to preserve the main aims of the Scheme as a whole, however, deferment will be permitted, except in cases of the kind mentioned in the Note annexed hereto, only in one or other of the following circumstances: -

1. Upon an agreement between the solicitor and counsel's clerk in relation to a particular case or in relation to cases in a particular category or for a particular client or in relation to all cases, whereby it is agreed that fees should be rendered and payable at each of the following stages in the case, viz., at the closing of the

Record, after completion of a Procedure Roll Debate, Proof or Jury Trial and after completion of a Hearing in the Inner House.

2.   Upon an agreement between the solicitor and counsel's clerk in relation to a particular case or in relation to cases in a particular category or for a particular client or in relation to all cases, whereby it is agreed that fees should be rendered and payable at certain prearranged periods in time, subject to a maximum of six months in relation to any such period.

3.   Upon an agreement between the solicitor and counsel's clerk in relation to a particular case or in relation to cases in a particular category or for a particular client or in relation to all cases, whereby it is agreed that fees should be rendered and payable at every point when a prearranged total of rendered and unpaid fees net of VAT has been reached in that case, subject to a maximum total sum at any one time net of VAT of £5,000 in relation to senior counsel and £3,500 in relation to junior counsel.

4.   Upon an agreement between the solicitor and counsel's clerk in relation to a particular case or in relation to cases in a particular category or for a particular client or in relation to all cases, whereby it is agreed that fees should be rendered and payable at every point when a prearranged global total of counsel's fees rendered and unpaid net of VAT has been reached in that case subject to a maximum total sum at any one time of £1,000.

It is emphasised that except in cases of the kind mentioned in the note annexed hereto, the Scheme and these Guidelines do not permit any agreement to be reached between counsel or his clerk and a solicitor whereby all fees for work in any case are to be deferred until its completion. If an advocate wishes to achieve deferment in circumstances other than those covered by these Guidelines he should consult first with the Chairman of Faculty Services Limited whom failing any other Faculty officer.

As aids to interpretation:-

1.   Examples of "completion" as defined in paragraph 6(2) of the Scheme are: -

   (a)   In relation to paragraph 1 above – the date of the Interlocutor closing the Record OR the date of the Interlocutor making avizandum at the end of a Procedure Roll Debate, Proof or Jury Trial or Hearing in the Inner House.

   (b)   In relation to paragraph 2 above – the expiry of the agreed period in time.

   (c)   In relation to paragraph 3 above – the issue of the proposed fee note which results in the agreed total being reached.

   (d)   In relation to a case of the kind mentioned in the Note annexed hereto – the date of the final Interlocutor.

   (e)   In relation to cases settled extra judicially – the date of authority being interposed to the Joint Minute.

2.   "good reason" in terms of paragraph 7 of the Scheme will depend on the particular circumstances of the case but may, for example, include a situation where a solicitor has had to instruct counsel in an emergency situation and has been assured at the time that adequate funds would be forthcoming to meet counsel's fees, but in the event this proves not to be so. On the other hand mere unwillingness on the part of the solicitor to obtain funds to meet counsel's fees would not be likely to amount to "good reason"

3.   "exceptional circumstances" in terms of paragraph 7(12) of the Scheme will depend on the particular circumstances of the case but may, for example, include a situation where a firm has persistently been the subject of action in terms of paragraph 7(10) and (11).

4.   "subscriber" means counsel who is a subscriber to Faculty Services Limited.

NOTE ANNEXED

1.   Petitions for the appointment of and work instructed on behalf of liquidators, trustees in bankruptcy, curators bonis, judicial factors, curators ad litem and the like.

2.   Multiple poindings.

3. Speculative cases.

Tables of Fees under the Legal Aid Acts

Part A — Legal aid under the Legal Aid (Scotland) Act 1967 and advice and assistance under the Legal Advice and Assistance Act 1972

Paragraph 3 (1) of Schedule 4 to the Legal Aid (Scotland) Act 1986 provides that nothing in the 1986 Act shall affect any legal aid under the 1967 Act or advice and assistance under the 1972 Act in respect of which an application was determined before 1 April 1987; and, notwithstanding the repeal by the 1986 Act of the 1967 Act and the 1972 Act, they and any schemes, regulations, orders or rules of court made under them are to continue to have effect for the purposes of such legal aid or advice and assistance.

Part B — Legal aid and advice and assistance under the Legal Aid (Scotland) Act 1986

1. Advice and assistance (including assistance by way of representation)

Advice and Assistance (Scotland) (Consolidation and Amendment) Regulations 1996 (SI 1996 No 2447)

[This Statutory Instrument is printed as amended by:

Advice and Assistance (Scotland) Amendment Regulations 1997 (SI 1997 No 726) which came into force on 1st April 1997;

Advice and Assistance (Scotland) Amendment Regulations 2000 (SSI 2000 No 181) which came into force on 7th July 2000;

The Advice and Assistance (Scotland) Amendment (No 2) Regulations 2004 (SSI 2004 No 262) which came into force on 23rd June 2004;

The Advice and Assistance (Scotland) Amendment (No 2) Regulations 2005 (SSI 2005 No 171) which came into force on 30th April 2005;

The Advice and Assistance (Scotland) Amendment (No 2) Regulations 2006 (SSI 2006 No 233) which came into force on 12th June 2006;

The Advice and Assistance (Scotland) Amendment Regulations 2007 (SSI 2007 No 60) which came into force on 1st May 2007;

The Criminal Legal Assistance (Fees and Information etc.) (Scotland) Regulations 2008 (SSI 2008 No 240) which came into force on 30th June 2008.]

Fees and outlays of solicitors

17.—(1) Subject to paragraph (2) below, fees and outlays allowable to the solicitor upon any assessment or taxation mentioned in regulations 18 and 19 in respect of advice or assistance shall, and shall only, be —

    (a) fees for work actually, necessarily and reasonably done in connection with the matter upon which advice and assistance was given, due regard being had to economy, calculated, in the case of assistance by way of representation, in accordance with the table of fees in Part I of Schedule 3 and, in any other case, in accordance with the table of fees in Part II of Schedule 3; and

    (b) outlays actually, necessarily and reasonably incurred in connection with that matter, due regard being had to economy, provided that, without prejudice to any other claims for outlays, there shall not be allowed to a solicitor outlays representing posts and incidents.

(2) The fees and outlays allowable to the solicitor under paragraph (1) above shall not exceed the limit applicable under section 10 of the Act as read with regulation 12.

(3) In the application of paragraph (1) above so far as concerning assistance by way of representation in relation to a summary criminal matter, there is to be taken into account time necessarily spent in travelling

to and from the relevant court (other than one in the town or other place where the solicitor has a place of business) or any other place visited for the purpose of preparing or conducting the defence.

(4) Paragraph (3) above does not apply if it would have been more economical to use a local solicitor (where that would have been reasonable in the interests of the client).

(5) This regulation (so far as concerning criminal matters) is subject to the Criminal Legal Aid (Fixed Payments) (Scotland) Regulations 1999.

Assessment and taxation of fees and outlays

18.—(1) Where the solicitor considers that the fees and outlays properly chargeable for the advice or assistance exceed any contribution payable by the client under the provisions of section 11 of the Act together with any expenses or property recovered or preserved under the provisions of section 12 of the Act as read with regulation 16, he shall, within one year of the date when the giving of advice and assistance was completed, submit an account to the Board:

Provided that, where civil legal aid has been made available to an applicant to whom in connection with the same matter advice or assistance has been given, the account for such advice and assistance shall be submitted to the Board at the same time as that for civil legal aid; and any work which is charged under civil legal aid shall not be charged in the advice and assistance account.

(2) The Board may accept an account for advice and assistance submitted outwith the period referred to in paragraph (1) above if it considers that there is a special reason for late submission.

(3) Where the Board receives an account in accordance with paragraph (1) above, it shall assess the fees and outlays allowable to the solicitor for the advice or assistance in accordance with regulation 17 and shall determine accordingly any sum payable out of the Fund and pay it to the solicitor.

(3A) Where the solicitor has given advice and assistance by way of a diagnostic interview then he shall, within 3 months of the date when the giving of the advice and assistance was completed, submit an account to the Board separate from any account or accounts submitted under paragraph (1). No account supplementary to that provided for in this paragraph may be submitted.

(4) If the solicitor is dissatisfied with any assessment of fees and outlays by the Board under paragraph (3) above, he may require taxation of his account by the auditor; the auditor shall tax the fees and outlays allowable to the solicitor for the advice or assistance in accordance with regulation 17, and such taxation shall be conclusive of the fees and outlays so allowable.

SCHEDULE 3

TABLE OF FEES ALLOWABLE TO SOLICITORS

PART I — TABLE OF FEES ALLOWABLE TO SOLICITORS FOR ASSISTANCE BY WAY OF REPRESENTATION

1.   Subject to paragraph 3 of this Part, the fees allowable to a solicitor for providing assistance by way of representation shall be for criminal matters and civil matters as follows—

   (a)   Omitted by SSI 2008 No 240.

   (b)   fees, as undernoted, for work other than or subsequent to that described in Schedule 1B to the Criminal Legal Aid (Fixed Payments) (Scotland) Regulations 1999.

   1.   The fee for —

(i) any time up to the first half hour spent by a solicitor appearing in court or conducting another hearing;	£27.40	£33.15
(ii) each quarter hour (or part thereof) subsequent to the first half hour spent in court or conducting another hearing.	£13.70	£16.60

   2.   The fee for —

(i) each quarter hour (or part thereof) spent by a solicitor in carrying out work other than that prescribed in paragraphs 1 and 3 to 5 hereof, provided that any time is additional to the total time charged for under paragraph 1 above;	£10.55	£12.75
(ii) for each quarter hour (or part thereof) spent by a solicitor's clerk in carrying out work other than that prescribed in paragraphs 3 to 5 hereof shall be	£5.25	£6.35.

3. The fee for —
    (i) each citation of a witness including execution thereof;
    (ii) framing and drawing precognitions and other necessary papers, subject to paragraph 4 (iii) below — per sheet (or part thereof);
    (iii) instructing messengers-at-arms and sheriff officers, including examining execution and settling fee;
    (iv) lengthy telephone calls (of over 4 and up to 10 minutes duration); and
    (v) letters, including instructions to counsel, subject to paragraph 4 (ii) below — per page (or part thereof). £6.00   £7.25

4. The fee for —
    (i) attendance at court offices for performance of formal work including each necessary lodging in or uplifting from court or each necessary enquiry for documents due to be lodged;
    (ii) short letters of a formal nature, intimations and letters confirming telephone calls;
    (iii) framing formal papers, including inventories and title pages — per sheet (or part thereof);
    (iv) revising papers drawn by counsel or where revisal ordered by court — per 5 sheets (or part thereof); and
    (v) short telephone calls (of up to 4 minutes duration),................................... £2.40   £2.90

5. Where a document is copied and it is necessary to take a copy of more than 20 sheets (whether 20 of 1 sheet, 5 of 4 sheets or whatever), a fee of 8 pence shall be paid for each sheet copied.

Interpretation

2. In this table —
    a "sheet" shall consist of 250 words or numbers;
    a "page" shall consist of 125 words or numbers.

Petition by debtor for sequestration

3. The fees allowable to a solicitor for providing assistance by way of representation in relation to a petition by a debtor for the sequestration of his estate under section 5(2)(a) of the Bankruptcy (Scotland) Act 1985 shall be —

    (a) £33.15 for any time spent by a solicitor appearing in court in connection with the petition; and
    (b) £54.45 for all other work in connection with the petition.

PART II — TABLE OF FEES ALLOWED TO SOLICITORS FOR ADVICE AND ASSISTANCE OTHER THAN ASSISTANCE BY WAY OF REPRESENTATION

1. The fees allowable to a solicitor shall be calculated for criminal matters and for civil matters and for children's matters arising out of Part II of the Children (Scotland) Act 1995 as follows:

		Criminal	Civil	Children
A.	Time occupied in carrying out work for the client other than work described in paragraphs B to E below —			
	(i) solicitor — per quarter hour (or part thereof).............................	£11.60	£12.75	£12.75
	(ii) solicitor's clerk — per quarter hour (or part thereof).................	£5.77	£6.35	£6.35
B.	For short letters of a formal nature, short telephone calls (of up to 4 minutes duration), framing formal documents such as inventories and engrossing formal documents for signature — per sheet (or part thereof)	£2.64	£2.90	£2.90
C.	For letters other than in B above — per page (or part thereof), framing non-formal documents other than precognitions — per sheet of 250 words (or part thereof) and lengthy telephone calls (of over 4 and up to 10 minutes duration)...	£6.60	£7.25	£7.25

D.　For taking and drawing precognitions

　　for the first sheet of 250 words or less .... £23.15　£25.50　£25.50

　　for each subsequent sheet of 250 words .... £23.15　£25.50　£25.50

　　for each subsequent sheet of less than 250 words .... £11.60　£12.75　£12.75

E.　Where a document is copied and it is necessary to take a copy of more than 20 sheets (whether 20 of 1 sheet, 5 of 4 sheets or whatever), a fee of 9 pence shall be paid for each sheet copied

2. Omitted by SSI 2008 No 240.

Interpretation

3. In this Table —

　a "sheet" shall consist of 250 words or numbers; and

　　a "page" shall consist of 125 words or numbers.

2. Criminal legal aid

NOTE: THE UNDERNOTED REGULATIONS APPLY SUBJECT TO THE PROVISIONS OF THE CRIMINAL LEGAL AID (FIXED PAYMENTS) (SCOTLAND) REGULATIONS 1999 (SI 1999 NO 491) — SEE PP 98–106.

Criminal Legal Aid (Scotland) (Fees) Regulations 1989 (SI 1989 No 1491)

[This Statutory Instrument is printed as amended by:

Criminal Legal Aid (Scotland) (Fees) Amendment Regulations 1990 (SI 1990 No 474) (counsel's fees);

Criminal Legal Aid (Scotland) (Fees) Amendment (No 2) Regulations 1990 (SI 1990 No 1035) (solicitors' fees);

Criminal Legal Aid (Scotland) (Fees) Amendment Regulations 1991 (SI 1991 No 566) (solicitors' fees) which came into force on 1st April 1991;

Criminal Legal Aid (Scotland) (Fees) Amendment Regulations 1992 (SI 1992 No 374) (solicitors' fees) which came into force on 1st April 1992;

Criminal Legal Aid (Scotland) (Fees) Amendment Regulations 1997 (SI 1997 No 719) which came into force on 1st April 1997;

The Scotland Act 1998 (Consequential Modifications) No 1 Order 1999 (SI 1999 No 1042) which came into force on 6th May 1999;

Criminal Legal Aid (Scotland) (Fees) Amendment Regulations 2002 (SSI 2002 No 246) which came into force on 17th June 2002;

Criminal Legal Aid (Youth Courts) (Scotland) Regulations 2003 (SSI 2003 No 249) which came into force on 2nd June 2003;

Criminal Legal Aid (Scotland) (Fees) Amendment Regulations 2004 (SSI 2004 No 264) which came into force on 28th June 2004;

Criminal Legal Aid (Scotland) (Fees) Amendment (No 2) Regulations 2004 (SSI 2004 No 316) which came into force on 2nd July 2004;

Criminal Legal Aid (Scotland) (Fees) Amendment Regulations 2005 (SSI 2005 No 113) which came into force on 25th March 2005;

Criminal Legal Aid (Scotland) (Fees) Amendment (No 2) Regulations 2005 (SSI 2005 No 584) which came into force on 10th December 2005;

Criminal Legal Aid (Scotland) (Fees) Amendment (No 3) Regulations 2005 (SSI 2005 No 656) which came into force on 29th January 2006;

Criminal Legal Aid (Summary Justice Pilot Courts and Bail Conditions) (Scotland) Regulations 2006 (SSI 2006 No 234) which came into force on 2nd June 2006;

Criminal Legal Aid (Scotland) (Fees) Amendment Regulations 2006 (SSI 2006 No 515) whcih came into force on 16th November 2006;

Criminal Legal Aid (Scotland) (Fees) Amendment Regulations 2007 (SSI 2007 No 180) which came into force on 29th March 2007;

Criminal Legal Assistance (Fees and Information etc.) (Scotland) Regulations 2008 (SSI 2008 No 240) which came into force on 30th June 2008.]

Fees allowance to solicitors: general provisions

4.—(1) Subject to the following provisions of this regulation and to regulations 5, 6 and 9, the fees allowable to solicitors shall be those specified in Schedule 1.

(2) Where a nominated solicitor represents two or more persons charged in the same indictment or complaint, or appealing against conviction or sentence in respect of the same indictment or complaint he shall submit one account in respect of all those persons.

(3) Where a nominated solicitor requires another solicitor, whether an Edinburgh solicitor in connection with an appeal or on a remit for sentence, or a solicitor at the place of the prison or the court, or a local solicitor for the purpose of local precognitions or inquiry, nevertheless only one account shall be submitted by the nominated solicitor (payment of the other solicitor being a matter for adjustment between the nominated solicitor and the other solicitor out of the fees payable hereunder), but in determining the sum to be allowed to the nominated solicitor account shall be taken also of the work carried out by that other solicitor.

(4) Where the work done by a solicitor constitutes a supply of services in respect of which value-added tax is chargeable, there may be added to the amount of fees allowed to the solicitor an amount equal to the amount of value-added tax chargeable.

Solicitors' fees for identification parades and judicial examinations

5.—(1) The duty solicitor or, where criminal legal aid may be provided by a solicitor other than the duty solicitor, the nominated solicitor shall be allowed, in respect of attendance at an identification parade to which section 21(4)(b) of the 1986 Act applies, fees at the following rates:

First hour of attendance — £93.80;

Each subsequent quarter hour — £11.82.

(2) The duty solicitor or the nominated solicitor shall be allowed in respect of representing an accused person at a judicial examination (whether a first examination or a further examination) to which sections 35 to 39 of the Criminal Procedure (Scotland) Act 1995 apply —

(a)   fees in accordance with the rates specified in regulation 6(1); and

(b)   fees in respect of any necessary waiting time or any other necessary work relating to the judicial examination, determined in accordance with regulation 7.

(3) Any fees allowed to a nominated solicitor under this regulation shall be in addition to any fees allowed to him under regulation 7.

Duty solicitors' fees

6.—(1) There shall be allowed to the duty solicitor representing accused persons in the sheriff or district court fees on the following scales:

(a)   for attendance at the first session of a court for the day, a sessional fee of £63 for the first case in which the accused pleads not guilty or which is adjourned under section 145 of the 1995 Act and £9 for each additional such case, subject to a maximum total fee of £140 for the session until its termination on completion of business for the day or on adjournment by the court, whichever is the earlier;

(aa) for attendance a that session, a fee of £70 for each case in which the accused pleads guilty;

(b)   for attendance at any other session of that court on the same day, a sessional fee of £63 for the first case in which the accused pleads not guilty or which is adjourned under section 145 of the 1995 Act and £9 for each additional such case, subject to a maximum total fee of £93 for each such other session;

(c)   for attendance at any other such session, a fee of £70 for each case in which the accused pleads guilty:

Provided that the fee according to the foregoing scale shall cover the appearance in court of the duty solicitor on behalf of the accused as well as any interview or interviews with the accused or others whether such interview or interviews take place during the same or another session.

(2) Where, following a plea of guilty or in circumstances where the accused has not been called on to plead, one or more adjournments are ordered by the court, and the duty solicitor requires to appear again, then an additional fee shall be payable to the duty solicitor in respect of —

(a)   additional interviews with the accused or others; and

(b)   attendances at court other than during the course of the duty solicitor's period of duty.

The amount of such additional fee calculated on the basis of the fees set out in Schedule 1 shall be such sum not exceeding £150 (of which the relevant fee of £70 under paragraph (1) is to form part) as shall form reasonable remuneration having regard to the additional work and time involved.

(3) There shall be allowed to the duty solicitor making, for an accused person in the sheriff or district court,

a preliminary plea to the competency or relevancy of the petition or complaint, or conducting any plea in bar of trial or any mental health proof, or any proof in mitigation or any proof of a victim statement an additional fee to be calculated on the basis of the fees set out in Schedule 1, the amount of such additional fee to be such sum not exceeding £150 as shall form reasonable remuneration having regard to the additional work and time involved.

(3A) In an exceptional case, the Board may pay to the duty solicitor such fees other than those specified in paragraph (2) or (3) (and to a higher limit) as it considers appropriate in the circumstances of the case.

(3B) Where fees are payable under this regulation, the duty solicitor is not entitled to separate payment in respect of any expenses incurred in travelling to and from the court (despite any entitlement to such payment that would arise but for this paragraph).

(3C) But paragraph (3B) does not prevent the Board paying such fees as are reasonably required for the purpose of securing the availability of a duty solicitor at a remote court.

(4) Where the duty solicitor represents an accused person before a court which has been designated by the sheriff principal as a youth court, domestic abuse court or summary justice pilot court, the maximum fees prescribed in paragraph (2) shall not apply.

Fees allowable to solicitors

7.—(1) Subject to the provisions of regulations 4, 5, 6 and 9, and paragraph (2) of this regulation, a solicitor shall be allowed such amount of fees as shall be determined to be reasonable remuneration for work actually and reasonably done, and travel and waiting time actually and reasonably undertaken or incurred, due regard being had to economy. The fees allowed shall be calculated in accordance with Schedule 1.

(2) In determining the fees specified in paragraph (1) above there shall be taken into account —

    (a) time necessarily spent at the court on any day in waiting for the case or the appeal to be heard, where such time had not been occupied in waiting for or conducting another case; and

    (b) time necessarily spent in travelling to and from the court at which the accused appears or the trial or appeal takes place (not being a court in the town or place where the solicitor has a place of business) and to and from the prison and any place visited for the purpose of preparing or conducting the defence or appeal;

Provided that it would not have been more economical to use a local solicitor unless it was reasonable in the interests of the client that the nominated solicitor or a solicitor assisting the nominated solicitor in terms of regulation 4(3) should attend personally.

Outlays allowable to solicitors

8.—(1) A solicitor shall be allowed the following outlays, due regard being had to economy —

    (a) expenses actually and reasonably incurred by himself or his clerk in travelling to and from the court at which the accused person appears or the trial or appeal takes place (not being a court in the town or place where the solicitor has a place of business) and to and from the prison and any place visited for the purpose of preparing or conducting the defence or appeal:

Provided that where public transport is not used a reasonable mileage allowance shall be treated as an outlay;

    (b) fees paid to witnesses who are not on the Crown list, which fees shall not exceed such sums as are considered by the Board to be reasonable having regard to the sums payable from time to time by the Crown to witnesses of the same categories; and

    (c) any out of pocket expenses actually and reasonably incurred, provided that without prejudice to any other claims for outlays there shall not be allowed to a solicitor outlays representing posts and incidents.

(2) Where a witness is a person giving evidence of fact or expert evidence and value-added tax is chargeable in respect of giving that evidence, and the witness adds an amount equal to the tax chargeable to his note of fee, the amount so added may be allowed to the solicitor as an outlay.

Submission of accounts

9.—(1) Subject to paragraph (2) accounts prepared in respect of fees and outlays allowable to solicitors and fees allowable to counsel shall be submitted to the Board not later than 4 months after the date of conclusion of the proceedings in respect of which that legal aid was granted.

(2) The Board may accept accounts submitted in respect of fees and outlays allowable to solicitors and fees allowable to counsel later than the 4 months referred to in paragraph (1) if it considers that there is a special reason for late submission.

Fees allowable to counsel

10.—(1) Counsel shall be allowed such fee as appears to the Board, or at taxation the auditor to represent reasonable remuneration, calculated in accordance with Schedule 2 or 3, for work actually and reasonably done, due regard being had to economy.

(2) Where work done by counsel constitutes a supply of services in respect of which value-added tax is chargeable, there may be added to the amount of fees allowable to counsel an amount equal to the amount of value-added tax chargeable thereon.

Taxation of fees and outlays

11.—(1) If any question or dispute arises between the Board and a solicitor or counsel as to the amount of fees or outlays allowable to the solicitor, or as to the amount of fees allowable to counsel, from the Fund in respect of legal aid in criminal proceedings in–

  (a) the High Court, including appeals, the matter shall be referred for taxation to the Auditor of the Court of Session;

  (b) the Judicial Committee of the Privy Council, the matter shall be referred for taxation to the Registrar of the Judicial Committee of the Privy Council; or

  (c) the sheriff or district court, the matter shall be referred for taxation to the auditor of the sheriff court for the district in which those proceedings took place.

(2) A reference to an auditor under this regulation may be made at the instance of the solicitor concerned or, where the question in dispute affects the fees allowable to counsel, of the counsel concerned, or of the Board and the auditor concerned shall give reasonable notice of the diet of taxation to the solicitor or counsel as appropriate and the Board.

(3) The Board and any other party to a reference under paragraph (1)(a) or (c) shall have the right to state written objections to the High Court or, as the case may be, the sheriff in relation to the report of the auditor within 14 days of issue of such report and the Board and any such other party may be heard thereon.

11A. —(1) In relation to proceedings in the Judicial Committee of the Privy Council, the Board and any other party to a reference to the auditor who is dissatisfied with all or part of a taxation shall have the right to lodge a petition to the Judicial Committee of the Privy Council within 14 days of the taxation setting out the items objected to and the nature and grounds of the objections.

(2) The petition shall be served on the Board, any such other party who attended the taxation and any other party to whom the auditor directs that a copy should be delivered.

(3) Any party upon whom such a petition is delivered may within 14 days after such delivery lodge a response to the petition which shall be served on the Board, any such other party who attended the taxation and any other party to whom the auditor directs that a copy should be delivered.

(4) The petition and responses, if any, shall be considered by a Board of the Judicial Committee of the Privy Council which may allow or dismiss the petition without a hearing, invite any or all of the parties to lodge submissions or further submissions in writing or direct that an oral hearing be held.

SCHEDULE 1   Regulation 7

DESCRIPTION OF WORK AND FEES FOR CALCULATING REMUNERATION OF SOLICITORS IN THE JUDICIAL COMMITTEE OF THE PRIVY COUNCIL, HIGH, SHERIFF AND DISTRICT COURTS

			Summary Procedure	*Solemn Procedure*
1.	The fee for —			
	(a)	any time up to the first half hour spent by a solicitor conducting a trial in court or conducting another hearing	£27.40	£34.02
	(b)	each quarter hour (or part thereof) subsequent to the first half hour spent in so conducting a trial or other hearing	£13.70	£17.01
2.	The fee for each quarter hour (or part thereof) spent by a solicitor in waiting time or meeting with the client, provided that any time is additional to the total time charged for under paragraph 1 above.		£10.55	£12.38
3.	The fee for—			
	(a)	each quarter hour (or part thereof) spent by a solicitor in carrying out work other than that prescribed in paragraphs 1, 2 and 4 to 6 hereof, provided that any time is additional to the total time charged for under paragraphs 1 and 2 above;...	£10.55	£11.82

(b)	each quarter hour (or part thereof) spent by a solicitor's clerk in carrying out work other than that prescribed in paragraphs 4 to 6 hereof.	£5.25	£5.88

4. The fee for—

(a) each citation of a witness including execution thereof;

(b) short formal letters, letters each having a similar nature, instructions and letters confirming telephone calls;

(c) instructing messengers at arms and sheriff officers, including examining execution and settling fee;

(d) lengthy telephone calls (of over 4 and up to 10 minutes' duration); and

(e) letters, including instructions to counsel - per page (or part thereof), subject to paragraph 5(b) below,

in each of paragraphs (a) (e). £6.00 £6.72

5. The fee for-

(a) attendance at court offices for performance of formal work including each necessary lodging in or uplifting from court or each necessary inquiry for documents due to be lodged;

(b) Short formal letters, letters each having a similar nature, intimations and letters confirming telephone calls;

(c) framing formal papers, including inventories and title pages - per sheet (or part thereof);

(d) revising papers drawn by counsel or where revisal ordered by court - per 5 sheets (or part thereof); and

(e) short telephone calls (of up to 4 minutes' duration),

in each of paragraphs (a) (e)... £2.40 £2.69

6. Where a document is copied and it is necessary to take a copy of more than 20 sheets (whether 20 of one sheet, 5 of 4 sheets or whatever) for each sheet copied a fee of £0.08 £0.09

Interpretation

7. In this Schedule—

"court" means the Judicial Committee of the Privy Council, the High Court, the sheriff court or the district court as the case may be;

a "sheet" shall consist of 250 words or numbers; and

a "page" shall consist of 125 words or numbers."

SCHEDULE 2

Regulation 10

FEES OF COUNSEL

Notes on the operation of Schedule 2

1. Subject to the following provisions of this Schedule, fees shall be calculated by the Board, and in the event of a question or dispute by the auditor, in accordance with the Table of Fees in this Schedule.

2. Where the Table of Fees does not prescribe a fee for any item of work or category of proceedings the Board, or as the case may be the auditor, shall allow such fee as appears appropriate to provide reasonable remuneration for the work with regard to all the circumstances, including the general levels of fees in the Table of Fees.

3. In the assessment and taxation of counsel's fees–

(a) counsel's fees are allowed only where the Board has sanctioned the employment of counsel or counsel is automatically available;

(b) junior counsel shall only be allowed the fees prescribed in Chapter 1 of Parts I to III of the Table of Fees even where sanction has been granted for the employment of senior counsel in the case, except in any case to which sub-paragraph (c) below applies;

(c) where a senior junior is representing an accused person in a multiple accused case at first instance and where any co-accused is represented by senior counsel, the fees payable to senior junior shall be those prescribed in the Table of Fees for junior as leader, and the fees payable to any junior counsel assisting senior junior shall be those of junior with leader;

(d) except on cause shown, fees for only two consultations in the case shall be allowed;

(e) except on cause shown, fees for senior counsel or, as the case may be, for both senior and junior counsel shall not be payable for attendance at hearings which do not require the attendance of senior or, as the case may be, both senior and junior counsel;

(f) the auditor shall not have regard to any information produced by counsel at taxation which was not made available to the Board at the time the Board made the offer to counsel which is subject to taxation;

(g) although counsel may keep records of professional services based on the number of hours expended on the work, counsel shall not be entitled to fees at an hourly rate in addition to the fees prescribed in the Table of Fees; and

(h) correspondence, telephone calls, written work (other than work for which fees are prescribed in the Table of Fees) and meetings between counsel acting for the same assisted person are not allowable as separate items and shall be subsumed within the fees set out for the conduct of a hearing.

Appeals in the High Court of Justiciary

4. The Board, or as the case may be the auditor, shall have power to increase any fee prescribed in Part II of the Table of Fees where satisfied that, because of the particular complexity or difficulty of the work or any other particular circumstances, such an increase is necessary to provide reasonable remuneration for the work. This power shall only be exercised in the following circumstances and subject to the following conditions:–

(a) the Board, or as the case may be the auditor, shall have regard to the general level of fees in Part II of the Table of Fees;

(b) the fees prescribed in Part II of the Table of Fees are the fees for a case of average complexity or difficulty requiring the involvement of junior counsel or, where appropriate, senior counsel and includes the level of preparation which would not be considered unusual for such a case;

(c) the factors which shall be taken into account in considering an increase in any fee are–

(i) novelty of the issues of law;

(ii) unusually complex issues of fact;

(iii) issues of considerable legal significance; and

(iv) unusually high level of preparation;

(d) counsel seeking an enhanced fee shall identify and vouch such factors under sub paragraph (c) above as apply to the case, and the Board, or as the case may be the auditor, shall require to be satisfied that the factors identified and vouched had a significant effect on the conduct of the case before allowing such a fee;

(e) in the event of an enhanced fee being allowed after taxation, the auditor shall specify each of the factors in sub paragraph (c) above which justify the enhanced fee, and the extent to which each of those factors justify the fee.

5. Subject to the provisions of paragraphs 6 to 10 below, the maximum fee which the Board, or as the case may be the auditor, can allow for an item of work, set out in paragraphs 1 and 2 of Chapters 1 and 2 of Part II of the Table of Fees, in a case involving the most complex or difficult work, and whatever the circumstances, shall be that set out in Chapter 3 of Part II of the Table of Fees.

6. Where a hearing as specified in paragraph 2(b) or (c) of Chapter 1 or 2 of Part II of the Table of Fees is set down for half a day, or longer, then the fee allowable for that hearing shall be the same as that specified in paragraph 2(a) of Chapter 1 or 2 of Part II of the Table of Fees. For cases in which the provisions of paragraph 5 above apply, the maximum fee allowable shall be as prescribed in paragraph (f) of Chapter 3 of Part II of the Table of Fees.

7. For a fee set out in paragraph 3 of Chapters 1 and 2 of Part II of the Table of Fees, the Board, or as the case may be the auditor, may allow a percentage increase not exceeding 100 per cent of the fees prescribed for a consultation, subject to the following conditions:–

(a) in determining an appropriate level of fee, regard shall be had to the length of the consultation and any unusually high level of preparation required which has not otherwise been reflected in a claim for an enhanced fee under paragraph 4 above, or for a separate fee for preparation claimed under paragraph 10 below; and

(b) no increase shall be allowed in respect of the travel element of the fees prescribed in paragraph 3 of Chapters 1 and 2 of Part II of the Table of Fees.

8. Any enhanced fee allowed by the Board, or as the case may be the auditor, in respect of paragraphs 4 and 5 above shall be proportionate to the maximum fee, and shall be set between the fee prescribed in Part II of the Table of Fees up to the maximum fee for the most complex and difficult case, the amount by which the fee is enhanced depending on the circumstances of the case.

9. Subject to paragraph 10 below, in any case where an unusually high level of preparation was required because of the particular complexity or difficulty of the work, this preparation shall be included within a claim for an enhanced fee under paragraph 4 above, and the Board, or as the case may be the auditor, shall only consider a claim for an enhanced fee in respect of preparation if the following apply:–

    (a) counsel seeking an enhanced fee in respect of preparation shall–

        (i)   identify which part of the claim for an enhanced fee relates to the factors specified in paragraph 4(c)(i) to (iii) above, and which part relates to preparation; and

        (ii) produce records providing a detailed summary of the nature of the work or, if applicable, the nature of the documentation perused, at each stage of the process, the time taken and when and where the work was undertaken; and

        (iii) retain and produce, if requested, any contemporaneous record or notes made in the course of preparation; and

    (b) in allowing an enhanced fee for preparation the Board, or as the case may be the auditor, must be satisfied that the level of preparation was necessary, reasonable and proportionate in all the circumstances of the case.

10. In exceptional cases involving extraordinary preparation, a separate fee in respect of that preparation may be allowed at the discretion of the Board, or as the case may be the auditor, but subject to the following conditions:–

    (a) such a fee shall only be payable to the extent that the preparation in respect of which the fee is claimed is not included in an enhanced fee for preparation under paragraph 9 above;

    (b) in allowing such a fee the Board, or as the case may be the auditor, must be satisfied that the level of preparation was necessary, reasonable and proportionate in all the circumstances of the case;

    (c) counsel shall produce records providing a detailed summary of the nature of the work or, if applicable, the nature of the documentation perused, at each stage of the process, the time taken and when and where the work was undertaken and shall retain and produce, if requested, any contemporaneous record or notes made in the course of preparation; and

    (d) where such a fee is allowed it shall be calculated by dividing the total time allowed into units of 6 hours, each unit payable at the rate of two thirds of the fee prescribed at paragraph 2(a) of Chapters 1 and 2 of Part II of the Table of Fees in this Schedule.

11. The Board, or as the case may be the auditor, shall have power to reduce any fee set out in Part II of the Table of Fees in this Schedule where satisfied that, because of any particular circumstances, a reduced fee is sufficient to provide reasonable remuneration for the work having regard to the general level of fees in the said Part II.

Proceedings in the High Court of Justiciary (other than appeals) and the Sheriff Court

12. Subject to paragraphs 13 to 15 below, the fees prescribed in Parts I and III of the Table of Fees in this Schedule shall include all preparation.

13. A fee for separate preparation shall be allowed only on the following conditions:–

    (a) such a fee is allowable only once in any case to junior or senior, or as the case may be junior and senior, counsel representing an applicant or assisted person, notwithstanding that the applicant or assisted person is represented by more than one junior or senior counsel during the course of the case;

    (b) in allowing such a fee the Board, or as the case may be the auditor, must be satisfied that the level of preparation was necessary, reasonable and proportionate in all the circumstances of the case; and

    (c) counsel shall produce records providing a detailed summary of the nature of the work or, if applicable, the nature of the documentation perused, at each stage of the process, the time taken and when and where the work was undertaken and shall retain and produce, if requested, any contemporaneous record or notes made in the course of preparation.

14. A fee for separate preparation shall be allowed only in any case–

    (a) where–

        (i)   the case is disposed of at a hearing under section 76 of the 1995 Act; or

        (ii) the case proceeds to trial,

    and the level of preparation is that to which paragraph 15 (d) or (e) below applies; or

    (b) where a plea of guilty is tendered, or a plea of not guilty is accepted, up to and including the first day of trial and the case does not proceed to trial, and the level of preparation is that to which paragraph 15 (c) or (e) below applies.

15. A fee for separate preparation allowed under paragraphs 13 and 14 above shall be calculated by reference to the total number of sheets of documentation as follows:–

(a) no fee for separate preparation for the first 1,000 sheets shall be allowed under any circumstances;

(b) each range set out in sub-paragraphs (c) and (d) below specifies a total number of days which may be allowed per total number of sheets within the range, and each day shall be paid at the rate of two-thirds of the fee prescribed for the conduct of a trial at paragraph 3 of Chapters 1 and 2 of Part I, or as the case may be, paragraph 2 of Chapters 1 and 2 of Part III of the Table of Fees in this Schedule depending on the nature of the charges and the status of counsel;

(c) the ranges are–

    (i) 3 days are allowable for 1,001 3,500 sheets;

    (ii) 5.5 days are allowable for 1,001 7,000 sheets;

    (iii) 7.5 days are allowable for 1,001 10,000 sheets;

(d) 2.5 days are allowable for 7,500–10,000 sheets;

(e) where the total number of sheets exceeds 10,000 counsel shall be entitled to a fee in respect of the total preparation reasonably undertaken having regard to all the circumstances, including the general level of fees prescribed in this paragraph; and

(f) a fee for separate preparation allowed under–

    (i) paragraph 14(a) above shall be calculated on the basis of sub-paragraph (d) or the proportion of the fee allowable under sub-paragraph (e) which is attributable to over 7.500 sheets; or

    (ii) paragraph 14(b) above shall be calculated on the basis of sub-paragraph (c) or (e) above.

16. Where a fee is claimed in respect of paragraph 1B(c) of Chapter 1 or 2 of Part I of the Table of Fees–

(a) information shall be provided by or on behalf of counsel as to the reason for the adjournment; and

(b) no fee shall be allowed by the Board or the auditor where satisfied that an adjournment was caused because the defence was not prepared to proceed, or where the preliminary hearing could have been altered in advance under section 75A(5) of the 1995 Act.

17. For the purposes of the fees prescribed in Parts I and III of the Table of Fees in this Schedule–

(a) a trial shall be taken to commence when the jury is empanelled;

(b) where the trial of an accused person proceeds in respect of more than one offence, the fee payable in terms of paragraphs 3 of Chapters 1 and 2 of Part I and paragraphs 2 of Chapters 1 and 2 of Part III shall be that for the offence for which the highest fee is prescribed;

(c) where counsel conducts a number of deferred sentences on the same day the prescribed fee shall be reduced by half for a second deferred sentence, and by a further half for a third and any subsequent deferred sentence;

(d) the fees allowed under Part III shall be no more than four fifths of the fees prescribed in Part I of the Table of Fees in this Schedule, and except on cause shown, fees for counsel in the Sheriff Court shall not be allowable for attendance at hearings which are routine or procedural only or which do not materially advance the case;

(e) the prescribed fees shall include all work undertaken in the case that day;

(f) fees for a waiting day shall be allowed on the basis of paragraph 18 below;

(g) the fees prescribed in Parts I and III cannot be increased or reduced in terms of paragraphs 4 to 11 above.

(h) where the trial of an accused person proceeds in respect of the offence of attempting to pervert the course of justice, the fee payable in terms of paragraph 3 of Chapter 1 or 2 of Part I and paragraph 2 of Chapter 1 or 2 of Part III shall be that for the offence to which the charge of attempting to pervert the course of justice relates. Where the offence to which the charge relates is not prescribed in Schedule 2, the fee payable shall be in terms of paragraph 3(b) of Chapter 1 or 2 of Part I and paragraph 2(b) of Chapter 1 or 2 of Part III; and

(i) where an accused person pleads guilty at a hearing fixed for trial before the jury is empanelled, or where the case is brought to an end by the Crown's acceptance of a plea of not guilty, or where, following the court deserting the trial *simpliciter* or *pro loco et tempore*, the indictment falls or, for any other reason, is not brought to trial and where no order is made by the court to postpone or appoint a further trial diet, the fee payable shall be two-thirds of the fee payable in terms of paragraph 3 of Chapter 1 or 2 of Part I and paragraph 2 of Chapter 1 or 2 of Part III.

17A. Where counsel claims a fee in respect of the first diet under paragraph 3(u) of Chapter 1 or 2 of Part III of the Table of Fees, the fee shall only be payable where a plea of guilty is tendered at that hearing or where the case is brought to an end by the Crown's acceptance of a plea of not guilty, withdrawal of the libel, desertion of the diet or by other means.

18. Where counsel claims a fee for a waiting day—

    (a)   the fee payable to junior counsel, depending on the status of counsel in the case, for such a day shall be–

        (i)   half of the fee prescribed at paragraph 4(a) of Chapter 1 of Part I of the Table of Fees or at paragraph 3(a) of Chapter 1 of Part III depending on the applicable court, where no travel for the purposes of paragraph 7 of Chapter 2 of Part I or paragraph 6 of Chapter 2 of Part III is incurred; or

        (ii)   two-thirds of the fee prescribed at either paragraph referred to in sub paragraph (a)(i) above, depending on the applicable court, where such travel is incurred;

    (b)   the fee payable to senior counsel for such a day shall be—

        (i)   half the fee prescribed at paragraph 4(a) of Chapter 2 of Part I of the Table of Fees or at paragraph 3(a) of Chapter 2 of Part III depending on the applicable court, where no travel for the purposes of paragraph 7 of those Chapters is incurred; or

    (ii)   two-thirds of the fee prescribed at either paragraph referred to in sub paragraph (b)(i) above, depending on the applicable court, where such travel is incurred;

    (c)   no other chargeable work shall be undertaken in the case that day; and

    (d)   provided that counsel remains available at court in case the trial proceeds that day, chargeable work in respect of other cases may be undertaken on that day, other than conducting a hearing or trial.

19. Where counsel claims a fee in respect of paragraph 2 of Chapter 1 or 2 of Part I, or paragraph 1B of Chapter 1 or 2 of Part III, of the Table of Fees—

    (a)   subject to sub-paragraph (b) below, no fee shall be payable under paragraph 1B, 3 or 4 of each Chapter of Part I, or paragraph 2 or 3 of each Chapter of Part III, of the Table of Fees; but

    (b)   a fee shall be payable for all post conviction hearings including hearings for which a prescribed fee is set out in paragraphs 4(j), (k), (l) and (m) of each Chapter of Part I, and paragraphs 3(j), (k), (l) and (m) of each Chapter of Part III, of the Table of Fees.

20. The supplementary fee for necessary travel specified in paragraph 7 of Chapters 1 and 2 of Part I and paragraph 6 of Chapters 1 and 2 of Part III of the Table of Fees is chargeable only as follows:–

    (a)   the travel undertaken must exceed 60 miles in either direction (120 mile round trip);

    (b)   the fee excludes travel costs;

    (c)   counsel shall, if required, produce records certifying the travel undertaken;

    (d)   the fee is chargeable only once per day in respect of the same journey irrespective of the number of cases for which the travel is undertaken;

    (e)   the fee is chargeable only once where counsel makes the outward and return journeys on the same day; and

    (f)   the fee is chargeable twice where, on cause shown and subject to the provisions of the other sub-paragraphs of this paragraph, counsel is required to travel and make the return journey on different days.

20A. Travel costs are chargeable as an outlay only in circumstances where a supplementary fee for travel is chargeable under paragraph 20.

21. The payment for necessary accommodation and subsistence specified under paragraph 8 of Chapters 1 and 2 of Part I, and paragraph 7 of the Chapters of Part III, of the Table of Fees is chargeable only in circumstances where a supplementary fee for travel is chargeable and on cause shown. Counsel shall, if required, produce records certifying the accommodation and subsistence costs incurred.

Interpretation

22. In this Schedule–

    "consultation" means a formal meeting with counsel on the instructions of the solicitor concerning a significant issue which advances the cause taking place usually, but not always, in the presence of the accused or an expert witness, including formal meetings with Crown Counsel taking place following the first preliminary hearing;

    "documentation" means Crown statements, precognitions, productions including defence productions and labels;

    "waiting day" means a day where counsel is required to attend court and does so but the trial does not proceed; and

    "sheet" shall consist of 250 words and numbers, or each minute of an un-transcribed tape.

TABLE OF FEES

PART I

FEES OF COUNSEL FOR PROCEEDINGS IN THE HIGH COURT OF JUSTICIARY

CHAPTER 1 –

JUNIOR COUNSEL

1A. *Written work*

(a) petition to Nobile Officium	£225.00
(b) drafting devolution minute	£150.00
(c) drafting section 275 application under the 1995 Act[3]	£150.00
(d) drafting specification of documents	£125.00
(e) drafting interrogatories	£125.00

1B. *Preliminary hearing*

(a) Preliminary hearing including managed meeting or equivalent communication with the Crown by whatever means and including any note on the line of evidence — Payable at one and a half times the full rate for a trial (paragraph 3 below) depending on category of case and status of counsel.

(b) further diet under section 72(9) of the 1995 Act — Payable at two thirds of the full rate for a trial (paragraph 3 below) depending on category of case and status of counsel.

(c) adjourned diet under section 75A of the 1995 Act, or continued diet — Payable at one-half of the full rate for a trial (paragraph 3 below) depending on category of case and status of counsel.

(d) attendance at managed meeting or work in connection with equivalent communication with the Crown by whatever means and including any note on the line of evidence where counsel does not attend preliminary hearing — Payable at one-half of the fee prescribed at paragraph 1B(a) above.

(e) conduct of preliminary hearing on receipt of detailed instructions not having been involved in pre hearing communication with the Crown — Payable at one-half of the fee prescribed at paragraph 1B(a) above.;

	Junior as leader	*Junior Alone*	*Junior with leader*
2. *Early Plea* Hearing under section 76 of the 1995 Act	£1,250.00	£1,250.00	£625.00

3. *Trial per day*

Category Charges Prosecuted in the High Court

(a) Murder, Multiple attempted murder, Culpable homicide, Rape, Assault and Robbery (involving commercial premises), Importation of controlled drugs, Fraud and related offences, Section 1 of the 1988 Act (causing death by dangerous driving), Section 3A of the 1988 Act (causing death by careless driving when under the influence of drink or drugs), Sedition, Treason, Offences under the 2000 Act, Torture, War crimes, Offences under the Explosive Substances Act 1883, sections 327 to 333 and 339(1A) of the Proceeds of Crime Act 2002 (Money Laundering), Firearms offences, Incest, Sodomy, Embezzlement, Lewd and Libidinous behaviour against children under the age of 12.	£750.00	£650.00	£450.00
(b) Attempted Murder, Assault to severe injury (with aggravations), Indecent Assault, Assault and Robbery (involving retail premises), Possession with intent to supply or being concerned in the supply of a Class A drug, Attempted Rape, Lewd and libidinous behaviour (other than	£617.50	£535.00	£375.00

under category (a) above), Offences under the Sexual Offences Act, Offences against Children under the 1995 Consolidation Act, Offences under section 16A of the 1995 Consolidation Act, Abduction and/or unlawful imprisonment, Extortion, Counterfeiting, Bribery and Corruption, Mobbing and rioting, Indecent or Obscene Publications, Environmental Protection prosecutions, Health and Safety offences, Intellectual Property offences, Offences under the Immigration Act 1971, Offences under section 52 or 52A of the Civic Government (Scotland) Act 1982

(c)	Possession with intent to supply or being concerned in the supply of a Class B or Class C drug, Assault to severe injury, Assault and robbery, Mobbing, Wilful fire raising, Housebreaking, Opening lockfast places, Bigamy, Contempt of Court, Perjury, Theft, Forgery, Uttering, Reset, Concealing a pregnancy, Deforcement of Sheriff's Officers, Malicious Mischief, Brothel keeping, Public Order Offences (stirring of racial hatred, wearing of uniforms, disrupting lawful meetings), Harassment, Road traffic offences (other than section 1 or 3A of the 1988 Act), Possession of offensive weapons, Violation of sepulchres	£495.00	£430.00	£305.00

4. *Miscellaneous Hearings*

(a)	fee for a day in court for miscellaneous hearings other than those for which a fee is prescribed	£360.00	£315.00	£225.00
(b)	preliminary diet	£360.00	£315.00	£225.00
(c)	hearing under section 275 of the 1995 Act	£360.00	£315.00	£225.00
(d)	hearing on specification of documents	£360.00	£315.00	£225.00
(e)	hearing on a devolution minute	£360.00	£315.00	£225.00
(f)	hearing on an application by the Crown for an extension of time	£360.00	£315.00	£225.00
(g)	hearing under section 72 of the 1995 Act	£180.00	£157.50	£112.50
(h)	hearing on a motion to adjourn	£180.00	£157.50	£112.50
(i)	hearing on an application for special measures	£180.00	£157.50	£112.50
(j)	confiscation diet in which substantial evidence is led or where full settlement is agreed where the confiscation proceedings follow acceptance of a guilty plea to the charge or charges categorised as below or follow a trial as specified in this Chapter in—			
	(i) paragraph 3(a)	£750.00	£650.00	£450.00
	(ii) paragraph 3(b)	£617.50	£535.00	£375.00
	(iii) paragraph 3(c)	£455.00	£395.00	£275.00
(k)	confiscation diet where no substantial evidence is led	£360.00	£315.00	£225.00
(l)	deferred sentence where mitigation is led	£360.00	£315.00	£225.00
(m)	deferred sentence where no mitigation is led	£180.00	£157.50	£112.50
(n)	remit for sentence	£360.00	£315.00	£225.00
(o)	adjourned trial diet	£180.00	£157.00	£112.00
(p)	adjourned trial diet (trial having commenced)	£360.00	£315.00	£225.00
(q)	trial within a trial	Payable at the full rate for a trial (paragraph 3 above) depending on category of case and status of counsel.		
(r)	examination of the facts in a case of insanity or diminished responsibility	Payable at the full rate for a trial (paragraph 3 above) depending on category of case and status of counsel.		
(s)	proof in mitigation	Payable at the full rate for a trial (paragraph 3 above) depending on category of case and status of counsel.		

(t) deferred sentence in which evidence is taken from an expert witness	Payable at the full rate for a trial (paragraph 3 above) depending on category of case and status of counsel.;		

5. *Fee for consultations, accused and counsel meetings and locus visits*

£210.00	£184.00	£135.00

6. *Fee for a necessary Note*

£50.00	£50.00	£50.00

7. *Travel*

Supplementary fee chargeable in addition to any of the above fees where necessary travel is undertaken within Scotland, including travel to a Procurator Fiscal's office or elsewhere to view productions	£100.00	£100.00	£100.00
Supplementary fee chargeable in addition to any of the above fees where necessary travel is undertaken furth of Scotland; and	£200.00	£200.00	£200.00

8. *Accommodation and associated subsistence*

Payment of necessary accommodation and associated subsistence per day	£100.00	£100.00	£100.00

CHAPTER 2 –

SENIOR COUNSEL

1. *Preliminary Hearing*

(a) preliminary hearing including managed meeting or equivalent communication with the Crown by whatever means and including any note on the line of evidence	Payable at the full rate for a trial (paragraph 3 below) depending on category of case and status of counsel.

1A. *Written work*

(a) petition to Nobile Officium	£225.00
(b) drafting devolution minute	£150.00
(c) drafting section 275 application under the 1995 Act(a)	£150.00
(d) drafting specification of documents	£125.00
(e) drafting interrogatories	£125.00

1B. *Preliminary hearing*

(a) Preliminary hearing including managed meeting or equivalent communication with the Crown by whatever means and including any note on the line of evidence	Payable at one and a half times the full rate for a trial (paragraph 3 below) depending on category of case and status of counsel.
(b) further diet under section 72(9) of the 1995 Act	Payable at two thirds of the full rate for a trial (paragraph 3 below) depending on category of case and status of counsel.
(c) adjourned diet under section 75A of the 1995 Act, or continued diet	Payable at one-half of the full rate for a trial (paragraph 3 below) depending on category of case and status of counsel.
(d) attendance at managed meeting or work in connection with equivalent communication with the Crown by whatever means and including any note on the line of evidence where counsel does not attend preliminary hearing	Payable at one-half of the fee prescribed at paragraph 1B(a) above.
(e) conduct of preliminary hearing on receipt of detailed instructions not having been involved in pre hearing communication with the Crown	Payable at one-half of the fee prescribed at paragraph 1B(a) above.

2. *Early Plea*

Hearing under section 76 of the 1995 Act	£1,250.00

3. *Trial (per day)*

Category Charges Prosecuted in the High Court

(a) Murder, Multiple attempted murder, Culpable homicide, Rape, Assault and Robbery (involving commercial premises), Importation of controlled drugs, Fraud and related offences, Section 1 of the 1988 Act (causing death by dangerous driving), Section 3A of the 1988 Act (causing death by careless driving when under the influence of drink or drugs), Sedition, Treason, Offences under the 2000 Act, Torture, War crimes, Offences under the Exploxive Substances Act 1883, sections 327 to 333 and 339(1A) of the Proceeds of Crime Act 2002 (Money Laundering), Firearms offences, Incest, Sodomy, Embezzlement, Lewd and Libidinous behaviour against children under the age of 12.   £900.00

(b) Attempted Murder, Assault to severe injury (with aggravations), Indecent Assault, Assault and Robbery (involving retail premises), Possession with intent to supply or being concerned in the supply of a Class A drug, Attempted Rape, Lewd and libidinous behaviour (other than under category (a) above), Offfences under the Sexual Offences Act, Offences against Children under the 1995 Consolidation Act, Offences under section 16A of the 1995 Consolidation Act, Abduction and/or unlawful imprisonment, Extortion, Counterfeiting, Bribery and Corruption, Mobbing and rioting, Indecent or Obscene Publications, Environmental Protection prosecutions, Health and Safety offences, Intellectual Property offences, Offences under the Immigration Act 1971, offences under section 52 or 52A of the Civic Government (Scotland) Act 1982   £700.00

(c) Possession with intent to supply or being concerned in the supply of a Class B or Class C drug, Assault to severe injury, Assault and robbery, Mobbing, Wilful fire raising, Housebreaking, Opening lockfast places, Bigamy, Contempt of Court, Perjury, Theft, Shameless Indecency, Offences under the SexualOffences Act 2003, Forgery, Concealing a pregnancy, Deforcement of Sheriff's Officers, Malicious mischief, Brothel keeping, Public order offences (stirring up racial hatred, wearing of uniforms, disrupting lawful meetings), Harassment, Road traffic offences (other than section 1 or 3A of the 1988 Act), Possession of offensive weapons, Violation of sepulchres   £560.00

4. *Miscellaneous Hearings*

(a)	fee for a day in court for miscellaneous hearings other than those for which a fee is prescribed	£410.00
(b)	preliminary diet	£410.00
(c)	hearing under section 275 of the 1995 Act	£410.00
(d)	hearing on specification of documents	£410.00
(e)	hearing on a devolution minute	£410.00
(f)	hearing on an application by the Crown for an extension of time	£410.00
(g)	hearing under section 72 of the 1995 Act	£205.00
(h)	hearing on a Motion to adjourn	£205.00
(i)	hearing on an application for special measures	£205.00
(j)	confiscation diet in which substantial evidence is led or where full settlement is agreed where the confiscation proceedings follow acceptance of a guilty plea to the charge or charges categorised as below or follow a trial as specified in this Chapter in–	
	(i) paragraph 3(a)	£900.00
	(ii) paragraph 3(b)	£700.00
	(iii) paragraph 3(c)	£515.00

(k)	confiscation diet where no substantial evidence is led	£410.00
(l)	deferred sentence where mitigation is led	£410.00
(m)	deferred sentence where no mitigation is led	£205.00
(n)	remit for sentence	£410.00
(o)	adjourned trial diet	£205.00
(p)	adjourned trial diet (trial having commenced)	£410.00
(q)	trial within a trial	Payable at the full rate for a trial (paragraph 3 above) depending on category of case.
(r)	examination of the facts in a case of insanity or diminished responsibility	Payable at the full rate for a trial (paragraph 3 above) depending on category of case.
(s)	proof in mitigation	Payable at the full rate for a trial (paragraph 3 above) depending on category of case.
(t)	deferred sentence in which evidence is taken from an expert witness	Payable at the full rate for a trial (paragraph 3 above) depending on category of case.

5. *Fee for consultations, accused and counsel meetings and locus visits*

£250.00

6. *Fee for a necessary Note*

£50.00

7. *Travel*

Supplementary fee chargeable in addition to any of the above fees   £100.00
where necessary travel is undertaken within Scotland, including
travel to a Procurator Fiscal's office or elsewhere to view productions

Supplementary fee chargeable in addition to any of the above fees   £200.00
where necessary travel is undertaken furth of Scotland

8. *Accommodation and associated subsistence*

Payment of necessary accommodation and associated subsistence   £100.00
per day

PART II

FEES OF COUNSEL IN APPEAL PROCEEDINGS

CHAPTER 1 –

JUNIOR COUNSEL

		Junior with leader	Junior alone
1.	*Appeals, written work*		
	(a) Opinion on appeal		£60.00
	(b) drafting grounds of appeal against conviction, including any note of appeal	£58.00	£82.00
	(c) drafting bill of suspension		£60.00
	(d) note of adjustments to stated case	£58.00	£82.00
	(e) revisal of stated case		£60.00
2.	*Appeals, conduct*		
	(a) hearing in appeal against conviction (per day)	£223.00	£315.00
	(b) hearing on stated case or bill of suspension related to conviction or conviction and sentence	£101.00	£132.00
	(c) hearing in appeal against sentence including fee for drafting note of appeal	£41.00	£91.00
	(d) appeal relating to granting of bail	£30.00	£30.00

3. *Consultations*

(a)	in Edinburgh	£71.00	£101.00
	additional fee if held in prison	£11.00	£11.00
(b)	elsewhere within 60 miles journey by road from Edinburgh	£132.00	£173.00
(c)	in Aberdeen, Inverness or Dumfries	£264.00	£315.00
(d)	elsewhere beyond 60 miles journey by road from Edinburgh, such fee as the Board or the auditor considers appropriate with regard to the journey involved and the level of fees prescribed in this paragraph		

CHAPTER 2 –

SENIOR COUNSEL

1. *Appeals, written work*

(a)	Opinion on appeal	£91.00
(b)	revising grounds of appeal against conviction, including any note of appeal	£112.00
(c)	revisal of bill of suspension	£91.00
(d)	note of adjustments to stated case	£112.00
(e)	revisal of stated case	£91.00

2. *Appeals, conduct*

(a)	hearing in appeal against conviction (per day)	£409.00
(b)	hearing on stated case or bill of suspension related to conviction or conviction and sentence	£203.00
(c)	hearing in appeal against sentence including revisal of note of appeal	£132.00
(d)	appeal relating to granting of bail	£30.50

3. *Consultations*

(a)	in Edinburgh	£153.00
	additional fee if held in prison	£11.00
(b)	elsewhere within 60 miles journey by road from Edinburgh	£244.00
(c)	in Aberdeen, Inverness or Dumfries	£469.00
(d)	elsewhere beyond 60 miles journey by road from Edinburgh, such fee as the Board or the auditor considers appropriate with regard to the journey involved and the level of fees prescribed in this paragraph	

CHAPTER 3 –

MAXIMUM FEES

		Junior with leader	Junior alone	Senior
(a)	Opinion on appeal	£100.00	£132.00	£200.00
(b)	drafting or revising grounds of appeal against conviction, including any note of appeal	£150.00	£200.00	£300.00
(c)	drafting bill of suspension	£75.00	£100.00	£150.00
(d)	note of adjustments to stated case	£75.00	£100.00	£150.00
(e)	revisal of stated case	£75.00	£100.00	£150.00
(f)	hearing in appeal against conviction (per day)	£625.00	£825.00	£1,250.00
(g)	hearing on stated case or bill of suspension related to conviction or conviction and sentence	£225.00	£300.00	£475.00
(h)	appeal against sentence including drafting note of appeal	£225.00	£300.00	£475.00
(i)	appeal relating to granting of bail	£30.50	£30.50	£30.50

PART III

FEES OF COUNSEL FOR PROCEEDINGS IN THE SHERIFF AND DISTRICT COURT

CHAPTER 1 –

JUNIOR COUNSEL

	Junior as leader	Junior alone	Junior with leader
1A. *Written work*			
(a) petition to Nobile Officium	£225.00	£225.00	£225.00
(b) drafting devolution minute	£150.00	£150.00	£150.00
(c) drafting section 275 application under the 1995 Act	£150.00	£150.00	£150.00
(d) drafting specification of documents	£125.00	£125.00	£125.00
(e) drafting interrogatories	£125.00	£125.00	£125.00
1B. *Early plea*			
Hearing under section 76 of the 1995 Act	£1,250.00	£1,250.00	£625.00
2. *Trial (per day)*			
Category Charges Prosecuted in the Sheriff Court			
(a) Culpable Homicide, Assault and Robbery (involving commercial premises), Importation of controlled drugs, Fraud and related offence, Section 1 of the 1988 Act (causing death by dangerous driving), Section 3A of the 1988 Act (causing death by careless driving when under the influence of drink or drugs) Sedition, Treason, Offences under the 2000 Act, Torture, War crimes, Rape, Multiple attempted murder, Offences under the Explosive Substances Act 1883, sections 372 to 333 and 339(1A) of the Proceeds of Crime Act 2002 (Money laundering, Firearms offences, Incest, Sodomy, Embezzlement, Lewd and libidinous behaviour against children under the age of 12	£647.50	£575.00	£360.00
(b) Attempted Murder, Assault to severe injury (with aggravations), Indecent assault, Assault and robbery (involving retail premises), Possession with intent to supply or being concerned in the supply of a class A drug, Attempted rape, Lewd and libidinous behaviour (other than under category (a) above), Offences under the Sexual Offences Act, Offences against children under the 1995 Consolidation Act, Offences under section 16A of the 1995 Consolidation Act, Abduction and/or unlawful imprisonment, Extortion, Counterfeiting, Bribery and corruption, Mobbing and rioting, Environmental protection prosecutions, Health and safety offences, Intellectual property offences, Indecent or obscene publications, Possession with intent to supply or being concerned in the supply of a class B or class C drug, Assault to severe injury, Assault and robbery, Wilful fire raising, Housebreaking, Opening lockfast places, Bigamy, Contempt of Court Perjury, Theft, Forgery, Uttering, Reset, Concealing a pregnancy, Deforcement of Sheriff's Officers, Malicious mischief, Brothel keeping, Public order offences (stirring up racial hatred, wearing of uniforms, disrupting lawful meetings) Harassment, Road traffic offences (other than section 1 or 3A of	£495.00	£430.00	£350.00

the 1988 Act), Possession of offensive weapons,
Violation of sepulchres, Offences under the Immigration
Act 1971, Offences under section 52 or 52A of the Civic
Government (Scotland) Act 1982

3. *Miscellaneous Hearings*

(a)	fee for a day in court for miscellaneous hearings other than those for which a fee is prescribed	£288.00	£252.00	£180.00
(b)	preliminary diet	£288.00	£252.00	£180.00
(c)	hearing under section 275 of the 1995 Act	£288.00	£252.00	£180.00
(d)	hearing on specification of documents	£288.00	£252.00	£180.00
(e)	hearing on a devolution minute	£288.00	£252.00	£180.00
(f)	hearing on an application by the Crown for an extension of time	£288.00	£252.00	£180.00
(g)	hearing under section 72 of the 1995 Act	£144.00	£126.00	£90.00
(h)	hearing on a Motion to adjourn	£144.00	£126.00	£90.00
(i)	hearing on an application for special measures	£144.00	£126.00	£90.00
(j)	confiscation diet in which substantial evidence is led or where full settlement is agreed where the confiscation proceedings follow acceptance of a guilty plea to the charge or charges categorised as below or follow a trial as specified in this Chapter in–			
	(i) paragraph 2(a)	£647.50	£575.00	£360.00
	(ii) paragraph 2(b)	£495.00	£430.00	£300.00
(k)	confiscation diet where no substantial evidence is led	£288.00	£252.00	£180.00
(l)	deferred sentence where mitigation is led	£288.00	£252.00	£180.00
(m)	deferred sentence where no mitigation is led	£144.00	£126.00	£90.00
(n)	adjourned trial diet	£144.00	£126.00	£90.00
(o)	adjourned trial diet (trial having commenced)	£288.00	£252.00	£180.00
(p)	trial within a trial	Payable at the full rate for a trial (paragraph 2 above) depending on category of case and status of counsel.		
(q)	examination of the facts in a case of insanity or diminished responsibility	Payable at the full rate for a trial (paragraph 2 above) depending on category of case and status of counsel.		
(r)	proof in mitigation	Payable at the full rate for a trial (paragraph 2 above) depending on category of case and status of counsel.		
(s)	deferred sentence in which evidence is taken from an expert witness	Payable at the full rate for a trial (paragraph 2 above) depending on category of case and status of counsel.		
(t)	first diet	Payable at the full rate for a trial (paragraph 2 above) depending on category of case and status of counsel.		

4. *Fee for consultations, accused and counsel meetings and locus visits*

	£178.00	£154.00	£108.00

5. *Fee for a necessary Note*

	£50.00	£50.00	£50.00

6. *Travel*

Supplementary fee chargeable in addition to any of the above fees where necessary travel is undertaken	£100.00	£100.00	£100.00

7. *Accommodation and associated subsistence*

Payment of necessary accommodation and associated subsistence per day	£100.00	£100.00	£100.00

CHAPTER 2 –

SENIOR COUNSEL

1A. *Written work*

(a)	petition to Nobile Officium	£225.00	£225.00	£225.00
(b)	drafting devolution minute	£150.00	£150.00	£150.00
(c)	drafting section 275 application under the 1995 Act	£150.00	£150.00	£150.00
(d)	drafting specification of documents	£125.00	£125.00	£125.00
(e)	drafting interrogatories	£125.00	£125.00	£125.00

1B. *Early plea*

Hearing under section 76 of the 1995 Act   £1,250.00   £1,250.00   £625.000

2. *Trial (per day)*

Category Charges Prosecuted in the Sheriff Court

(a) Culpable Homicide, Assault and Robbery (involving commercial premises i.e.   £720.00
banks, post offices, warehouses etc.), Importation of Controlled Drugs, Fraud
and related offence. Section 1 of the 1988 Act (causing death by dangerous
driving), Section 3A of the 1988 Act (causing death by careless driving when
under the influence of drink or drugs), Sedition, Treason, Offences under
the 2000 Act, Torture, War crimes, Rape, Multiple attempted murder (other
than under category (a) above)

(b) Attempted Murder, Assault to severe injury (with aggravations), Indecent   £560.00
assault, Assault and robbery (involving retail premises), Possession with
intent to supply or being concerned in the supply of a class A drug,
Attempted rape, Lewd and libidinous behaviour (other than under category
(a) above), Offences under the Sexual Offences Act, Offences against
children under the 1995 Consolidation Act Offences under section 16A of
the 1995 Consolidated Act, Abduction and/or unlawful imprisonment,
Extortion, Counterfeiting, Bribery and corruption, Mobbing and rioting,
Mobbing, Environmental protection prosecutions, Health and safety
offences, Intellectual property offences, Indecent or obscene publications,
Possession with intent to supply or being concerned in the supply of a
class B or class C drug, Assault to severe injury, Assault and robbery,
Wilful fire raising, Housebreaking, Opening lockfast places, Bigamy,
Contempt of Court, Perjury, Theft, Forgery, Uttering, Reset, Concealing
a pregnancy, Deforcement of Sheriff's Officers, Malicious mischief,
Brothel keeping, Public order offences (stirring up racial hatred, wearing
of uniforms, disrupting lawful meetings), Harassment, Road traffic
offences (other than section 1 or 3A of the 1988 Act), Possession of
offensive weapons, Violation of sepulchres, Offences under the Immigration
Act 1971, Offences under section 52 or 52A of the Civic Government
(Scotland) Act 1982"

3. *Miscellaneous Hearings*

(a)	fee for a day in court for miscellaneous hearings other than for which a fee is prescribed	£328.00
(b)	preliminary diet	£328.00
(c)	hearing under section 275 of the 1995 Act	£328.00
(d)	hearing on specification of documents	£328.00
(e)	hearing on a devolution minute	£328.00
(f)	hearing on an application by the Crown for an extension of time	£328.00
(g)	hearing under section 72 of the 1995 Act	£164.00
(h)	hearing on a motion to adjourn	£164.00
(i)	hearing on an application for special measures	£164.00
(j)	confiscation diet in which substantial evidence is led or where full settlement is agreed where the confiscation proceedings follow acceptance of a guilty plea to the charge or charges categorised as below or follow a trial as specified in this Chapter in–	
	(i) paragraph 2(a)	£720.00
	(ii) paragraph 2(b)	£560.00
	(iii) paragraph 2(c)	£328.00
(k)	confiscation diet where no substantial evidence is led	£328.00

(l) deferred sentence where mitigation is led	
(m) deferred sentence where no mitigation is led	£328.00
(n) adjourned trial diet	£164.00
(o) adjourned trial diet (trial having commenced)	£164.00
(p) trial within a trial	£328.00
	Payable at the full rate for a trial (paragraph 2 above) depending on category of case.
(q) examination of the facts in a case of insanity or diminished responsibility depending on category of case.	Payable at the full rate for a trial (paragraph 2 above)
(r) proof in mitigation	Payable at the full rate for a trial (paragraph 2 above) depending on category of case.
(s) deferred sentence in which evidence is taken from an expert witness	Payable at the full rate for a trial (paragraph 2 above) depending on category of case.
(t) first diet	Payable at the full rate for a trial (paragraph 2 above) depending on category of case.

4. *Fee for consultations, accused and counsel meetings and locus visits*

£200.00

5. *Fee for a necessary Note*

£50.00

6. *Travel*

Supplementary fee chargeable in addition to any of the above fees where necessary travel is undertaken within Scotland, including travel to a Procurator Fiscal's office or elsewhere to view productions

£100.00

Supplementary fee chargeable in addition to any of the above fees where necessary travel is undertaken furth of Scotland

£200.00

7. *Accommodation and associated subsistence*

Payment of necessary accommodation and associated subsistence per day

£75.00

SCHEDULE 3

Regulation 4

FEES OF COUNSEL FOR PROCEEDINGS IN THE JUDICIAL COMMITTEE OF THE PRIVY COUNCIL

Notes on the operation of Schedule 3

1. Subject to the following provisions of this Schedule, fees shall be calculated by the Board, and in the event of a question or dispute by the auditor, in accordance with the Table of Fees in this Schedule.

2. In the assessment and taxation of counsel's fees–

    (a) where higher fees than those set out in the Table of Fees are sought, they must be explained in a note from counsel;

    (b) for proceedings under paragraph 1 of the Table of Fees–

        (i) subject to any higher fees allowable under sub-paragraph (a), no other payments are permitted;

        (ii) there is a working assumption that a single fee is allowed for one junior counsel even where sanction is authorised for two counsel and that it would only be in the most exceptional cases that fees are allowable for two counsel; and

        (iii) a fee for senior counsel may be allowed instead of junior counsel if it is held to be necessary because of the difficulty or complexity of the case or for other good reason; and

    (c) for proceedings under paragraph 2 of the Table of Fees–

        (i) counsel's fees are allowed only where the Board has sanctioned the employment of counsel or where counsel is automatically available;

        (ii) except on cause shown, the auditor shall not have regard to any information produced by counsel at taxation which was not made available to the Board at the time the Board made the offer to counsel which is subject to taxation;

(iii) in cases where junior counsel has undertaken most of the work on a particular item the auditor shall allow such fee to senior and junior counsel as appears appropriate to provide reasonable remuneration for the work;

(iv) there is a working assumption that counsel for an appellant commands a higher fee than counsel for a respondent;

(v) only one counsel's fee is permitted on a petition of appeal and on attending judgment; and

(vi) the brief fee shall include all work on the brief, the case and the first day of attendance at the Judicial Committee.

TABLE OF FEES

	Junior Counsel	Senior Counsel
1. *Petition for leave to appeal*		
(a) Drafting petition for leave to appeal	£800.00	£1000.00
(b) Preparing respondents' objections	£550.00	£750.00
(c) Attending Judicial Committee	£1100.00	£1600.00
2. *Appeals and References*		
(a) Drafting Petition of appeal	£75.00	£75.00
(b) Statement of Facts and Issues	£1750.00	£3500.00
(c) Authorities	£600.00	£1200.00
(d) Consultations (each, up to a maximum of three)	£350.00	£700.00
(e) Brief (based on a 1 day hearing)	£6250.00	£12500.00
(f) Brief (based on a 2 day hearing)	£8000.00	£16000.00
(g) Refresher (from day two of the hearing)	£1250.00	£2500.00
(h) Judgment	£150.00	£150.00

NOTE: WHERE THE UNDERNOTED REGULATIONS APPLY, THE FIXED PAYMENTS REPLACE THE FEES AND OUTLAYS PAYABLE IN TERMS OF THE CRIMINAL LEGAL AID (SCOTLAND) (FEES) REGULATIONS 1989 (SI 1989 NO 1491) — SEE PP 79–98.

The Criminal Legal Aid (Fixed Payments) (Scotland) Regulations 1999 (SI 1999 No 491)

[These Regulations are printed as amended by:
The Scotland Act 1998 (Consequential Modifications) (No 2) Order 1999 (SI 1999 No 1820) which came into force on 1st July 1999;
Criminal Legal Aid (Fixed Payments) (Scotland) Amendment Regulations 1999 (SSI 1999 No 48) which came into force on 1st October 1999;
Criminal Legal Aid (Fixed Payments) (Scotland) Amendment Regulations 2001 (SSI 2001 No 307) which came into force on 15th October 2001;
Criminal Legal Aid (Fixed Payments) (Scotland) Amendment Regulations 2002 (SSI 2002 No 247) which came into force on 17th June 2002;
Criminal Legal Aid (Fixed Payments) (Scotland) Amendment (No 2) Regulations 2002 (SSI 2002 No 442) which came into force on 1st November 2002.]
Criminal Legal Aid (Youth Courts) (Scotland) Regulations 2003 (SSI 2003 No 249) which came into force on 2nd June 2003;
Criminal Legal Aid (Fixed Payments) (Scotland) Amendment Regulations 2004 (SSI 2004 No 51) which came into force on 11th March 2004;
Criminal Legal Aid (Fixed Payments) (Scotland) Amendment (No 2) Regulations 2004 (SSI 2004 No 126) which came into force on 2nd April 2004;
Criminal Legal Aid (Fixed Payments) (Scotland) Amendment (No 3) Regulations 2004 (SSI 2004 No 263) which came into force on 28th June 2004;
Criminal Legal Aid (Fixed Payments) (Scotland) Amendment Regulations 2005 (SSI 2005 No 93) which came into force on 23rd March 2004;
Criminal Legal Aid (Summary Justice Pilot Courts and Bail Conditions) (Scotland) Regulations 2006 (SSI 2006 No 234) which came into force on 12th June 2006;
The Criminal Legal Assistance (Fees and Informaiton etc.) (Scotland) Regulations 2008 (SSI 2008 No 240) which came into force on 30th June 2008.]

Citation and commencement

1. These Regulations may be cited as the Criminal Legal Aid (Fixed Payments) (Scotland) Regulations 1999 and shall come into force on 1st April 1999.

Interpretation

2.—(1) In these Regulations, unless the context otherwise requires—

"the Act" means the Legal Aid (Scotland) Act 1986;

"the 1995 Act" means the Criminal Procedure (Scotland) Act 1995;

"diet of deferred sentence" includes those diets where the case has been adjourned for inquiries or reports under sections 201 (power of court to adjourn case before sentence) and 203 (reports) respectively of the 1995 Act;

"adjourned trial diet" means a diet that follows a rial that has commenced by the leading of evidence;

"assisted person" means a person to whom criminal legal aid or (as the case may be) assistance by way of representation has been made available in relation to the proceedings in question;

"continued diet" means a diet which takes place on a separate date from the diet at which a victim statement is laid before the court;

"excluded proceedings" means—

(a) summary proceedings arising following a reduction from solemn proceedings;

(b) proceedings in relation to which legal aid is only available by virtue of section 22(1)(a) of the Act (identification parades held by or on behalf of the prosecutor in contemplation of criminal proceedings);

(c) proceedings in relation to which legal aid is only available by virtue of section 22(1)(c) of the Act (assisted person in custody or liberated by police on undertaking to appear), except where those proceedings are before a court which has been designated as a drug court by the sheriff principal;

(d) proceedings in relation to which legal aid is only available by virtue of section 22(1)(da) of the Act (plea of insanity in bar of trial);

(e) proceedings in relation to which legal aid is only available by virtue of section 22(1)(db) of the Act (examination of facts);

(f) proceedings in relation to which legal aid is made available by virtue of regulation 15 of the Criminal Legal Aid (Scotland) Regulations 1996 (matters of special urgency);

(g) any reference in connection with proceedings under article 234 of the EEC Treaty;

(h) any reference on a devolution issue under paragraph 9 of Schedule 6 to the Scotland Act 1998;

(i) proceedings under section 9 of the Extradition Act 1989;

(j) proceedings under section 5 of the International Criminal Court Act 2001;

(k) proceedings in relation to which legal aid is only available by virtue of section 22(1) (dd) of the Act (solicitor appointed by court for person accused of sexual offence);

(l) proceedings in an appeal to the High Court under section 174(1) (appeals relating to preliminary pleas) of the 1995 Act.

"proof in mitigation" includes those diets where a proof in mitigation take place at the same time as a proof of a victim statement;

"relevant ABWOR" means assistance by way of representation provided by a solicitor in relation to summary criminal proceedings other than excluded proceedings;

"relevant criminal legal aid" means criminal legal aid provided by a solicitor in relation to summary proceedings other than excluded proceedings;

"victim statement" means a statement made for the purposes of section 14 of the Criminal Justice (Scotland) Act 2003.

(2) In these Regulations, unless the context otherwise requires, any reference to a numbered regulation is to one of these Regulations.

(3) For the purposes of these Regulations, a trial, proof in mitigation or proof of a victim statement shall be taken to commence when the first witness is sworn.

Application

3.—(1) For the purposes of these regulations, the references in section 33(3A) and (3B) of the Act to criminal legal assistance relate to relevant criminal legal aid and relevant ABWOR.

(2) These Regulations shall apply—

    (a)   in respect of relevant criminal legal aid first made available in terms of sections 22 or 24(7) of the Act, only in relation to any case where criminal legal aid is first so available on or after 1st April 1999; and

    (b)   in respect of relevant criminal legal aid first made available otherwise, only in relation to any case where an application for criminal legal aid is granted on or after that date.

(3) These Regulations apply also in respect of relevant ABWOR.

Fixed payments allowable to solicitors

4.—(1) There shall be made to a solicitor who provides relevant criminal legal aid in summary proceedings, in respect of the professional services provided by him and the outlays specified in paragraph (2) below, and in accordance with the provisions of this regulation, the fixed payments specified in Schedule 1 or 1A.

(1A) In the application of paragraph (1) above in relation to the assisted person's case, fixed payments are payable under one of those Schedules only (as alternatives to each other) where–

    (a)   Schedule 1 is for the purpose of–

        (i)   cases in the JP court (other than before a stipendiary magistrate);

        (ii)   cases in the JP court (before a stipendiary magistrate) or the sheriff court which proceed beyond the first 30 minutes of a trial;

    (b)   Schedule 1A is for the purpose of cases in the JP court (before a stipendiary magistrate) or the sheriff court which do not so proceed.

(1B) Those Schedules are to be read and applied accordingly.

(1C) There is to be made (in accordance with the other provisions of this regulation) to a solicitor who provides relevant ABWOR in summary proceedings, in respect of the professional services provided by the solicitor and the outlays mentioned in paragraph (2) below, the fixed payments specified in Schedule 1B.

(1D) Schedule 1B is for the purpose of cases in the JP court (before a stipendiary magistrate or otherwise) or the sheriff court.

(2) The outlays specified in this paragraph are all outlays in connection with—

    (a)   the taking, drawing, framing and perusal of precognitions;

    (b)   the undertaking by another solicitor of any part of the work; and

    (c)   photocopying.

(3) Except where proceedings have been brought under section 185 of the 1995 Act, for the purposes of the reference to summary proceedings in paragraph (1) above the following are to be treated as a single matter

    (a)   a single summary complaint or complaints which arise out of the same incident; and

    (b)   proceedings under sections 27(1)(e) and 28 of the 1995 Act (breach of bail conditions) arising out of the complaint or complaints referred to in sub-paragraph (a).

(4) Where in such proceedings a solicitor acts for more than one assisted person a separate fixed payment shall be made to him in respect of each such assisted person, in accordance with paragraph (5) below.

(5) Where a solicitor represents 2 or more assisted persons he shall be paid in respect of the first assisted person 100% of such of the fixed payments as are appropriate to that assisted person, in respect of a second assisted person 40% of the appropriate fixed payments, and in respect of a third and each subsequent assisted person 20% of those payments.

(6) Where a solicitor represents an assisted person who has been remanded in custody at or subsequent to the first calling of the case and that assisted person is at any time during that remand under 21 years of age the fixed payment specified in paragraph 1 of Part 1 of Schedule 1 shall be increased by £100.

(7) Where the Board grants an application for a change of solicitor under regulation 17(3) of the Criminal Legal Aid (Scotland) Regulations 1996 there shall be paid to each of the solicitors who act for the assisted person in the relevant proceedings

    (a)   an equal part of the total amount payable under paragraph 1 of Part 1 of Schedule 1 or (as the case may be) under paragraph 1 of Schedule 1A; and

    (b)   where Schedule 1 applies the amounts payable under paragraphs 2 to 13 of Part 1 of Schedule 1 shall be payable to the solicitor who carries out the work described in those paragraphs;

(c)   where Schedule 1A applies, the amounts payable under paragraph 1 of Schedule 1A so far as applying by reference to paragraphs 10 and 10AA of Part 1 of Schedule 1, or under paragraph 2 of Schedule 1A, are payable to the solicitor who carries out the work concerned (despite, in the case of paragraph 1 of Schedule 1A, the reference in sub paragraph (a) above to that paragraph).

(7A) Paragraph (7) above is subject to paragraph (1A) above (and, accordingly, does not affect the restriction imposed by it).

(7B) Where, in relation to relevant ABWOR, there is a change of solicitor by virtue of regulation 14A(2) and (3) of the Advice and Assistance (Scotland) Regulations 1996, there is to be paid–

(a)   to each of the solicitors who act for the assisted person in the relevant proceedings, an equal part of the total amount payable under paragraph 1 or 2 of Part 1 of Schedule 1B; and

(b)   to the solicitor who carries out work described in the other paragraphs of that Part of that Schedule, the amount payable under those paragraphs in respect of the work.

(8) Where the work done by a solicitor constitutes a supply of services in respect of which value added tax is chargeable, there may be added to the amount of payments allowed to the solicitor an amount equal to the amount of value added tax chargeable.

(9) Where a solicitor represents an assisted person (having relevant criminal legal aid) in a court which has been designated as a drug court by the sheriff principal —

(a)   Part 1 of Schedule 1 shall not apply to those proceedings; and

(b)   where that assisted person has been remanded in custody at or subsequent to the first calling of the case and is at any time during that remand under 21 years of age, there shall be payable in addition to the fixed payments specified in Part 2 of Schedule 1 a payment of £100.

(10) Where a solicitor represents an assisted person (having relevant ABWOR) in a court which has been so designated–

(a)   Part 1 of Schedule 1B does not apply; and

(b)   the fixed payment specified in Part 2 of that Schedule is payable instead.

Exceptional cases

4A.—(1) A solicitor who provides relevant criminal legal aid shall —

(a)   where the circumstances prescribed at paragraph (3) exist; and

(b)   subject to the conditions prescribed at paragraph (5),

instead of receiving the fixed payments specified in Schedule 1, be paid out of the Fund in accordance with regulations made under section 33(2) and (3) of the Act.

(2) It shall be for the Board to determine whether the circumstances prescribed at paragraph (3) exist, and whether the conditions prescribed at paragraphs (5) and (9) are met.

(3) The circumstances referred to in paragraph (1)(a) are where an assisted person would be deprived of the right to a fair trial in any case because of the amount of the fixed payments payable for the criminal legal assistance provided.

(4) The factors to be taken into account by the Board in considering whether the circumstances prescribed at paragraph (3) exist shall include —

(a)   the number, nature and location of witnesses;

(b)   the number and nature of productions;

(c)   the complexity of the law (including procedural complexity);

(d)   whether the assisted person, or any witnesses, may be unable to understand the proceedings because of age, inadequate knowledge of English, mental illness, other mental or physical disability or otherwise.

(5) The conditions referred to in paragraph (1)(b) are as follows —

(a)   the solicitor providing relevant criminal legal aid shall make an application to the Board —

(i)   in such manner and form; and

(ii)   containing such information,

as it may specify, at as early a stage in the provision of the relevant criminal legal aid as is reasonably practicable and that solicitor shall, if required by the Board to do so, supply such further information or such documents as the Board may require to enable it to determine the application; and

(b) that solicitor shall keep proper records of all professional services provided by way of an outlays incurred in the provision of that relevant criminal legal aid, whether before or after the Board exercises its power to determine whether the conditions prescribed at paragraph (5)(a) are met.

(6) An application for a review under section 33(3K) of the Act shall —

(a) be signed by the applicant;

(b) subject to paragraph (7), be lodged with the Board within 15 days of the time when notice of refusal of the application was given to the applicant;

(c) include a statement of any matters which the applicant wishes the Board to take into account in reviewing the application; and

(d) be accompanied by such additional precognitions and other documents as the applicant considers to be relevant to the review.

(7) Paragraph (6)(b) shall not apply where the Board considers that there is a special reason for it to consider a late application for review.

(8) Where the Board has granted an application for a change of solicitor under regulation 17(3) of the Criminal Legal Aid (Scotland) Regulations 1996[3], any solicitor who provided relevant criminal legal aid prior to that grant shall, where the Board has determined that the circumstances prescribed in Schedule 1, be paid out of the Fund in accordance with regulations made under section 33(2) and (3) of the Act.

(9) A solicitor to whom paragraph (8) applies shall only be paid where that solicitor has kept proper records of all professional services provided by way of and outlays incurred in the provision of that relevant criminal legal aid.

Submission of accounts

5.—(1) A claim for a fixed payment in accordance with these Regulations shall be made by submitting to the Board not later than 4 months after the date of conclusion of the proceedings in respect of which the relevant legal aid or assistance was granted, an account specifying the fixed payments which are claimed in relation to the proceedings, together with any fees and outlays which are claimed in relation to those proceedings by virtue of the Criminal Legal Aid (Scotland) (Fees) Regulations 1989 or Advice and Assistance (Scotland) Regulations 1996.

(2) The Board may accept accounts submitted later than the 4 months referred to in paragraph (1) if it considers that there is special reason for late submission.

SCHEDULE 1 PART 1 Regulation 4

	Where professional services are provided in relation to proceedings in the District Court (other than where proceedings are set down to proceed before a Stipendiary Magistrate)	*Where professional services are provided in relation to proceedings in the Sheriff Court (other than proceedings in a Court specified in Schedule 2) or the District Court (where proceedings are set down to proceed before a Stipendiary Magistrate)*	*Where professional services are provided in relation to proceedings in the Sheriff Court and those proceedings are brought in a Court specified in Schedule 2*
1. All work up to and including: (i) any diet at which a plea of guilty is made and accepted or plea in mitigation is made: (ii) the first 30 minutes of	£315 (where criminal legal aid has been made available in the circumstances referred to in paragraphs 11 or 12 below £290)	£515 (where criminal legal aid has been made available in the circumstances referred to in paragraphs 11 or 12 below £490)	£565 (where criminal legal aid has been made available in the circumstances referred to in paragraphs 11 or 12 below £540)

	Where professional services are provided in relation to proceedings in the District Court (other than where proceedings are set down to proceed before a Stipendiary Magistrate)	Where professional services are provided in relation to proceedings in the Sheriff Court (other than proceedings in a Court specified in Schedule 2) or the District Court (where proceedings are set down to proceed before a Stipendiary Magistrate)	Where professional services are provided in relation to proceedings in the Sheriff Court and those proceedings are brought in a Court specified in Schedule 2
conducting a proof in mitigation, or a proof of a victim statement, other than in the circumstances where paragraph 3 below applies; (iii) the first 30 minutes of conducting any trial; and (iiia) a first or second diet of deferred sentence; and (iv) advising, giving an opinion and taking final instructions on the prospects of an appeal against conviction, sentence, other disposal or acquittal, together with any subsequent or additional work other than that specified in paragraphs 2–13 below.			
2. All work mentioned in paragraph 1 above that is done in connection with a complaint under section 27(1)(b) of the 1995 Act.	£157.50	£257.50	£257.50
3. All work done in connection with a grant of legal aid under section 23(1)(b) of the Act ncluding ithe first 30 minutes of conducting a proof in mitigation, or a proofof a victim statement.	£25	£50	£50

SCHEDULE 1 PART 1   Regulation 4

	Where professional services are provided in relation to proceedings in the District Court (other than where proceedings are set down to proceed before a Stipendiary Magistrate)	*Where professional services are provided in relation to proceedings in the Sheriff Court (other than proceedings in a Court specified in Schedule 2) or the District Court (where proceedings are set down to proceed before a Stipendiary Magistrate)*	*Where professional services are provided in relation to proceedings in the Sheriff Court and those proceedings are brought in a Court specified in Schedule 2*
4. Conducting a trial or proof in mitigation for the first day (after the first 30 minutes).	£50	£100	£100
4A. Conducting an adjourned trial diet, during which no evidence is led, where there was no intention nor anticipation that evidence would be led, the only matter in consideration being the determination of the further procedure of the trial proceedings.	£25	£50	£50
4B. Conducting an adjourned trial diet, during which no evidence is led, where there was an intention and an anticipation that the trial would proceed through the continued leading of evidence.	£50	£100	£100
5. Conducting a trial or proof in mitigation for the second day	£50	£200	£200
6. Conducting a trial or proof in mitigation for the third and subsequent days (per day)	£100	£400	£400
7. Representation in court at a continued diet following a victim statement having been laid before the court		£50	

	Where professional services are provided in relation to proceedings in the District Court (other than where proceedings are set down to proceed before a Stipendiary Magistrate)	*Where professional services are provided in relation to proceedings in the Sheriff Court (other than proceedings in a Court specified in Schedule 2) or the District Court (where proceedings are set down to proceed before a Stipendiary Magistrate)*	*Where professional services are provided in relation to proceedings in the Sheriff Court and those proceedings are brought in a Court specified in Schedule 2*
where the court determines sentence or fixes a proof of a victim statement, or adjourns such a proof without hearing evidence.			
8. Conducting a proof of a victim statement where there has been no trial or proof in mitigation for the first day (after the first 30 minutes), and thereafter for subsequent days (per day).		£200	
9. Conducting a proof of a victim statement at a continued diet following a concluded trial or proof in mitigation (per day).		£200	
10. Representation in court at a diet of deferred sentence or per appearance in a court which has been designated as a youth court by the sheriff principal, at a hearing in respect of a community supervision order, or per appearance at a hearing in a court which has been designated as a domestic abuse court by the sheriff principal.	£25	£50	£50
10A. Omitted by SSI 2008 No 240	—		—

SCHEDULE 1 PART 1   Regulation 4

	Where professional services are provided in relation to proceedings in the District Court (other than where proceedings are set down to proceed before a Stipendiary Magistrate)	*Where professional services are provided in relation to proceedings in the Sheriff Court (other than proceedings in a Court specified in Schedule 2) or the District Court (where proceedings are set down to proceed before a Stipendiary Magistrate)*	*Where professional services are provided in relation to proceedings in the Sheriff Court and those proceedings are brought in a Court specified in Schedule 2*
10AA. Representation at a first or second diet of deferred sentence (one only) at which the court considers a report required under section 203 of the 1995 Act and where the case is disposed of (as an additional payment).	£25	£25	£25
11. All work done where the accused is in custody and has tendered a plea of not guilty until determination of the application for legal aid.	£25	£25	£25
12. All work done by virtue of section 24(7) of the Act until determination of the application for legal aid.	£25	£25	£25
13. All work done in connection with a bail appeal under section 32 of the 1995 Act, or an appeal under section 201(4) of the 1995 Act.	£50	£50	£50
14. All work done in connection with an application for bail subject to a movement restriction condition under section 24A of the 1995 Act.	—	£50	—

"SCHEDULE 1A

	Where professional services are provided in relation to proceedings in the Sheriff Court or the JP court (where proceedings are set down to proceed before a Stipendiary Magistrate)	Where professional services are provided in relation to proceedings in the Sheriff Court and those proceedings are brought in a Court specified in Schedule 2
1. All work up to and including– (a) any diet at which a plea of guilty is made and accepted or plea in mitigation is made; (b) the first 30 minutes of conducting any trial; (c) a first or second diet of deferred sentence; and (d) advising, giving an opinion and taking final instructions on the prospects of an appeal against conviction, sentence, other disposal or cquittal, together with any s ubsequent or a dditional work other than that of the kind specified in paragraphs 10 to 12 of Part 1 of Schedule 1 above.	£515 (where criminal legal aid has been made available in the circumstances referred to in paragraphs 11 or 12 of Part 1 of Schedule 1 above, £490)	£515 (where criminal legal aid has been made available in the circumstances referred to in paragraphs 11 or 12 of Part 1 of Schedule 1 above, £490)
2. All work mentioned in paragraph 1 above that is done in connection with a complaint under section 27(1)(b) of the 1995 Act.	£257.50	£257.50

SCHEDULE 1B PART 1

	Where professional services are provided in relation to proceedings in the JP court (other than where proceedings are set down to proceed before a StipendiaryMagistrate)	Where professional services are provided in relation to proceedings in the Sheriff Court or the JP court (where proceedings are set down to proceed before a Stipendiary Magistrate)
1. All work up to and including–		£515
(a) any diet at which a plea of guilty is made and accepted or plea in mitigation is made;		
(b) the first 30 minutes of conducting a proof in mitigation, or a proof of a victim statement, other than in the circumstances where paragraph 3 below applies;		
(c) a first or second diet of deferred sentence; and		
(d) advising, giving an opinion and taking final instructions on the prospects of an appeal against conviction, sentence, other disposal or acquittal, together with any subsequent or additional work other than that specified in paragraphs 8 and 9 below.		
2. All work prior to, and attendance at–	£150	
(a) any diet at which a plea to the competency or relevancy of the complaint or proceedings, or a plea in bar of trial, is tendered;		
(b) any diet at which a question within the meaning of Rule 31.1 of the Act of Adjournal		

Where professional services are provided in relation to proceedings in the JP court (other than where proceedings are set down to proceed before a StipendiaryMagistrate)	*Where professional services are provided in relation to proceedings in the Sheriff Court or the JP court (where proceedings are set down to proceed before a Stipendiary Magistrate)*

(Criminal Procedure Rules) 1996 is raised;

(c) any diet from or to which the case has been adjourned under section 145 of the 1995 Act;

(d) any diet at which there is tendered a plea of guilty or a plea in mitigation is made;

(e) any diet at which the court is considering the accused's plea of guilty to the charges and where there has been no change of plea; and

(f) any diet at which the court is considering the accused's change to plea of guilty to the charges, and where no application for criminal legal aid has been made, together with–

(i) the first 30 minutes of conducting a proof in mitigation;

(ii) a first or second diet of deferred sentence;

(iii) any subsequent or additional work other than that specified in paragraphs 4 and 8 to 13 below.

3. All work mentioned £75   £257.50
in paragraph 1 or 2
above that is done
in connection with
a complaint under
section 27(1)(b) of
the 1995 Act.

SCHEDULE 1B PART 1

	Where professional services are provided in relation to proceedings in the JP court (other than where proceedings are set down to proceed before a StipendiaryMagistrate)	Where professional services are provided in relation to proceedings in the Sheriff Court or the JP court (where proceedings are set down to proceed before a Stipendiary Magistrate)
4. Conducting a proof in mitigation for the first day (after the first 30 minutes).	£50	£100
5. Representation in court at a continued diet following a victim statement having been laid before the court where the court determines sentence or fixes a proof of a victim statement, adjourns such a proof without hearing evidence.		£50
6. Conducting a proof of a victim statement where there has been no proof in mitigation for the first day (after the first 30 minutes), and thereafter for subsequent days (per day).		£200
7. Conducting a proof of a victim statement at a continued diet following a concluded trial or proof in mitigation (per day).		£200
8. Representation in court at a diet of deferred sentence or, per appearance, in a court which has been designated as a youth court by the Sheriff Principal, at a hearing in respect of a community supervision order, or per appearance at a hearing in a court which has been designated as a domestic abuse court by the Sheriff Principal.	£25	£50

SCHEDULE 1B PART 1

	Where professional services are provided in relation to proceedings in the JP court (other than where proceedings are set down to proceed before a StipendiaryMagistrate)	Where professional services are provided in relation to proceedings in the Sheriff Court or the JP court (where proceedings are set down to proceed before a Stipendiary Magistrate)
9. Representation at a first or second diet of deferred sentence (one only) at which the court considers a report required under section 203 of the 1995 Act and where the case is disposed of (as an additional payment).	£25	£25
10. All work done in connection with a bail appeal under section 32 of the 1995 Act, or on appeal under section 201(4) of the 1995 Act.	£50	£50
11. All work done in connection with an application for bail subject to a movement restriction condition under section 24A of the 1995 Act.		£50
12. Conducting a special reasons proof or hearing on exceptional hardship (where both, they to be regarded as one only even if conducted separately).	£150	£150
13. Conducting a back-duty proof (but only if in the case no fee is payable under paragraph 12 above).	£50	£50

PART 2

	Where professional services are provided in relation to proceedings in a sheriff court which has been designated as a drug court by the Sheriff Principal
1. All work done in connection with any appearance of an assistance person (per appearance).	£50

SCHEDULE 1 PART 2

	Where professional services are provided in relation to proceedings in a Sheriff Court which has been designated as a drug court by a Sheriff Principal
1. All work done under section 22(1)(c) of the Act up to and including the first appearance of an assisted person.	£100
2. All work done (other than work done in terms of paragraph 1) in 101 (per appearance)	£50

SCHEDULE 2 PART 2

Campeltown	Oban
Dunoon	Portree
Fort William	Rothesay
Kirkwall	Stornoway
Lerwick	Wick
Lochmaddy	

3. Civil Legal Aid

Civil Legal Aid (Scotland) (Fees) Regulations 1989 (SI 1989 No 1490)

[This Statutory Instrument is printed as amended by:

Civil Legal Aid (Scotland) (Fees) Amendment Regulations 1990 (SI 1990 No 473) (counsel's fees);

Civil Legal Aid (Scotland) (Fees) Amendment (No 2) Regulations 1990 (SI 1990 No 1036) (solicitors' fees);

Civil Legal Aid (Scotland) (Fees) Amendment Regulations 1991 (SI 1991 No 565) (solicitors' and counsel's fees) which came into force on 1st April 1991;

Civil Legal Aid (Scotland) (Fees) Amendment Regulations 1992 (SI 1992 No 372) (solicitors' and counsel's fees) which came into force on 1st April 1992;

Civil Legal Aid (Scotland) (Fees) Amendment Regulations 1994 (SI 1994 No 1015) (solicitors' fees) which came into force on 5th May 1994;

Civil Legal Aid (Scotland) (Fees) Amendment (No 2) Regulations 1994 (SI 1994 No 1233) (solicitors' fees) which came into force on 27th May 1994;

Civil Legal Aid (Scotland) (Fees) Amendment Regulations 1995 (SI 1995 No 1044) which came into force on 5th May 1995;

Civil Legal Aid (Scotland) (Fees) Amendment Regulations 1997 (SI 1997 No 689) which came into force on 1st April 1997;

The Scotland Act 1998 (Consequential Modifications) (No 1) Order 1999 (SI 1999 No 1042) which came into force on 6th May 1999;

Civil Legal Aid (Scotland) (Fees) Amendment Regulations 2002 (SSI 2002 No 496) which came into force on 1st December 2002;

Civil Legal Aid (Scotland) (Fees) Amendment Regulations 2003 (SSI 2003 No 178) which came into force on 1st October 2003;

The Civil Legal Aid (Scotland) (Fees) Amendment Regulations 2007 (SSI 2007 No 14) which came into force on 10th February 2007;

The Civil Legal Aid (Scotland) (Fees) Amendment (No 2) Regulations 2007 (SSI 2007 No 181) which came into force on 29th March 2007;

The Civil Legal Aid (Scotland) (Fees) Amendment (No 3) Regulations 2007 (SSI 2007 No 438) which came into force on 1st November 2007;

The Civil Legal Aid (Scotland) (Fees) Amendment Regulations 2009 (SSI 2009 No 203) which came into force on 22nd June 2009.]

Fees and outlays allowable to solicitors

4. Subject to the provisions of regulations 5 and 7 regarding the calculation of fees, regulations 6 and 7 regarding the calculation of outlays, and the provisions of regulation 8 regarding the submission of accounts, a solicitor shall be allowed such amount of fees and outlays as shall be determined by the Board to be reasonable remuneration for work actually, necessarily and reasonably done and outlays actually, necessarily and reasonably incurred, for conducting the proceedings in a proper manner, as between solicitor and client, third party paying.

5.—(1) A solicitor's fees in relation to proceedings in the Court of Session shall be calculated in accordance with Schedule 5.

(2) A solicitor's fees in relation to proceedings in the sheriff court–

    (a) shall, subject to sub-paragraphs (b) and (c), be calculated in accordance with chapters I and II of Schedule 6;

    (b) which are listed in Schedule 7 shall be calculated in accordance with Schedule 5; and

    (c) which consist of a summary cause or executry business shall be calculated in accordance with chapter III or IV respectively of Schedule 2.

(2A) For the purpose of calculating the fees set out in Schedule 6, a unit has the value of £21.00.

(2B) Where a solicitor does work which comes within chapter I of Schedule 6 (undefended cases) and, in the same case, does work which comes within chapter II of that Schedule (defended cases) the fee for all work in that case shall be calculated on the basis of the fees set out in chapeter II of that Schedule.

(2C) Subject to paragraph (2D), the Board may at its discretion allow a fee additional to the fees prescribed in chapter II of Schedule 6 where it is satisfied that any of the circumstances prescribed in chapter III of that Schedule exists, and have a significant effect on the conduct of the case.

(2D) The additional fee allowable in accordance with paragraph (2C) shall be 15% of the fee authorised by Chapter II of Schedule 6 in respect of each of the circumstances specified in paragraphs 1 to 5A of Chapter III of that Schedule and 20% of the said fee authorised in respect of each of the circumstances specified in paragraphs 6 and 7 of said Chapter III, up to a maximum in any case of 50% of that fee.

(2E) Fees for sequestration in bankruptcy (other than summary sequestrations) shall be chargeable only on the basis of Schedule 3 and fees for summary sequestrations shall be chargeable only on the basis of 80 per cent of the fees in that Schedule.

(3) A solicitor's fees in relation to proceedings in the Judicial Committee of the Privy Council, under paragraph 10, 12 or 13(b), 32 or 33 of Schedule to the Scotland Act 1998, House of Lords, Employment Appeal Tribunal, Lands Valuation Appeal Court, Scottish Land Court or Lands Tribunal for Scotland or before the Child Support Commissioners or the Social Security Commissioners, shall be calculated in accordance with Schedule 5.

(4) In all Court of Session proceedings a fee, additional to those set out in Schedule 5 and not exceeding 50 per cent of those fees, may be allowed at the discretion of the court to cover the responsibility undertaken by a solicitor in the conduct of the proceedings. In the sheriff court, in proceedings of importance or requiring special preparation, the sheriff may allow a percentage increase in a cause on the Summary Cause Roll, not exceeding 100 per cent, of the fees authorised by Schedules 2 or 3 to cover the responsibility undertaken by the solicitor in the conduct of the proceedings. The Court of Session in deciding whether to allow an additional fee and the auditor in determining that fee or the sheriff in fixing the amount of a percentage fee increase shall take into account the following factors —

    (a) the complexity of the proceedings and the number, difficulty or novelty of the questions involved;

    (b) the skill, specialised knowledge and responsibility required of and the time and labour expended by the solicitor;

    (c) the number and importance of the documents prepared or perused;

    (d) the place and circumstances of the proceedings or in which the solicitor's work of preparation for and conduct of it has been carried out;

    (e) the importance of the proceedings or the subject matter thereof to the client;

    (f) the amount or value of money or property involved;

    (g) the steps taken with a view to settling the proceedings, limiting the matters in dispute or limiting the scope of any hearing; and

    (h) any other fees and allowances payable to the solicitor in respect of other items in the same proceedings and otherwise charged for in the account.

(5) The auditor of the Court of Session shall have power to increase or decrease any inclusive fee set out in Schedule 1 in any appropriate circumstances.

(6) The auditor shall have the power to apportion any fees set out in Schedules 1, 2 or 6 between solicitors in appropriate circumstances or to modify any such fees in the case of a solicitor acting for more than one party in the same proceedings or in the case of the same solicitor acting in more than one proceeding arising out of the same circumstances or in the event of the proceedings being settled or disposed of at a stage when the work covered by any inclusive fee has not been completed.

(7) Where work done by a solicitor constitutes a supply of services in respect of which value-added tax is chargeable, there may be added to the amount of fees calculated in accordance with the foregoing paragraphs of this regulation an amount equal to the amount of value-added tax chargeable.

6.   A solicitor's outlays shall include a charge in respect of posts and incidents of 12 per cent of the amount of the fees allowable to the solicitor in Schedules 1 and 2 (excluding any amount added in accordance with regulations 5 (4) and (7)). In Schedule 5 or 6, without prejudice to any other claims for outlays, a solicitor shall not be allowed outlays representing posts and incidents.

7.   Where any work is carried out in the preparation for or conduct of the proceedings and that work could more economically have been done by instructing a local solicitor, only such fees and outlays shall be allowed as would have been allowable if a local solicitor had been instructed, including reasonable fees for instructing and corresponding with him, unless it was reasonable in the interests of the client that the solicitor in charge of the proceedings, or a solicitor or clerk authorised by him, should attend personally.

Accounts in respect of solicitors' fees and outlays

8.—(1) Subject to paragraph (2) below, accounts prepared in respect of fees and outlays allowable to solicitors shall be submitted to the Board not later than 6 months after the date of completion of the proceedings in respect of which that legal aid was granted.

(2) The Board may accept accounts submitted in respect of fees and outlays later than the 6 months referred to in paragraph (1) if they consider that there is a special reason for late submission.

Fees allowable to counsel

9.   Subject to the provisions of regulation 10 regarding calculation of fees, counsel may be allowed such fees as are reasonable for conducting the proceedings in a proper manner, as between solicitor and client, third party paying.

10.—(1) Counsel's fees in relation to proceedings in the Court of Session shall be calculated in accordance with Schedule 4.

(2) Counsel's fees for any work in relation to proceedings in the sheriff court, Judicial Committee of the Privy Council, House of Lords, Employment Appeal Tribunal, Lands Valuation Appeal Court, Scottish Land Court or Lands Tribunal for Scotland, or before the Child Support Commissioners or the Social Security Commissioners shall be 90 per cent of the amount of fees which would be allowed for that work on a taxation of expenses between solicitor and client, third party paying, if the work done were not legal aid.

(2A) The fees of a solicitor — advocate for any work in relation to proceedings in the House of Lords or the Judicial Committee of the Privy Council, shall be 90 per cent of the amount of fees which would be allowed for that work on a taxation of expenses between solicitor and client, third party paying, if the work done were not legal aid.

(3) Where work done by counsel constitutes a supply of services in respect of which value-added tax is chargeable, there may be added to the amount of fees calculated in accordance with the foregoing paragraphs of this regulation an amount equal to the amount of value-added tax chargeable thereon.

Payments to account

11.—(1) A solicitor acting for, or counsel instructed on behalf of, a person receiving civil legal aid may prior to the completion of the proceedings for which the legal aid was granted submit a claim to the Board, in such form and complying with such terms and containing such information as the Board may require for assessment purposes, for payment of sums to account of his fees necessarily and reasonably incurred in connection with these proceedings.

(2) When assessing the fee payable to a solicitor in respect of legal aid the Board may have regard to any payment, or payments, made to account under advice and assistance in relation to the same matter and, where the work in respect of which such payment, or payments, is made might reasonably have been carried out under legal aid, it may reduce the amount of the fee payable accordingly.

(Regulation 11(2) is amended insofar as it relates to payments to solicitors)

(5) The making of a claim under this regulation shall not be regarded as an account of expenses nor shall the claim affect in any way the provisions of regulation 8 above with regard to the submission and acceptance of accounts prepared in respect of fees and outlays allowable to solicitors.

(6) Where payment has been made in accordance with the provisions of this regulation but the payment made exceeds in the case of any solicitor acting for the assisted person the total fees and outlays allowable to that solicitor in respect of the legal aid or in the case of any counsel instructed on behalf of the assisted person the total fees allowable to that counsel in respect of the legal aid, the excess shall be repaid to the Fund by such solicitor or counsel as the case may be:

Provided that where by reason of a failure to comply with the requirements of regulation 8 above with regard to submission of an account of his fees and outlays the amount of the fees and outlays allowable to a solicitor to whom payment has been made under this regulation cannot be ascertained, the Board may require such solicitor to repay to the Fund the whole amount paid under this regulation or such part thereof which it is satisfied may have been overpaid to the solicitor.

Taxation of fees and outlays

12.—(1) If any question or dispute arises between the Board and a solicitor or counsel as to the amount of fees or outlays allowable to the solicitor, or as to the amount of fees allowable to counsel, from the Fund under these Regulations, other than regulation 11 above, the matter shall be referred for taxation by the auditor.

(2) A reference to the auditor under paragraph (1) above may be at the instance of the solicitor concerned or, where the question or dispute affects the fees allowable to counsel, of the counsel concerned, or of the Board, and the auditor shall give reasonable notice of the diet of taxation to the solicitor or counsel as appropriate and to the Board.

(3) Subject to regulaton 12A the Board and any other party to a reference to the auditor under paragraph (1) above shall have the right to state written objections to the court in relation to the auditor's report within 14 days of the issue of that report, and may be heard thereon; and where the court is the Court of Session rule 349 of the Act of Sederunt (Rules of Court, consolidation and amendment) 1965 shall apply to the determination of any such objections.

(4) For the purposes of this regulation the expression "the court" means —

    (a) in relation to any report of the Auditor of the Court of Session, the Court of Session;

    (b) in relation to any report of the auditor of a sheriff court, the sheriff; and

    (c) in relation to any report of the Auditor of the Scottish Land Court, the Chairman of the Scottish Land Court.

12A.—(1) In relation to proceedings in the Judicial Committee of the Privy Council, the Board and any other party to a reference to the auditor who is dissatisfied with all or part of a taxation shall have the right to lodge a petition to the Judicial Committee of the Privy Council within 14 days of the taxation setting out the items objected to and the nature and grounds of the objections.

(2) The petition shall be served on the Board, any such other party who attended the taxation and any other party to whom the auditor directs that a copy should be delivered.

(3) Any party upon whom such a petition is delivered may within 14 days after such delivery lodge a response to the petition which shall be served on the Board, any such other party who attended the taxation and any other party to whom the auditor directs that a copy should be delivered.

(4) The petition and responses, if any, shall be considered by a Board of the Judicial Committee of the Privy Council of the Privy Council which may allow or dismiss the petition without a hearing, invite any or all of the parties to lodge submissions or further submissions in writing or direct that an oral hearing be held.

SCHEDULE 1

Regulation 5

FEES OF SOLICITORS FOR PROCEEDINGS IN THE COURT OF SESSION

1. In this Schedule, unless the context otherwise requires —

    "the court" means the Court of Session; and

    "session fee" means the fee set out in paragraph 21 of Part V of the Table of Fees in this Schedule.

TABLE OF FEES

PART I — UNDEFENDED ACTIONS (OTHER THAN CONSISTORIAL ACTIONS)

£

1. Inclusive fee to pursuer's solicitor in all undefended cases where no proof is led, to cover all work from taking instructions up to and including obtaining extract decree 95.80

PART II — UNDEFENDED CONSISTORIAL ACTIONS (OTHER THAN ACTIONS TO WHICH PART III APPLIES)

1. Fee for all work (other than precognitions) up to and including the calling of summons in court 136.20

Note: Precognitions to be charged as in Part V, paragraph 5 of this Schedule

2. *Incidental procedures*

   Fixing diet, enrolling action, preparation for proof, citing witnesses, etc 77.10

3. *Amendment*

   (a) Where summons amended, where re-service is not ordered, and motion is not starred 19.40

   (b) Where summons amended, where re-service is not ordered and motion is starred 28.40

   (c) Where summons amended and re-service is ordered 36.00

4. *Commissions to take evidence on interrogatories*

   (a) Basic fee to cover all work up to and including lodging completed interrogatories 28.40

   (b) Additional fee for completed interrogatories, including all copies — per sheet 6.05

5. *Commissions to take evidence on open commission*

   (a) Basic fee to solicitor applying for commission but excluding attendance at execution thereof 32.10

   (b) Attendance at execution of commission — per half hour 16.50

6. Where applicable the fees set out in paragraphs 6, 7, 10, 14, 16 and 21 of Part V of this Schedule may be charged

7. Proof and completion fee — excluding accounts of expenses but including instructing counsel for proof, attendance at proof, settling with witnesses, borrowing and returning productions, procuring interlocutor, and obtaining extract decree of divorce 95.80

8. Accounts

   Framing and lodging account and attending taxation 30.60

PART III — UNDEFENDED CONSISTORIAL ACTIONS: AFFIDAVIT PROCEDURE

1. In any undefended action of divorce or separation where —

   (a) the facts set out in section 1(2)(b) (unreasonable behaviour) of the Divorce (Scotland) Act 1976 are relied upon; and

   (b) the pursuer seeks to prove those facts by means of affidavits,

   the pursuer's solicitor may in respect of the work specfied in column 1 of Table A in this paragraph charge, in a case where he is an Edinburgh solicitor acting alone, the inclusive fee specfied in respect of that work in column 2 of that Table, and, in any other case, the inclusive fee specfied in respect of that work in column 3 of that Table.

TABLE A

Column 1 *Work done*	Column 2 *Inclusive fee Edinburgh solciitor acting alone*	Column 3 *Inclusive fee any other case*
1. All work to and including calling of the summons	£198.60	£227.10
2. All work from calling to and including swearing affidavits	£141.90	£170.40
3. All work from swearing affidavits to and including sending extract decree	£42.60	£63.80
4. All work to and including sending extract decree	£383.20	£461.20
Add session fee to item 4	of 7.5 %	of 10%

2. In any undefended action of divorce or separation where —

    (a) the facts set out in section 1(2)(a) (adultery), 1(2)(c) (desertion), 1(2)(d) (two years' non-cohabitation and consent) or 1(2)(e) (five years' non-cohabitation) of the Divorce (Scotland) Act 1976 are relied on; and

    (b) the pursuer seeks to prove these facts by means of affidavits,

the pursuer's solicitor may in respect of the work specified in column 1 of Table B in this paragraph charge, in a case where he is an Edinburgh solicitor acting alone, the inclusive fee specified in respect of that work in column 2 of that Table, and, in any other case, the inclusive fee specified in respect of that work in column 3 of that Table.

TABLE B

Column 1 *Work done*	Column 2 *Inclusive fee Edinburgh solciitor acting alone*	Column 3 *Inclusive fee any other case*
1. All work to and including calling of the summons	£163.20	£191.60
2. All work from calling to and including swearing affidavits	£78.10	£99.30
3. All work from swearing affidavits to and including sending extract decree	£42.60	£63.80
4. All work to and including sending extract decree	£282.80	£354.70
Add session fee to item 4	of 7.5 %	of 10%

3. If —

    (a) the pursuer's solicitor charges an inclusive fee under either paragraph 1 or paragraph 2 of this Part; and

    (b) the action to which the charge relates includes a conclusion relating to an ancillary matter,

in addition to that fee, he may charge in respect of the work specified in column 1 of Table C in this paragraph the inclusive fee specified in respect of that work in column 2 of that Table.

TABLE C

Column 1 *Work done*	Column 2 *Inclusive fee*
1. All work to and including calling of the summons	£39.80
2. All work from calling to and including swearing affidavits	£45.40
4. All work under items 1 and 2	£85.10
Add session fee to item 3 of 7.5% in the case of an Edinburgh solicitor acting alone and 10% in any other case.	

PART IV — OUTER HOUSE PETITIONS

A. *Unopposed petitions*   £

1. Fee for all work, including precognitions and all copyings, up to and obtaining extract decree —

    (a) in the case of an Edinburgh solicitor acting alone 200.70

    (b) in any other case 280.10

Note: Outlays including duplicating charges to be allowed in addition.

B. *Opposed petitions*

2. Fee for all work (other than precognitions) up to and including lodging petition, obtaining and executing warrant for service 136.20

Note: Outlays including duplicating charges to be allowed in addition.

3. Where applicable, the fees set out in paragraphs 5, 6, 7, 10, 12, 14, 18, 19, 20 and 21 of Part V of this Schedule may be charged.

4. Reports —

    (a) For each report by Accountant of Court 24.00

    (b) For any other report as under Part V, paragraph 6 of this Schedule.

5. Obtaining Bond of Caution.. 24.00

PART V — DEFENDED ACTIONS

1. *Instruction fee*   £

    (a) To cover all work (apart from precognitions) until lodgement of open record 188.60

    (b) Instructing re-service where necessary 20.20

    (c) If counter-claim lodged, additional fee for solicitor for each party................................... 39.80

2. *Record fee*

    (a) To cover all work in connection with adjustment and closing of record including subsequent work in connection with By Order Adjustment Roll 200.70

    (b) To cover all work as above, so far as applicable, where action settled or disposed of before record closed 125.00

    (c) If consultation held before record closed, additional fees may be allowed as follows:

        (i) Arranging consultation.. 20.20

        (ii) Attendance at consultation — per half hour.. 16.50

    (d) Additional fee (to include necessary amendments) to the solicitors for the existing pursuer and each existing defender, to be allowed for each pursuer, defender or third party brought in before the record is closed, each of.. 59.10

    (e) Additional fee to the solicitors for existing pursuer and each existing defender, to be allowed for each pursuer, defender, or third party brought in after the record is closed, each of 88.30

3. *Procedure Roll or Debate Roll*

    (a) Preparing for discussion and all work incidental thereto including instruction of counsel 39.80

    (b) Attendance at court — per half hour 16.50

    (c) Advising and work incidental thereto 30.00

4. *Adjustment of issues and counter-issues*

    (a) Fee to solicitor for pursuer to include all work in connection with and incidental to the lodging of an issue, and adjustment and approval thereof 38.20

    (b) If one counter-issue, additional fee to solicitor for pursuer 10.60

    (c) If more than one counter-issue, additional fee to solicitor for pursuer for each additional counter-issue 4.55

£

(d) Fee to solicitor for defender or third party for all work in connection with lodging of counter-issue and adjustment and approval thereof 38.20

(e) Fee to solicitor for defender or third party for considering issue where no counter-issue lodged 10.60

(f) Fee to solicitor for defender or third party for considering each additional counter-issue 4.55

5. *Precognitions*

Taking and drawing precognitions — per sheet 19.40

Note: (i)   In addition each solicitor shall be entitled to charge for copies of the precognitions for the use of counsel and himself.

         (ii)   Where a skilled witness prepares his own precognition or report the solicitor shall be allowed, for revising and adjusting it, half of the taking and drawing fee per sheet.

6. *Reports obtained under order of court excluding auditor's report*

(a) Fee for all work incidental thereto 42.00

(b) Additional fee per sheet of report to include all copies required (maximum £42.35) 6.05

7. *Specification of documents*

(a) Basic fee to cover instructing counsel, revising and lodging and all incidental procedures to obtain a diligence up to and including obtaining interlocutor 39.80

(b) Fee to opponent's solicitor 19.40

(c) If commission executed, additional fee — per half hour 16.50

(d) If alternative procedure adopted, fee per person upon whom order served 15.80

8. *Commission to take evidence on interrogatories*

(a) Basic fee to solicitor applying for commission to cover all work up to and including lodging report of commission with completed interrogatories and cross interrogatories 80.10

(b) Basic fee to opposing solicitor if cross-interrogatories lodged 64.40

(c) Fee to opposing solicitor if no cross-interrogatories lodged 24.00

(d) Additional fee to solicitor for each party for completed interrogatories or cross-interrogatories, including all copies — per sheet 6.05

9. *Commission to take evidence on open commission*

(a) Basic fee to solicitor applying for commission up to and including lodging report of commission, but excluding attendance at execution thereof 88.30

(b) Basic fee to opposing solicitor 39.80

(c) Attendance at execution of commission — per half hour 16.50

10. *Miscellaneous motions where not otherwise covered by this Schedule*

(a) Where attendance of counsel and/or solicitor not required 10.60

(b) Where attendance of counsel and/or solicitor required, inclusive of instruction of counsel — not exceeding half hour 30.00

(c) Thereafter attendance fee — per additional half hou 16.50

11. *Incidental procedure (not chargeable prior to approval of issue or allowance of proof)*

Fixing diet, obtaining note on the line of evidence, etc, borrowing and returning process, lodging productions, considering opponent's productions, and all other work prior to the consultation on the sufficiency of evidence 112.40

12. *Amendment of record*

(a) Amendment of conclusions only — fee to solicitor for pursuer 30.00

(b) Amendment of conclusions only — fee to solicitor for opponent 10.60

(c) Amendment of pleadings after record closed, where no answers to the amendment are lodged — fee to solicitor for proposer 43.50

£

(d) In same circumstances — fee to solicitor for opponent 20.20

(e) Amendment of pleadings after record closed where answers are lodged — fee for solicitor for each party lodging answers 102.50

(f) Fee for adjustment of minute and answers, where applicable, to be allowed in addition to solicitor for each party 56.20

13. *Preparation for trial or proof to include fixing consultation on the sufficiency of evidence and attendance thereat, fee-funding precept, adjusting minute of admissions, citing witnesses, all work checking and writing up process, and preparing for trial or proof*

(a) If action settled before trial or proof, or the trial or proof lasts only one day, to include, where applicable, instruction of counsel 272.50

(b) For each day or part of a day after the first, including instruction of counsel 24.00

(c) To cover preparing for adjourned diet and all work incidental as in (a), if diet postponed more than 5 days 49.50

14. *Copying fees* —

Where a document is copied and it is necessary to take a copy of more than 20 sheets (whether 20 of 1 sheet, 5 of 4 sheets or whatever), for each sheet copied a fee of 0.08

Note: a "sheet" shall consist of 250 words or numbers.

15. *Settlement by tender — fees for solicitor for either party*

(a) Basic fee for lodging, or for considering, first tender 59.10

(b) Fee for lodging, or for considering, each further tender 39.80

(c) Additional fee if tender accepted 39.80

16. *Extra-judicial settlement*

Fee inclusive of joint minute (not based on a judicial tender) 102.50

17. *Proof or trial*

Attendance fee — per half hour 16.50

18. *Accounts* — to include framing and lodging account, intimating diet, and attending taxation, uplifting account and noting and intimating taxations 71.80

19. *Ordering and obtaining extract* 15.00

20. *Final procedure*

(a) If case goes to trial or proof, to include all work to close of litigation, so far as not otherwise provided for, including in particular settling with witnesses and procuring and booking verdict, or attendance at judgment 80.10

(b) If case disposed of before trial or proof 24.00

21. *Session fee — to cover communications with client and counsel*

(a) Where no correspondent — 7.5% of total fees (including copying fees) allowed on taxation.

(b) Where correspondent involved — 10% of total fees (including copying fees) allowed on taxation.

PART VI — INNER HOUSE BUSINESS

1. *Reclaiming motions*   £

(a) Fee for solicitor for appellant for all work up to interlocutor sending case to roll 59.10

(b) Fee for solicitor for respondent 30.00

(c) Additional fee for solicitor for each party for every 50 pages of appendix 24.70

2. *Appeals from inferior courts* £

    (a) Fee for solicitor for appellant 71.80

    (b) Fee for solicitor for respondent 35.20

    (c) Additional fee for solicitor for each party for every 50 pages of appendix 24.70

3. *Summar or Short Roll*

    (a) Preparing for discussion, instructing counsel, and preparing appendix 59.10

    (b) Attendance fee — per half hour 16.50

4. Where applicable the fees set out in Part V of this Schedule may be charged.

5. *Special cases and Inner House petitions*

    According to circumstances of the case.

6. Obtaining Bond of Caution 24.00

PART VII — ADMIRALTY AND COMMERCIAL CASES, SEQUESTRATION IN BANKRUPTCY,
APPLICATIONS FOR SUMMARY TRIAL UNDER SECTION 26 OF THE COURT OF SESSION ACT 1988
AND CASES REMITTED FROM THE SHERIFF COURT

The fees shall be based on this Schedule or Schedule 3 according to the circumstances.

SCHEDULE 2

Regulation 5

FEES OF SOLICITORS FOR PROCEEDINGS IN THE SHERIFF COURT

1. Subject to the following provisions of this Schedule fees shall be calculated in accordance with the Table of Fees in this Schedule.

2. Chapter III of the Table of Fees in this Schedule shall have effect subject to the following provisions:—

    (a) in paragraph 2 of Part I and paragraph 7 of Part II, no fee is allowable for attendance at a continuation of the first calling, unless specifically authorised by the court;

    (b) in Part I, in relation to actions for reparation there are allowable such additional fees for precognitions and reports as are necessary to permit the framing of the summons;

    (c) in Part II, in respect of paragraph 22 (final procedure),no fee shall be allowed in respect of accounts of expenses when the hearing on the claim for expenses takes place immediately on the sheriff or sheriff principal announcing his decision;

    (d) unless the sheriff, on an incidental application in that behalf, otherwise directs, all fees chargeable under Chapter III shall be reduced by 50% in respect of—

        (i) undefended actions for recovery of heritable property;

        (ii) actions under the Tenancy of Shops (Scotland) Act 1949(3) or section 3 of the Sheriff Courts (Civil Jurisdiction and Procedure) (Scotland) Act 1963(4).

2A. In Chapter III of the Table of Fees in this Schedule—

    "attendance at court" means waiting for and conducting any hearing unless specifically provided for elsewhere in the Chapter;

    "half hour" shall be read as if immediately followed by the words "(or part thereof)";

    "a page" consists of 125 words or numbers; and

    "a sheet" consists of 250 words or numbers.

TABLE

Actions	Percentage Reduction
1. For recovery of possession of heritable property in undefended actions	50%
2. Under the following enactments:-	50%
(i) Tenancy of Shops (Scotland) Act 1949, and	
(ii) Section 3 of the Sheriff Courts (Civil Jurisdiction and Procedure) (Scotland) Act 1963	

Provided that for the purposes of this sub-paragraph "value", in relation to any action in which a counter-claim has been lodged, is the total of the sums craved in the writ and in the counter-claim.

3. In this Schedule "process fee" means the fee set out in paragraph 23 of Chapter II of the Table of Fees in this Schedule.

TABLE OF FEES

NOTE

THE UNDERNOTED FEES APPLY ONLY TO CAUSES COMMENCED ON OR AFTER 1ST JANUARY 1994. THE FEES APPLICABLE TO CAUSES COMMENCED BEFORE 1ST JANUARY 1994 CAN BE FOUND IN THE FEES SUPPLEMENT 1998 AT PAGES 109–116.

CHAPTER I — UNDEFENDED ACTIONS (OTHER THAN ACTIONS TO WHICH CHAPTER III OR IV APPLIES)

Part I — All actions except those actions of divorce or separation and aliment to which Part II applies

£

1. Actions (other than those specified in paragraph 2 of this Part) in which decree is granted without proof —

Inclusive fee to cover all work from taking instructions up to and including obtaining extract decree 79.30

In cases where settlement is effected after service of a writ but before the expiry of the period of notice 65.90

Note: If the pursuer's solicitor elects to charge this inclusive fee he shall endorse a minute to that effect on the initial writ before ordering extract decree. Outlays such as court dues for deliverance and posts shall be chargeable in addition and taxation shall be unnecessary.

2. Actions of separation and aliment (not being actions to which Part II of this Chapter applies), adherence and aliment or custody and aliment where proof takes place —

Inclusive fee to cover all work from taking instructions up to and including obtaining extract decree 280.10

Part II — Actions of divorce or separation and aliment where proof is by means of affidavits

1. In any undefended action of divorce or of separation and aliment where —

   (a)   the facts set out in section 1(2)(b) (unreasonable behaviour) of the Divorce (Scotland) Act 1976 are relied upon; and

   (b)   the pursuer seeks to prove those facts by means of affidavits,

the pursuer's solicitor may in respect of the work specified in column 1 of Table A in this paragraph charge the inclusive fee specified in respect of that work in column 2 of that Table.

TABLE A

Column 1 *Work done*	Column 2 *Inclusive fee*
1. All work to and including the period of notice	£198.60
2. All work from the period of notice to and including swearing affidavits	£141.90
3. All work from swearing affidavits to and including sending extract decree	£42.60
4. All work to and including sending extract decree	£383.20
Add process fee to item 4	of 10%

2. In any undefended action of divorce or separation and aliment where —

    (a) the facts set out in section 1(2)(a) (adultery), 1(2)(c) (desertion), 1(2)(d) (two years' non-cohabitation and consent) or 1(2)(e) (five years' non-cohabitation) of the Divorce (Scotland) Act 1976 are relied on; and

    (b) the pursuer seeks to prove those facts by means of affidavits,

the pursuer's solicitor may in respect of the work specified in column 1 of Table B in this paragraph charge the inclusive fee specified in respect of that work in column 2 of that Table.

TABLE B

Column 1 *Work done*	Column 2 *Inclusive fee*
1. All work to and including the period of notice	£163.20
2. All work from the period of notice to and including swearing affidavits	£78.10
3. All work from swearing affidavits to and including sending extract decree	£42.60
4. All work to and including sending extract decree	£283.80
Add process fee to item 4	of 10%

3. If —

    (a) the pursuer's solicitor charges an inclusive fee under either paragraph 1 or paragraph 2 of this Part; and

    (b) the action to which the charge relates includes a crave relating to an ancillary matter,

in addition to that fee, he may charge in respect of the work specified in column 1 of Table C in this paragraph the inclusive fee specified in respect of that work in column 2 of that Table.

TABLE C

Column 1 *Work done*	Column 2 *Inclusive fee*
1. All work to and including the period of notice	£77.30
2. All work from the period of notice to and including swearing affidavits	£45.40
3. All work under items 1 and 2	£122.60
Add process fee to item 3	of 10%

CHAPTER II — DEFENDED ACTIONS (OTHER THAN ACTIONS TO WHICH CHAPTER III OR IV APPLIES)

£

1. *Instruction fee —*

    (a) To cover all work (except as hereinafter otherwise specially provided for in this Chapter) to the lodging of defences including copying 217.30

    (b) Additional fee where separate statement of facts and counterclaim and answers lodged 40.20

2. *Precognitions* — taking and drawing — per sheet 19.00

Note: Where a skilled witness prepares his own precognition or report, the solicitor shall be allowed half of above drawing fee for revising and adjusting it.

3. *Productions —*

    (a) For lodging productions — each inventory 20.60

    (b) For considering opponent's productions — each inventory 10.30

4. *Adjustment fee* — To cover all work (except as otherwise specially provided for in this Chapter) in connection with the adjustment of the Record including making up and lodging certified copy Record —

    (a) Fee to solicitor for any party 99.90

    (b) Fee to each original party's solicitor if action settled before Options Hearing 58.70

    (c) Additional fee to each original party's solicitor if additional defender brought in before Options Hearing 24.70

    (d) Additional fee to each original party's solicitor if additional defender brought in after Options Hearing 31.90

5. *Fee for framing affidavits* — per sheet 8.25

6. *Options Hearing* — Fee to include preparation for and conduct of Options Hearing (or First Hearing in defended family actions) and noting interlocutor —

    (a) Where hearing does not exceed one half hour 82.40

    (b) Where hearing exceeds one half hour — for every extra quarter hour 12.40

    (c) For lodging and intimating or for considering note of basis of preliminary plea — for each note lodged 20.60

7. *Additional Procedure* — For all work subsequent to Options Hearing including preparation for and attendance at procedural hearing —

    Where hearing does not exceed one half hour 82.40

    For every extra quarter hour 12.40

8. *Debate (other than on evidence) —*

    (a) Where counsel not employed —

        (i) To include preparation for and all work in connection with any hearing or debate other than on evidence 62.80

        (ii) For conduct of debate — per quarter hour 11.30

    (b) Where counsel employed, fee to solicitor appearing with counsel — per quarter hour . 8.25

9. *Interim Interdict Hearings —*

    (a) Preparation for each hearing — each party 39.10

    (b) Fee to conduct hearing — per quarter hour 11.30

    (c) If counsel employed, fee to attend hearing per quarter hour 8.25

10. *Reports obtained under order of court, excluding auditor's report —*

    (a) Fee for all work incidental thereto 43.30

    (b) Additional fee per sheet of report to include all copies required (maximum £28.25) 5.65

11. *Commissions to take evidence —* £

    (a) On interrogatories —

        (i) Fee to solicitor applying for commission to include drawing, intimating and lodging motion, drawing and lodging interrogatories, instructing commissioner and all incidental work (except as otherwise specially provided for in this Chapter) but excluding attendance at execution of commission 119.50

        (ii) Fee to opposing solicitor if cross-interrogatories prepared and lodged 79.30

        (iii) If no cross-interrogatories lodged 23.70

    (b) Open Commissions —

        (i) Fee to solicitor applying for commission to include all work (except as otherwise specially provided in this Chapter) up to lodging report of commission but excluding attendance thereat 79.30

        (ii) Fee to solicitor for opposing party 40.20

        (iii) Fee for attendance at execution of commission — per quarter hour 11.30

        (iv) If counsel employed, fee for attendance of solicitor — per quarter hour 8.25

        (v) Travelling time — per quarter hour 8.25

12. *Specification of documents —*

    (a) Fee to cover drawing, intimating and lodging specification and relative motion —

        (i) Where motion unopposed 41.30

        (ii) Where motion opposed — additional fee per quarter hour 11.30

    (b) Fee for considering opponent's specification and relative motion —

        (i) Where motion not opposed 23.70

        (ii) Where motion opposed — additional fee per quarter hour 11.30

    (c) Fee for citation of havers, preparation for and attendance before commissioner at execution of commission —

        (i) Where attendance before commissioner does not exceed 1 hour 43.30

        (ii) For each additional quarter hour after the first hour 14.00

    (d) If optional procedure adopted — fee per person upon whom order is served 10.30

    (e) Fee for perusal of documents recovered — per quarter hour 11.30

13. *Amendment of Record —*

    (a) (i) Fee to cover drawing, intimating and lodging minute of amendment and relative motion 39.10

        (ii) Fee for perusal of answers 15.50

        (iii) Fee for any court appearance necessary — per quarter hour 11.30

    (b) (i) Fee to opposing solicitor — for perusing minute of amendment 31.90

        (ii) Fee for preparation of answers 15.50

        (iii) Fee for any court appearance necessary — per quarter hour 11.30

    (c) Fee for adjustment of minute and answers where applicable to be allowed in addition to each party 39.10

14. *Motions and minutes —*

    (a) Fee to cover drawing, intimating and lodging any written motion or minute, including a reponing note, and relative attendances at court (except as otherwise provided in for in this Chapter) —

        (i) Where opposed 55.60

        (ii) Where unopposed (including for each party a joint minute other than under paragraph 20(b)) 23.70

£

　(b)　Fee to cover considering opponent's written motion, minute or reponing note and relative attendances at court —

　　(i)　Where motion, minute or reponing note opposed 55.60

　　(ii)　Where motion, minute or reponing note unopposed 20.60

15. *Hearing Limitation* —

Fee to include work (except as otherwise specially provided for in this Chapter) undertaken with a view to limiting the scope of any hearing, and including the exchange of documents, precognitions and expert reports, agreeing any fact, statement or document not in dispute, preparing and intimating any Notice to Admit or Notice of Non- Admission and preparing and lodging any Joint Minute, not exceeding 195.70

16. *Procedure preliminary to proof* —

　(a)　Fee to cover all work, preparing for proof (except as otherwise specially provided in this Chapter) —

　　(i)　If action settled or abandoned not later than 14 days before the diet of proof 127.70

　　(ii)　In any other case 233.80

　(b)　Fee to cover preparing for adjourned diet and all incidental work as in (a) if diet postponed for more than 6 days, for each additional diet 51.50

　(c)　Fee for attendance inspecting opponent's documents — per quarter hour 12.40

17. *Conduct of proof*

　(a)　Fee to cover conduct of proof and debate on evidence if taken at close of proof — per quarter hour 11.30

　(b)　If counsel employed, fee to solicitor appearing with counsel — per quarter hour 8.25

18. *Debate on evidence*

　(a)　Where debate on evidence not taken at conclusion of proof, fee for preparing for debate 39.10

　(b)　Fee for conduct of debate — per quarter hour 11.30

　(c)　If counsel employed, fee to solicitor appearing with counsel — per quarter hour 8.25

19. *Appeals*

　(a)　To sheriff principal —

　　(i)　Fee to cover instructions, marking of appeal or noting that appeal marked, noting diet of hearing thereof and preparation for hearing 119.50

　　　If counsel employed, restricted to 68.00

　　(ii)　Fee to cover conduct of hearing — per quarter hour 11.30

　　　If counsel employed, fee to solicitor appearing with counsel — per quarter hour 8.25

　(b)　To Court of Session —

Fee to cover instructions, marking appeal or noting that appeal marked and instructing Edinburgh correspondents 39.10

20. *Settlements*

　(a)　Judicial tender —

　　(i)　Fee for preparation and lodging or for consideration of minute of tender 43.30

　　(ii)　Fee on acceptance of tender, to include preparation and lodging or consideration of minute of acceptance and attendance at court when decree granted in terms thereof 35.00

　(b)　Extra-judicial settlement —

Fee to cover negotiations resulting in settlement, framing or revising joint minute and attendance at court when authority interponed thereto 80.30

　(c)　Whether or not fees are payable under (a) or (b) above where additional work has been undertaken with a view to effecting settlement, including offering settlement, although settlement is not agreed — not exceeding 80.30

21. *Final procedure*   £

   (a) Fee to cover settling with witnesses, enquiries for cause at avizandum, noting final interlocutor 59.70

   (b) Fee to cover drawing account of expenses, arranging, intimating and attending diet of taxation and obtaining approval of auditor's report and adjusting account with opponent where necessary, ordering, procuring and examining extract decree or adjusting account with opponent 47.90

   (c) Fee to cover considering opponent's account of expenses and attending diet of taxation or adjusting account with opponent 15.00

22. *Copying fees*

Where a document is copied and it is necessary to take a copy of more than 20 sheets (whether 20 of 1 sheet, 5 of 4 sheets or whatever), for each sheet copied a fee of 0.08

Note: A "sheet" shall consist of 250 words or numbers.

23. *Process fee*

Fee to cover all consultations between solicitor and client during the progress of the cause and all communications, written or oral, passing between them:

10% on total fees (including copying fees) allowed on taxation.

24. *Instruction of counsel*

   (a) Fee for instructing counsel to revise pleadings 24.70

   (b) Fee for instructing counsel to attend court 51.50

   (c) Fee for attending consultation with counsel —

      (i) Where total time engaged does not exceed one hour 51.50

      (ii) For each additional quarter hour 11.30

Note: In each case to cover all consultations, revisal of papers and all incidental work.

CHAPTER III

Part I —Undefended Actions

1. The fee for citation, service or re-service after the first citation—

   (a) to any destination by post £6.74

   (b) by advertisement £19.01

2. The fee for attendance at court.. £19.01

3. The fee for all other work... £53.50

Part II —Defended Actions

1. The instruction fee—

(a) for the pursuer's solicitor, including taking instructions, framing summons and statement of claim, obtaining warrant for service, enquiring for the form of response and noting defence ... £81.16

(b) for the defender's solicitor, for all work from taking instructions (including instructions for a counter-claim) up to and including lodging the form of response £81.16

2. Where an additional defender or third party enters the cause, an additional fee for each of the original parties' solicitors for all consequent work £40.61

3. The fee for citation, service or re-service, except as provided for in paragraph 19(e), by—

(a) post, to a destination—

      (i) within the United Kingdom, Isle of Man, Channel Islands or the Republic of Ireland £6.74

      (ii) other than one specified in paragraph (i) £14.42

(b) sheriff officer, to include instructing sheriff officer, perusing execution of citation and settling sheriff officer's fee £6.74

(c) advertisement, to include framing and instructing the advertisement £21.11

4. In connection with the first hearing of the cause—

(a) the fee for attendance at court, including noting the outcome of the hearing £70.17

(b) if waiting for and conducting the hearing exceeds an hour and a half, the fee for attendance at court for each subsequent half hour £21.11

5. The fee for attendance at court, except as specifically provided for elsewhere in this Chapter, per half hour...... £21.11

6. The fee for drawing precognitions, including instructions, attendances with witnesses and all relative meetings and correspondence, per sheet £31.27

7. The fee for perusing, revising and adjusting a report or precognition prepared by a skilled witness, per sheet...... £15.64

8. In connection with reports commissioned by order of Court, the fee for—

(a) all incidental work, including instructing the report £21.11

(b) each half hour perusing the report £21.11

9. The fee, per inventory, for—

(a) lodging productions £31.27

(b) perusing the opposition's productions £14.42

10. The fee for framing affidavits, per sheet...... £15.64

11. Except as provided for by paragraphs 17, 18 and 19 the fee for—

(a) drawing, intimating and lodging any written minute or incidental application including any relative attendance at court, where that minute or application is—

    (i)   opposed £44.53

    (ii) unopposed £26.74

(b) considering a written minute or incidental application intimated by the opposition including any relative attendance at court, where that minute or application is—

    (i)   opposed £36.63

    (ii) unopposed £21.11

12. In connection with a hearing to which paragraph 11 applies, if waiting for and conducting that hearing exceeds half an hour, the fee for attendance at court for each subsequent half hour..... £21.11

13. In connection with a proof the fee for all work, except as specifically provided for elsewhere in this Chapter, preparatory to—

(a) the first scheduled proof, if—

    (i)   the cause is settled or abandoned 7 or more days before the scheduled proof £73.26

    (ii) paragraph (i) does not apply £87.96

(b) any adjourned proof, if the postponement from the hearing previously scheduled exceeds 6 days and—

    (i)   the cause is settled or abandoned 7 or more days before the scheduled proof £36.63

    (ii) paragraph (i) does not apply £43.98

14. The fee for each half hour inspecting the opposition's documents either at court or at a place fixed by the opposition £21.11

15. In connection with a proof or a trial and debate on evidence taken at the close of proof, the fee for each half hour—

(a) conducting that hearing £21.11

(b) waiting in court for that hearing £11.22

16. In connection with a debate on evidence not taken at the close of proof, the fee for—

(a) all preparatory work £49.06

(b) attendance at court, per half hour £21.11

17. In connection with a minute of judicial tender—

(a) the fee for consideration of, preparing and lodging the minute £44.53

(b) on acceptance of the tender, the fee for consideration of, preparing and lodging the minute of acceptance and attendance at court when decree is granted in terms of that minute £31.27

(c) on rejection of the tender, the fee for considering it £31.27

18. The fee for each party where the case is settled extra-judicially, including all relative negotiations, framing or revising the joint minute and attendance at court when authority is interponed thereto £73.26

19. In connection with an incidental application for commission and diligence to recover documents or an order under section 1 of the Administration of Justice (Scotland) Act 1972(6), the fee for—

(a) drawing, intimating and lodging the application and, where relevant, specification and any relative attendance at court, where the application is—

     (i)   opposed £48.95

     (ii)   unopposed £26.74

(b) considering the application and, where relevant, specification intimated by the opposition and any relative attendance at court, where the application is—

     (i)   opposed £36.63

     (ii)   unopposed £21.11

(c) each subsequent half hour, where attendance at court exceeds half an hour £21.11

(d) citing havers and preparing for and appearing before the commissioner or sheriff at the execution of the commission, per half hour £21.11

(e) serving an order on each person, if optional procedure is adopted £14.42

(f) each half hour perusing the documents recovered £21.11

20. In connection with an open commission to take evidence, the fee for—

(a) all work, excluding attendance at the commission, by the—

     (i)   solicitor applying for the commission £49.06

     (ii)   the opposing solicitor £21.11

(b) each half hour attending the execution of the commission £21.11

21. In connection with an appeal, the fee for—

(a) all work, including preparation for any hearing £100.17

(b) attendance at court for a hearing on adjustments or for the appeal hearing, per half hour £21.11

22. At the conclusion of the cause, the fee for—

(a) settling with witnesses and noting the final decree £44.53

(b) the successful party to cover drawing the account of expenses, arranging, intimating and attending a diet of taxation and obtaining approval of the auditor's report and, where necessary, ordering, procuring and examining extract decree or adjusting account with opponent £44.53

(c) the unsuccessful party to cover considering the opponent's account of expenses and, where necessary, adjusting the account with opponent or attending a diet of taxation £21.11

Chapter IV — Executry Business

                                                                                       £

1. *Petition for decree dative*

Inclusive fee for taking instructions to present petition, drawing petition and making necessary copies, lodging and directing publication, attendance at court, moving for decreedative, extracting decree where necessary and all matters incidental to petition 33.70

2. *Restriction of Caution*

Inclusive fee for taking instructions to prepare petition, drawing petition and making necessary copies, lodging, instructing advertisement and all matters incidental to petition ... 33.70

3. Fees for other work shall be chargeable according to Schedule 3.

SCHEDULE 3

Regulation 4

TABLE OF DETAILED FEES CHARGEABLE BY SOLICITORS FOR PROCEEDINGS IN THE COURT OF SESSION AND SHERIFF COURT

£

1. The fee for —

   (a) Any time up to the first half hour spent by a solicitor conducting a proof or hearing 28.20

   (b) Each quarter hour (or part thereof) subsequent to the first half hour 14.10

2. The fee for —

   (a) Each quarter hour (or part thereof) spent by a solicitor in carrying out work other than that prescribed in paragraphs 1 and 3 to 6 hereof, provided that any time is additional to the total time charged for under paragraph 1 above 10.90

   (b) Each quarter hour (or part thereof) spent by a solicitor's clerk in carrying out work other than that prescribed in paragraphs 3 to 6 hereof 5.40

3. The fee for —

   Framing affidavits — per sheet (or part thereof) 9.25

4. The fee for —

   (a) Framing and drawing all necessary papers, other than affidavits or papers of a formal character

   (b) Each citation of a party, witness or haver including execution thereof

   (c) Instructing messengers-at-arms and sheriff officers, including examining execution and settling fee

   (d) Agency accepting service of any writ

   (e) Lodging first step of process

   (f) Lengthy telephone calls (of over 4 minutes and up to 10 minutes duration)

   (g) Letters including instructions to counsel — per page (or part thereof), subject to paragraph 5(f) below

   (h) Perusing any document (other than a letter) consisting of not more than 12 sheets — for the first 2 sheets and each 2 sheets thereafter —

   Note: Where the document perused consists of more than 12 sheets the fee for perusing the whole document shall be charged in accordance with paragraph 2 above.

   in each of sub-paragraphs (a)-(h) 6.20

5. The fee for —

   (a) Attendance at court offices for carrying out formal work including making up process and each necessary lodging in (other than first step), uplifting from or borrowing of process (to include return of same) or enquiry for documents due to be lodged;

   (b) Revising papers drawn by counsel, open and closed records etc or where revisal ordered — per 5 sheets (or part thereof);

   (c) Framing formal papers such as inventories, title pages and accounts of expenses per sheet (or part thereof);

   (d) Certifying or signing a document;

   (e) Short telephone calls (of up to 4 minutes duration);

   (f) Short letters of a formal nature, intimations, and letters confirming telephone calls — in each of sub-paragraphs (a) to (f) 2.45

6. Where a document is copied and it is necessary to take a copy of more than 20 sheets (whether 20 of 1 sheet, 5 of 4 sheets or whatever), for each sheet copied a fee of 0.08

Interpretation

In this Table —

    "court" means court or tribunal as the case may be;

    a "sheet" shall consist of 250 words or numbers; and

    a "page" shall consist of 125 words or numbers.

SCHEDULE 4

Regulation 10

FEES OF COUNSEL FOR PROCEEDINGS IN THE COURT OF SESSION

1. Subject to the following provisions of this Schedule, the fees of counsel and of solicitor-advocates shall be calculated in accordance with the Table of Fees in this Schedule and the fee of a solicitor-advocate for undertaking an item of work shall be —

    (a) where he is acting as a junior solicitor-advocate, the same as that allowable to a junior counsel for undertaking an item of work equivalent to that undertaken by the solicitor-advocate; or

    (b) where he is acting as a senior solicitor-advocate, the same as that allowable to a senior counsel for undertaking an item of work equivalent to that undertaken by the solicitor-advocate.

2. Where the Table of Fees in this Schedule does not prescribe a fee for any class of proceedings or any item of work, the auditor shall allow such fee as appears to him appropriate to provide reasonable remuneration for the work with regard to all the circumstances, including the general levels of fees in the said Table of Fees.

3. Where the Table of Fees in this Schedule prescribes a range of fees, the auditor shall (subject to paragraphs 4 and 5 of this Schedule) allow such fee within that range as appears to him to provide reasonable remuneration for the work.

4. The auditor shall have power to increase any fee set out in the Table of Fees in this Schedule where he is satisfied that because of the particular complexity or difficulty of the work or any other particular circumstances such an increase is necessary to provide reasonable remuneration for the work.

5. The auditor shall have power to reduce any fee set out in the Table of Fees in this Schedule where he is satisfied that because of any particular circumstances a reduced fee is sufficient to provide reasonable remuneration for the work.

TABLE OF FEES

CHAPTER I — JUNIOR COUNSEL

Part I — Undefended Actions of Divorce or Separation — Affidavit Procedure

£

1. *Summons or other initiating writ*

    (a) Subject to sub-paragraph (b) below the fees shall be —

(i)	where the facts set out in section 1(2)(b) (unreasonable behaviour) of the Divorce (Scotland) Act 1976 are relied on	31.40
(ii)	where the facts set out in section 1(2)(a) (adultery) or section 1(2)(c) (desertion) of the said Act are relied on and the action is not straightforward	31.40
(iii)	where the facts set out in the said section 1(2)(a) (adultery) or section 1(2)(c) (desertion) are relied on and the action is straightforward	25.20
(iv)	where the facts set out in section 1(2)(d) (2 years' non-cohabitation and consent) or 1(2)(e) (5 years' non-cohabitation) of the said Act are relied on	25.20

£

    (b)   Where common law interdict and/or any order under the Matrimonial Homes (Family Protection) (Scotland) Act 1981 or any other ancillary order is also sought, the fee shall be within the following range:

          From 31.40

          To 58.20

2. *Minute*

    (a)   Minute involving arrangements for a child or children and/or financial provision 23.20

    (b)   Any other minute 18.00

3. *By Order Roll appearance* 18.00

4. *All other work*

    The fees specified in Part IV shall apply.

Part II — Consistorial Actions other than those to which Part I Applies

1. *Summons or other initiating writ*

    The fees specified in Part I shall apply.

2. *Minute for pursuer relating to custody, aliment or access* 25.80

3. *Defences or answers*

    (a)   Defences or answers in purely skeleton form to preserve rights of parties 14.40

    (b)   Answers to minute 23.20

    (c)   The fee for defences or answers to which sub-paragraph (a) or (b) does not apply shall be within the following range:

          From 25.20

          To 52.50

4. *Joint minute regulating custody, aliment or access*

    Framing or adjusting the minute 22.10

5. *By Order Roll appearance* 18.00

6. *All other work*

    The fees specified in Part IV shall apply.

Part III — Petitions

1. *Petition (including any revisals thereto)*

    (a)   Petition for interdict 65.90

    (b)   Other Outer House petitions 44.30

    (c)   Inner House petition: such fee shall be allowed as appears to the auditor to provide reasonable remuneration for the work.

2. *Answers (including any revisals thereto)*

    (a)   Petition for interdict 65.90

    (b)   Other Outer House petitions 40.70

    (c)   Inner House petitions: such fee shall be allowed as appears to the auditor to provide reasonable remuneration for the work.

3. *All other work*

    The fees specified in Part IV shall apply.

Part IV — Ordinary Actions £

1. *Summons (including any revisals thereto)*

    (a) Straightforward cases 55.10

    (b) Other cases 72.60

2. *Defences (including any revisals thereto)*

    (a) Where in purely skeleton form to preserve rights of parties 14.40

    (b) Otherwise the fee shall be within the following range, having regard to nature of summons:

         From 55.10

         To 72.60

3. *Adjustment of record*

    (a) Adjustment fee (each occasion) 23.20

    (b) Additional adjustment fee, where skeleton defences require to be amplified, where additional parties are introduced, etc 55.10

4. *Specification of documents*

    Standard calls only 23.20

5. *Minutes, etc*

    (a) Formal amendments or answers 21.10

    (b) Amendments or answers other than formal 37.10

    (c) Revising and signing tender or acceptance 9.25

    (d) Note of exceptions 23.20

    (e) Abandonment, sist, restriction, etc 11.30

    (f) Issue or counter issue 11.30

6. *Notes*

    (a) Note on quantum only 58.20

    (b) Note advising on tender or extra-judicial offer, where not merely confirming advice at consultation 65.90

    (c) Note on line of evidence 65.90

    (d) The fee for other types of note shall be within the following range:

         From 22.10

         To 65.90

7. *Consultations*

    (a) Before proof or trial, or otherwise involving a significant degree of preparation or lengthy discussion —

         (i) Junior alone 80.30

         (ii) Junior with Senior 44.30

    (b) Other consultations —

         (i) Junior alone 65.90

         (ii) Junior with Senior 37.10

8. *Motions*

    (a) Unopposed motions on By Order (Adjustment) Roll, etc 11.30

    (b) Opposed motions —

         Attendance for up to half hour 23.10

         Attendance for each subsequent half hour or part thereof 18.00

    (c) Motions on By Order Roll (including advice) 21.10

9. *Procedure Roll, proof or jury trial*   £

   (a) Junior alone — per day 240.50

   (b) Junior with Senior — per day 182.80

10. *Inner House*

   (a) Single Bills

      (i)   Unopposed 18.00

      (ii) Opposed — Attendance for each half hour or part thereof 25.80

   (b) Reclaiming motion

      (i)   Junior opening or appearing alone — per day 256.00

      (ii) Junior otherwise — per day 197.80

   (c) Motion for new trial

      (i)   Junior alone — per day 256.00

      (ii) Junior with Senior — per day 197.80

11. *Attendance at judgment*

   (a) Outer House 21.10

   (b) Inner House 25.80

CHAPTER II — SENIOR COUNSEL

CONSISTORIAL ACTIONS, PETITIONS AND ORDINARY ACTIONS

1. *Revisal of pleading*   £

   (a) Revisal of summons, defences, petition or answers 96.30

   (b) Adjustment fee (open record) (each occasion) 37.10

2. *Minutes, etc — revisal fees*

   (a) Amendments (other than formal) or answers 40.70

   (b) Admissions, tender or acceptance (in appropriate cases) 11.30

   (c) Note of exceptions 11.30

3. *Notes*

   (a) Note on quantum only 87.60

   (b) Advice on tender or extra-judicial offer where not merely confirming advice at consultation 96.30

   (c) Note on line of evidence (revisal) 96.30

   (d) The fee for other notes shall be within the following range:

      From 30.40

      To 96.30

4. *Consultations*

   (a) Before proof or trial, or otherwise involving a significant degree of preparation or lengthy discussion 116.40

   (b) Other consultations 96.30

5. *Day in court*

   (a) Inner House — per day 343.50

   (b) Outer House — per day 320.80

SCHEDULE 5

Regulations 5 and 6

TABLE OF DETAILED FEES CHARGEABLE BY SOLICITORS FOR PROCEEDINGS IN THE COURT OF SESSION, PROCEEDINGS IN THE COURT OF SESSION, PROCEEDINGS LISTED AT REGULATION 5(3) AND PROCEEDINGS IN THE SHERIFF COURT LISTED IN SCHEDULE 7

1. The fee for –

    £

  (a) Any time to the first half hour spent by a solicitor conducting a proof or hearing 37.58

  (b) Each quarter hour (or part thereof) subsequent to the first half hour 18.79

2. The fee for –

  (a) Each quarter hour (or part thereof) spent by a solicitor in carrying out work other than that prescribed in paragraphs 1 and 3 to 6 hereof, provided that any time is additional to the total time charged for under paragraph 1 above 14.53

  (b) Each quarter hour (or part thereof) spent by a solicitor's clerk in carrying out work other than that prescribed in paragraphs 3 to 6 hereof 7.18

3. The fee for –

  Framing affidavits – per sheet (or part thereof) 12.32

4. The fee for –

  (a) Framing and drawing all necessary papers, other than affidavits or papers of a formal character

  (b) Each citation of a party, witness or haver including execution thereof

  (c) Instructing messengers-at-arms and sheriff officers, including examining execution and settling fee

  (d) Agency accepting service of any writ

  (e) Lodging first step of process

  (f) Lengthy telephone calls (of over 4 minutes and up to 10 minutes duration)

  (g) Letters, including instructions to counsel – per page (or part thereof), subject to paragraph 5(f) below

  (h) Perusing any document (other than a letter) consisting of not more than 12 sheets – for the first 2 sheets and each 2 sheets thereafter-

Note: Where the document perused consists of more than 12 sheets the fee for perusing the whole document shall be charged in accordance with paragraph 2 above

  in each of sub paragraphs (a)–(h) 8.29

5. The fee for –

  (a) Attendance at court offices for carrying out formal work including making up process and each necessary lodging in (other than first step) uplifting from or borrowing of process (to include return of same) or enquiry for documents due to be lodged

  (b) Revising papers drawn by counsel, open and closed records etc. or where revisal ordered – per 5 sheets (or part thereof)

  (c) Framing formal papers such as inventories, title pages and accounts of expenses per sheet (or part thereof)

  (d) Certifying or signing a document

  (e) Short telephone calls (of up to 4 minutes duration)

  (f) Short letters of a formal nature, intimations, and letters confirming telephone calls

  in each of sub paragraphs (a) to (f) 3.26

6. Where an exceptional amount of copying proves necessary, for each sheet a fee of 0.09

Interpretation

In this Table –

    'court' means court or tribunal as the case may be;

    a 'sheet' shall consist of 250 words or numbers;

    a 'page' shall consist of 125 words or numbers; and

    'exceptional' means the production of more than 20 output copy sheets (whether 20 of 1 sheet, 5 of 4 sheets or whatever) when a document has been copied.

SCHEDULE 6

Regulations 5 and 6

TABLE OF FEES CHARGEABLE BY SOLICITORS FOR PROCEEDINGS IN THE SHERIFF COURT (EXCEPT SUMMARY CAUSE AND EXECUTRY PROCEEDINGS AND THE PROCEEDINGS LISTED IN SCHEDULE 7)

CHAPTER I

SHERIFF COURT CIVIL FEES (UNDEFENDED)

Notes on the operation of Chapter I

Payment of the fees set out in the table in this chapter is subject to the following provisions.

1. A fee is payable under paragraph 2 of Part I where it can be demonstrated that following the grant of legal aid significant work was undertaken by the solicitor by way of negotiation with the opponent and/or the opponent's solicitor. Where this fee is claimed the work done must be clearly documented on the file, for perusal, if required, by the Board.

2. The factors that the Board or, as the case may be, the Auditor shall take into account in assessing a claim based on any of the paragraphs within Part I are a lengthy meeting or series of meetings or correspondence or other communication between the parties which, together, justify the conclusion that, but for this significant work, the case would have proceeded further at potential cost to the Fund or the parties.

3. The fee provided in paragraph 2 of Tables A to C includes all the costs incurred in the swearing of affidavits, including defender's affidavits where appropriate.

4. A fee is payable under either Table A or Table B. The fee under Table C relating to matters ancillary to those in Tables A and B is payable only once.

5. The fees payable under this chapter include all travel to court, except as otherwise provided for by paragraph 6.

6. In addition to the fees payable under Part II of this chapter, travel time is payable at 0.8 units per 15 minutes and is allowable only in relation to an attendance at court, subject to the following conditions:–

    (a) the solicitor claiming travel time is a solicitor with whom the client has had significant contact in relation to the conduct of the case;

    (b) the solicitor's attendance is necessary for the advancement of the case;

    (c) the distance travelled is at least 10 miles in each direction from the solicitor's normal place of work;

    (d) when payment for travel time is claimed for more than one case, the time shall be apportioned equally among the various cases for which the solicitor attended court (including non legally aided cases).

7. Travel expenses may be incurred only where travel time is chargeable.

8. Where it would be more cost effective to travel by public transport the solicitor shall do so.

Work Done	Inclusive Fee in Units

PART I – NEGOTIATION

1. Cases where settlement is effected without an action being raised where through negotiation, discussion, voluntary disclosure, meetings, correspondence and, as the case may be, other forms of participation by the solicitor a negotiated settlement is reached and minute of agreement or separation agreement, as the case may be, is entered into (subject to a maximum charge of 19); or

        10–19

2. Cases where settlement is not effected but where without an action being raised the outcome or disposal is effected through negotiation, discussion, voluntary disclosure, meetings, correspondence and, as the case may be, other forms of participation by the solicitor (subject to a maximum charge of 10).

        5–10

PART II – ALL ACTIONS EXCEPT THOSE ACTIONS OF DIVORCE OR SEPARATION AND ALIMENT TO WHICH PART III APPLIES

	Inclusive fee in Units

1. Actions (other than those specified in paragraph 2 of this Part) in which decree is granted without proof–

        10–19

Inclusive fee to cover all work from taking instructions up to and including obtaining extract decree.

        10

Note: In cases where settlement is effected after service of a writ but before the expiry of the period of notice.

        5

Additional fee to cover–

(a) drawing, intimating and lodging any written motion for or minute (including any Motion for an interim Order) or diligence, including the first quarter hour of argument, even if involving appearances on different dates (to include instructing service and implementation);

        6

(b) thereafter, waiting for or attending by solicitor at the conduct of any hearing not otherwise prescribed (including any continued hearing and ancillary hearing on expenses or other miscellaneous subsequent hearing) per quarter hour.

        1

To framing all necessary affidavits per sheet (to include notarial fee unless on cause shown the affidavit cannot be notarised within the principal agent's firm, in which case a fee to the external notary is 1 unit).

        1

Note: Charges levied by notaries outwith the United Kingdom shall be payable according to the circumstances of the case; and

affidavits in this Part do not include those required to prove a divorce.

Report Fee – to instructing (if required) perusing and taking instructions on any report extending to at least four sheets obtained from a professional or expert person, either–

(i) where the report is commissioned by the solicitor for the assisted person; or

(ii) where the report is commissioned by order of Court.

Attendance at Hearing – Paragraph 19 of the Notes on the operation of Chapter II in relation to the calculation of time shall apply in relation to attendance of a hearing under Part II of Chapter I.

2. Actions of separation and aliment (not being actions to which Part III of this chapter applies) or residence and aliment where proof takes place–

inclusive fee to cover all work from taking instructions up to and including obtaining extract decree.

        20

(a) 1976 *c.*39.

PART III – ACTIONS OF DIVORCE OR SEPARATION AND ALIMENT WHERE PROOF
IS BY MEANS OF AFFIDAVITS

1.　In any undefended action of divorce or separation and aliment where–

   (a)　the facts set out in section 1(2)(b) (unreasonable behaviour) of the Divorce (Scotland) Act 1976(**a**) are relied upon; and

   (b)　the pursuer seeks to prove those facts by means of affidavits,

the pursuer's solicitor may in respect of the work specified in column 1 of Table A in this paragraph charge the inclusive fee specified in respect of that work in column 2 of that Table.

TABLE A

Column 1	Column 2
	Inclusive fee in Units
1.　All work to and including the period of notice.	16
2.　All work from the period of notice to and including swearing affidavits.	13
3.　All work from swearing affidavits to and including sending extract decree.	3
4.　All work to and including sending extract decree.	32

2.　In any undefended action of divorce or separation and aliment where–

   (a)　the facts set out in section 1(2) (adultery), 1(2)(d) (one year's non-cohabitation and consent) or 1(2)(e) (two years' non-cohabitation) of the Divorce (Scotland) Act 1976(**b**) are relied on; and

   (b)　the pursuer seeks to prove those facts by means of affidavits,

the pursuer's solicitor may, in respect of the work specified in column 1 of Table B in this paragraph, charge the inclusive fee specified in respect of that work in column

TABLE B

Column 1	Column 2
	Inclusive fee in Units
1.　All work to and including the period of notice.	13
2.　All work from the period of notice to and including swearing affidavits.	8
3.　All work from swearing affidavits to and including sending extract decree.	3
4.　All work to and including sending extract decree.	24

3.　If–

   (a)　the pursuer's solicitor charges an inclusive fee under paragraph 1 or 2 of this Part; and

   (b)　the action to which the fee relates includes a crave relating to an ancillary matter,

in addition to that fee, he may charge in respect of the work specified in column 1 of Table C in this paragraph the inclusive fee specified in respect of that work in column 2 of that Table.

(**b**) Section 1(2)(d) and (e) was amended by the Family Law (Scotland) Act 2006 (asp 2), section 11.

TABLE C

Column 1	Column 2
	Inclusive fee in Units
1. All work to and including the period of notice.	6
2. All work from the period of notice to and including swearing affidavits.	3.5
3. All work under items 1 and 2.	9.5

CHAPTER II

SHERIFF COURT CIVIL FEES (DEFENDED)

Notes on the operation of chapter II

Payment of the fees set out in the table in this chapter is subject to the following provisions.

1. In assessing any account lodged with the Board on a solicitor and client, third party paying basis, regard shall be had to-

    (a) what would be considered reasonable in a judicial taxation, on a party and party basis, for conducting the proceedings in a proper manner; and

    (b) any work or expense specifically sanctioned, certified or authorised by the Board.

2. It shall be competent for the Auditor to disallow any fee which he shall judge irregular or unnecessary.

3. In the taxation of accounts where counsel is employed-

    (a) counsel's fees are allowed only where the Board has sanctioned the employment of counsel;

    (b) except on cause shown, fees to counsel for only two consultations in the course of the cause are allowed; and

    (c) except on cause shown, fees to counsel shall not be payable for attendance at hearings which are routine or procedural or which do not advance the cause.

4. A fee in respect of a Minute of Amendment is only payable to the solicitor bringing the amendment where–

    (a) the Minute was necessary due to a new development in the case;

    (b) relevant information which was previously unknown to the solicitor came to the solicitor's attention; or

    (c) the work could not have been done at an earlier stage in the proceedings.

5. The fees set out in this chapter include-

    (a) all correspondence, telephone calls or communication of whatever nature with the Board;

    (b) all fees incurred by any other solicitor in relation to work done in any part of the case, which shall not be a chargeable outlay; and

    (c) copyings,

and include not only the work expressly set out within the terms of each paragraph but also (unless specifically provided for) all meetings, correspondence, precognitions, negotiation ancillary thereto, and all posts and incidental expenses.

6. The fee under paragraph 1(d) is payable on each transfer of agency but is not payable where an advice and assistance account in respect of the same matter is charged to the Board or the client. Where there is a transfer of agency, the solicitor from whom agency is transferred shall be paid the whole fee for work done by that solicitor in respect of any paragraph or sub-paragraph; and where work done under any paragraph or sub-paragraph is only partially completed by that solicitor, the fee payable in respect of that work shall be apportioned equally between the solicitor from whom agency is transferred and the solicitor to whom agency is transferred.

7. A fee is payable under paragraph 2(a)(i), (ii) or (iii); more than one fee cannot be claimed. The fee under paragraph 2(a)(ii) is only payable where it is unlikely that the action would have settled without the input of the solicitor and the solicitor certifies that settlement took place in consequence of one or both of the following circumstances:-

(a) settlement was expressed within an extraneous Minute of Agreement or a Joint Minute (other than a Joint Minute for dismissal or decree simpliciter) encompassing an outcome materially different from the terms of any interim order of court in force immediately prior to the execution of that Joint Minute or Minute of Agreement;

(b) settlement followed upon an exercise of sustained negotiation involving a significant level of discussion between solicitor, the client or the opponent (or their agent) taking place after the conclusion of the work payable under paragraph 1 and clearly documented on the file for perusal, if required, by the Board.

7A. The fee under paragraph 2(a)(iii) is payable only where–

(a) no settlement is achieved but an outcome or disposal is reached and the solicitor can demonstrate that an exercise of sustained negotiation involving a significant level of discussion between the solicitor, the client and, as the case may be, the opponent (or the opponent's agent) took place;

(b) the Board is satisfied that all the additional work carried out by the solicitor was reasonable and necessary in all the circumstances of the case; and

(c) the work is clearly documented on the file and may be persued by the Board as required.

8. The factors that the Board or, as the case me be, the Auditor shall take into account in assessing a claim based on paragraph 2(a)(ii) or (iii) will be a lengthy meeting or series of meetings or correspondence or other communication between the parties which, together, justify the conclusion that, but for this significant work, the case would have proceeded further at potential cost to the Fund or the parties.

9. The fee under paragraph 3(a) is payable only in relation to time engaged in the conduct of the hearing and any continued hearing including a hearing under Rule 18.3 of the Ordinary Cause Rules in Schedule 1 to the Sheriff Courts (Scotland) Act 1907. The conduct of the hearing is the actual time involved in the substantive argument and does not include any formal attendance at a hearing for the purpose of seeking an adjournment or other formal attendance not devoted to the stating of the argument

10. The fee payable under paragraph 3(a)(i) includes the first quarter hour of argument, even if involving appearances on different dates. The fee is not chargeable on a quarter hour block but rather on the total number of minutes taken up in argument at a hearing or continued hearings.

11. The fee payable under paragraph 4(a) includes the notarial fee unless, on cause shown, the affidavit cannot be notarised within the principal agent's firm, in which case a fee of one unit is payable to the external notary. Charges levied by notaries outwith the United Kingdom shall be paid according to the circumstances of the case.

12. The fees under paragraph 4(b), (c), (d) and (e) are payable only once in any case.

13. The fee under paragraph 4(e) is payable only where the settlement conference or negotiation takes place in one location or by telephone. This fee is payable in relation to one meeting (including a continued meeting) in relation to any case and is payable only where

(a) negotiation commences at least 14 days prior to the proof; and

(b) the fee under paragraph 4(f) is not charged in the case,

and where this fee is claimed the work done should be clearly documented on the file, for perusal, if required, by the Board.

14. The fee under paragraph 4(f) is payable only where no other attendance fee is charged in relation to any appearance at which authority is interponed to the Joint Minute and is not payable in addition to any fee under paragraph 5(a)(ii) to (iii).

14A. The fee under paragraph 4(k) in contentious contact dispute cases is payable only where the additional work is necessary as a result of a material issue and not due to ones party's refusal to resolve any contact issue.

14B. The fee under paragraph 4(k) is payable in respect of each of the circumstances specified in that sub-paragraph.

15. The fee under paragraph 5(a) is only payable once in any case and the fee under paragraph 5(a)(iii) includes preparation for a debate on evidence.

16. The fee under paragraph 5(b) is payable only in respect of a debate in law.

17. Omitted by SSI 2007/14.

18. Notwithstanding paragraph 5(e), the taking of an appeal to the Sheriff Principal is a distinct proceeding and shall require a separate application for civil legal aid and nothing in this table shall imply otherwise.

19. The fee under paragraph 6 is payable on the total time engaged per day and is payable cumulatively between waiting and conduct time, rounded up too the nearest 15 minutes. The fee is payable-

(a) from the time appointed by the court for the hearing; or

(b) from the conclusion of any other business (including non legal aid cases) ending prior to the hearing,

whichever is the shorter.

20. The fees payable under this chapter include all travel to court, except as otherwise provided for by paragraph 21.

21. In addition to the fees payable under this chapter, travel time, is payable at 0.8 units per 15 minutes and is allowable only in relation to an attendance at court, subject to the following conditions:-

(a) the solicitor claiming travel time is a solicitor with whom the client has had significant contact in relation to the conduct of the case;

(b) the solicitor's attendance is necessary for the advancement of the case;

(c) the distance travelled is at least 10 miles in each direction from the solicitor's normal place of work;

(d) when payment for travel time is claimed for more than one case, the time shall be apportioned equally among the various cases for which the solicitor attended court (including non legally aided cases).

22. Travel expenses may only be incurred where travel time is chargeable.

23. Where it would be more cost effective to travel by public transport the solicitor shall do so.

24. Unless otherwise prescribed no fee is allowable unless the work for which the fee is payable has been completed in its entirety.

Fee Payable	Units

1. Instruction Fee

(a) To cover all work from the taking of instructions to the conclusion of proceedings where no fee is payable under paragraph (b). — 10

(b) To cover all work from the taking of instructions to– — 20

  (i) commence proceedings until the lodging of a Notice of Intention to Defend or the first appearance of the defender; or

  (ii) to defend proceedings until the date appointed for the lodging of defences, the making of an order dispensing with written defences, the first appearance of the defender or the issue of the usual procedural timetable (except as specifically provided below).

(c) Counterclaim – Additional fee where a counterclaim is lodged. — 4

(d) Transfer of Agency – receiving instructions after a transfer of agency, where defences have, or should already have been, lodged, to include familiarising the incoming agent with the file. — 8

2. Progress Fees

(a) (i) To cover all additional work (including adjustment and attendance at Options Hearing) from the conclusion of the work in Paragraph 1 until the allowance of a Proof or Debate or other court hearing fixed for the purpose of settlement (except as specifically provided below); — 19

  (ii) To cover all additional work (e.g. negotiation, discussion, voluntary disclosure and all meetings and correspondence) involving the active participation of agents and resulting, prior to the allowance of a Proof, Debate, or other court hearing fixed for the purpose of settlement, in the negotiated settlement of the action (except as specifically provided below); or — 19

  (iii) To cover all additional work (e.g. negotiation, discussion, voluntary disclosure and all meetings and correspondence) involving the active participation of agents where, prior to the allowance of a Proof or Debate, or other court hearing fixed for the purpose of settlement, an outcome or disposal is effected (subject to a maximum charge of 10 units) (except as specifically provided below); — 10

(b) Fee to cover all work for the preparation and attendance at any Continued Options Hearing including the preparation of an amended Record. — 2

3. Motions and Minutes etc.

(a) Fee to cover drawing, intimating, lodging, receiving and opposing (if so advised) any reponing note or written motion or minute (including Motions for interim orders) for any party-

    (i) where opposed or unopposed and involving a hearing before the Sheriff, to include the first quarter hour of argument, even if involving appearances on different dates   6

    (ii) where unopposed and not involving a hearing   2

    (iii) thereafter attendance fee per quarter hour, including any continuation of the diet ordered by the Sheriff to allow a minute of amendment to be received and answered   1

(b) Fee to cover drawing, or receiving Minute of Amendment, in addition to motion fee, if appropriate-

    (i) where assisted person is party bringing amendment and no answers lodged;   4

    (ii) where amendment is sought by another party and no answers lodged by assisted person;   2

    (iii) where answered, to include adjustment as required, for any party.   6

(c) Specification of Documents, in addition to motion fee, if appropriate-

    (i) fee to cover drawing, intimating and lodging Specification   4

    (ii) fee to opposing solicitor.   2

4. Miscellaneous Fees

(a) Affidavits – to framing all necessary affidavits, per sheet.   1

(b) Contact Arrangements – fee arranging or attempting to arrange interim contact arrangements where appropriate.   6

(c) Notice to Admit – preparing and serving/receiving a Notice to admit and serving a counter notice if required.   4

(d) Joint Minute of Admissions – preparing and/or considering and executing a joint minute of admissions with a view to avoiding unnecessary evidence or disposing of some (but not all) craves.   4

(e) Settlement conference/negotiation – participating in a settlement conference or negotiation after the allowance of a proof or debate where the solicitor making the claim is authorised in advance by the client to participate, per quarter hour (subject to a maximum charge of 8 units).   1

(f) Extra Judicial Settlement – fee to cover work to formalise settlement.   8

(g) Minute of Agreement – to drawing/revising Minute of Agreement necessary to accomplish or record overall settlement per sheet (subject to a maximum charge of 8 units).   1

(h) Report Fee – to instructing (if required) perusing and taking instructions on any report extending to at least four sheets obtained from a professional or expert person, either

    (i) where the report is commissioned by the solicitor for the assisted person; or   4

    (ii) the report is commissioned by order of Court.

(i) Additional Procedure – additional fee where Additional Procedure invoked in terms of Chapter 10 of the Ordinary Cause Rules in Schedule 1 to the Sheriff Courts (Scotland) Act 1907 (to include attendance at any procedural hearing(s).   4

(j) Additional fee where the action involves a third party minuter at any stage.   4

(k) Additional fee where the action involves–   4

    (i) a complex financial dispute leading to protracted negotiations;

    (ii) a complex pension sharing arrangement; or

    (iii) a contentious contact dispute.

(l) Peremptory diet – fee to cover all work in connection with a peremptory diet (excluding attendance at court).   3

5. Preparation

(a) *Preparation for proof or evidential child welfare hearing*

    (i) If action settled or abandoned not later than 14 days before the diet of proof or evidential child welfare hearing.   18

    (ii)   Where the action settles within 14 days of, or on the day of, or after the diet of proof or evidential child welfare hearing but without evidence being lead.   24

    (iii)   In any other case where evidence is led (to include settling with witnesses and enquiring for cause at avizandum (if required).   36

(aa) *Preparation for Child Welfare Hearing*

    (i)   Fee to cover all work preparing for first hearing   6

    (ii)   Fee to cover all work preparing for each subsequent hearing   3

(b)   Preparation for Debate- Fee to cover all work in connection with preparing for any debate, where such debate takes place prior to proof or Proof Before Answer.   8

(c)   Omitted by SSI 2007/14.

(d)   Commission to Take Evidence – Fee to cover all work preparing for the taking of evidence or executing specification on open commission or proceeding as provided in (iii) below-

    (i)   For solicitor arranging commission.   8

    (ii)   For opposing solicitor.   4

    (iii)   If optional procedure adopted-fee for each person on whom specification is served.   1

    (iv)   Fee for perusing documents recovered-per quarter hour.   1

(e)   Preparing for Appeal – Fee to cover all work preparing for an appeal to the Sheriff Principal (to include marking appeal or noting marking of appeal).   12

6.   Conduct & Waiting

To waiting for or attending by solicitor at the conduct of any hearing not otherwise prescribed (including any continued hearing and ancillary hearing on expenses or other miscellaneous subsequent hearing) per quarter hour.   1

CHAPTER III

CIRCUMSTANCES IN WHICH THE BOARD MAY ALLOW A FEE ADDITIONAL TO THE FEES PRESCRIBED IN CHAPTER II

1.   That the assisted person's inadequate knowledge of English—

    (a)   required instructions through an interpreter; or

    (b)   significantly increased the duration of meetings necessary to take instructions.

2.   That although able to attend at the solicitor's office the assisted person suffered throughout or for a significant period of the case from—

    (a)   a severe substance abuse problem; or

    (b)   a mental disorder within the meaning of section 328 of the Mental Health (Care and Treatment) (Scotland) Act 2003.

3.   That the assisted person suffered from a physical disability which necessitated a significantly lengthier process than would normally have been encountered in the taking and obtaining of instructions.

4.   That the assisted person was, for a significant period in relation to the overall duration of the case, unable to attend at the solicitor's office by reason of disability, illness or imprisonment.

5.   That the nature or circumstances of the case necessitated significant attendance to its progress outwith normal office hours.

5A.   That the assisted person or any other witness in the case is a vulnerable witness in terms of section 11 of the Vulnerable Witnesses (Scotland) Act 2004 and this has necessitated significant additional work in seeking, or opposing, or implementing a special measure for the taking of evidence from a vulnerable witness by virtue of sections 11, 12, 13 and 18(1)(a) and/or (b) of that Act.

6.   That the law in relation to the matter at issue was particularly complex and involved an area of law with which a solicitor engaged in general court practice would be unlikely to be familiar.

7.   That the case raised unusually complex issues of fact, including detailed consideration of extensive documentary evidence.

Note on the application of Chapter III

(a) Except where an uplift is granted under paragraph 5, 6 or 7 above, the element of the solicitor's fee subject to an uplift will exclude any amount charged in relation to time spent waiting or appearing at, court.

(b) Only 1 of paragraphs 2, 3 and 4 may be claimed in any case.

(c) An uplift may not be granted under paragraph 7 above where a fee under paragraph 4(k) of the table of fees in Chapter II of Schedule 6 is claimed.

(d) the solicitor of an assisted person, who is a vulnerable witness, may not claim in respect of the assisted person the additional fee under paragraphs 2, 3 or 4, if there is a claim under paragraph 5A in respect of the assisted person as a vulnerable witness.

SCHEDULE 7

Regulation 5

SHERIFF COURT PROCEEDINGS FOR WHICH FEES FOR WORK DONE SHALL ONLY BE PAYABLE UNDER SCHEDULE 5

Adoptions;

conveyancing work required to implement an Order of the Court;

division and sale of heritable property

exceptional cases;

fatal accident inquiries;

minute procedure in a closed process;

proceedings arising under the Mortgage Rights (Scotland) Act 2001

proceedings where the assisted person is a curator *ad litem*;

proceedings where the assisted person is a third party minuter;

work carried out under Regulation 18 of the Civil Legal Aid (Scotland) Regulations 2002 in a case which does not proceed to a grant of civil legal aid;

work in connection with a motion for modification of expenses of the assisted person, drafting and submitting an account of expenses, or disputing (on receipt) an opponent's account of expenses, including attendance at taxation and taking/opposing Notes of Objections, including taxations instructed by the Board; and

work in connection with letters of inhibition;

work in connection with the registration and enforcement of a decree;

summary applications.

Interpretation

1.—(1) For the purposes of this Schedule an "exceptional case" means any case certified as such by the Board on the application of the solicitor involved.

(2) The solicitor involved may apply to the Board not later than 4 months after the conclusion of a case to have it certified as an exceptional case.

(3) The Board will certify a case as exceptional only if satisfied that—

(a) the other party, or as the case may be at least one of the other parties, was a party litigant;

(b) there were concurrent proceedings before a children's hearing;

(c) the solicitor involved had to apply for a transfer of agency after the fixing of a diet of proof, debate or any other hearing fixed for the purposes of settlement; or

(d) payment in accordance with Schedule 6 would not provide reasonable remuneration for the word actually, necessarily and reasonably done because the case involved—

(i) unusual court procedure for which a fee is not otherwise prescribed; or

(ii) a significantly greater volume of work than is usual for a case of that type.

SOLICITORS' OUTLAYS

Table of Fees payable in the Court of Session and Offices connected therewith

Court of Session etc Fees Order 1997 (SI 1997 No 688)

[This Table of Fees is printed as amended by:

The Court of Session etc. Fees Amendment Order 1999 (SI 1999 No 755) which came into force on 1st April 1999;

The Court of Session etc. Fees Amendment Order 2002 (SI 2002 No 270) which came into force on 1st July 2002;

The Court of Session etc. Fees Amendment Order 2007 (SSI 2007 No 319) which came into force on 16th July 2007;

The Court of Session etc. Fees Amendment Order 2008 (SSI 2008 No 236) which came into force on 6th June 2008;

The Court of Session etc Fees Amendment Order 2009 (SSI 2009 No 88) which came into force on 1st August 2009.]

Exemption of certain persons from fees in simplified divorce applications

5. A fee regulated by this Order shall not be payable by a person if—

   (a) the person or his or her partner is in receipt of income support under the Social Security Contributions and Benefits Act 1992;

   (b) the person is in receipt of an income-based jobseeker's allowance (payable under the Jobseekers Act 1995);

   (c) the person is in receipt of civil legal aid within the meaning of section 13(2) of the Legal Aid (Scotland) Act 1986 in respect of the matter in the Table of Fees in connection with which the fee is payable;

   (d) the fee is payable in connection with a simplified divorce or dissolution of a civil partnership application and the person is in receipt of advice and assistance from a solicitor under the Legal Aid (Scotland) 1986 in respect of that application;

   (e) the person's solicitor is undertaking work in relation to the matter in the Table of Fees in connection with which the fee is payable on the basis of any regulations made under section 36 of the Legal Aid (Scotland) Act 1986 providing for legal aid in a matter of special urgency;

   (f) the person or his or her partner is in receipt of guarantee credit under the State Pension Credit Act 2002;

   (g) the person or his or her partner is in receipt of working tax credit, provided that—

      (i) child tax credit is being paid to the party, or otherwise following a claim for child tax credit made jointly by the members of a couple (as defined in section 3(5A) of the Tax Credits Act 2002) which includes the party; or

      (ii) there is a disability element or severe disability element (or both) to the tax credit received by the party; or

     and that the gross annual income taken into account for the calculation of the working tax credit is £16,642 or less.

   (h) the person or his or her partner is in receipt of income-related employment and support allowance under the Welfare Reform Act 2007.

Exemption of certain motions from fees

5A.—(1) This article applies to motions which are enrolled in the process of the cause or made orally at the bar in accordance with rule 23.2 of the Rules of Court (enrolment of motions).

(2) The fees specified in items B26 and C24 of the Table of Fees shall not be payable in respect of motions which operate solely so as to activate further steps of procedure and any opposition to such motions.

(3) Without prejudice to the generality of paragraph (2) above, motions which are exempt from the payment of fees include motions under the following rules of the Rules of Court—

   (a) rule 19.1 (decrees in absence);

   (b) rule 22.3(5)(a) (closing record);

(c)   rule 36.13 (death, disability, retiral, etc. of Lord Ordinary);

(d)   rules 37.1(2)(b), 37.1(6) and 37.1(7) (applications for jury trial);

(e)   rule 37.10 (application of verdicts);

(f)   rule 38.17(1) (orders for hearing);

(g   rule 40.7(3) (procedure following transmission of appeal process);

(h)   rule 40.11(1)(a) (early disposal of appeal) but only insofar as the motion relates to rule 40.7A (required application for early disposal of appeal against interlocutor other than final judgment);

(i)   rule 40.15(1) (orders for hearing of appeal);

(j)   rule 41.15(1) (motions for hearing of appeals); and

(k)   rule 41.22(1) (motion for further procedure).

Calculation of fees payable

5B.—(1) Subject to article 5A above, the fees specified in items B26 and C24 of the Table of Fees shall be payable in addition to those fees which are specified in items B2, B6 and C5 of the Table of Fees.

(2) The fees specified in items B26 and C24 of the Table of Fees shall not be payable in addition to those fees which are specified in items B9, B10 and B13 and C10, of the Table of Fees.

SCHEDULE

TABLE OF FEES

(Fees payable from 1st April 2009)

PART I – FEES IN THE CENTRAL OFFICE OF THE COURT

Column 1 *(Matters)*	Column 2 *(Fee payable)* £	Column 3 *(Fee formerly payable)* £
A. Signeting		
Signeting of any writ or summons, if attendance is necessary outwith the normal office hours........	100.00	100.00
B. General Department		
1. Appeal, summons, or other writ or step by which any cause or proceeding, other than a family action, is originated in either the Inner or Outer House – fee (to comprehend signeting in normal office hours)............	175.00	170.00
2. Defences, answers or other writ (including a joint minute) or step in process or enrolment or opposition to a motion in a pending process by which a party other than an originating party first makes an appearance in a course or proceeding other than a family action............	175.00	170.00
3. Writ by which a family action is originated (other than a simplified divorce or dissolution of a civil partnership application) – inclusive fee (to comprehend signeting within normal office hours and, if applicable, issue to the pursuer of an extract in terms of item G5(a) of this Table, and to the defender, if appropriate, of a duplicate thereof)............	135.00	130.00
4. Simplified divorce or dissolution of a civil partnership application (inclusive of all procedure other than that specified in item B5 of this Table)............	100.00	100.00
5. In relation to a simplified divorce or dissolution of a civil partnership application, citation of any persons under rule 16.1(1)(a)(i), (ii) or (iii), as applied by rule 49.76, of the Rules of Court, or intimation to any person or persons under rule 16.1(1)(a)(i), (ii) or (iii), as applied by rule 49.76, of those Rules, where such intimation is required.	£10 plus Messengers at Arms' fee	Charge of the sheriff officer to serve document plus £10

	Column 1	Column 2	Column 3
	(Matters)	(Fee payable) £	(Fee formerly payable) £
6.	Defences, answers or other writ (including a joint minute) or step in process or enrolment of or opposition to a motion in a pending process by which a party other than an originating party first makes appearance in a family action.........	135.00	130.00
7.	Fee for initial lodging of affidavits in a family action where proof by affidavit evidence has been allowed	60.00	55.00
8.	Special case–..		
	For each party...	90.00	85.00
	Maximum fee payable per case..	355.00	345.00
9.	Application by minute or motion for variation of an order in a family action...	30.00	30.00
10.	Answers or opposition to an application under item B9 of this Table...............	30.00	30.00
11.	Letter of request to a foreign court...	45.00	45.00
12.	Citation of each jury, to include outlays incurred in citing and countermanding – payable on receipt of instruments for issue of precept	245.00	240.00
13.	Reclaiming motion – fee payable by party enrolling motion............................	175.00	170.00
14.	Closed record – fee payable by each party on the lodging of the closed record or, where no closed record is lodged, when mode of enquiry is determined	85.00	85.00
15.	Allowing proof, etc. – fee payable by each party on diet of proof, jury trial, procedure roll or summar roll hearing being allowed..	45.00	45.00
16.	For the items in B17 to B25, except B22 and B23 where there is no fee for the first 30 minutes, the fee is payable by each party appearing at the hearing –		
	For every 30 minutes or part thereof		
17	Proof or Procedure Roll (B16 applies)...	45.00	40.00
18.	Summar Roll (B16 applies)...	95.00	40.00
19.	Jury Trial (B16 applies)..	45.00	40.00
20.	Outer House hearing (other than Proof or Procedure Roll, Jury Trial, Motion Roll hearing or hearings out of hours) (B16 applies)	45.00	40.00
21.	Inner House hearing (other than Summar Roll, Single Bills hearing or hearings out of hours) (B16 applies)...	95.00	95.00
22.	Motion Roll hearing (B16 applies)..	45.00	40.00
23.	Single Bills hearing (B16 applies)	95.00	95.00
24.	Outer House hearings out of hours (B16 applies)..	55.00	55.00
25.	Inner House hearings out of hours (B16 applies)	120.00	120.00
26.	Fee payable by any party enrolling a motion or making a motion orally at the bar and any party opposing any such motion...	45.00	45.00

C. Petition Department

1.	Petition of whatever nature presented to Inner or Outer House other than a petition under item C3 or C4 of this Table, whether in respect of the first or any subsequent step of process, and any application for registration or recognition of a judgment under the Civil Jurisdiction and Judgments Act 1982.................	175.00	170.00
2.	Additional fee payable when a petition in terms of item C1 of this Table is presented outwith normal office hours...	100.00	100.00

Column 1 (Matters)	Column 2 (Fee payable) £	Column 3 (Fee formerly payable) £
3. Petition to be admitted as a notary public:		
For each applicant	130.00	130.00
4. Petition to be admitted as a solicitor:		
For each applicant	130.00	130.00
5. Answers, objection or other writ (including a joint minute) or step in process or enrolment or opposition to a motion in a pending process by which a party other than an originating party first makes appearance in a proceeding to which item C1 of this Table applies	175.00	170.00
6. Caveat	45.00	45.00
7. Fiat	45.00	45.00
8. Registering official copies of orders of courts in England and Wales or Northern Ireland	15.00	15.00
9. (Omitted by SSI 2009 No 88)		
10. Reclaiming motion – fee payable by party enrolling motion	175.00	170.00
11. Closed record – fee payable by each party on the lodging of the closed record or, when no closed record is lodged, when mode of enquiry is determined	85.00	85.00
12. Allowing proof, etc. – fee payable by each party on diet of proof, procedure roll, summar roll or judicial review hearing being allowed	45.00	45.00
13. (Omitted by SSI 2009 No 88)		
14. For the items in C15 to C23, except C21 where there is no fee for the first 30 minutes, the fee is payable by each party appearing at the hearing–		
For every 30 minutes or part thereof	45.00	40.00
15. Proof, Procedure Roll or other Hearing (C14 applies)	45.00	40.00
16. Summar Roll (C14 applies)	95.00	40.00
17. (Omitted by SSI 2009 No 88)		
18. Outer House hearing (C14 applies)	45.00	40.00
19. Inner House hearing (other than Summar Roll, Single Bills hearing or hearings out of hours) (C14 applies)	95.00	95.00
20. Motion Roll hearing (C14 applies)	45.00	55.00
21. Single Bills hearing (C14 applies)	95.00	95.00
22. Outer House hearings out of hours (C14 applies)	55.00	55.00
23. Inner House hearings out of hours (C14 applies)	120.00	120.00
24. Fee payable by any party enrolling a motion or making a motion orally at the bar; and any party opposing any such motion	45.00	45.00
25. Lodging of notice of appointment or intention to appoint an administrator out of court under the Insolvency Act 1986	175.00	170.00
D. *Court for hearing appeals relating to the registration of electors*		
Appeal – inclusive fee	175.00	170.00
E. *Election Court*		
1. Parliamentary election petition	175.00	170.00
2. Statement of matters	15.00	15.00
3. Any other petition, application, answers or objections submitted to the court	45.00	45.00
4. Certificate of judgement	45.00	45.00

	Column 1 (Matters)	Column 2 (Fee payable) £	Column 3 (Fee formerly payable) £
F.	*Lands Valuation Appeal Court*		
1.	Appeal – inclusive fee	175.00	170.00
2.	Answers – inclusive fee	175.00	170.00
G.	*Extracts Department*		
1.	Extract decree following upon a summons, petition or appeal, or after protestation of a note, and whether in absence or otherwise	50.00	45.00
2.	Extract of admission as a solicitor	40.00	40.00
3.	Extract of protestation	40.00	40.00
4.	Certificate under the Civil Jurisdiction and Judgments Act 1982	40.00	40.00
5.	Documentation evidencing divorce, nullity or dissolution of marriage or civil partnership:		
	(a) Extract from Consistorial Register of Decrees of decree pronounced on or after 23rd September 1975 if not issued in terms of item B3 or B4 of this Table	25.00	25.00
	(b) Certificate of divorce in decree pronounced prior to 23rd September 1975	25.00	25.00
	(c) Certified copy interlocutor in decree pronounced prior to 23rd September 1975	25.00	25.00
6.	Extract from the Register of Acts and Decrees – per sheet or part thereof	25.00	25.00
7.	Sealing and certifying any document for exhibition in a foreign jurisdiction or otherwise	25.00	25.00
8.	Acknowledgement of receipt of a notice under section 19(6) or 21(2) of the Conveyancing and Feudal Reform (Scotland) Act 1970	40.00	40.00
9.	(Omitted by SSI 2009 No 88)		

Part II — Fees in the Office of the Accountant of Court

H. *Office of the Accountant of Court*

I. In factories

		Column 2	Column 3
1.	For registering case and receiving and delivering up bond of caution–		
	(a) in Court of Session appointments	30.00	30.00
	(b) in Sheriff Court appointments	20.00	20.00
2.	For examining factor's inventory – 0.333% of the value of the estate as disclosed		
	(a) minimum fee payable	20.00	20.00
	(b) maximum fee payable	590.00	575.00
3.	For auditing each account–		
	(a) basic fee	10.00	10.00
	(b) additional percentage fee on the factor's commission as fixed (or what would have been the factor's full commission if chargeable or fully allowed)	17.5%	17.5%
4.	For reporting re discharge, special powers or on other special matters	105.00	105.00
5.	For report on scheme of division	105.00	105.00
6.	For certificate under seal	25.00	25.00

	Column 1	Column 2	Column 3
	(Matters)	*(Fee payable)*	*(Fee formerly payable)*
		£	£

II. In Consignations

7.	For lodging consignation	20.00	15.00
8.	For producing or delivering up consignation–		
	(a) basic fee	20.00	15.00
	(b) additional fee for every £100 or part thereof uplifted	1.00	1.00
	(c) maximum fee payable	60.00	60.00

III. Liquidations

9.	For uplifting bond of caution	5.00	5.00

PART III — FEES IN THE OFFICE OF THE AUDITOR OF THE COURT OF SESSION

I. Office of the Auditor of the Court of Session

1. Taxing accounts of expenses incurred in judicial proceedings (including proceedings in the High Court of Justiciary) remitted to the Auditor of the Court of Session for taxation:

(a)	Auditor's fee on lodging account for taxation	35.00	34.00
(b)	Auditor's fee for taxing accounts for expenses etc.		
(i)	up to £400	20.00	18.00
(ii)	for every additional £100 or part thereof	5.00	5.00

Note: fee to be determined by the Auditor of the Court of Session on amount of account as submitted

2. Fee for assessing account remitted to the Auditor to determine whether an additional fee should be paid 230.00 226.00

3. Fee for cancellation of diet of taxation–

(a)	where written notice of cancellation received by receiving party after 4.00 pm on the fourth working day prior to the diet of taxation	50% of fee that would have been payable under item I1(b) of this Table	75% of fee that would have been payable under item I1(b) of this Table
(b)	where written notice of cancellation received by receiving party after 4.00 pm on the working day before or the day of the diet of taxation	50% of fee that would have been payable under item I1(b) of this Table	75% of fee that would have been payable under item I1(b) of this Table

Column 1	Column 2	Column 3
(Matters)	(Fee payable)	(Fee formerly payable)
	£	£

PART IV — FEES COMMON TO ALL OFFICES

J. Miscellaneous

	Column 2	Column 3
1. Certified copy of proceedings for appeal to the House of Lords......	175.00	170.00
2. Certifying of any other document (plus copying charges if necessary)......	15.00	15.00
3. Recording, extracting, engrossing or copying– all documents (exclusive of search fee)–		
(a) Copying of each document up to 10 pages	5.00	5.00
• for each page or part thereof (in excess of 10 pages)	0.50	0.50
(b) Copy of each document copied to CD or in electronic form	5.00	5.00
4. Searches – for any search of records or archives:		
(a) Up to 30 minutes	15.00	15.00
(b) For more than 30 minutes up to 2 hours	35.00	35.00
(c For each additional 30 minutes (in excess of 2 hours)	10.00	10.00
(d) In addition, correspondence fee where applicable	10.00	10.00
5. Captions:		
(a) Marking caption when ordered	10.00	10.00
(b) Warrant for caption when issued	10.00	10.00

Bankruptcy Fees (Scotland) Regulations 1993 (SI 1993 No 486)

[This Table of Fees is printed as amended by:

The Bankruptcy Fees (Scotland) Amendment Regulations 1999 (SI 1999 No 752) which came into force on 1st April 1999;

The Bankruptcy Fees (Scotland) Amemdment Regulations 2007 (SSI 2007 No 220) which came into force on 1st April 2007;

The Bankruptcy Fees (Scotland) Amemdment Regulations 2008 (SSI 2008 No 35) which came into force on 1st February 2008;

The Bankruptcy Fees (Scotland) Amemdment (No 2) Regulations 2008 (SSI 2008 No 79) which came into force on 1st April 2008;

The Bankruptcy Fees (Scotland) Amemdment Regulations 2009 (SSI 2008 No 97) which came into force on 1st April 2009.]

SCHEDULE

TABLE OF FEES

PART I

Column 1	Column 2	Column 3
(Functions)	(Rates) payable)	(Former rates)
1. In respect of the exercise by the Accountant in Bankruptcy of that office's functions as interim trustee in a sequestration where the Accountant in Bankruptcy is not appointed as trustee in that sequestration—		
(a) in respect of each of the first five hours of work;	£39 per hour	£37 per hour
(b) in respect of each subsequent hour of work	£69 per hour	£66 per hour

	Column 1	Column 2	Column 3
	(Functions)	*(Rates)* *payable)*	*(Former* *rates)*

2. In respect of the exercise by the Accountant in Bankruptcy of that office's functions as interim trustee or trustee in a sequestration, other than in respect of the realisation of assets in the sequestrated estate—

   (a) in respect of each of the first 21 hours of work; .... £39 per hour   £37 per hour

   (b) in respect of each subsequent hour of work .... £69 per hour   £66 per hour

3. In respect of the exercise by the Accountant in Bankruptcy of that office's functions as trustee in a sequestration in relation to the realisation of assets in the sequestrated estate—

   (a) in respect of the total price paid in a transaction by the purchaser of heritable property, including any interest paid thereon, but after the deduction of any sums paid to secured creditors in respect of their securities over that property—

     (i) on the first £10,000 or fraction thereof; .... 5% of that amount   *(No change)*

     (ii) on the next £10,000 or fraction thereof; .... 1% of that amount   *(No change)*

     (iii) on all further sums; .... 0.5% of that amount   *(No change)*

   (b) in respect of the proceeds of the sale of moveable property, after the deduction of the expenses of sale and any sums paid to secured creditors in respect of their securities over that property. .... 5% of that amount   *(No change)*

4. In respect of the exercise by the Accountant in Bankruptcy of that office's functions as trustee in relation to the payment of dividends to creditors. .... £78 plus £39 in respect of each creditor who is paid a dividend   £74 plus £37 in respect of each creditor who is paid a dividend

PART II

	Column 1	Column 2	Column 3
	(Matters)	*(Fee* *payable)* £	*(Fee* *formerly* *payable)* £

1. For registering award of sequestration 20.00   19.00

2. For admistration of a creditor's petition .... 100.00   None

3. For supervising proceedings in sequestration—

   (a) where commissioners have been elected; 139.00   132.00

   (b) where no commissioners have been elected; 210.00   200.00

   (c) where the Accountant in Bankruptcy is the trustee 139.00   132.00

Column 1 (Matters)	Column 2 (Fee payable) £	Column 3 (Fee formerly payable) £
4. For supervising payment of dividend to creditors where no commissioners have been elected......	69.00	66.00
5. For any special report to the court	69.00	66.00
6. For considering and issuing a determination in an appeal against a determination of commissioners as to the outlays and remuneration payable to a permanent trustee	5% of the sum remaining on deduction from the sum of outlays and remuneration determined by the Accountant in Bankruptcy of any outlays incurred by way of statutory fees, trading expenses or expenses of realisation	*(No change)*
7. For issuing a determination fixing the outlays and remuneration payable to— (a) an interim trustee; or (b) a permanent trustee	17.5% of the sum remaining on deduction from the sum of outlays and remuneration determined of any outlays incurred by way of statutory fees, trading expenses or expenses of realisation	*(No change)*
8. For examination of the sederunt book and related work, in connection with the discharge of a permanent trustee	36.00	34.00
9. For granting a certificate of discharge to an interim trustee	36.00	34.00
10. For granting a certificate of discharge to a debtor	11.00	10.00
11. For providing a certified copy of an entry in the register of insolvencies	24.00	23.00
12. For the certifying of any other document (excluding copying charges)	17.00	16.00
13. For providing a copy of any document— (a) by photocopying— (i) 10 pages or less	11.00	10.00
(ii) each page after first 10	0.32	0.30
(b) in an electronic medium or by printout from records held on computer — per document	£0.13	£0.12
14. For searches in the register of insolvencies— (a) where the search is carried out by staff of the Accountant in Bankruptcy — for each search in respect of a debtor	17.00	16.00
(b) where searches are carried out by remote direct access by computer — for each day from 0000 hours to 2359 hours	17.00	16.00
(c) where searches are carried out by remote direct access by computer — for each year or part thereof	4,200.00	4,000.00
(d) where searches are carried out by remote direct access by computer by non profit making bodies established in the UK including the Scottish Executive, UK Government Departments, Police and Credit Unions, on proof to the satisfaction of the Accountant in Bankruptcy of non profit making status	nil *(No change)*	
(e) where searches are carried out by remote direct access by computer by persons acting as agents of the Accountant in Bankruptcy	nil *(No change)*	

	Column 1	Column 2	Column 3
	(Matters)	*(Fee payable)*	*(Fee formerly payable)*
		£	£
15.	For attendance at any meeting of creditors — fee per hour or part thereof, including travelling time	69.00	66.00
16.	For calling any meeting of creditors	36.00	34.00
17.	For attendance at any examination of the debtor — fee per hour or part thereof, including travelling time	69.00	66.00
18.	In respect of protected trust deeds—		
	(a) for registering a protected trust deed	36.00	34.00
	(b) for supervision of the trustee of a protected trust deed	200.00	*(No change)*
19.	For auditing the accounts of a trustee under a protected trust deed and fixing the trustee's remuneration.	5% of the sum remaining on deduction from the sum of outlays and remuneration determined of any outlays incurred by way of statutory fees, trading expenses or expenses of realisation	*(No change)*
20.	For lodging any unclaimed dividend in an appropriate bank or institution set aside for payment to a creditor or creditors, in respect of each creditor on consignation	13.00	12.00
21.	For uplifting any sum lodged in an appropriate bank or institution, in respect of each creditor on consignation	13.00	12.00
22.	For determination of a debtor application	100.00	*(No change)*
23.	For an application for a bankruptcy restrictions order	250.00	*(No change)*
24.	For accepting and issuing a bankruptcy restrictions undertaking	150.00	*(No change)*
25.	For registering a court order appointing a replacement trustee	19.00	*(No change)*
26.	For petitioning for the replacement of a trustee acting in more than one sequestration	200.00	*(No change)*

Table of Fees payable in the High Court of Justiciary

High Court of Justiciary Fees Order 1984 (SI 1984 No 252)

[This Schedule is printed as amended by:

High Court of Justiciary Fees Amendment Order 1991 (SI 1991 No 331) which came into force on 1st April 1991;

High Court of Justiciary Fees Amendment Order 1992 (SI 1992 No 412) which came into force on 1st April 1992;

High Court of Justiciary Fees Amendment Order 1993 (SI 1993 No 426) which came into force on 1st April 1993;

High Court of Justiciary Fees Amendment Order 1994 (SI 1994 No 3266) which came into force on 1st February 1995;

High Court of Justiciary Fees Amendment Order 1996 (SI 1996 No 516) which came into force on 1st April 1996;

High Court of Justiciary Fees Amendment Order 1999 (SI 1999 No 753) which came into force on 1st April 1999;

High Court of Justiciary Fees Amendment Order 2007 (SI 2007 No 321) which came into force on 16th July 2007;

High Court of Justiciary Fees Amendment Order 2008 (SSI 2008 No 237) which came into force on 1st August 2008.]

SCHEDULE

TABLE OF FEES

Column 1 (Matters)	Column 2 (Fee payable) £	Column 3 (Fee formerly payable) £
1. Petitions to the Nobile Officium and applications for criminal letters (inclusive fee covering all steps in procedure)	85.00	65.00
2. Extract convictions, per sheet or part thereof	35.00	26.00
3. Certified copy of any other document	15.00	11.00
4. Copying–		
(a) of each document up to 10 pages	5.00	—
(b) each further page or part thereof (in excess of 10 pages)	0.50	0.20
(c) of each document copied to CD or in electronic form	5.00	3.00
5. Searches – for any search of records or archives–		
(a) up to 30 minutes	15.00	11.00
(b) for more than 30 minutes up to 2 hours	35.00	29.00
(c) each additional 30 minutes (in excess of 2 hours)	10.00	8.00
(d) In addition, correspondence fee where applicable	10.00	8.00

Table of Fees payable in the Judicial Committee of the Privy Council

The Judicial Committee (Devolution Issues) Rules Order 1999
(SI 1999 No 665)

SCHEDULE

TABLE OF FEES

		£
1.	Lodging—	
	(a) a petition for special leave to appeal	75.00
	(b) a petition of appeal	60.00
	(c) any other petition or motion	45.00
	(d) a reference by a court	nil
	(e) any other reference	60.00
2.	Entering appearance—	
	(a) in the case of a reference by a court	50.00
	(b) in any other case	20.00
3.	Lodging Case	180.00
4.	Lodging affidavit	15.00
5.	Committee Report on appeal or reference	45.00
6.	Original Order of the Judicial Committee	30.00
7.	Office Copy of Committee Order	10.00
8.	Taxing fee	5% of the sum allowed

Table of Fees payable in the Sheriff Court

Sheriff Court Fees Order 1997 (SI 1997 No 687)

[This Table of Fees is printed as amended by:

The Sheriff Court Fees Amendment Order 1999 (SI 1999 No 754) which came into force on 1st April 1999;

The Sheriff Court Fees Amendment Order 2002 (SSI 2002 No 269) which came into force on 1st July 2002;

The Sheriff Court Fees Amendment Order 2003 (SSI 2003 No 97) which came into force on 12th March 2003;

The Sheriff Court Fees Amendment Order 2007 (SSI 2007 No 318) which came into force on 16th July 2007;
The Sheriff Court Fees Amendment Order 2008 (SSI 2008 No 239) which came into force on 1st April 2009;
The Sheriff Court Fees Amendment Order 2009 (SSI 2009 No 89) which came into force on 6th March 2009.]

SCHEDULE

TABLE OF FEES

PART I — COMMISSARY PROCEEDINGS

Column 1 (Matters)	Column 2 (Fee payable) £	Column 3 (Fee formerly payable) £
1. Petition for —		
(a) appointment of executor,		
(b) restriction of caution,		
(c) special warrant,		
(d) sealing up of repositories or the like, or		
(e) appointment of Commissary factor	15.00	15.00
2. Sealing up repositories or the like, per hour	25.00	25.00
3. (a) Receiving and examining inventory of estate, except where sub paragraph (b) or (c) of this paragraph applies —		
(i) where the amount of the estate vested in or belonging beneficially to the deceased, of which confirmation is required, or for which resealing under the Colonial Probates Act 1892 is required does not exceed —		
• £5,000	No fee	No fee
• £50,000	195.00	190.00
(ii) where the amount of the said estate exceeds £50,000	195.00	190.00
(b) Receiving and examining additional or corrective inventory of estate or inventory of estate *ad non executa*	195.00	19.00
(c) Receiving and examining inventory of estate where it is	The fees payable shall be 50% of those specified in sub paragraph (a) or (b) of this paragraph. If confirmation is subsequently required the remaining 50% of the fees specified in sub paragraph (a) or (b) shall be payable	The fees payable shall be 50% of those specified in sub paragraph (a) or (b) of this paragraph. If confirmation is subsequently required the remaining 50% of the fees specified in sub paragraph (a) or (b) shall be payable

	Column 1	Column 2	Column 3
	(Matters)	*(Fee payable)* £	*(Fee formerly payable)* £
	declared that confirmation is not required:		
4.	Commissary copying and extracting		
(1)	Issuing certificate of confirmation		
(a)	if ordered when lodging inventory each certificate	5.00	5.00
(b)	If ordered subsequent to lodging inventory —		
	(i) first certificate including search fee	15.00	15.00
	(ii) each subsequent certificate	5.00	5.00
(2)	Copy or duplicate confirmation–		
(a)	if ordered when lodging inventory	10.00	10.00
(b)	if ordered subsequent to lodging inventory —		
	(i) first duplicate including search fee	20.00	20.00
	(ii) each subsequent duplicate if ordered at the same time as the first duplicate	10.00	10.00
(3)	Certified extract confirmation and will (if any) —		
(a)	if ordered when lodging inventory	20.00	20.00
(b)	if ordered subsequent to lodging inventory —		
	(i) first certified extract including search fee	30.00	30.00
	(ii) each subsequent certified extract if ordered at the time of the first certified extract	20.00	20.00
(4)	Copy will—		
(a)	if ordered when lodging inventory	5.00	5.00
(b)	if ordered subsequent to lodging inventory —		
	(i) first copy including search fee	15.00	15.00
	(ii) each subsequent copy, if ordered at the same time as the first copy	5.00	5.00

PART II — SHERIFF COURT PROCEEDINGS

Initial Writ

5.	Initial writ in any proceedings not being proceedings for which any other paragraph of this Table prescribes a fee...	80.00	75.00

European order for payment in terms of EU Regulation 1896/2006

5A.	Application for European order for payment.....................................	80.00	75.00

Divorce and dissolution of civil partners

6.	Initial writ in an action of divorce or dissolution of a civil partnership (other than a simplified divorce or dissolution of a civil partnership application)	120.00	120.00

Application for Simplified Divorce and simplified dissolution of civil partnership

7.	Any application (inclusive of all procedures other than those specified at paragraphs 8 and 9)	90.00	90.00
8.	Citation of, or intimation to, any person or persons by sheriff officer	10plus sheriff officer's fee	10plus sheriff officer's fee
9.	Subsequent application upon change of circumstances by party........................	25.00	25.00

Column 1 (Matters)	Column 2 (Fee payable) £	Column 3 (Fee formerly payable) £
Summary warrant		
10. Application for summary warrant	60.00	55.00
Bankruptcy		
11. Petition for sequestration of estates	95.00	90.00
12. Petition for discharge of a bankrupt or application for approval of composition or deed of arrangement	30.00	25.00
13. Miscellaneous applications including appeals under the Bankruptcy (Scotland) Act 1985	45.00	45.00
14. Act and warrant of trustee	40.00	35.00
15. Application (written or oral) for discharge of trustee	30.00	25.00
Declarator and Petitions for completion of title for the Sheriff of Chancery		
16. Applications for Declarator and Petitions for completion of title to the Sheriff of Chancery	185.00	180.00
17. Issue of chancery extract	90.00	85.00
Summary cause		
18. Summons summary cause (including small claim and European small claim procedure)—		
(a) actions for payment of money less than £200 (or 250 euros for European Small Claims)	15.00	15.00
(b) other actions	65.00	60.00
(c) in relation to a small claim summons, citation of, or intimation to, any party by sheriff officer	10 plus sheriff officer's fee	10 plus sheriff officer's fee
(d) on the marking of an appeal	45.00	45.00
Criminal procedure		
19. Complaint	30.00	25.00
Road Traffic Offenders Act 1988		
20. Petition for removal of disqualification	75.00	75.00
Miscellaneous		
21. Application under section 4 of the Requirements of Writing (Scotland) Act 1995	15.00	15.00
22. Caveat	30.00	25.00
23. Any proceedings under section 12 or 18 of the Civil Jurisdiction and Judgments Act 1982	20.00	20.00
24. Note in a liquidation or judicial factory	30.00	25.00
Defender's responses		
25. First writ, reponing note or attendance to state a defence, or oppose an interim order (fee payable by each defender or compearer)		
(a) in proceedings to which paragraph 5 of this Table applies	80.00	75.00
(b) in an action of divorce or dissolution of a civil partnership (other than a simplified divorce or dissolution of civil partnership)	120.00	120.00

	Column 1	Column 2	Column 3
	(Matters)	*(Fee payable)* £	*(Fee formerly payable)* £

Civil court procedure

Payable by pursuer

26. Lodging of a certified copy record under the standard procedure of the Ordinary Cause Rules 1993 .... 95.00 — 90.00

27. Lodging of a certified closed record under the additional procedure of the said Rules .... 95.00 — 90.00

28. Fixing of a proof, a debate or a hearing in a summary or miscellaneous application on the merits of the cause .... 40.00 — 40.00

29. For each day or part thereof of proof, debate or hearing in a summary or miscellaneous application on the merits of the cause (not payable if the proof, debate or hearing does not proceed on that day) .... 95.00 — 90.00

30. Endorsing of a minute in Form F27 in terms of rule 33.29(1)(b) of the said Rules .... 55.00 — 55.00

Payable by any party(including pursuer)

31. Lodging of a written motion or minute; and the lodging of any written opposition to any such motion or minute .... 40.00 — 35.00

32. Marking an appeal to the Sheriff Principal in any proceedings (other than as provided for in paragraph 18(d) of this Table) .... 95.00 — 90.00

Sheriff court books

33. Recording protest of a bill or promissory note (NOTE: Extract to be charged as in paragraph 38 of this Table.) .... 20.00 — 20.00

34. Preservation of deeds, each deed (NOTE: This includes recording and engrossing. If extracts are required, a separate fee is to be charged as in paragraph 38 of this Table) .... 10.00 — 10.00

Miscellaneous office procedures

35. Lodging each set of plans or other Parliamentary deposit .... 60.00 — 55.00

36. Inspection of report of auction and the auditor of court's report .... 15.00 — 10.00

37. Search and report service as instructed by a trade protection society, licensed credit reference agency or trade publication of protests, of relevant court records as allowed by appropriate said Rules as amended, with the fees below payable in advance —

    (a) weekly for twelve months .... 280.00 — 275.00

    (b) twice weekly for twelve months .... 560.00 — 545.00

    (c) four times weekly for twelve months .... 1,125.00 — 1,095.00

38. Recording, engrossing, extracting or copying of all documents except as provided for at paragraph 4 of this Table (if a search is required an additional fee will be charged as per paragraph 39 of this Table)

    (a) by photocopying or otherwise producing a printed or typed copy —

        (i) Up to 10 pages .... 5.00 — 5.00

        (ii) Each page or part thereof (in excess of 10 pages) .... 50.50 — 50.50

    (b) for a copy of a document on a computer disc or in other electronic form .... 5.00 — 5.00

Note: Recording in Sheriff Court Register of Deeds to be charged as in paragraph 38(a)

Column 1 (Matters)	Column 2 (Fee payable) £	Column 3 (Fee formerly payable) £
39. Searches: for each search of records or archives, except as provided for at paragraph 4 of this Table—		
(a) up to 30 minutes	15.00	15.00
(b) for more than 30 minutes up to 2 hours	35.00	35.00
(c) for each additional 30 minutes (in excess of 2 hours)	10.00	10.00
(d) In addition, correspondence fee where applicable	10.00	10.00

PART III — AUDITOR OF COURT

	Column 2 £	Column 3 £
40. For taxing accounts of expenses incurred in judicial proceedings remitted to the auditor of court for taxation —		
(1) auditor's fee on lodging account for taxation...............................	35.00	34.00
(2) auditor's fee for taxing accounts of expenses etc. —		
(a) up to £400	19.00	18.00
(b) for every additional £100 or part thereof	5.00	5.00

Note: Fee to be determined by auditor of court on amount of account as submitted.

	Column 2	Column 3
(3) fee for cancellation of diet of taxation —		
(a) where written notice of cancellation received by receiving party within three working days of diet	50% of fee that would have been payable under sub-paragraph (2) of this paragraph	50% of fee that would have been payable under sub-paragraph (2) of this paragraph
(b) where written notice of cancellation received by receiving party on the working day before or the day of the diet	75% of fee that would have been payable under sub paragraph (2) of this paragraph	75% of fee that would have been payable under sub paragraph (2) of this paragraph

Table of Fees payable to Messengers-at-Arms

Act of Sederunt (Fees of Messengers-at-Arms) (No 2) 2002
(SSI 2002 No 566))

[This Schedule is printed as amended by:

Act of Sederunt (Fees of Messengers-at-Arms) 2004 (SSI 2004 No 515) which came into force on 1st January 2005;

Act of Sederunt (Fees of Messengers-at-Arms) 2005 (SSI 2005 No 582) which came into force on 1st January 2006;

Act of Sederunt (Fees of Messengers-at-Arms) 2006 (SSI 2006 No 540) which came into force on 1st January 2007;

Act of Sederunt (Fees of Messengers-at-Arms) 2007 (SSI 2007 No 532) which came into force on 1st January 2008;

Act of Sederunt (Fees of Messengers-at-Arms) 2008 (SSI 2008 No 481) which came into force on 12th January 2009.]

SCHEDULE 1
GENERAL REGULATIONS

1. Subject to the following paragraphs, the fees payable to a messenger-at-arms shall be calculated in accordance with the Table of Fees in this Schedule and shall be payable in respect of all forms of service or intimation of a document, citation of a person or execution of diligence and all other work authorised by the court and executed by a messenger-at-arms during the normal business hours of 9.00 am to 5.00 pm.

2. Fees in relation to service or intimation of a document, citation of a person or diligence which, of necessity, is executed outwith normal business hours shall be surcharged by the levying of an additional fee of —

(a) 33⅓ per cent of the fee specified in the Table of Fees, where it is executed on a week day between the hours of 5.00 pm and 10.00 pm; and

(b) 75 per cent of the fee specified in the Table of Fees, where it is executed on a week day after 10.00 pm or before 9.00 am or on a Saturday, Sunday or a public holiday.

3.—(1) There shall be three bands of charge in the Table of Fees in accordance with which fees shall be payable.

(2) The three bands of charge shall be —

(a) Band 1 — up to 12 miles;

(b) Band 2 — over 12 miles and up to 18 miles; and

(c) Band 3 — over 18 miles.

(3) A fee is payable in respect of one band of charge only for any item.

(4) Unless by special arrangement between a messenger-at-arms and the instructing agent, the bands of charge shall be calculated according to the distance from the place of business of the nearest messenger-at-arms to the place of execution.

4. An additional fee may be negotiated between the messenger-at-arms and the instructing agent by prior agreement in the following circumstances:

(a) where the messenger-at-arms is standing by awaiting the delivery or uplifting of a document for immediate service;

(b) where the messenger-at-arms has to instruct an huissier or other officer of court outwith Scotland to serve a document; or

(c) where there is no prescribed fee and the importance, urgency and value of the work involved necessitates an additional fee.

5. All reasonable outlays, including postage and any recorded delivery costs in respect of items 1(b) and 1(c) in the Table of Fees, necessarily incurred by a messenger-at-arms in carrying out lawful instructions shall be charged in addition to a fee specified in the Table of Fees.

6. Every fee note rendered by a messenger-at-arms shall be so detailed that the fees charged by him may

be easily checked against the Table of Fees; and any fees agreed under paragraph 4 above and any allowable outlays shall be clearly narrated as such. The fee note shall be reviewed by the messenger-at-arms to ensure that it is fair and reasonable in the circumstances and shall be adjusted by him if necessary.

7. Discounting of fees is permitted only between messengers-at-arms.

8. Any restriction or modification made by a messenger-at-arms of fees recoverable from a person shall be passed on to that person only.

9. Time shall be charged in units of 30 minutes or part thereof; and, except in relation to time under paragraph 10, 11 or 12 below —

   (*a*) time shall apply from the end of the first hour at the place of execution until completion; or

   (*b*) time shall apply after the messenger-at-arms has travelled a distance of 30 miles from his place of business until he returns to a distance of 30 miles from that place.

10. Where a messenger-at-arms has to use a ferry, he and any witness shall be allowed the necessary cost of the ferry, all reasonable subsistence and the time for boarding, crossing and returning, which shall be charged on a time basis.

11. Where a messenger-at-arms is required to attend before a notary public, commissioner or other person or as a witness, a fee for such attendance by the messenger-at-arms and any witness shall be chargeable on a time basis.

12. Where enquiries are necessary in order to execute service, intimation, citation, diligence or any other work authorised by the court, a fee for such enquiries shall be chargeable on a time basis.

13.—(1) Where, in an attachment, the appraised value of an article exceeds the sum recoverable, the fee specified in the Table of Fees shall be calculated in accordance with the sum recoverable and not the appraised value.

(2) Where, in an attachment, a debtor or other occupier of the premises claims that goods are subject to a hire purchase agreement or are otherwise the property of someone other than the debtor, but refuses, or is unable, to produce evidence to that effect, the messenger-at-arms may poind the goods and shall add a note on the schedule of the poinding stating that the debtor has claimed that the goods are subject to a hire purchase agreement or are otherwise the property of someone other than the debtor, as the case may be.

14. A messenger-at-arms supplying services to any person in respect of which fees are payable to him under this Schedule shall —

   (*a*) if he is a taxable person within the meaning of the Value Added Tax Act 1983; and

   (*b*) if the supply is a taxable supply within the meaning of that Act,

make charges to that person in addition to the charges in respect of that fee, being such additional charge as amounts to the value-added tax payable under that Act in respect of the supply of those services.

15. In this Schedule, unless the context otherwise requires —

   "the Act of 2002" means the Debt Arrangement and Attachment (Scotland) Act 2002 (asp 7)

   "the Act of 1987" means the Debtors (Scotland) Act 1987;

   "apprehension" means apprehending, detaining and taking to and from court or prison;

   "arranging" means accepting instructions, checking for competency, reserving time, advising instructing agent, making all necessary arrangements, intimation and service (where necessary) prior to execution;

   "possession" means searching, taking possession and delivery;

   "postal diligence" means service of any diligence, which may be served by post, by registered post or the first class recorded delivery service;

   "postal service" means service or intimation by registered post or the first class recorded delivery service;

   "service" means service or intimation of any document under a rule of court or an order of the court and includes accepting instructions, preparation, postage and service or intimation of any ancillary form or other ancillary document.

TABLE OF FEES

Item		Band 1 £	Band 2 £	Band 3 £
1.	*Service or intimation of a document*			
(a)	Service			
	(i) each person at a different address	52.30	88.70	112.00
	(ii) each additional person at the same address or additional copy required to be served or intimated under the Act of 1987 and the Act of 2002	17.50	17.50	17.50
(b)	Postal service	25.25	25.25	25.25
(c)	Postal diligence	38.45	38.45	38.45
2.	*Inhibitions*			
(a)	Inhibition only			
	(i) each person at a different address	55.05	88.70	112.00
	(ii) each additional person at the same address	28.55	28.55	28.55
(b)	Inhibition and service			
	(i) each person at a different address	72.45	105.95	129.70
	(ii) each additional person at the same address	46.05	46.05	46.05
(c)	Inhibition, service and interdict			
	(i) each person at a different address	175.90	175.90	175.90
	(ii) each additional person at the same address	74.80	74.80	74.80
3.	*Interdicts (including non-harassment orders under the Protection from Harassment Act 1997)*			
(a)	Interdict only			
	(i) each person at a different address	129.70	129.70	129.70
	(ii) each additional person at the same address	28.50	28.50	28.50
(b)	Interdict and service			
	(i) each person at a different address	147.30	147.30	147.30
	(ii) each additional person at the same address	46.05	46.05	46.05
(c)	Interdict, service and inhibition			
	(i) each person at a different address	175.90	175.90	175.90
	(ii) each additional person at the same address	74.80	74.80	74.80
4.	*Attachments*			
(a)	Serving notice of entry	9.80	9.80	9.80
(b)	Arranging attachment and endeavouring but being unable to execute same for whatever reason	73.45	73.45	73.45
(c)	Arranging and executing attachment where appraised value is—			
	(i) £605 or under	86.00	86.00	86.00
	(ii) over £605 and up to £2,431	133.35	133.35	133.35
	(iii) over £2,431 and up to £24,493 — 10% of the appraised value			
	(iv) over £24,493 and up to £122,453 — 10% of the first £24,493, 5% thereafter			
	(v) over £122,453 — 10% of the first £24,493, 5% thereafter up to £122,453 and 1% thereafter			
(d)	Reporting attachment	8.20	8.20	8.20

Item			Band 1 £	Band 2 £	Band 3 £
5.	*Attachments of motor vehicle, heavy plant or machinery*				
	(a)	Arranging and executing attachment where appraised value is—			
		(i) £605 or under	86.00	86.00	86.00
		(ii) over £605 and up to £2,690	133.35	133.35	133.35
		(iii) over £2,695 and up to £122,453 — 5% of the appraised value			
		(iv) over 122,453 5% of the first £122,453 and 1% thereafter			
	(d)	Reporting attachment	8.20	8.20	8.20
6.	*Sequestrations for rent, poinding of the ground*				
	(a)	Arranging for the sequestration or poinding of the ground and endeavouring but being unable to execute same for whatever reason	70.20	70.20	70.20
	(b)	Arranging and effecting sequestration or poinding of the ground	129.70	129.70	129.70
7.	*Auctions*				
	(a)	(i) Arranging auction, preparing advertisement and giving public notice	21.30	21.30	21.30
		(ii) Serving copy of warrant of auction and intimating the place and date of auction and if necessary the date of removal of attached effects as in item 1 (a) or (b) above, as the case may be			
	(b)	(i) Officers and witness attending auction sale and being unable to execute same for whatever reason	70.20	70.20	70.20
		(ii) Officers and witness attending auction sale	129.70	129.70	129.70
8.	*Ejections*				
	(a)	Arranging ejection	70.20	70.20	70.20
	(b)	Arranging and executing ejection	109.05	109.05	109.05
9.	*Taking possession of effects*				
	(a)	Arranging possession	70.20	70.20	70.20
	(b)	Arranging and effecting possession	129.70	129.70	129.70
10.	*Apprehensions*				
	(a)	Arranging apprehension	70.20	70.20	70.20
	(b)	Arranging and apprehending	129.70	129.70	129.70
11.	*Taking possession of children*				
	(a)	Arranging to take possession	70.20	70.20	70.20
	(b)	Taking possession of each child	129.70	129.70	129.70
12.	*Arresting vessels, aircraft and cargo*				
	(a)	Arranging to arrest	70.20	70.20	70.20
	(b)	Arranging and effecting arrestment	214.55	214.55	214.55

Item	Band 1 £	Band 2 £	Band 3 £
13. Miscellaneous			
(a) Making any report or application under the Act of 1987 or the Act of 2002 with the exception of reporting an attachment	16.25	16.25	16.25
(b) Granting any receipt required to be issued under the Act of 1987 or the Act of 2002	8.20	8.20	8.20
(c) Arranging locksmith or tradesman to be in attendance	5.20	5.20	5.20
(d) Granting certificate of displenishment or providing any other certificate or report, registering any document or making any application to a court or the creditor	16.25	16.25	16.25
(e) Executing warrant to open lockfast places	16.25	16.25	16.25
(f) Time			
(i) with witness £26.10 per unit			
(ii) without witness £19.50 per unit			
(g) Photocopies			
(i) first page of document £1.85			
(ii) subsequent pages per page £1.00			

Table of Fees payable to Sheriff Officers

Act of Sederunt (Fees of Sheriff Officers) (No 2) 2002 (SSI 2002 No. 567)

[This Schedule is printed as amended by:

Act of Sederunt (Fees of Sheriff Officers) 2003 (SSI 2003 No 538) which came into force on 1st January 2004;

Act of Sederunt (Fees of Sheriff Officers) 2004 (SSI 2004 No 513) which came into force on 1st January 2005;

Act of Sederunt (Fees of Sheriff Officers) 2005 (SSI 2005 No 538) which came into force on 1st January 2006;

Act of Sederunt (Fees of Sheriff Officers) 2006 (SSI 2006 No 539) which came into force on 1st January 2007;

Act of Sederunt (Fees of Sheriff Officers) 2007 (SSI 2006 No 550) which came into force on 14th January 2008;
Act of Sederunt (Fees of Sheriff Officers) 2008 (SSI 2008 No 430) which came into effect on 26th January 2009.]

SCHEDULE 1

GENERAL REGULATIONS

1. Subject to the following paragraphs, the fees payable to a sheriff officer in relation to an ordinary cause or a summary cause, as the case may be, shall be calculated in accordance with the Table of Fees in this Schedule and shall be payable in respect of (a) all forms of service or intimation of a document, citation of a person or execution of diligence and all other work authorised by the court and (b) recovery of rates, charges or taxes by summary warrant, any of which is executed by a sheriff officer during the normal business hours of 9.00 am to 5.00 pm.

1A. Column A of the Table of Fees specifies the fees payable in relation to —

  (a) a summary cause commenced before 14th January 2008; and

  (b) a summary cause commenced on or after that date where the value of the claim when the cause is commenced is £1,500 or less (exclusive of interest and expenses).

1B. A summary cause falling within paragraph (c) of section 35(1) of the Sheriff Courts (Scotland) Act 1971 (actions *ad factum praestandum* and actions for the recovery of possession of heritable or moveable property)(**4**) falls within paragraph (b) of general regulation 1A where it contains no additional or alternative crave for decree for payment of money or where the value of such crave is £1,500 or less (exclusive of interest and expenses).

1C. Column B of the Table of Fees specifies the fees payable in relation to —

  (a) a summary cause not falling within general regulation 1A; and

  (b) an ordinary cause.

2. Fees in relation to service or intimation of a document, citation of a person or diligence which, of necessity, is executed outwith normal business hours shall be surcharged by the levying of an additional fee of —

  (a) 33⅓ per cent of the fee specified in the Table of Fees, where it is executed on a week day between the hours of 5.00 pm and 10.00 pm; and

  (b) 75 per cent of the fee specified in the Table of Fees, where it is executed on a week day after 10.00 pm or before 9.00 am or on a Saturday, Sunday or a public holiday.

3.—(1) There shall be three bands of charge in the Table of Fees in accordance with which fees shall be payable.

  (2) The three bands of charge shall be —

  (a) Band 1 — up to 12 miles;

  (b) Band 2 — over 12 miles and up to 18 miles; and

  (c) Band 3 — over 18 miles.

  (3) A fee is payable in respect of one band of charge only for any item.

  (4) Unless by special arrangement between a sheriff officer and the instructing agent, the bands of charge shall be calculated according to the distance between the court house where the warrant was granted and the place of execution or the distance from the place of business of the nearest sheriff officer within the district to the place of execution, whichever is the lesser.

4. An additional fee may be negotiated between a sheriff officer and the instructing agent by prior agreement in the following circumstances —

  (a) where the sheriff officer is standing by awaiting the delivery or uplifting of a document for immediate service;

(b)   where the sheriff officer has to instruct an huissier or other officer of court outwith Scotland to serve a document; or

(c)   where there is no prescribed fee and the importance, urgency and value of the work involved necessitates an additional fee

5.   All reasonable outlays, including postage and any recorded delivery costs in respect of items 1(b) and 1(c) in the Table of Fees, necessarily incurred by a sheriff officer in carrying out lawful instructions shall be charged in addition to a fee specified in the Table of Fees in this Schedule.

6.   Every fee note rendered by a sheriff officer shall be so detailed that the fees charged by him may be easily checked against the Table of Fees; and any fees agreed under paragraph 4 above and any allowable outlays shall be clearly narrated as such. The fee note shall be reviewed by the sheriff officer to ensure that it is fair and reasonable in the circumstances and shall be adjusted by him if necessary.

7.   Discounting of fees is permitted only between sheriff officers.

8.   Any restriction or modification made by a sheriff officer of fees recoverable from a person shall be passed on to that person only.

9.   Time will be charged in units of 30 minutes or part thereof; and, in respect of the following items in the Table of Fees, shall apply from the end of the first hour at the place of execution until completion: 2. 5(c), 6(b)(i) and (ii), 7(b), 8(b), 9(b), 10(b) and 11(b).

10.   Where a sheriff officer has to use a ferry, he and any witness shall be allowed the necessary cost of the ferry, all reasonable subsistence and the time for boarding, crossing and returning, which shall be charged on a time basis.

11.   Where a sheriff officer is required to attend before a notary public, commissioner or other person or as a witness, a fee for such attendance by the sheriff officer and any witness shall be chargeable on a time basis.

12.   Where enquiries are necessary in order to execute service, intimation, citation, diligence or any other work authorised by the court, a fee for such enquiries shall be chargeable on a time basis.

13.   Where personal service is to be carried out under item 1(a)(i) in the Table of Fees and more than one visit is required, each additional visit shall be charged at 50 per cent of the fee specified in that item.

14.—(1)   Where, in an attachment, the appraised value of an article exceeds the sum recoverable, the fee specified in the Table of Fees in this schedule shall be calculated in accordance with the sum recoverable and not the appraised value.

(2) Where, in an attachment, a debtor or other occupier of the premises claims that goods are subject to a hire purchase agreement or are otherwise the property of someone other than the debtor, but refuses or is unable to produce evidence to that effect, the sheriff officer may attach the goods and shall add a note on the schedule of the attachment stating that the debtor has claimed that the goods are subject to a hire purchase agreement or are otherwise the property of someone other than the debtor, as the case may be.

15.   The fees payable to a sheriff officer in respect of recovery of rates, charges or taxes by summary warrant shall be calculated in accordance with the fees specified in Column B of the Table of Fees.

16.   A sheriff officer supplying services to any person in respect of which fees are payable to him under this Schedule shall —

(a)   if he is a taxable person within the meaning of the Value Added Tax Act 1983; and

(b)   if the supply is a taxable supply within the meaning of that Act,

make charges to that person in addition to the charges in respect of that fee, being such additional charge as amounts to the value-added tax payable under the Act in respect of the supply of those services.

17.   In this Schedule, unless the context otherwise requires —

"the Act of 2002" means the Debt Arrangement and Attachment Act 2002 (asp 17);

"the Act of 1987" means the Debtors (Scotland) Act 1987;

"apprehension" means apprehending, detaining and taking to and from court or prison;

"arranging" means accepting instructions, checking for competency, reserving time, advising instructing agent, making all necessary arrangements, intimation and service (where necessary) prior to execution;

"possession" means searching, taking possession and delivery;

"postal diligence" means service of any diligence, which may be served by post, by registered post or the first class recorded delivery service;

"postal service" means service or intimation by registered post or the first class recorded delivery service;

"service" means service or intimation of any document under a rule of court or an order of the court and includes accepting instructions, preparation, postage and service or intimation of any ancillary form or other ancillary document.

TABLE OF FEES

Item	Column A			Column B		
	Band 1 £	Band 2 £	Band 3 £	Band 1 £	Band 2 £	Band 3 £
1. *Service or intimation of a document*						
(a) Service						
(i) each person at a different address	28.85	45.50	57.65	47.10	69.35	90.40
(ii) each additional person at the same address or additional copy required to be served or intimated under the Act of 1987 and the Act of 2002	9.65	9.65	9.65	15.70	15.70	15.70
(b) Postal service	13.60	13.60	13.60	23.00	23.00	23.00
(c) Postal diligence	21.10	21.10	21.10	34.65	34.65	34.65
2. *Interdicts (including non-harassment orders under the Protection from Harassment Act 1997 and anti-social behaviour order under the Crime and Disorder Act 1998)*						
(a) Interdict only						
(i) each person at a different address				129.70	129.70	129.70
(ii) each additional person at the same address				28.55	28.55	28.55
(b) Interdict and service						
(i) each person at a different address				145.70	145.70	145.70
(ii) each additional person at the same address				44.40	44.40	44.40
3. *Attachments*						
(a) Serving notice of entry	6.35	6.35	6.35	9.80	9.80	9.80
(b) Arranging attachment and endeavouring but being unable to execute the same for whatever reason	50.20	50.20	50.20	73.45	73.45	73.45
(c) Arranging and executing attachment where appraised value is —						
(i) £605 or under	86.00	86.00	86.00	86.00	86.00	86.00
(ii) Over £605 and up to £2,431	133.35	133.35	133.35	133.35	133.35	133.35
(iii) Over £2,431 and up to £24,493 10% —of the appraised value						
(iv) Over £24,493 and up to £122,453 — 10% of the first £122,453, 5% thereafter						
(v) Over £117,348 — 10% of the first £24,493, 5% thereafter up to £122,453 and 1% thereafter						
(d) Reporting attachment	8.20	8.20	8.20	8.20	8.20	8.20
4. *Attachment of motor vehicles, heavy plant or machinery*						
(a) Arranging and executing attachment where appraised value is						
(i) £605 or under	86.00	86.00	86.00	86.00	86.00	86.00
(ii) Over £605 and up to £2,690	133.35	133.35	133.35	133.35	133.35	133.35
(iii) Over £2,690 and up to £122,453 — 5% of the appraised value						
(iv) Over £122,453 — 5% of the first £122,453, and 1% thereafter						
(b) Reporting attachment	8.20	8.20	8.20	8.20	8.20	8.20

Item	Column A			Column B		
	Band 1 £	Band 2 £	Band 3 £	Band 1 £	Band 2 £	Band 3 £
5. *Sequestrations for rent, poinding of ground*						
(a) Arranging for the sequestration or poinding of the ground and endeavouring but being unable to execute same for whatever reason	46.75	46.75	46.75	70.20	70.20	70.20
(b) Arranging and effecting sequestration where the appraised value is —						
(i) £605 or under	82.60	82.60	82.60			
(ii) Over £605 and up to £2,431	129.70	129.70	129.70			
(iii) Over £2,431 as in item 3(c)(iii) above						
(c) Arranging and effecting ordinary sequestration or poinding of the ground				129.70	129.70	129.70
(d) Service — as in item 1(a) or (b) above, as the case may be						
6. *Auctions*						
(a) (i) Arranging auction, preparing advertisement and giving public notice	21.30	21.30	21.30	21.30	21.30	21.30
(ii) Intimating the place and date of auction and if necessary the date of removal of attached items as in item 1(a) or (b) above as the case may be						
(b) (i) Officer and witness attending auction but auction not executed for whatever reason	46.75	46.75	46.75	70.20	70.20	70.20
(ii) Officer and witness attending auction	129.70	129.70	129.70	129.70	129.70	129.70
7. *Ejections*						
(a) Arranging ejection	46.75	46.75	46.75	70.20	70.20	70.20
(b) Arranging and executing ejection	96.05	96.05	96.05	109.00	109.00	109.00
8. *Taking possession of effects*						
(a) Arranging possession	46.75	46.75	46.75	70.20	70.20	70.20
(b) Arranging and effecting possession	96.05	96.05	96.05	129.70	129.70	129.70
9. *Apprehensions*						
(a) Arranging apprehension				70.20	70.20	70.20
(b) Arranging and apprehending				129.70	129.70	129.70
10. *Taking possession of children*						
(a) Arranging to take possession				70.20	70.20	70.20
(b) Arranging and taking possession of each child				129.70	129.70	129.70
11. *Arresting vessels, aircraft and cargo*						
(a) Arranging to arrest	46.75	46.75	46.75	70.20	70.20	70.20
(b) Arranging and effecting arrestment	118.00	118.00	118.00	214.55	214.55	214.55

Item	Column A			Column B		
	Band 1 £	Band 2 £	Band 3 £	Band 1 £	Band 2 £	Band 3 £
12. *Miscellaneous*						
(a) Making any report or application under the Act of 1987 or the Act of 2002 with the exception of reporting an attachment	16.25	16.25	16.25	16.25	16.25	16.25
(b) Granting any receipt required to be issued under the Act of 1987 and the Act of 2002	8.20	8.20	8.20	8.20	8.20	8.20
(c) Arranging locksmith or tradesman to be in attendance	5.20	5.20	5.20	5.20	5.20	5.20
(d) Granting certificate of displenishment or providing any other certificate or report, registering any document or making any application to a court or the creditor	16.25	16.25	16.25	16.25	16.25	16.25
(e) Executing warrant to open lockfast places	16.25	16.25	16.25	16.25	16.25	16.25
(f) Time						
(i) with witness — £26.10 per unit						
(ii) without witness — £19.50 per unit						
(g) Photocopies						
(i) first page of document — £1.85						
(ii) subsequent pages — per page —£1.00						

Table of Fees payable in the Scottish Land Court

Scottish Land Court (Fees) Order 1996 (SI 1996 No 680)

[Came into force on 1st April 1996.]

SCHEDULE

TABLE OF FEES

	£
(1) Small Landholders (Scotland) Acts 1886 to 1931 and Crofters (Scotland) Act 1993	
(a) Application for a record of a holding or a croft	
Principal application (each applicant)	60.00
For each respondent	10.00
(b) Recording agreements for loan by —	
(i) The Scottish Office Agriculture, Environment And Fisheries Department And	
(ii) Highlands And Islands Enterprise	
Each agreement	70.00
(c) Other applications	
Principal application	28.00
When more than one applicant (each additional applicant)	18.00
For each respondent	4.00
(d) Appeals and motions for rehearing	
Each appellant or motioner	50.00
Each respondent	6.00
(e) Hearing and inspection fee payable by applicant in all applications. For each day or part thereof the court sits or inspects	60.00
(f) Additional fee	
(i) Where the application is granted, dismissed or withdrawn after the hearing order has been received by each party but before the commencement of the hearing — payable by the applicant	70.00
(iii) Where the principal clerk of court executes a conveyance following upon an order of the court under section 16(2) of the crofters (scotland) act 1993 — payable by the applicant	65.00
(2) Agricultural Holdings (Scotland) Act 1991	
(a) Valuation of sheep stocks	
Awards not exceeding £100	6.00
Awards exceeding £100:	
For the first £100 thereof	6.00
For every additional £100 or part thereof	3.00
Where application dismissed or withdrawn before valuation	75.00
(b) Arbitration as to rents	
Rental as fixed by court, not exceeding £500	50.00
Rental as fixed by court exceeding £500:	
For The First £500	50.00
For every additional £100 or part thereof	7.50
Where application dismissed or withdrawn before rent fixed	80.00

		£
(c)	Appeals against award by an arbiter	
	Fee payable on lodging appeal	65.00
	Rental as fixed by court not exceeding £500	30.00
	Rental as fixed by court exceeding £500:	
	For the first £500	30.00
	For every additional £100 or part thereof	3.00
	Where application dismissed or withdrawn before rent fixed	85.00
(d)	Claims for compensation	
	Awards not exceeding £100	12.00
	Awards exceeding £100:	
	For the first £100 thereof	12.00
	For every additional £100 or part thereof	5.00
	Where application dismissed or withdrawn before compensation fixed	80.00
(e)	Other applications	
	Principal application	100.00
	When more than one applicant (each additional applicant)	50.00
	For each respondent	45.00
(f)	Appeals and motions for rehearing	
	Each Appellant Or Motioner	60.00
(g)	Hearings And Inspections	
	For every day or part thereof the court sits or inspects — payable by the applicant	120.00
(h)	Additional fee	
	Where the application is granted, dismissed or withdrawn after the hearing order has been received by each party but before the commencement of the hearing — payable by the applicant	120.00

(3) Miscellaneous

(a)	for making a copy or copies of the principal application or any part of it, or any order in it, or any original deed, writ, or document in process	
	For each sheet	1.20
	For certifying such copy	7.00
(b)	Applications not otherwise specified	
	Principal application	100.00
	When more than one applicant (each additional applicant)	50.00
	For each respondent	45.00
(c)	Hearings And Inspections	
	For every day or part thereof the court sits or inspects — payable by the applicant	120.00
(d)	Additional Fee	
	Where the application is granted, dismissed or withdrawn after the hearing order has been received by each party but before the commencement of the hearing — payable by the applicant .	120.00
(e)	Search Fee	
	For searches in records arising from postal or other enquiries — for each search	9.00

Table of Fees payable in the Lands Tribunal for Scotland

Lands Tribunal for Scotland Rules 1971 (SI 1971 No 218)

[This Schedule is printed as amended by:

the Lands Tribunal for Scotland (Amendment) (Fees) Rules 1993 (SI 1993 No 296) which came into force on 1st April 1993;

the Lands Tribunal for Scotland (Amendment) (Fees) Rules 1994 (SI 1994 No 218) which came into force on 1st April 1994;

the Lands Tribunal for Scotland (Amendment) (Fees) Rules 1995 (SI 1995 No 308) which came into force on 1st April 1995;

the Lands Tribunal for Scotland (Amendment) (Fees) Rules 1996 (SI 1996 No 519) which came into force on 1st April 1996.

the Lands Tribunal for Scotland (Amendment) (Fees) Rules 2003 (SI 2003 No 521) which came into force on 1st November 2003;

the Lands Tribunal for Scotland Amendment (Fees) Rules 2004 (SSI 2004 No 480) which came into force on 28th November 2004.]

SCHEDULE 2

FEES

Applications etc.	£
1. On an application under the Conveyancing and Feudal Reform (Scotland) Act 1970 —	
(i) section 1 (land obligations) — initial application	130.00
(ii) section 1 — subsequent application	65.00
(iii) section 4 (feu duties)	75.00
2. On an application relating to disputed compensation under Part III of these Rules or where the Tribunal is acting under a reference by consent under section 1(5) of the Lands Tribunal Act 1949 —	
(i) where the disputed amount does not exceed £20,000.00 being either a lump sum or a rent or other annual payment	78.00
(ii) where the disputed amount exceeds £20,000.00 being either a lump sum or a rent or other annual payment	130.00
(iii) where the application or reference does not involve a disputed amount	78.00
3. On an appeal under section 1(3A) of the Lands Tribunal Act 1949 (valuation for rating) —	
(i) where the net annual value does not exceed £10,000.00	100.00
(ii) where the net annual value exceeds £10,000.00 but not £50,000.00	150.00
(iii) where the net annual value exceeds £50,000.00 but not £100,000.00	300.00
(iv) where the net annual value exceeds £100,000.00	500.00
4. On an appeal under section 1(3BA) of the Lands Tribunal Act 1949 (non-referral of valuation appeal or complaint)	78.00
5. On an appeal under section 25 of the Land Registration (Scotland) Act 1979 (appeal from action or omission of the Keeper of the Registers of Scotland)	78.00
6. On any other application (not being an appeal under Part IV or Part VA or a reference under Part V of these Rules)	52.00

Hearing fees, etc.

7. (a) On the hearing of an application under section 1 of the Conveyancing and Feudal Reform (Scotland) Act 1970 — £155.00 for each day on which the Tribunal sits

    (b) On the making of an order under—

       (i) section 1 of the Conveyancing and Feudal Reform (Scotland) Act 1970 — £88.00

       (ii) section 4 of that Act — £88.00

8. On the hearing of an application under Part III or an appeal under Part VC of these Rules or where the Tribunal is acting under a reference by consent —

    (a) Where the amount is determined in terms of a lump sum— £50.00 in respect of every £5,000.00 or part of £5,000.00 of such lump sum but not less than £155.00 for each day on which the Tribunal sits and not exceeding in any case £5,000.00

    (b) Where the amount is determined in terms of rent or other annual payment — £50.00 in respect of every £500.00 or part of £500.00 of such rent or other annual payment but not less than £155.00 for each day on which the Tribunal sits and not exceeding in any case £5,000.00

    (c) Where there is a settlement as to amount, for each day on which the Tribunal sits — £155.00

9. On the hearing of any other application or appeal or reference including the hearing of preliminary pleas-in-law or legal debates in which no fee is payable by reference to an amount determined — £155.00 for each day on which the Tribunal sits

Miscellaneous fees

10. On certifying a copy of an order or determination of the Tribunal — £7.50

11. For each sheet of a copy of all or part of any document — £1.20

12. On a case for the decision of the Court of Session or the Lands Valuation Appeal Court (in respect of references under Part VC of these Rules) — an application for appeal by way of stated case (to include drafting of case and any necessary copies) — £55.00

13. On the placing of an advertisement under section 1 of the Conveyancing and Feudal Reform (Scotland) Act 1970 (*Note:* advertisements are invariably required in applications involving (a) missing superiors, (b) alcohol and (c) major developments which may have widespread implications) — 100 per cent of the cost of the advertisement in an appropriate newspaper (charge is restricted to the cost of one advertisement irrespective of the number of advertisements placed)

14. On an application for the cancellation of a hearing — £75.00

15. On an application during the course of proceedings which is not specifically referred to in the above table of fees (*eg* an application for (i) an extension to the period in which answers or adjustments are required to be lodged, or (ii) the continuation or sisting of an application) — £35.00

16. On an application under section 90 or 91 of the Title Conditions (Scotland) Act 2003 — £150.00

17. On an application under the Land Reform (Scotland) Act 2003 — £150.00

18. On a referral under section 86(5) of the Title Conditions (Scotland) Act 2003 or section 44 of the Abolition of Feudal Tenure etc. (Scotland) Act 2000	£150.00
19. On the hearing of an application or referral under items 16,17, or 18 above	£155 for each day on which the Tribunal sits
20. On the making of an order under the Abolition of Feudal Tenure etc. (Scotland) Act 2000, the Land Reform (Scotland) Act 2003 or the Title Conditions (Scotland) Act 2003	£88 plus 100% of the cost of registering the order where the Tribunal is obliged to do so
21. For placing an advertisement in connection with applications under section 20 of the Abolition of Feudal Tenure etc. (Scotland) Act 2000 and sections 90 and 91 of the Title Conditions (Scotland) Act 2003	100% of the cost of the advertisement in an appropriate newspaper (charge is restricted to the cost of one advertisement irrespective of the number of advertisements placed)
22. On making representatives as respects an application under section 90(1) or 91 of the Title Conditions (Scotland) Act 2003	£25
23 On a referral under section 102 of the Title Conditions (Scotland) Act 2003	£150

Table of Fees payable to the Edinburgh Gazette

Authorised Scale of Charges for Notices and Advertisements

[Rates from 1st December 2008.]

	Submitted in defined electronic format		All Other Formats		Includes Voucher copy
	excl VAT	incl VAT	excl VAT	incl VAT	incl VAT
1. *Notice of Application for Winding up by the Court*	47.00	54.05	62.50	71.88	72.83
2. *All Other Corporate and Personal Insolvency Notices* (2–5 Related Companies will be charged at double the single company rate) (6–10 Related Companies will be charged at treble the single company rate)	47.00	55.05	62.50	71.88	72.83
3. *Water Resources, Control of Pollution (PPC); and Listed Buildings in Conservation Areas, Local Plans, Stopping Up and Conversion of Roads Notices where there are more than 5 addresses or roads*	94.00	108.10	125.00	143.75	144.70
4. *All Other Notice Types* Up to 20 lines	47.00	54.05	62.50	71.88	72.83
Additional 5 Lines or fewer	18.25	20.99	18.25	20.99	N/A
6. *Proofing* – per notice (Copy must be submitted at least one week prior to publication)	Free	Free	31.25	35.94	N/A
7. *Late Advertisements* accepted after 9.30 am, 1 day prior to publication	31.25	35.94	31.25	35.94	N/A
8. *Withdrawal of Notices* after 9.30 am, 1 day prior to publication	47.00	54.05	62.50	71.88	N/A
9. *Voucher Copy* of the newspaper for advertiser's files	0.95	0.95	0.95	0.95	

A logo or brand can be displayed for £50 plus VAT. An annual subscription to the printed copy is available for £88.20. PDFs of the Edinburgh Gazette and Company Law Supplement are available from TSO. Electronic datafeeds are available for many notice types.

All Notices and Advertisements should reach the Edinburgh Gazette Office before 9.30 am, the working day prior to publication. Notices and Advertisements received after that time will be inserted if circumstances permit.

The Edinburgh Gazette is published every Tuesday and Friday (except Bank holidays).

The Edinburgh Gazette, TSO Scotland, 26 Rutland Square, Edinburgh EH1 2BW
Tel: 0131 659 7032/Fax: 0131 659 7039
or email notices to
edinburgh.gazette@tso.co.uk

Published in the UK by The Stationery Office Limited (TSO) under the superintendence of Carol Tullo, the Queen's Printer for Scotland.

Table of Fees payable in the Registers of Scotland Executive Agency

Fees in the Registers of Scotland Order 1995 (SI 1995 No 1945)

[This Table of Fees is printed as amended by:

The Fees in the Registers of Scotland Amendment Order 1999 (SI 1999 No 1085) which came into force on 21st April 1999;

The Fees in the Registers of Scotland Amendment Order 2001 (SI 2001 No 163) which came into force on 15th May 2001;

The Fees in the Registers Amendment Order 2004 (SSI 2004 No 507) which came into force on 26th Novembr 2004;

The Fees in the Registers Amendment Order 2005 (SSI 2005 No 580) which came into force on 28th Novembr 2005;

The Fees in the Registers of Scotland Amendment Order 2009 (SSI 2009 No 171) which came into force on the 31st May 2009.]

SCHEDULE

TABLE OF FEES IN THE REGISTERS OF SCOTLAND

PART 1 — LAND REGISTER OF SCOTLAND

1. Registration fees

A. Interests in land other than heritable securities

(1) Where an application is made to which paragraph (3) applies the fee will, subject to paragraphs (4) to (7), be caluclated on the amount of the consideration or the value, whichever is the greater, of the interest in land created, granted or transferred to which the application relates.

(2) Subject to paragraphs (8) to (10) and Part III of this Schedule, thee fee for an application to which paragraph (3) applies will be at the rates shown in Table A or, where the application is made using the ARTL System, Table B in Part IV of this Schedule.

(3) This paragraph applies to an application for registration of –

    (a) an unregistered interest in land in pursuance of section 2(1) of the Act;

    (b) the creation over a registered interest in land of a liferent or an incorporal heritable right in pursuance of section 2(3) of the Act; or

    (c) any transfer of a registered interest in land (not being a heritable security) in pursuance of section 2(4) of the Act.

(4) Where the application is to register an interest or interests in land excambed the fee will be calculated on the value of the interest in land created, granted or transferred to which the application relates.

(5) Where the consideration consists of a yearly or periodical payment, the consideration will be calculated at 10 years' purchase.

(6) Where the application is to register the grant of an interest in land in long lease the fee will be calculated on the consideration (if any) provided for that grant plus ten times the relevant rent.

(7) Where the application is made to register the assignation of an interest in land in long lease, the fee will be calculated on the consideration (if any) provided for the assignation plus ten times the annual rent payable at the date the application is made.

(8) Where a single application affects a number of title sheets (for the avoidance of doubt, in the case of an application to register a transfer of part of a registered interest in land, not including any title sheet created as a result of the application or amended to include the part transferred), the fee will be at the rates shown in Table A in Part IV of this Schedule, plus an additional fee of Åí30 for every title sheet affected other than the first.

(9) Where the application is made to give effect to a survivorship destination only, Åí30.

(10) Where an application is made by a fire and rescue authority, joint fire and rescue board, local authority, police authority, valuation authority, Health Board, Special Health Board or the Scottish Children's Reporter Administration as unregistered holder of a registered interest in land to complete its title to that interest in land in terms of section 3(6) of the Act, Åí30 for each title sheet affected.

B. Heritable securities

Where application is made for_

(a)   registration of the creation over a registered interest in land of a heritable security in pursuance of section 2(3) of the Act; or

(b) registration of any other dealing with a heritable security in pursuance of section 2(4) of the Act,

Åí30 or, where application is made using the ARTL System, Åí20 for each title sheet affected.".

2. Reports

When application is made —

(a) on Form 10 for a report prior to first registration 28.50
(b) on Form 11 for continuation of report prior to first registration 16.50
(c) on Form 12 for a report over registered subjects 28.50
(d) on Form 13 for continuation of report over registered subjects 16.50
(e) on Form 14 for a report to ascertain whether or not subjects have been registered.................. 28.50
(f) on Form P16 for comparison of a bounding description with the Ordnance Map separately from item (a) above 28.50
(g) on Form P17 for comparison of the boundaries on the title plan with the Ordnance Map separately from item (c) above 28.50
(h) on Form P16 for comparison of a bounding description with the Ordnance Map in conjunction with item (a) above, a combined fee of 41.00
(i) on Form P17 for comparison of the boundaries on the title plan with the Ordnance Map in conjunction with item (c) above, a combined fee of.. 41.00

3. Miscellaneous services

A. Applications made

Where application is made_

(a) on Form 5 for noting of an overriding interest etc... £30.00
for each title sheet affected
(b) on Form 9 for rectification of the register... £30.00
(c) for checking the boundaries of adjoining properties... £20.00
(d) for withdrawal of an application under rule 11 of the Land Registration (Scotland) Rules 2006 .. £30.00
(e) for the provision of information from a deed or document in the Land Register archive, for each such deed or document.. £8.00

Where the application is to register a Tree Preservation Order or a Compulsory Purchase Order, £30 for each title sheet affected.

B. Applications rejected

Where the application is rejected under rule 13 of the Land Registration (Scotland) Rules 2006.. £30.00

Part II — GENERAL REGISTER OF SASINES
RECORDING FEES

A. Conveyances

(1) Where the recording of a deed or document to which paragraph (3) applies is made, the fee will, subject to paragraphs (4) to (6), be calculated on the amount of the consideration or value, whichever is the greater, of the heritable subjects transferred, passing or to which the recording relates.

(2) Subject to paragraph (7) and Part III of this Schedule, the fee will be at the rates shown in Table A in Part IV of this Schedule.

(3) This paragraph applies to the recording of–

(a)   a conveyance, including absolute conveyance, voluntary or judicial, either for a consideration or as a gift or in implement of trust or other purpose;

(b) a long lease;

(c) completion of title by decree or by notice of title; and

(d) all other deeds transferring an absolute right to heritable subjects.

(4) Where the consideration consists of a yearly or periodical payment, the consideration will be calculated at 10 years' purchase.

(5) Where the application is to record the grant of a long lease the fee will be calculated on the consideration (if any) provided for the grant plus ten times the relevant rent.

(6) Where an assignation of a long lease is recorded, the fee will be calculated on the consideration (if any) provided for the assignation plus ten times the annual rent payable at the date an application for recording is made.

(7) Where application is made to record a notice of title_

(a) along with another deed granting a long lease or a servitude over the whole or any part of the same subjects,

(b) on behalf of a fire and rescue authority, joint fire and rescue board, local authority, police authority, valuation authority or the Scottish Children's Reporter Administration, completing title as statutory successor of a previous authority,

(c) on behalf of a Health Board or Special Health Board, completing title as transferee in terms of an order made under section 2 of the National Health Service (Scotland) Act 1978,

£30.

B. Heritable securities

In respect of the recording of a heritable security, including the constitution, transfer, postponement, corroboration or extinction of a security, £30.

C. Recording by memorandum

Where any writ is presented in the Register of Sasines for recording by memorandum, £30 for each memorandum.

Part III — Fees for Registrations and Recordings in both the Land and Sasine Registers

1. Recording and Registration Fees for Single Transactions effected by more than One Deed and/or Application

A. Interests in land other than heritable securities

Where a single transaction is given effect to in a deed or deeds presented for recording in the Register of Sasines and/or by an application or applications for registration in the Land Register, and due notice is given to the Keeper of the nature of that transaction,

(a) where the transaction is first given effect to by a deed presented in the Register of Sasines, the fee to be charged for the first deed presented will be calculated on the amount of the consideration, or the total value of the heritable interest created, granted or transferred, whichever is the greater, and shall be at the rates shown in Table A in Part IV of this Schedule, plus a fee of £30 for every related deed presented in the Register of Sasines and for every title sheet affected by a related application for registration in the Land Register; or

(b) where the transaction is first given effect to by an application for registration in the Land Register, the fee to be charged in respect of the first application will be calculated on the amount of the consideration, or the total value of the interest in land created, granted or transferred, whichever is the greater, and shall be at the rates shown in Table A in Part IV of this Schedule, plus a fee of £30 for every other title sheet affected by that application and by every other related application, and for every related deed presented for recording in the Register of Sasines.";

B. Heritable securities

Where a single transaction is given effect to in a deed or deeds presented for recording in the Register of Sasines and/or by application or applications for registration in the Land Register, and due notice of the nature of that transaction is given to the Keeper, £30 in respect of that transaction, deed or application, plus £30 for every related application or every related deed presented in the Retister of Sasines and for each title sheed attected by every related application for registration in the Land Register.

Note: In this Part, "related" means giving effect to the same single transaction.

C. Dual registration

Where an application for registration in the Land Register or for recording a deed, notice or order in the Register of Sasines comprises an application for dual registration or an application for variation of a title condition and no fee is provided in respect of such application under Heads A and B of Parts I and II a fixed fee shall be charged in respect of that application

2. Miscellaneous

A. Industrial and Provident Society receipts

Where application is made for registration or recording of receipts under the Industrial and Provident Societies Act 1965, 25 pence.

B. Other Deeds and Events

Where application is made for registration or recording of other deeds and events not included under paragraphs A or B of Parts I and II or paragraph C of this Part, £30 for each title sheet affected or each deed recorded in the Register of Sasines.

TABLE A

Consideration or value	£	Fee £
Not exceeding	50,000	30
	100,000	100
	150,000	200
	200,000	300
	300,000	400
	500,000	500
	700,000	600
	1,000,000	700
	2,000,000	1,000
	3,000,000	3,000
	5,000,000	5,000
Exceeding	5,000,000	7,500

TABLE B (ARTL applications)

Consideration or value	£	Fee £
Not exceeding	50,000	20
	100,000	75
	150,000	150
	200,000	225
	300,000	300
	500,000	375
	700,000	450
	1,000,000	550
	2,000,000	800
	3,000,000	2,500
	5,000,000	4,500
Exceeding	5,000,000	7,000

PART V — REGISTER OF INHIBITIONS AND ADJUDICATIONS

Registration Fees   £

For each document 15.00

PART VI — REGISTER OF DEEDS ETC., REGISTER OF PROTESTS AND REGISTER OF JUDGMENTS

Registration Fees   £

For a document 10.00

Note: The extracting and authentication of the first or only extract is included in the fees.

PART VII — REGISTER OF SERVICE OF HEIRS

Omitted by SSI 2006 No 600.

PART VIII — REGISTER OF THE GREAT SEAL

Registration Fees   £

1. For a charter of incorporation 250.00

2. For a Crown grant of land

    (1) unsealed deed 60.00

    (2) sealed deed 250.00

3. For a Commission 630.00

PART IX — REGISTER OF THE CACHET SEAL

For each impression 30.00

PART X — REGISTER OF THE QUARTER SEAL

Registration Fees   £

For each Gift of Ultimus Haeres.. 130.00

PART XI — OTHER FEES

1. For each Certificate issued under the Civil Jurisdiction and Judgments Act 1982 .... 30.00

2. For each Certificate of Custody when a deed is retained for permanent preservation 20.00

PART XII — FEES APPLICABLE TO ALL REGISTERS

FEES FOR THE PROVISION OF INFORMATION

A. General Register of Sasines

1. Presentment Book   £

    (a) Per search against a name... 1.80

    (b) Per search against an address 1.80

    (c) Per search against a minute number 1.80

2   Minute Book

    (a) Per search against a name... 1.80

    (b) Per search against an address 1.80

    (c) Per search against a minute number 1.80

3. Search Sheet

    (a) Per search against a name... Nil

    (b) Per search against an address... Nil

    (c) Per search by search sheet number 1.80

    (d) Per view of any individual search sheet 1.80

    (e) The provision of information from any other index, volume, document or process 1.80

Note: No fee will be charged for a search under number 1, 2 or 3 above which produces a nil return.

B. Land Register of Scotland

1. Application Record   £

    (a) Per search against a name... 1.80

    (b) Per search against an address... 1.80

    (c) Per search against an application number 1.80

    (d) Per search against a title number 1.80

2.   Title Sheet   £

    (a) Per search against a name 1.80

    (b) Per search against an address 1.80

    (c) Per search against a title number 1.80

    (d) Per view of the title sheet affecting one interest in land 1.80

Note: Where on the same occasion a view of the title sheet is made against an entry identified in the course of an initial search as per 2(a) and (b), no fee is payable in respect of the initial search

3.   Index Map

    (a) Per search by navigation .... Nil

    (b) Per search by address .... Nil

    (c) Per search by title number .... Nil

    (d) Per search by grid reference .... Nil

    (e) Per seed rectangle search £1.80

    (f) Per seed point search £1.80

Note: Where on the same occasion a view of the title sheet is made against an entry identified in the course of an initial search as per 3(e) and (f), no fee is payable in respect of the initial search

4.   The provision of information from any other index, volume, document or process 1.80

5.   Per property price search .... Nil

C.   Books of Council and Session

For each search in the Register of Deeds or Register of Judgements Index against:

1.   a name 1.80

2.   a pursuer/petitioner 1.80

3.   a defender/respondent 1.80

4.   a judgement number 1.80

D.   Register of Inhibitions and Adjudications

1.   For each group of 6 names or fewer searched against 1.80

2.   For provision of a paper copy of the daily minutes (per day) 19.50

3.   Per search of a specified minute number 1.80

Note: A search includes a print disclosing relevant entries if requested within 7 working days of the date of the original search.

EXTRACTING AND COPYING FEES   £

1.   For a plain copy or duplicate 8.00

2.   For an official extract or certified copy 15.00

3.   For an official extract obtained from the National Archives of Scotland 5.00

4.   For an office copy 15.00

5.   For each additional copy of any deed or document requested at the same time as registration
     in the General Register of Sasines or Book of Council and Session of that document 8.00

3.   *Other Services*

For any service not listed above. .... A fee being the full value of the work and materials involved

DATA EXTRACTIONS

Data Extraction Fee per County is based on the table below

1.   For information on Sales for Consideration comprising reports in a
     spreadsheet format containing a data extraction of residential sales ....   A fee of £4.50 per month for the whole of Scotland

2. For information on Land Values comprising reports in a spreadsheet of
   sales from the Land Register of Scotland, per Land Values script............ A fee of £622 per month for
   the whole of Scotland

3. For information on a particular Creditor or Legal AgentComprising a
   spreadsheet list of deeds submitted to LRS by Creditor or Legal Agent ... A fee of £100 per month or
   £100 per quarter

4. For a Data Set of Registration County Boundaries .... A fee of £100

5. For information on General Register of Sasines minutes............................ A fee of £252 per month for
   the whole of Scotland

Breakdown of Data Extraction Costs by Registration County

	Land Values	Sales for Consideration
Aberdeen	£42.00	£29.00
Angus	£23.00	£17.00
Argyll	£9.00	£7.00
Ayr	£38.00	£27.00
Banff	£10.00	£7.00
Berwick	£5.00	£4.00
Bute	£5.00	£4.00
Caithness	£8.00	£6.00
Clackmannan	£5.00	£4.00
Dumbarton	£23.00	£17.00
Dumfries	£10.00	£7.00
East Lothian	£9.00	£7.00
Fife	£39.00	£27.00
Glasgow	£68.00	£48.00
Inverness	£14.00	£10.00
Kincardine	£8.00	£6.00
Kinross	£5.00	£4.00
Kirkcudbright	£5.00	£4.00
Lanark	£56.00	£40.00
Midlothian	£80.00	£57.00
Moray	£16.00	£12.00
Nairn	£5.00	£4.00
Orkney & Zetland	£8.00	£6.00
Peebles	£5.00	£4.00
Perth	£15.00	£11.00
Renfrew	£35.00	£24.00
Ross & Cromarty	£18.00	£13.00
Roxburgh	£5.00	£4.00
Selkirk	£5.00	£4.00
Stirling	£23.00	£17.00
Sutherland	£5.00	£4.00
West Lothian	£15.00	£11.00
Wigtown	£5.00	£4.00
Scotland	£622.00	£450.00

REPORTS

1. For a report on Post Code Sectors or District comprising the average price
   and volume of sales. .... A fee of £105 per month
   or £105 per quarter

Note:

The information for each stated time period aims to cover all sales of properties, where applications are
received for registration with Registers of Scotland in that period.

The reports includes both cash sales and properties bought with a mortgage, and right to buy sales of council
houses to sitting tenants. The analysis aims to exclude single sales of blocks of properties.

Calculations in standard reports are based on transactions between £20,000 and £1,000,000. Bespoke
Reports can be for sales from £5,000 upwards.

Table of Fees payable in The National Archives of Scotland

Act of Sederunt (Fees in the National Archives of Scotland) 2003
(SSI 2003 No 234)

This Table of Fees is printed as amended by: Act of Sederunt (Fees in the National Archives of Scotland) 2005 (SSI 2005 No 77) which came into force on 1st March 2005.)

SCHEDULE
TABLE OF FEES

PART I — INSPECTION FEES

Column 1	Column 2
For the inspection of each volume, document or process, and the production of associated copies for each document or process therein	£6.00
Note: Fees are remitted for the inspection of records for historical or literary purposes in terms of section 10 of the Public Records (Scotland) Act 1937.	

PART II — SEARCH FEES

Column 1	Column 2
For personal searches in the records, for each search	£40.00
Notes:	
(1) The Keeper of the Records of Scotland may carry out a search in the records of the National Archives of Scotland for any person, and for any search the Keeper shall —	
(i) impose an additional charge based on the cost of carrying out that search, which cost shall include the cost of any copying requested or required as part of that search;	
(ii) provide an estimate to that person of the amount of that additional charge; and	
(iii) require that person to pay a deposit of a sum not exceeding £40 before carrying out that search.	
(2) The Keeper of the Records of Scotland may reduce or waive the charge or deposit payable for any search.	

PART III — COPYING FEES

Column 1	Column 2
1. Reprographic services, including digital images and output to microfilm and microfiche, are provided on a cost recovery basis, and National Archives of Scotland will provide an estimate of the cost on request.	As estimated
Notes:	
(1) A minimum charge of £6.00 will be payable for any of the above services.	
(2) An additional charge may be payable for work of unusual difficulty, or requiring special attention.	
2. Authentication: for each extract or certified copy, in addition to the reprographic charge and handling charge.	£4.00

PARTY LITIGANTS

Act of Sederunt (Expenses of Party Litigants) 1976 (SI 1976 No 1606)

[Amended by Act of Sederunt (Expenses of Party Litigants) (Amendment) 1983 (SI 1983 No 1438).]

2.—(1) Where in any proceedings in the Court of Session or the sheriff court, any expenses of a party litigant are ordered to be paid by any other party to the proceedings or in any other way, the auditor may, subject to the following provisions of this Rule, allow as expenses such sums as appear to the auditor to be reasonable having regard to all the circumstances in respect of —

  (*a*) work done which was reasonably required in connection with the cause, up to the maximum of two- thirds of the sum allowable to a solicitor for that work under the table of fees for solicitors in judicial proceedings; and

  (*b*) outlays reasonably incurred for the proper conduct of the cause.

(2) Without prejudice to the generality of paragraph (1) above, the circumstances to which the auditor shall have regard in determining what sum, if any, to allow in respect of any work done, shall include —

  (*a*) the nature of the work;

  (*b*) the time taken and the time reasonably required to do the work;

  (*c*) the amount of time spent in respect of which there is no loss of earnings;

  (*d*) the amount of any earnings lost during the time required to do the work;

  (*e*) the importance of the cause to the party litigant;

  (*f*) the complexity of the issues involved in the cause.

(3) In this Rule —

  (*a*) the word "auditor" includes any person taxing or otherwise determining a claim for expenses incurred in any proceedings in the Court of Session or in the sheriff court;

  (*b*) the expression "remunerative time" in relation to a litigant, means time when he is earning or would have been earning but for work done in or in connection with proceedings in court;

  (*c*) the expression "leisure time" in relation to a litigant, means time other than remunerative time.

  (*d*) the expression "table of fees for solicitors in judicial proceedings" means —

    (i) in relation to a cause in the Court of Session, the table of fees in Rule 347 of the Rules of Court in force at the time the work is done; and

    (ii) in relation to an ordinary action in the sheriff court, the table of fees in Schedule 2 to the Act of Sederunt (Alteration of Sheriff Court Fees) 1971 in force at the time the work is done.

STAMPS AND TAXES

Stamp Duty and Stamp Duty Land Tax

A. The following provisions apply to instruments executed before 1st October 1999.

For provisions applying to instruments executed on or after 1st October 1999, see section B below.

Unless otherwise stated, references are to Stamp Act 1891, as amended.

Agreement for lease or tack or for any letting. *See* "Lease", and sec. 75 (as amended by Finance Act 1984, sec. 111).

Agreement for lease. *See* "Lease" and Finance Act 1994, sec. 240.

Agreement for sale. *See* "Conveyance or transfer on sale" and sec. 59.

Annuity, conveyance in consideration of. *See* "Conveyance or transfer on sale", and sec. 56.

Purchase of. *See* "Conveyance or transfer on sale", "Bond, covenant or instrument" and sec. 60.

Instruments relating to, upon any other occasion. *See* "Bond, covenant or instrument".

Appointment of a new trustee, and appointment in execution of a power of any property, or of any use, share, or interest in any property, by any instrument not being a will. — Duty payable is nil.

A conveyance of the trust property is exempt provided it is certified under the Stamp Duty (Exempt Instruments) Regulations 1987 (*see below*).

Assignation, upon a sale or otherwise. *See* "Conveyance or transfer on sale".

Assurance. *See* "Policy".

Assumption of new trustee (and conveyance). *See* "Appointment."

Attorney, Letter or Power of. — Duty payable is nil.

Bearer instrument

Finance Act 1963, sec. 59 [repealed by FA 1999 in relation to bearer instruments issued on or after 1 October 1999]. See replacemnet provisions at FA 1999, sec 113

(1) Inland bearer instrument (other than deposit certificate for overseas stock). — Duty of an amount equal to three times the transfer duty.

(2) Overseas bearer instrument (other than deposit certificate for overseas stock or bearer instrument by usage). — Duty of an amount equal to three times the transfer duty.

(3) Instrument excepted from paragraph (1) or (2) of this heading. — Duty of 10p for every £50 or part of £50 of the market value.

(4) Inland or overseas bearer instrument given in substitution for a like instrument duly stamped *ad valorem* (whether under this heading or not). — Duty of 10p.

Exemptions

(a) Instrument constituting, or used for transferring stock which is exempt from all stamp duties on transfer by virtue of general exemption (1) in this Schedule or of any other enactment.

(b) Bearer letter of allotment, bearer letter of rights, scrip, scrip certificate to bearer or other similar instrument, to bearer. (With effect from 25th March 1986 this exemption was repealed — Finance Act 1986, sec. 80.)

(c) Renounceable letter of allotment, letter of rights or other similar instrument where the rights under the letter or instrument are renounceable not later than six months after the issue of the letter or instrument (Finance Act 1985, sec. 85, Sched. 24).

Paired shares

See Finance Act 1988, sec. 143, as amended by Finance Act 1990, sec. 112 for the detailed provisions which apply where the Articles of Association of a United Kingdom company and the equivalent constitution of a foreign incorporated company each provide that no share of that company shall be transferred except as part of a unit consisting of one share of each company.

Bond in relation to any annuity upon the original creation and sale thereof. *See* "Conveyance or transfer on sale", and sec. 60.

Bond, covenant, or instrument of any kind whatsoever

The charge to duty under paras. (1) and (2) — securities for annuities other than superannuation annuities and for certain other periodic sums — was abolished as from 1st August 1971 except as regards instruments increasing the rent reserved by another instrument (Finance Act 1971, sec. 64).

The charge to duty under para. (3) was abolished by Finance Act 1989, sec. 173(1) in relation to instruments made after 31st December 1989.

Conveyance or transfer on sale of any property.

Definition

The Stamp Act 1891, sec. 54 [repealed by FA 1999, sec 139], provides that "Conveyance on sale" includes every instrument and every decree or order, whereby any property or any estate or interest in any property upon the sale thereof is transferred to or vested in a purchaser.

The definition includes a decree or order for or having the effect of an order for foreclosure, provided that (*a*) the *ad valorem* stamp shall not exceed the duty on a sum equal to the value of the property, and where the decree or order states that value, that statement is conclusive; (*b*) where *ad valorem* stamp is paid on the decree or order, any conveyance following is exempt from *ad valorem* duty.

By Finance Act 1900, sec. 10, a conveyance on sale made for any consideration in respect whereof it is chargeable with *ad valorem* duty, and in further consideration of a covenant by the purchaser to make, or of his having previously made, any substantial improvement of or addition to the property, or of any covenant relating to the subject matter of the conveyance, is not chargeable, with any duty in respect of such further consideration.

Stamp duty is chargeable on VAT inclusive consideration in respect of certain commercial property transactions. See Statement of Practice SP11/91.

Statement of Practice (SP8/93) issued on 12th July 1993 sets out the practice of the Commissioners for HMRC in relation to the stamp duty chargeable on the conveyance of a new or partly constructed building.

Stock and securities

Sec. 55 provides that where the consideration, or part of the consideration, consists of any stock or marketable security, the conveyance is to be charged with *ad valorem* duty in respect of the value of the stock or security.

It is immaterial whether, at the time of the execution of the conveyance on sale, the stock or marketable security is or has been issued or is to be issued; and in a case where the stock or marketable security is to be issued, when it is to be, or is, issued and whether the issue is certain or contingent. Where the consideration, or part of the consideration, consists of any security not being a marketable security, the conveyance is to be charged with *ad valorem* duty in respect of the amount due on the date thereof for principal and interest on the security.

Consideration of periodic payments

Sec. 56 provides that where the consideration, or part of the consideration, consists of money payable periodically for a definite period not exceeding 20 years, so that the total amount to be paid can be previously ascertained, the conveyance is charged in respect of that consideration with *ad valorem* duty on such total amount.

Where the consideration, or part of the consideration, consists of money payable periodically for a definite period exceeding 20 years, or in perpetuity, or for any indefinite period not terminable with life, the conveyance is charged in respect of that consideration with *ad valorem* duty on the total amount, which will or may be payable during 20 years after the date of the instrument.

Where the consideration, or any part of the consideration, consists of money payable periodically during any life or lives, the conveyance is charged in respect of that consideration with *ad valorem* duty on the amount which will or may be payable during the period of 12 years after the date of the instrument.

Consideration of a debt

Sec. 57, as amended by Finance Act 1980, sec. 102, provides that where property is conveyed wholly or partially in consideration for a debt due to the transferee, the consideration for the transfer is the amount of the value of the property if less than the face value of the debt. Where this rule applies conveyances must be adjudicated. Sec. 57 still applies if the debt is only part of the consideration. (See Statement of Practice SP6/90.)

Property conveyed in separate parcels

Sec. 58 provides that where property contracted to be sold for one consideration for the whole is conveyed to the purchaser in separate parcels by different instruments, the consideration is apportioned in such manner as the parties think fit, so that a distinct consideration for each separate parcel is set forth in the conveyance thereof, and such conveyance is charged with *ad valorem* duty in respect of such distinct consideration.

Where property contracted to be purchased for one consideration for the whole by two or more persons jointly, or by any person for himself and others, or wholly for others, is conveyed in parcels by separate instruments to the persons by or for whom the same was purchased for distinct parts of the consideration, the conveyance of each separate part or parcel is charged with *ad valorem* duty in respect of the distinct part of the consideration therein specified.

Where there are several instruments for completing the purchaser's title to the property sold, the principal conveyance only is charged with *ad valorem* duty, and the others are charged with such other duty as they may be liable to, but not exceeding the *ad valorem* duty in respect of the principal instrument.

Sub-sales

Sec. 58(4), (5) and (6) provide that where a person having contracted for the purchase of any property, but not having obtained a conveyance, contracts to sell to any other person, and the property is conveyed immediately to the sub-purchaser, the conveyance is charged with *ad valorem* duty in respect of the consideration moving from the sub-purchaser or last sub-purchaser whether higher or lower than the original price.

Where a person having contracted for the purchase of any property, but not having obtained a conveyance, contracts to sell the whole or any part or parts to any other person or persons, and the property is in consequence conveyed by the original seller to different persons in parcels, the conveyance of each parcel is charged with *ad valorem* duty in respect only of the consideration moving from the sub-purchaser thereof, without regard to the amount of value of the original consideration.

Where a sub-purchaser takes an actual conveyance of the interest of the person immediately selling to him, which is chargeable with *ad valorem* duty in respect of the consideration moving from him, and is stamped accordingly, any conveyance to be afterwards made to him of the same property by the original seller is chargeable only with such other duty as it may be liable to, but not exceeding the *ad valorem* duty.

Finance Act 1984, sec. 112, amends the provisions of subs. (6) so that, for sub-sales entered into after 19th March 1984, these provisions will not apply where the chargeable consideration is less than the value of the property immediately before the sub-sale. It was amended by Finance Act 1985, sec. 82.

Contracts chargeable as conveyances

Sec. 59 Repealed by FA 1999, s. 139 and Sch. 20, Pt. V(2) in relation to instruments executed, or bearer instruments issued, on or after 1 October 1999 but as regards unit trust schemes subject to FA 1999, Sch. 20, Pt. V(2), para. 2. The repeal took effect from 6 February 2000 as regards unit trust schemes, by virtue of FA 1999, s. 122(4) and Sch. 19.

Creation of annuities, etc.

Sec. 60 provides that where upon the sale of any annuity or other right not before in existence such annuity or other right is not created by actual grant or conveyance, but is only secured by bond, covenant, contract or otherwise, the bond or other instrument, or some one of such instruments, is charged with the same duty as an actual grant or conveyance.

Ascertainment of principal writ

Sec. 61 provides that where there is a disposition or assignation executed by the seller, and any other instrument is executed for completing the title, the disposition or assignation is deemed the principal instrument.

In any other case the parties may determine for themselves which of several instruments is to be deemed the principal instrument, and may pay the *ad valorem* duty thereon accordingly.

Voluntary conveyance

The *ad valorem* duty on gifts inter vivos was abolished by Finance Act 1985, sec. 82. Conveyances by way of gift are, with effect from 1st May 1987, exempt from duty — *see* Stamp Duty (Exempt Instruments) Regulations 1987.

Sales of land where the consideration is unascertainable

Where in an instrument executed after 7th December 1993 the consideration for a sale of land is unascertainable, the transfer will be liable to *ad valorem* duty on the market value of the property immediately before the transfer was executed. (Finance Act 1994, sec. 242)

Conveyance or Transfer of any kind not hereinbefore described 50p

AD VALOREM DUTY ON CONVEYANCE OR TRANSFER ON SALE OR PREMIUM FOR A LEASE

From 16th March 1999 to 27th March 2000, the rates of stamp duty payable in respect of transfers of land and buildings (unless the transfer is pursuant to a contract made on or before 9th March 1999) (Finance Act 1999, Sch 13 para 4) are as undernoted:

Consideration or premium		Instrument certified at £60,000	Instrument certified at £250,000	Instrument certified at £500,000	Instrument not certified
Exceeds	Does not exceed				
–	£60,000	nil	–	–	£3.50 per £100 or part thereof
£600,000	£250,000	–	1 per 100 or part thereof	–	£3.50 per £100 or part thereof
£250,00	£500,00	–	–	£2.50 per 100 or part thereof	£3.50 per £100 or part thereof
£500,00	–	–	–	–	£3.50 per £100 or part thereof

(1) An instrument which is "certified" at a particular amount is one which contains a statement certifying that the transaction effected by the instrument does not form part of a larger transaction or series of transactions in respect of which the amount or value, or aggregate amount or value, of the consideration exceeds that amount. For the purpose of determining the amount at which an instrument is to be certified the consideration for any sale or contract or agreement for the sale of goods, wares or merchandise should (except where the instrument is itself an actual conveyance or transfer of the goods, wares or merchandise, with or without other property) be disregarded. *If not in gremio of the deed, the certificate should be signed by all granters.*

Note: Conveyances of exempt property will not require the certificate of value provided for under Finance Act 1958, sec. 34 (4) (Finance Act 1991, sec. 113).

(2) Transfers of stock or marketable securities

With effect from 27th October 1986 the stamp duty payable was reduced to 50p for every £100 of consideration.

CREST — the system of paperless share transfers was introduced in July 1996.

Finance Act 1996, sec. 186, provides that stamp duty shall not be chargeable on an instrument effecting a transfer of securities if the transferee is a member of an electronic transfer system and the instrument is in a form which will, in accordance with the rules of the system, ensure that the securities are changed from being held in certificated form to being held in uncertificated form so that title to them may become transferable by means of the system.

Paperless transfers are liable to stamp duty reserve tax rather than stamp duty. For the detailed provisions, see Finance Act 1996, secs. 187–196, and Finance Act 1997, Part VI.

(3) Bearer shares

The rate of stamp duty on the issue of inland bearer instruments was reduced to 1.5% on or after 27th October 1986, and the rate was similarly reduced in relation to overseas bearer instruments on the first transfer in the United Kingdom on or after that date.

(4) Voluntary conveyances

The duty on such conveyances is abolished (Finance Act 1985, sec. 82), but see Stamp Duty (Exempt Instruments) Regulations 1987.

(5) Charities

No duty is chargeable on conveyances or transfers on sale, voluntary dispositions and leases, made to bodies of persons or trusts established for charitable purposes only. The instrument must be adjudicated (Finance Act 1982, sec. 129).

(6) Loan capital

Certain transfers are exempt (Finance Act 1986, sec. 79).

(7) Sale of houses at discount by local authority

See Finance Act 1981, sec. 107 (as amended by Finance Act 1984, sec. 110). Stamp duty is payable on discounted value. This relief is now available in transactions with Housing Action Trusts established under the Housing Act 1988.

(8) Divorce

Transfer of property between spouses in connection with the legal break-up of a marriage are exempt, but see Stamp Duty (Exempt Instruments) Regulations 1987.

(9) Death

Deeds of family arrangement and deeds of variation are exempt, but see Stamp Duty (Exempt Instruments) Regulations 1987.

(10) Unit trusts

Stamp duty is not chargeable on or after the 27th July 1989 in respect of the transfer of any unit in an authorised unit trust scheme, the funds of which can only be invested, such that the trustees are chargeable on income under Sched. C or under Sched. D Case III (Finance Act 1989, sec. 174).

Transfers of property between associated bodies

The provisions regarding relief from stamp duty are contained in Finance Act 1930, sec. 42, as amended by Finance Act 1995, sec. 132.

Rent to Loan Schemes

The Finance Act 1993 sec. 203 provides where:-

(a) a person exercises the right to purchase a house by way of the rent to loan scheme under Part III of the Housing (Scotland) Act 1987, and

(b) in pursuance of the exercise of that right a heritable disposition of the house is executed in favour of him,

The consideration for the sale shall be taken to be equal to the price which, by virtue of section 62 of the Housing (Scotland) Act 1987, would be payable for the house if the person were exercising the right to purchase under section 61 of that Act.

Exempt instruments

Under the Stamp Duty (Exempt Instruments) Regulations 1987 which came into force on 1st May 1987 many documents formerly liable to 50p duty are now exempt subject to a certificate (it is not necessary for these documents to be submitted for adjudication). The documents once certified can be sent directly to the registrar or other person who needs to act upon them, and should not be sent to the Stamp Office.

The documents which are exempt are as follows:

(a) The vesting of property subject to a trust in the trustees of the trust on the appointment of a new trustee, or in the continuing trustees on the retirement of a trustee.

(b) The conveyance or transfer of property the subject of a specific devise or legacy to the beneficiary named in the will (or his nominee).

(c) The conveyance or transfer of property which forms part of an intestate's estate to the person entitled on intestacy (or his nominee).

(d) The appropriation of property within sec. 84 (4) of the Finance Act 1985 (death: appropriation in satisfaction of a general legacy of money) or sec. 84 (5) or (7) of that Act (death: appropriation in satisfaction of any interest of surviving spouse and in Scotland also of any interest of issue).

(e) The conveyance or transfer of property which forms part of the residuary estate of a testator to a beneficiary (or his nominee) entitled solely by virtue of his entitlement under the will.

(f) The conveyance or transfer of property out of a settlement in or towards satisfaction of a beneficiary's interest, not being an interest acquired for money or money's worth, being a conveyance or transfer constituting a distribution of property in accordance with the provisions of the settlement.

(g) The conveyance or transfer of property on and in consideration only of marriage to a party to the marriage (or his nominee) or to trustees to be held on the terms of a settlement made in consideration only of the marriage.

(h) The conveyance or transfer of property within sec. 83 (1) of the Finance Act 1985 (transfers in connection with divorce etc).

(i) The conveyance or transfer by the liquidator of property which formed part of the assets of the company in liquidation to a shareholder of that company (or his nominee) in or towards satisfaction of the shareholder's rights on a winding-up.

(j) The grant in fee simple of an easement in or over land for no consideration in money or money's worth.

(k) The grant of a servitude for no consideration in money or money's worth.

(l) The conveyance or transfer of property operating as a voluntary disposition *inter vivos* for no consideration in money or money's worth nor any consideration referred to in sec. 57 of the Stamp Act 1891 (conveyance in consideration of a debt etc).

(m) The conveyance or transfer of property by an instrument within sec. 84 (1) of the Finance Act 1985 (death: varying disposition).

(n) The declaration of any use or trust of or concerning a life policy, or property representing, or benefits arising under, a life policy.

Certificate of exemption

The certificate should be included as part of the document or endorsed upon the document or firmly attached to the document (if prepared separately); and should include the category into which the document falls and a sufficient description of the document where the certificate is separate but physically attached. It should also be signed by the transferor or grantor, or by a solicitor on his behalf. (An authorised agent of the transferor or grantor who is not a solicitor may also sign provided he states the capacity in which he signs, confirms that he is authorised and that he has knowledge of the facts of the transaction.)

A suggested form of words is:

"I/We hereby certify that this instrument falls within category ... [*here insert the appropriate letter*] in the Schedule to the Stamp Duty (Exempt Instruments) Regulations 1987."

Counterpart. *See* "Duplicate or counterpart".

Covenant in relation to any annuity upon the original creation and sale thereof. *See* "Conveyance or transfer on sale", and sec. 60.

Covenant in relation to any annuity (*except upon the original creation and sale thereof*) or to other periodical payments. See "Bond, covenant or instrument".

Covenant. Any separate deed of covenant. — Duty payable is nil.

Crown. Where any conveyance, transfer or lease is made to a minister of the Crown, no duty shall be chargeable on such instrument executed on or after 1st August 1987.

Declaration of any use or trust of or concerning any property by any writing, not being a will or an instrument chargeable with *ad valorem* duty as a unit trust instrument — Duty payable is 50p.

Disposition containing constitution of feu or ground annual right. *See* "Conveyance or transfer on sale", and sec. 56.

Disposition of any property or of any right or interest therein not described in this schedule. — Duty payable is 50p.

Divorce. Transfers of property between spouses (Finance Act 1985, sec. 83).

With effect from 1st May 1987, such instruments are now exempt from duty, if certified — *see* Stamp Duty (Exempt Instruments) Regulations 1987.

Duplicate or counterpart of any instrument chargeable with any duty.

Where such duty does not amount to 50p, *the* same duty as the original instrument. In any other case the duty payable is 50p (Finance Act 1974, Sched. 11.- Repealed by FA 1999, s. 139 and Sch. 20, Pt. V(2) in relation to instruments executed, or bearer instruments issued, on or after 1 October 1999 but as regards unit trust schemes subject to FA 1999, Sch. 20, Pt. V(2), para. 2. The repeal took effect from 6 February 2000 as regards unit trust schemes, by virtue of FA 1999, s. 122(4) and FA 1999, Sch. 19.)

Sec. 72 provides that the duplicate or counterpart of an instrument chargeable with duty (except the counterpart of an instrument chargeable as a lease such counterpart not being executed by or on behalf of any lessor or grantor) is not deemed duly stamped unless it is stamped as an original instrument, or unless it appears by some stamp impressed thereon that the full and proper duty has been paid upon the original instrument of which it is the duplicate or counterpart.

Exchange or excambion, instruments effecting.

Sec. 73 provides that where upon the exchange of any heritable property for any other heritable property or upon the partition or division of any heritable property, any consideration exceeding in amount or value one hundred pounds is paid or given, for equality the principal or only instrument is charged with the same *ad valorem* duty as a conveyance on sale for the consideration, and with that duty only, and where there are several instruments for completing the title of either party, the principal instrument is to be ascertained, and the other instruments are to be charged with duty in the manner hereinbefore provided in the case of several instruments of conveyanceIn any other case the duty payable is 50p.

From 8th December 1993, the head of charge "Exchange" no longer applies. (Sec. 73 of the Stamp Act 1891 was repealed by FA 1999, sec. 139 and Sch. 20, Pt. V(2) in relation to instruments executed, or bearer instruments issued, on or after 1 October 1999 but as regards unit trust schemes subject to FA 1999, Sch. 20, Pt. V(2), para. 2. The repeal took effect from 6 February 2000 as regards unit trust schemes, by virtue of FA 1999, s. 122(4) and Sch. 19.)

Factory in the nature of a letter or power of attorney. — Duty payable is nil. (Abolished by Finance Act 1985, sec. 85, Sched. 24.)

Family arrangements, deeds of family arrangement.

With effect from 1st May 1987, all qualifying deeds of family arrangement and similar instruments are exempt from duty if certified — *see* Stamp Duty (Exempt Instruments) Regulations 1987.

Fixed Duties. In relation to instruments executed on or after 1 October 1999 the amount of fixed stamp duty is £5 (Finance Act 1999, sec. 112(2))

Feu contract or charter. *See* "Conveyance or transfer on sale" under sub-heading Consideration of periodic payments, and sec. 56(2).

Gift. Duty payable is nil. (But *see* Stamp Duty (Exempt Instruments) Regulations 1987.)

Ground annual, contract of. *See* "Conveyance or transfer on sale" (under sub-heading Consideration of periodic payments).

Insurance. *See* Policy

Lease

Para. 1, was repealed by Finance Act 1963, Sched. 14, Part IV.

Para. 2 provides that, for any definite term less than a year:

(*a*) of any furnished house or apartments where the rent for such term exceeds £500, the duty payable is £1.00; and

(*b*) of any lands, tenements, or heritable subjects except or otherwise than aforesaid — the duty payable is the same as for a lease for a year at the rent reserved for the definite term.

Para. 3 provides that, for any other definite term or for any indefinite term:

Of any lands, tenements, or heritable subjects —

Where the consideration, or any part of the consideration, moving either to the lessor or to any other person, consists of any money, stock security or other property. (Finance Act 1994, sec. 241 (5) – was repealed by FA 1999, sec. 139 and Sch 20 Pt. V(2)).

In respect of such consideration, the same duty as a conveyance on a sale for the same consideration.

Where the consideration, or any part of the consideration, is any rent:

In respect of such consideration — If the rent, whether reserved as a yearly rent or otherwise, is at a rate or average rate: See table below.

TABLE OF STAMP DUTIES ON LEASES

Annual Rent		Term not exceeding 7 years or indefinite	Term exceeding 7 years but not exceeding 35 years	Term exceeding 35 years but not exceeding 100 years	Term exceeding 100 years
Exceeds	Does not exceed				
£	£	£	£	£	£
	5	NIL	0.10	0.60	1.20
5	10	NIL	0.20	1.20	2.40
10	15	NIL	0.30	1.80	3.60
15	20	NIL	0.40	2.40	4.80
20	25	NIL	0.50	3.00	6.00
25	50	NIL	1.00	6.00	12.00
50	75	NIL	1.50	9.00	18.00
75	100	NIL	2.00	12.00	24.00
100	150	NIL	3.00	18.00	36.00
150	200	NIL	4.00	24.00	48.00
200	250	NIL	5.00	30.00	60.00
250	300	NIL	6.00	36.00	72.00
300	350	NIL	7.00	42.00	84.00
350	400	NIL	8.00	48.00	96.00
400	450	NIL	9.00	54.00	108.00
450	500	NIL	10.00	60.00	120.00
500		50p per £50 or part of £50	1 per £50 or part of £50	£6 per £50 or part of £50	£12 per £50 or part of £50

This table is only applicaable for leases entered into before 1 December 2003.

Para. 4 provides that, on a lease any other kind whatsoever not herein before described, the duty payable is £2.00.

Where a lease attracts VAT, stamp duty is charged on the VAT inclusive consideration. See Statement of Practice SP11/91.

See Statement of Practice (8/93) in relation to stamp duty chargeable on the lease of a new or partly constructed building.

Leases between associated bodies — the provisions regarding relief from stamp duty are contained in Finance Act 1995, sec. 134.

See secs. 75 and 77.

If there is a consideration consisting of money, stock or security other than rent (*i.e.*, a grassum) it is chargeable with the same duty as the consideration in a conveyance on sale, and, if the rent does not exceed £300 a year, the same certificates of value, with the inclusion of the words "other than rent" after the word "consideration" and the same reduced rates of duty apply.

Note: For documents executed on or after 16th March 1993, the level of rent is increased to £600 a year.

Agreements for not more than 35 years or indefinite term

Sec. 75 (1) provides that an agreement for a lease or with respect to the letting of any lands, tenements, or heritable subjects, for any term not exceeding 35 years, or for any indefinite term, is charged with the same duty as if it were an actual lease or tack made for the term and consideration mentioned in the agreement.

Note: For the purposes of the said heading a lease granted for a fixed term and thereafter until determined shall be treated as a lease for a definite term equal to the fixed term together with such further period as must elapse before the earliest date at which the lease can be determined (Finance Act 1963, sec. 56 (3)).

Agreement entered into after 19th March 1984

If an agreement for a lease is entered into on or after 20th March 1984 it is chargeable as if it were the actual lease irrespective of the length of the term. Where the duty has been paid on an agreement for a lease the duty payable on the subsequent lease is reduced by the amount of duty paid on the agreement.

Where there is a conveyance or transfer of a freehold or leasehold interest subject to an agreement for a lease for more than 35 years, the conveyance or instrument of transfer is not to be taken as duly stamped unless the duty on the agreement is denoted on the conveyance, transfer or lease (Finance Act 1984, sec. 111).

Agreements for lease

Agreements for lease executed on or after 6th May 1994 can be submitted at the same time as the lease to which they relate without incurring a penalty for late stamping. This will apply as long as both lease and agreement are submitted within 30 days of the date of execution of the lease. (Finance Act 1994, sec. 240).

This provision applies to a lease which is in conformity with the agreement – i.e. relates to substantially the same property and term. From 6th May 1994 such a lease will not be duly stamped for the purposes of the Stamp Act unless either:-

    (i)   it is certified to the effect that there was no prior agreement, or

    (ii) it is denoted with a stamp showing that duty has been paid on the relevant agreement, or that the agreement was not liable to duty.

Penal rent or surrender of existing leases

Sec. 77 (1) provides that a lease or agreement for a lease, or with respect to any letting, is not charged with any duty in respect of any penal rent, or increased rent in the nature of a penal rent, thereby reserved or agreed to be reserved or made payable, or by reason of being made in consideration of the surrender or abandonment of any existing lease or agreement of or relating to the same subject-matter.

Subs. (2) provides that a lease made for any consideration in respect whereof it is chargeable with *ad valorem* duty, and in further consideration either of a covenant by the lessee to make, or of his having previously made, any substantial improvement of or addition to the property, or of any covenant relating to the matter of the lease, is not charged with any duty in respect of such further consideration. (*See* Revenue Act 1909, sec. 8.)

Subs. (5) provides that an instrument whereby the rent reserved by any other instrument chargeable with duty and duly stamped as a lease is increased, is not to be charged with duty otherwise than as a lease in consideration of the additional rent.

Further stamp duty may be payable on a Deed varying the terms of a lease so as to provide for payment of VAT by way of additional rent. See Statements of Practice SP11/91.

Agreements to surrender leases

Surrenders or renunciations of leases evidenced by a deed are chargeable to *ad valorem* duty. However, at present, where there is no deed and the lease is surrendered or renounced by operation of law, no charge to duty may arise. For agreements made after 7th December 1993 where there is no deed evidencing the surrender or the renunciation, the agreement to surrender or renounce will itself be chargeable to *ad valorem* duty. The charge will apply to any document evidencing the agreement or renunciation, whether it is a formal agreement or simply a letter outlining the terms of the procedure to be followed. (Finance Act 1994, sec. 243).

Shared ownership transactions

Certain leases are to be charged under "Conveyance or transfer on Sale". *See* Finance Act 1980, sec. 97, as amended by Finance Act 1981, sec. 108. Finance Act 1987, sec. 54, extends the foregoing provisions to include unregistered housing associations as lessees and private landlords who have taken over public housing estates.

Grant of a lease or tack where the premium or rent is unascertainable

Where in an instrument executed after 7th December 1993 the consideration for the grant of a lease is unascertainable, the transfer will be liable to ad valorem duty on the market value of the property immediately before the transfer was executed. Where the rent, or part of the rent, under a lease or tack is unascertainble, lease duty will be charged on the market rent of that property at the date the instrument is executed. (Finance Act 1994, sec. 242).

Note: This proposal applies only to land, it does not apply to sales of shares or other property.

Letter or Power of Attorney, and commission, factory, mandate, or other instrument in the nature thereof — duty payable is nil.

Loan capital

As from 1st August 1986 stamp duty is not chargeable on any transfer of loan capital except —

(1) where the loan capital at the time it is transferred carries a right (exerciseable then or later) of conversion into shares or other securities or to the acquisition of shares or other securities, including loan capital of the same description;

(2) where the loan capital at the time it is transferred or at earlier time carries or has carried —

(*a*) a right to interest the amount of which: (i) exceeds a reasonable commercial return on the nominal amount of the capital; or (ii) falls or has fallen to be determined to any extent by reference to the results of, or any part of, a business or to the value of any property; or

(*b*) a right on re-payment to an amount which exceeds the nominal amount of the capital and is not reasonably comparable with what is generally acceptable (in respect of a similar nominal amount of capital) under the terms of issue of loan capital listed in the Official List of The Stock Exchange.

Index linked loan capital also comes within the exemption (Finance Act 1986, sec. 79).

Non-exempt transfers are chargeable at the rate of 50p for every £100 or part of £100.

Mandate

Duty payable is nil.

Notice of title

Duty payable is nil.

Partition or division. Instruments effecting.

In the case specified in sec. 73, see that section. (See Finance Act 1994, sec 241).

In any other case, the duty payable is 50p.

Partnership, contract of. — Duty payable is nil.

Dissolution of, or entry or retirement of partners. Claims for stamp duty may arise as for sale. A certificate of value may be required. But a partition of assets is not a sale

Policy of insurance other than life insurance

Duty payable is nil.

Policy of life insurance

Stamp duty in respect of life policies, superannuation policies and purchased life annuities ceased to be chargeable on instruments made after 31st December 1989 (Finance Act 1989, sec. 173).

Assignation of life policy. See "Assignation".

Power of attorney

Duty payable is nil.

Release or renunciation of any property, or of any right or interest in any property

Upon a sale. *See* "Conveyance or transfer on sale".

In any other case, the duty payable is 50p.

Resignation of trustee

Duty payable is nil.

Revocation of any use or trust of any property by any writing, not being a will

Duty payable is nil.

Transfer

See "Conveyance or transfer on sale".

Trust deed for creditors

The duty payable is 50p. If by firms and partners, the duty is 50p for firm and 50p for each partner.

See "Declaration".

Unit trust instrument

This duty was abolished by Finance Act 1988, sec. 140, with effect from 22nd March 1988 as respects any trust instrument executed, or any property becoming trust property on or after that date.

Unit trusts: no stamp duty is chargeable on or after 27th July 1989 in respect of the transfer of any unit in an authorised unit trust scheme, the funds of which can only be invested such that the trustees are chargeable on income under Sched. C. or under Sched. D. Case III (Finance Act 1989, sec. 174).

Voluntary disposition

Duty payable is nil.

See Stamp Duty (Exempt Instruments) Regulations 1987.

B. Stamp duty land tax

The stamp duty land tax regime came into effect (subject to transitional provisions) on 1 December 2003. The main provisions relating thereto are contained in the Finance Act 2003 as amended.

Finance Act 2003

Amount of tax chargeable

55 Amount of tax chargeable: general

(1) The amount of tax chargeable in respect of a chargeable transaction is a percentage of the chargeable consideration for the transaction.

(2) That percentage is determined by reference to whether the relevant land—

(a) consists entirely of residential property (in which case Table A below applies), or

(b) consists of or includes land that is not residential property (in which case Table B below applies),

and, in either case, by reference to the amount of the relevant consideration.

Table A: Residential

Relevant consideration	Percentage
Not more than £175,000	0
More than £175,000 but not more than £250,000	1
More than £250,000 but not more than £500,000	3
More than £500,000	4

Table B: Non-residential or mixed

Relevant consideration	Percentage
Not more than £150,000	0
More than £150,000 but not more than £250,000	1
More than £250,000 but not more than £500,000	3
More than £500,000	4

(Special rules apply to land situated in a designated disadvantaged area)

(3) For the purposes of subsection (2)—

(a) the relevant land is the land an interest in which is the main subject-matter of the transaction, and

(b) the relevant consideration is the chargeable consideration for the transaction, subject as follows.

(4) If the transaction in question is one of a number of linked transactions—

(a) the relevant land is any land an interest in which is the main subject-matter of any of those transactions, and

(b) the relevant consideration is the total of the chargeable consideration for all those transactions.

(5) This section has effect subject to—

section 74 (collective enfranchisement by leaseholders), and

section 75 (crofting community right to buy),

(which provide for the rate of tax to be determined by reference to a fraction of the relevant consideration).

(6) In the case of a transaction for which the whole or part of the chargeable consideration is rent this section has effect subject to section 56 and Schedule 5 (amount of tax chargeable: rent).

(7) References in this Part to the "rate of tax" are to the percentage determined under this section.

56 Amount of tax chargeable: rent

Schedule 5 provides for the calculation of the tax chargeable where the chargeable consideration for a transaction consists of or includes rent.

Schedule 5

Stamp duty land tax: amount of tax chargeable: rent

1. This Schedule provides for calculating the tax chargeable—

(a) in respect of a chargeable transaction for which the chargeable consideration consists of or includes rent, or

(b) where such a transaction is to be taken into account as a linked transaction.

2.—(1) Tax is chargeable under this Schedule in respect of so much of the chargeable consideration as consists of rent.

(2) The tax chargeable is the total of the amounts produced by taking the relevant percentage of so much of the relevant rental value as falls within each rate band.

(3) The relevant percentages and rate bands are determined by reference to whether the relevant land—

(a) consists entirely of residential property (in which case Table A below applies), or

(b) consists of or includes land that is not residential property (in which case Table B below applies).

Table A: Residential

Rate bands from 1 December 2003 to 16 March 2005	*Percentage*
£0 to £60,000	0
Over £60,000	1
Rate bands from 17 March 2005 to 22 March 2006	*Percentage*
£0 to £120,000	0
Over £120,000	1
Rate bands from 22 March 2006	*Percentage*
£0 to £125,000	0
Over £125,000	1

Table B: Non-residential or mixed	
Rate bands	*Percentage*
£0 to £150,000	0
Over £150,000	1

(Special rules apply to land situated in a designated disadvantaged area)

(4) For the purposes of sub-paragraphs (2) and (3)—

(a) the relevant rental value is the net present value of the rent payable over the term of the lease, and

(b) the relevant land is the land that is the subject of the lease.

(5) If the lease in question is one of a number of linked transactions for which the chargeable consideration consists of or includes rent, the above provisions are modified.

(6) In that case the tax chargeable is determined as follows.

First, calculate the amount of the tax that would be chargeable if the linked transactions were a single transaction, so that—

(a) the relevant rental value is the total of the net present values of the rent payable over the terms of all the leases, and

(b) the relevant land is all land that is the subject of any of those leases.

Then, multiply that amount by the fraction:

$$\frac{\text{NPV}}{\text{TNPV}}$$

where—

NPV is the net present value of the rent payable over the term of the lease in question, and

TNPV is the total of the net present values of the rent payable over the terms of all the leases.

3. The net present value (v) of the rent payable over the term of a lease is calculated by applying the formula:

$$v = \sum_{i=1}^{n} \frac{r_i}{(1+T)^i}$$

where—

ri is the rent payable in year i,

i is the first, second, third, etc year of the term,

n is the term of the lease , and

T is the temporal discount rate (see paragraph 8).

8—(1) For the purposes of this Schedule the "temporal discount rate" is 3.5% or such other rate as may be specified by regulations made by the Treasury.

(2) Regulations under this paragraph may make any such provision as is mentioned in subsection (3)(b) to (f) of section 178 of the Finance Act 1989 (c 26) (power of Treasury to set rates of interest).

(3) Subsection (5) of that section (power of Inland Revenue to specify rate by order in certain circumstances) applies in relation to regulations under this paragraph as it applies in relation to regulations under that section.

9—(1) Where in the case of a transaction to which this Schedule applies there is chargeable consideration other than rent, the provisions of this Part apply in relation to that consideration as in relation to other chargeable consideration (but see paragraph 9A).

(2) If the relevant rental figure exceeds £600 a year, the 0% band in the Tables in subsection (2) of section 55 does not apply and any case that would have fallen within that band is treated as falling within the 1% band. [sub-paras 2, 2A and 3 repelaed by FA 2008, sec 92]

(2A) For the purposes of sub-paragraph (2) the relevant rental figure is—

(a) the annual rent in relation to the transaction in question, or

(b) if that transaction is one of a number of linked transactions for which the chargeable consideration consists of or includes rent, the total of the annual rents in relation to all those transactions.

(3) In sub-paragraph (2A) the "annual rent" means the average annual rent over the term of the lease or,

if—

(a) different amounts of rent are payable for different parts of the term, and

(b) those amounts (or any of them) are ascertainable at the effective date of the transaction, the average annual rent over the period for which the highest ascertainable rent is payable.

(4) Tax chargeable under this Schedule is in addition to any tax chargeable under section 55 in respect of consideration other than rent.

(5) Where a transaction to which this Schedule applies falls to be taken into account for the purposes of that section as a linked transaction, no account shall be taken of rent in determining the relevant consideration.

9A (1) This paragraph applies in the case of a transaction to which this Schedule applies where there is chargeable consideration other than rent.

(2) If—

(a) the relevant land consists entirely of land that is nonresidential property, and

(b) the relevant rent is at least £1,000, the 0% band in Table B in section 55(2) does not apply in relation to the consideration other than rent and any case that would have fallen within that band is treated as falling within the 1% band.

(3) Sub-paragraphs (4) and (5) apply if—

(a) the relevant land is partly residential property and partly non-residential property, and

(b) the relevant rent attributable, on a just and reasonable apportionment, to the land that is non-residential property is at least £1,000.

(4) For the purpose of determining the amount of tax chargeable under section 55 in relation to the consideration other than rent, the transaction (or, where it is one of a number of linked transactions, that set of transactions) is treated as if it were two separate transactions (or sets of linked transactions), namely—

(a) one whose subject-matter consists of all of the interests in land that is residential property, and

(b) one whose subject-matter consists of all of the interests in land that is non-residential property.

(5) For that purpose, the chargeable consideration attributable to each of those separate transactions (or sets of linked transactions) is the chargeable consideration so attributable on a just and reasonable apportionment.

(6) In this paragraph "the relevant rent" means—

(a) the annual rent in relation to the transaction in question, or

(b) if that transaction is one of a number of linked transactions for which the chargeable consideration consists of or includesrent, the total of the annual rents in relation to all of those transactions.

(7) In sub-paragraph (6) the "annual rent" means the average annual rent over the term of the lease or, if—

(a) different amounts of rent are payable for different parts of the term, and

(b) those amounts (or any of them) are ascertainable at the effective date of the transaction, the average annual rent over the period for which the highest ascertainable rent is payable.

(8) In this paragraph "relevant land" has the meaning given in section 55(3) and (4). [inserted by FA 2008, sec 92]

C. The following provisions apply to instruments executed on or after 28th March 2000 except, with certain exceptions, one giving effect to a contract made before 21st March 2000.

These provisions are contained in the Finance Act 1999 as amended by the Finance Act 2000.

However, with effect from 1 December 2003, the stamp duty land tax regime (see Part B) came into force, subject to transitional provisions.

Instruments chargeable and rates of duty as contained in Schedule 13 of Finance Act 1999 as amended by the Finance Act 2000 and subseqent Acts.

CONVEYANCE OR TRANSFER ON SALE

Charge

1.—(1) Stamp duty is chargeable on a transfer on sale.

(2) For this purpose "transfer on sale" includes every instrument, and every decree or order of a court or commissioners, by which any property, or any estate or interest in property, is, on being sold, transferred to or vested in the purchaser or another person on behalf of or at the direction of the purchaser.

(3) Sub-paragraph (1) is subject to sub-paragraphs (3A) to (6)

(3A) Stamp duty is not chargeable under sub-paragraph (1) on a transfer of stock or marketable securities where—

(a) the amount or value of the consideration for the sale is £1,000 or under, and

(b) the instrument is certified at £1,000.

(4) Where a company acquires any shares in itself by virtue of section 162 of the Companies Act 1985 (power of company to purchase own shares) or otherwise, sub-paragraph (1) does not apply to any instrument by which the shares are transferred to the company.

(5) Where a company holds any shares in itself by virtue of section 162A of that Act (treasury shares) or otherwise, sub-paragraph (1) does not apply to any instrument to which sub-paragraph (6) applies [as amended by FA 2008, sch 32, para 10].

(6) This sub-paragraph applies to any instrument for the sale or transfer of any of the shares by the company, other than an instrument which, in the absence of sub-paragraph (5), would be an instrument in relation to which—

(a) section 67(2) of the Finance Act 1986 (transfer to person whose business is issuing depositary receipts etc), or

(b) section 70(2) of that Act (transfer to person who provides clearance services etc), applied.

Rates of duty

2. Duty under this Part is chargeable by reference to the amount or value of the consideration for the sale.

3. In the case of a transfer of stock or marketable securities the rate is 0.5%.

4. In the case of any other transfer on sale the rates of duty are as follows—

1.	Where the amount or value of the consideration is £175,000 or under and the instrument is certified at £175,000	Nil
2.	Where the amount or value of the consideration is £250,000 or under and the instrument is certified at £250,000	1%
3.	Where the amount or value of the consideration is £500,000 or under and the instrument is certified at £500,000	3%
4.	Any other case	4%

5. The above provisions are subject to any enactment setting a different rate or setting an upper limit on the amount of duty chargeable.

Meaning of instrument being certified at an amount

6.—(1) The references in paragraphs 1(3A) and 4 above to an instrument being certified at a particular amount mean that it contains a statement that the transaction effected by the instrument does not form part of a larger transaction or series of transactions in respect of which the amount or value, or aggregate amount or value, of the consideration exceeds that amount.

(2) For this purpose a sale or contract or agreement for the sale of goods, wares or merchandise shall be disregarded—

(a) in the case of an instrument which is not an actual transfer of the goods, wares or merchandise (with or without other property);

(b) in the case of an instrument treated as such a transfer only by virtue of paragraph 7 (contracts or agreements chargeable as conveyances on sale);

and any statement as mentioned in sub-paragraph (1) shall be construed as leaving out of account any matter which is to be so disregarded.

Contracts or agreements chargeable as conveyances on sale

7.—(1) A contract or agreement for the sale of—

(a)   any equitable estate or interest in property, or

(b)   any estate or interest in property except—

    (i)   lands, tenements, hereditaments or heritages, or property locally situate out of the United Kingdom,

    (ii)   goods, wares or merchandise,

    (iii)   stock or marketable securities,

    (iv)   any ship or vessel, or a part interest, share or property of or in any ship or vessel, or

    (v)   property of any description situated outside the United Kingdom.

is chargeable with the same *ad valorem* duty, to be paid by the purchaser, as if it were an actual conveyance on sale of the estate, interest or property contracted or agreed to be sold.

(2) Where the purchaser has paid *ad valorem* duty and before having obtained a transfer of the property enters into a contract or agreement for the sale of the same, the contract or agreement is chargeable, if the consideration for that sale is in excess of the consideration for the original sale, with the *ad valorem* duty payable in respect of the excess consideration but is not otherwise chargeable.

(3) Where duty has been paid in conformity with sub-paragraphs (1) and (2), the transfer to the purchaser or sub-purchaser, or any other person on his behalf or by his direction, is not chargeable with any duty.

(4) In that case, upon application and upon production of the contract or agreement (or contracts or agreements) duly stamped, the Commissioners shall either—

(a)   denote the payment of the *ad valorem* duty upon the transfer, or

(b)   transfer the *ad valorem* duty to the transfer.

8.—(1) Where a contract or agreement would apart from paragraph 7 not be chargeable with any duty and a transfer made in conformity with the contract or agreement is presented to the Commissioners for stamping with the *ad valorem* duty chargeable on it—

(a)   within the period of six months after the execution of the contract or agreement, or

(b)   within such longer period as the Commissioners may think reasonable in the circumstances of the case,

the transfer shall be stamped accordingly, and both it and the contract or agreement shall be deemed to be duly stamped.

(2) Nothing in this paragraph affects the provisions as to the stamping of a transfer after execution.

9.—The *ad valorem* duty paid upon a contract or agreement by virtue of paragraph 7 shall be repaid by the Commissioners if the contract or agreement is afterwards rescinded or annulled or is for any other reason not substantially performed or carried into effect so as to operate as or be followed by a transfer.

[**NOTE** — By virtue of the Finance Act 2001, sec 92, no stamp duty shall be chargeable on a transfer of an estate or interest in land, or a lease of land, if the land is situated in a disadvantaged area, and the instrument is executed on or after a date to be specified by the Treasury. The specified date is 30 November 2001 (by virtue of SI 2001/3748). Finance Act 2002, sec 116, Sch 37 abolishes the duty on instruments executed after 23rd April 2002 relating to goodwill.]

LEASE

Charge

1.   Stamp duty is chargeable on a lease.

Rates of duty

2.   In the case of a lease for a definite term less than a year the duty is as follows—

    1.   Lease of furnished dwelling-house or apartments where the rent for the term exceeds £5000   £5

    2.   Any other lease of land   The same duty as for a lease for a year at the rent reserved for the definite term

3.—(1) In the case of a lease for any other definite term, or for an indefinite term, the duty is determined as follows.

(2) If the consideration or part of the consideration moving to the lessor or to any other person consists of any money, stock, security or other property, the duty in respect of that consideration is the same as that on a conveyance on a sale for the same consideration.

But if—

(a) part of the consideration is rent, and

(b) that rent exceeds £600 a year,

the duty is calculated as if paragraph 1 of the Table in paragraph 4 of Part I of Schedule 13 to the Finance Act 1999 were omitted.

(3) If the consideration or part of the consideration is rent, the duty in respect of that consideration is determined by reference to the rate or average rate of the rent (whether reserved as a yearly rent or not), as follows:—

1.	Term not more than 7 years or indefinite—	Nil
	(a) if the rent is £5000 or less	1%
	(b) if the rent is more than £5000	
2.	Term more than 7 years but not more than 35 years	2%
3.	Term more than 35 years but not more than 100 years	12%
4.	Term more than 100 years	24%

[The amending provisions in relation to leases of not more than seven years apply to instruments executed on or after 1st October 1999. Transitional provisions are contained in Schedule 32 of the Act for instruments executed on or after 1st October 1999 but before 28th March 2000.]

4. Stamp duty of £5 is chargeable on a lease not within paragraph 2 or 3 above.

Agreement for a lease charged as a lease

5.—(1) An agreement for a lease is chargeable with the same duty as if it were an actual lease made for the term and consideration mentioned in the agreement.

(2) Where duty has been duly paid on an agreement for a lease and subsequent to that agreement a lease is granted which either—

(a) is in conformity with the agreement, or

(b) relates to substantially the same property and term as the agreement,

the duty which would otherwise be charged on the lease is reduced by the amount of the duty paid on the agreement.

(3) Sub-paragraph (1) does not apply to missives of let in Scotland that constitute an actual lease.

Subject to that, references in this paragraph to an agreement for a lease include missives of let in Scotland.

Lease for fixed term and then until determined

6.—(1) For the purposes of this Part a lease granted for a fixed term and thereafter until determined is treated as a lease for a definite term equal to the fixed term together with such further period as must elapse before the earliest date at which the lease can be determined.

(2) Paragraph 5 (agreement for a lease charged as a lease) shall be construed accordingly.

[**NOTE** — By virtue of the Finance Act 2001, sec 92, no stamp duty shall be chargeable on a conveyance or transfer of an estate or interest in land, or a lease of land, if the land is situated in a disadvantaged area, and the instrument is executed on or after a date to be specified by the Treasury. The specified date is 30 November 2001 (by virtue of SI 2001/3748)]

OTHER INSTRUMENTS

Transfer otherwise than on sale

[repealed by FA 2008, sch 32 para 10 with effect for instruments executed on or after
13 March 2008 and not stamped before 19 March 2008]

1.— (1) Stamp duty of £5 is chargeable on a transfer of property otherwise than on sale.

(2) IN SUB-PARAGRAPH (1) "TRANSFER" INCLUDES EVERY INSTRUMENT, AND EVERY DECREE OR ORDER OF
A COURT OR COMMISSIONERS, BY WHICH ANY PROPERTY IS TRANSFERRED TO OR VESTED IN ANY PERSON.

Declaration of use or trust

*[repealed by FA 2008, sch 32 para 10 with effect for instruments executed on or after
13 March 2008 and not stamped before 19 March 2008]*

2.— (1) Stamp duty of £5 is chargeable on a declaration of any use or trust of or concerning property unless
the instrument constitutes a transfer on sale.

(2) This does not apply to a will.

Dispositions in Scotland

3.—(1) The following are chargeable with duty as a conveyance on sale—

(a) a disposition of heritable property in Scotland to singular successors or purchasers;

(b) a disposition of heritable property in Scotland to a purchaser containing a clause declaring all or
any part of the purchase money a real burden upon, or affecting, the heritable property thereby
disported, or any part of it;

(c) a disposition in Scotland containing constitution of feu or ground annual right.

(2) A disposition in Scotland of any property, or any right or interest in property, that is not so
chargeable is chargeable with stamp duty of £5.[repealed by FA 2008, sch 32 para 10 with effect for
instruments executed on or after 13 March 2008 and not stamped before 19 March 2008]

Duplicate or counterpart

4.—(1) A duplicate or counterpart of an instrument chargeable with duty is chargeable with duty of
£5.[repealed by FA 2008, sch 32 para 10 with effect for instruments executed on or after 13 March 2008 and
not stamped before 19 March 2008]

(2) The duplicate or counterpart of an instrument chargeable with duty is not duly stamped unless—

(a) it is stamped as an original instrument, or

(b) it appears by some stamp impressed on it that the full and proper duty has been paid on the original
instrument of which it is the duplicate or counterpart.

(3) Sub-paragraph (2) does not apply to the counterpart of an instrument chargeable as a lease, if that
counterpart is not executed by or on behalf of any lessor or grantor.

Instrument increasing rent

5.—(1) An instrument (not itself a lease)

(a) by which it is agreed that the rent reserved should be increased, or

(b) which confirms or records any such agreement made otherwise than in writing,

is chargeable with the same duty as if it were a lease in consideration of the additional rent made payable
by it.

(2) Sub-paragraph (1) does not apply to an instrument giving effect to provision in the lease for
periodic review of the rent reserved by it.

Partition or division

6.—(1) Where on the partition or division of an estate or interest in land consideration exceeding £100 in
amount or value is paid or given, or agreed to be paid or given, for equality, the principal or only instrument
by which the partition or division is effected is chargeable with the same *ad valorem* duty as a conveyance
on sale for the consideration, and with that duty only.

(2)   Where there are several instruments for completing the title of either party, the principal instrument is to be ascertained, and the other instruments shall be charged with duty, as provided by sections 58(3) and 61 of the Stamp Act 1891 in the case of several instruments of conveyance.

(3)   Stamp duty of £5 is chargeable on an instrument effecting a partition or division to which the above provisions do not apply.[repealed by FA 2008, sch 32 para 10 with effect for instruments executed on or after 13 March 2008 and not stamped before 19 March 2008]Release or renunciation

7.—Stamp duty of £5 is chargeable on a release or renunciation of property unless the instrument constitutes a transfer on sale.[repealed by FA 2008, sch 32 para 10 with effect for instruments executed on or after 13 March 2008 and not stamped before 19 March 2008]

Surrender

8.—Stamp duty of £5 is chargeable on a surrender of property unless the instrument constitutes a transfer on sale.[repealed by FA 2008, sch 32 para 10 with effect for instruments executed on or after 13 March 2008 and not stamped before 19 March 2008]

General Exemptions

1.   The following are exempt from stamp duty under Schedule 13 to the Finance Act 1999—

(a)   transfers of shares in the government or parliamentary stocks or funds or strips (within the meaning of section 47 of the Finance Act 1942) of such stocks or funds;

(b)   instruments for the sale, transfer, or other disposition (absolutely or otherwise) of any ship or vessel, or any part, interest, share or property of or in a ship or vessel;

(c)   testaments, testamentary instruments and dispositions *mortis causa* in Scotland;

(d)   renounceable letters of allotment, letters of rights or other similar instruments where the rights under the letter or other instrument are renounceable not later than six months after its issue.

2.   Stamp duty is not chargeable under Schedule 13 to the Finance Act 1999 on any description of instrument in respect of which duty was abolished by—

(a)   section 64 of the Finance Act 1971 or section 5 of the Finance Act (Northern Ireland) 1971 (abolition of duty on mortgages, bonds, debentures etc.), or

(b)   section 173 of the Finance Act 1989 (life insurance policies and superannuation annuities).

3.   Nothing in Schedule 13 to the Finance Act 1999 affects any other enactment conferring exemption or relief from stamp duty.

Bearer Instruments

Charge on issue of instrument

1.—(1)   Stamp duty is chargeable—

(a)   on the issue of a bearer instrument in the United Kingdom, and

(b)   on the issue of a bearer instrument outside the United Kingdom by or on behalf of a UK company.

(2)   This is subject to the exemptions in Part II of Schedule 15 to the Finance Act 1999.

Charge on transfer of stock by means of instrument

2.—Stamp duty is chargeable on the transfer in the United Kingdom of the stock constituted by or transferable by means of a bearer instrument if duty was not chargeable under paragraph 1 on the issue of the instrument and—

(a)   duty would be chargeable under Part 1 of Schedule 13 (transfer on sale) if the transfer were effected by an instrument other than a bearer instrument, or

(b)   the stock constituted by or transferable by means of a bearer instrument consists of units under a unit trust scheme.

Meaning of "bearer instrument"

3.—In Schedule 15 to the Finance Act 1999 "bearer instrument" means—

(a) a marketable security transferable by delivery;

(b) a share warrant or stock certificate to bearer or instrument to bearer (by whatever name called) having the like effect as such a warrant or certificate;

(c) a deposit certificate to bearer;

(d) any other instrument to bearer by means of which stock can be transferred; or

(e) an instrument issued by a non-UK company that is a bearer instrument by usage.

Rates of duty

4.—The duty chargeable under this Schedule is 1. 5% of the market value of the stock constituted by or transferable by means of the instrument, unless paragraph 5 or 6 applies.

5.—In the case of—

(a) a deposit certificate in respect of stock of a single non-UK company, or

(b) an instrument issued by a non-UK company that is a bearer instrument by usage (and is not otherwise within the definition of "bearer instrument" in paragraph 3),

the duty is 0.2% of the market value of the stock constituted by or transferable by means of the instrument.

6.—In the case of an instrument given in substitution for a like instrument stamped *ad valorem* (whether under Schedule 15 to the Finance Act 1999 or not) the duty is £5.[repealed by FA 2008, sch 32 para 10 with effect for instruments executed on or after 13 March 2008 and not stamped before 19 March 2008]

Ascertainment of market value

7.—(1) For the purposes of duty under paragraph 1 (charge on issue of instrument) the market value of the stock constituted by or transferable by means of the instrument is ascertained as follows.

(2) If the stock was offered for public subscription (whether in registered or in bearer form) within twelve months before the issue of the instrument, the market value shall be taken to be the amount subscribed for the stock.

(3) In any other case the market value shall be taken to be—

(a) the value of the stock on the first day within one month after the issue of the instrument on which stock of that description is dealt in on a stock exchange in the United Kingdom, or

(b) if stock of that description is not so dealt in, the value of the stock immediately after the issue of the instrument.

8.—(1) For the purposes of duty under paragraph 2 (charge on transfer of stock by means of instrument) the market value of the stock constituted by or transferable by means of the instrument is ascertained as follows.

(2) In the case of a transfer pursuant to a contract of sale, the market value shall be taken to be the value of the stock on the date when the contract is made.

(3) In any other case, the market value shall be taken to be the value of the stock on the day preceding that on which the instrument is presented to the Commissioners for stamping, or, if it is not so presented, on the date of the transfer.

Meaning of "deposit certificate"

9.—In this Schedule a "deposit certificate" means an instrument acknowledging the deposit of stock and entitling the bearer to rights (whether expressed as units or otherwise) in or in relation to the stock deposited or equivalent stock.

Bearer instruments by usage

10.—(1) In Schedule 15 to the Finance Act 1999 a "bearer instrument by usage" means an instrument—

(a) which is used for the purpose of transferring the right to stock, and

(b) delivery of which is treated by usage as sufficient for the purposes of a sale on the market, whether that delivery constitutes a legal transfer or not.

(2) A bearer instrument by usage is treated—

(a) as transferring the stock on delivery of the instrument, and

(b) as issued by the person by whom or on whose behalf it was first issued, whether or not it was then capable of being used for transferring the right to the stock without execution by the holder.

Meaning of "company", "UK company" and "non-UK company"

11.—In Schedule 15 to the Finance Act 1999—

"company" includes any body of persons, corporate or unincorporate;

"UK company" means

(a) a company that is formed or established in the United Kingdom other than an SE which has its registered office outside the United Kingdom following a transfer in accordance with Article 8 of Council Regulation (EC) 2157/2001 on the Statute for a European Company (Societas Europaea)), or

(b) an SE which has its registered office in the United Kingdom following a transfer in accordance with Article 8 of that Regulation; and

"non-UK company" means a company that is not a UK company.

Meaning of "stock" and "transfer"

12.—(1) In Schedule 15 to the Finance Act 1999 "stock" includes securities.

(2) References in that Schedule to stock include any interest in, or in any fraction of, stock or in any dividends or other rights arising out of stock and any right to an allotment of or to subscribe for stock.

(3) In that Schedule "transfer" includes negotiation, and "transferable", "transferred" and "transferring" shall be construed accordingly.

PART II—EXEMPTIONS

Substitute instruments

12A (1) Stamp duty is not chargeable on a substitute instrument.

(2) A substitute instrument is a bearer instrument given in substitution for a like instrument stamped ad valorem (whether under this Schedule or otherwise) ("the original instrument").

(3) The substitute instrument shall not be treated as duly stamped unless it appears by some stamp impressed on it that the full and proper duty has been paid on the original instrument." [inserted by FA 2008, sch 32, with effect for instruments executed on or after 13 March 2008 and not stamped before 19 March 2008]

Foreign loan securities

13.—Stamp duty is not chargeable on a bearer instrument issued outside the United Kingdom in respect of a loan which is expressed in a currency other than sterling and which is not—

(a) offered for subscription in the United Kingdom, or

(b) offered for subscription with a view to an offer for sale in the United Kingdom of securities in respect of the loan.

Stock exempt from duty on transfer

14.—Stamp duty is not chargeable under Schedule 15 to the Finance Act 1999 on an instrument constituting, or used for transferring, stock (other than units in a unit trust) that is exempt from all stamp duties on transfer.

Instruments in respect of which duty previously abolished

15.—Stamp duty is not chargeable under Schedule 15 to the Finance Act 1999 on any description of instrument in respect of which duty was abolished by—

(a) section 64 of the Finance Act 1971 or section 5 of the Finance Act (Northern Ireland) 1971 (abolition of duty on mortgages, bonds, debentures etc.), or

(b) section 173 of the Finance Act 1989 (life insurance policies and superannuation annuities).

Renounceable letters of allotment

16.—Stamp duty is not chargeable under Schedule 15 to the Finance Act 1999 on renounceable letters of allotment, letters of rights or other similar instruments where the rights under the letter or other instrument are renounceable not later than six months after its issue.

Instruments relating to non-sterling stock

17.—(1) Stamp duty is not chargeable under Schedule 15 to the Finance Act 1999 on the issue of an instrument which relates to stock expressed—

(a) in a currency other than sterling, or

(b) in units of account defined by reference to more than one currency (whether or not including sterling),

or on the transfer of the stock constituted by or transferable by means of any such instrument.

(2) Where the stock to which the instrument relates consists of a loan for the repayment of which there is an option between sterling and one or more other currencies, sub-paragraph (1) applies if the option is exercisable only by the holder of the stock and does not apply in any other case.

18.—Where the capital stock of a company is not expressed in terms of any currency, it shall be treated for the purposes of paragraph 17 as expressed in the currency of the territory under the law of which the company is formed or established.

19.—(1) A unit under a unit trust scheme or a share in a foreign mutual fund shall be treated for the purposes of paragraph 17 as capital stock of a company formed or established in the territory by the law of which the scheme or fund is governed.

(2) A "foreign mutual fund" means a fund administered under arrangements governed by the law of a territory outside the United Kingdom under which subscribers to the fund are entitled to participate in, or receive payments by reference to, profits or income arising to the fund from the acquisition, holding, management or disposal of investments.

(3) In relation to a foreign mutual fund "share" means the right of a subscriber, or of another in his right, to participate in or receive payments by reference to profits or income so arising.

Variation of original terms or conditions

20.—Where a bearer instrument issued by or on behalf of a non-UK company in respect of a loan expressed in sterling—

(a) has been stamped *ad valorem*, or

(b) has been stamped in accordance with paragraph 12A, or, or

(c) has been stamped with the denoting stamp referred to in paragraph 21(2)(b) below,

duty is not chargeable under Schedule 15 to the Finance Act 1999 by reason only that the instrument is amended on its face pursuant to an agreement for the variation of any of its original terms or conditions.

PART III—SUPPLEMENTARY PROVISIONS

Duty chargeable on issue of instrument

21.—(1) This paragraph applies where duty is chargeable under paragraph 1 of above.

(2) The instrument—

(a) shall before being issued be produced to the Commissioners together with such particulars in writing of the instrument as the Commissioners may require, and

(b) shall be deemed to be duly stamped if and only if it is stamped with a particular stamp denoting that it has been produced to the Commissioners.

(3) Within six weeks of the date on which the instrument is issued, or such longer time as the Commissioners may allow, a statement in writing containing the date of the issue and such further particulars as the Commissioners may require in respect of the instrument shall be delivered to the Commissioners.

(4) The duty chargeable in respect of the instrument shall be paid to the Commissioners on delivery of that statement or within such longer time as the Commissioners may allow.

22.—(1) If default is made in complying with paragraph 21—

(a)   the person by whom or on whose behalf the instrument is issued, and

(b)   any person who acts as the agent of that person for the purposes of the issue,

are each liable to a penalty not exceeding the aggregate of £300 and the duty chargeable.

(2) Those persons are also jointly and severally liable to pay to Her Majesty—

(a)   the duty chargeable, and

(b)   interest on the unpaid duty from the date of the default until the duty is paid.

Duty chargeable on transfer of stock by means of instrument

23.—(1) This paragraph applies where duty is chargeable under paragraph 2 of above.

(2) Where the instrument is presented to the Commissioners for stamping—

(a)   the person presenting it, and

(b)   the owner of the instrument,

shall furnish to the Commissioners such particulars in writing as the Commissioners may require for determining the amount of duty chargeable.

(3) If the instrument is not duly stamped each person who in the United Kingdom—

(a)   transfers any stock by or by means of the instrument, or

(b)   is concerned as broker or agent in any such transfer,

is liable to a penalty not exceeding the aggregate of £300 and the amount of duty chargeable.

(4) Those persons are also jointly and severally liable to pay to Her Majesty—

(a)   the duty chargeable, and

(b)   interest on the unpaid duty from the date of the transfer in question until the duty is paid.

Supplementary provisions as to interest

24.—(1) The following provisions apply to interest under paragraph 22(2) or 23(4).

(2) If an amount is lodged with the Commissioners in respect of the duty, the amount on which interest is payable is reduced by that amount.

(3) Interest is payable at the rate prescribed under section 178 of the Finance Act 1989 for the purposes of section 15A of the Stamp Act 1891 (interest on late stamping).

(4) The amount of interest shall be rounded down (if necessary) to the nearest multiple of £5.

No interest is payable if the amount is less than £25.

(5) The interest shall be paid without any deduction of income tax and shall not be taken into account in computing income or profits for any tax purposes.

Penalty for false statement

25.—A person who in furnishing particulars under this Part wilfully or negligently furnishes particulars that are false in any material respect is liable to a penalty not exceeding the aggregate of £300 and twice the amount by which the stamp duty chargeable exceeds that paid.

26.—An instrument in respect of which duty is chargeable under paragraph 2 of above which—

(a)   h as been stamped *ad valorem*, or

(b)   has been stamped with a stamp indicating that it is chargeable with a fixed duty under paragraph 6 (instrument in substitution for one stamped *ad valorem*) and has been stamped under that paragraph,[repealed by FA 2008, sch 32 para 10 with effect for instruments executed on or after 13 March 2008 and not stamped before 19 March 2008]

shall be treated as duly stamped for all purposes other than paragraph 25.

Regulations applicable to Instruments Generally

Stamp Act 1891 (as amended by Finance Act 1999)

Charge of duty upon instruments

Sec. 2.—Except where express provision is made to the contrary all stamp duties are to be denoted by impressed stamps only.

Sec. 3.—(1) Every instrument written upon stamped material is to be written in such manner, and every instrument partly or wholly written before being stamped is to be so stamped, that the stamp may appear on the face of the instrument, and cannot be used for or applied to any other instrument written upon the same piece of material.

    (2) If more than one instrument be written upon the same piece of material, every one of the instruments is to be separately and distinctly stamped with the duty with which it is chargeable.

Sec. 4.—Except where express provision to the contrary is made by this or any other Act:

    (*a*) an instrument containing or relating to several distinct matters is to be separately and distinctly charged, as if it were a separate instrument with duty in respect of each of the matters;

    (*b*) an instrument made for any consideration in respect whereof it is chargeable with *ad valorem* duty, and also for any further or other valuable consideration, is to be separately and distinctly charged, as if it were a separate instrument with duty in respect of each of the considerations.

Sec. 5.—All the facts and circumstances affecting the liability of any instrument to duty, or the amount of the duty with which any instrument is chargeable, are to be fully and truly set forth in the instrument; and every person who, with intent to defraud Her Majesty:

    (*a*) executes any instrument in which all the said facts and circumstances are not fully and truly set forth; or

    (*b*) being employed or concerned in or about the preparation of any instrument, neglects or omits fully and truly to set forth therein all the said facts and circumstances;

shall incur a penalty not exceeding £3,000.

Sec. 6.—(1) Where an instrument is chargeable with *ad valorem* duty in respect of

    (*a*) any money in any foreign or colonial currency, or

    (*b*) any stock or, marketable security

    the duty shall be calculated on the value, on the day of the date of the instrument, of the money in British currency according to the current rate of exchange, or of the stock or security according to the average price thereof.

    (2) Where an instrument contains a statement of current rate of exchange, or average price, as the case may require, and is stamped in accordance with that statement, it is, so far as regards the subject matter of the statement, to be deemed duly stamped, unless or until it is shown that the statement is untrue, and that the instrument is in fact insufficiently stamped.

Denoting stamps

Sec. 11.— Where the duty with which an instrument is chargeable depends in any manner upon the duty paid upon another instrument, the payment of such last mentioned duty shall, upon application to the commissioners, and production of both the instruments, be denoted on the first-mentioned instrument in such manner as the commissioners think fit. (*See* Finance Act 1984, sec.111).

Adjudication stamps

Sec. 12.—(1) Subject to such regulations as the commissioners may think fit to make, the commissioners may be required by any person to adjudicate with reference to any executed instrument upon the questions:

    (*a*) whether it is chargeable with any duty;

    (*b*) with what amount of duty it is chargeable.

    (*c*) whether any penalty is payable for late stamping, and

    (*d*) what penalty is in their opinion correct and adequate.

(2) The Commissioners may require to be furnished with an abstract of the instrument and with such evidence as they may require as to the facts and circumstances relevant to those questions.

(3) The Commissioners shall give notice of their decision upon those questions to the person by whom the adjudication was required.

(4) If the Commissioners decide that the instrument is not chargeable with any duty, it may be stamped with a particular stamp denoting that it has been the subject of adjudication and is not chargeable with any duty.

(5) If the Commissioners decide that the instrument is chargeable with duty and assess the amount of duty chargeable, the instrument when stamped in accordance with their decision may be stamped with a particular stamp denoting that it has been the subject of adjudication and is duly stamped.

(6) Every instrument stamped in accordance with subsection (4) or (5) shall be admissible in evidence and available for all purposes notwithstanding any objection relating to duty.

Sec 12A. (1) An instrument which has been the subject of adjudication by the Commissioners under section 12 shall not, if it is unstamped or insufficiently stamped, be stamped otherwise than in accordance with the Commissioners' decision on the adjudication.

(2) If without reasonable excuse any such instrument is not duly stamped within 30 days after the date on which the Commissioners gave notice of their decision, or such longer period as the Commissioners may allow, the person by whom the adjudication was required is liable to a penalty not exceeding £300.

(3) A statutory declaration made for the purposes of section 12 shall not be used against the person making it in any proceedings whatever, except in an inquiry as to the duty with which the instrument to which it relates is chargeable or as to the penalty payable on stamping that instrument.

(4) Every person by whom any such declaration is made shall, on payment of the duty chargeable upon the instrument to which it relates, and any interest or penalty payable on stamping, be relieved from any penalty to which he may be liable by reason of the omission to state truly in the instrument any fact or circumstance required by this Act to be so stated.

Sec 13.—(1) A person who is dissatisfied with a decision of the Commissioners on an adjudication under section 12 may appeal against it.

(2) The appeal must be brought within 30 days of notice of the decision on the adjudication being given under section 12(3).

(3) An appeal may only be brought on payment of—

(a) duty and any penalty in conformity with the Commissioners' decision, and

(b) any interest that in conformity with that decision would be payable on stamping the instrument on the day on which the appeal is brought.

(4) An appeal which relates only to the penalty payable on late stamping may be brought to the Special Commissioners in accordance with section 13A.

(5) Any other appeal may be brought in accordance with section 13B to the High Court of the part of the United Kingdom in which the case has arisen.

The following provisions apply in relation to instruments executed on or after 1st October 1999.

Sec 15.—(1) An unstamped or insufficiently stamped instrument may be stamped after being executed on payment of the unpaid duty and any interest or penalty payable.

(2) Any interest or penalty payable on stamping shall be denoted on the isntrument by a particular stamp.

Sec 15A.—(1) Interest is payable on the stamping of an instrument which—

(a) is chargeable with *ad valorem* duty, and

(b) is not duly stamped within 30 days after the day on which the instrument was executed (whether in the United Kingdom or elsewhere).

(2) Interest is payable on the amount of the unpaid duty from the end of the period of 30 days mentioned in subsection (1)(b) until the duty is paid.

If an amount is lodged with the Commissioners in respect of the duty, the amount on which interest is payable is reduced by that amount.

(3) Interest shall be calcualted at the rate applicable under section 178 of the Finance Act 1989 (power of Treasury to prescribe rates of interest).

(4) The amount of interest shall be rounded down (if necessary) to the nearest multiple of £5.

No interest is payable if that amount is less than £25.

(5) Interest under this section shall be paid without any deduction of income tax and shall not be taken into account in computing income or profits for any tax purposes.

Sec 15B.—(1) A penalty is payable on the stamping of an instrument which is not presented for stamping within 30 days after—

   (a)   if the instrument is executed in the United Kingdom or relates to land in the United Kingdom, the day on which it is so executed;

   (b)   if the instrument is executed outside the United Kingdom and does not relate to land in the United Kingdom, the day on which it is first received in the United Kingdom.

(1A) For the purposes of subsection (1) every instrument that (whether or not it also relates to any other transaction) relates to a transaction which to any extent involves land in the United Kingdom is an instrument relating to land in the United Kingdom.

(2) If the instrument is presented for stamping within one year after the end of the 30-day period mentioned in subsection (1), the maximum penalty is £300 or the amount of the unpaid duty, whichever is less.

(3) If the instrument is not presented for stamping until after the end of the one-year period mentioned in subsection (2), the maximum penalty is £300 or the amount of the unpaid duty, whichever is greater.

(4) The Commissioners may, if they think fit, mitigate or remit any penalty payable on stamping.

(5) No penalty is payable if there is a reasonable excuse for the delay in presenting the instrument for stamping.

Allowance for Spoiled Stamps

Stamp Duties Management Act 1891 (as amended by Finance Act 1999)

Note: The commissioners may by concession allow repayment where a duplicate has been stamped, or free stamp a duplicate, where a stamped instrument has been lost.

Procedure for obtaining allowance

Sec. 9. Allowance is to be made by the commissioners for stamps spoiled in the cases hereinafter mentioned:

(1) The stamp on any material inadvertently and undesignedly spoiled, obliterated, or by any means rendered unfit for the purpose intended, before the material bears the signature of any person or any instrument written thereon is executed by any party.

(4) The stamp on any bill of exchange signed by or on behalf of the drawer which has not been accepted or made use of in any manner whatever or delivered out of his hands for any purpose other than by way of tender for acceptance.

(5) The stamp on any promissory note signed by or on behalf of the maker which has not been made use of in any manner whatever or delivered out of his hands.

(6) The stamp on any bill or promissory note which from any omission or error has been spoiled or rendered useless, although the same, being a bill of exchange, may have been accepted or indorsed, or being a promissory note may have been delivered to the payee, provided that another completed and duly stamped bill or promissory note is produced identical in every particular, except in the correction of the error or omission, with the spoiled bill or note.

(7) The stamp used for any of the following instruments: that is to say —

(*a*) an instrument executed by any party thereto, but afterwards found to be absolutely void from the beginning;

(*b*) an instrument executed by any party thereto, but afterwards found unfit, by reason of any error or mistake therein, for the purpose originally intended;

(*c*) an instrument executed by any party thereto which has not been made use of for any purpose whatever, and which, by reason of the inability or refusal of some necessary party to sign the same or to complete the transaction according to the instrument, is incomplete and insufficient for the purpose for which it was intended;

(*d*) an instrument executed by any party thereto, which by reason of the refusal of any person to act under the same, or for want of registration within the time required by law, fails of the intended purpose or becomes void;

(*e*) an instrument executed by any party thereto which becomes useless in consequence of the transaction intended to be thereby effected being effected by some other instrument duly stamped.

Provided as follows:

(*a*) that the application for relief is made within two years after the stamp has been spoiled or become useless, or in the case of an executed instrument after the date of the instrument, or, if it is not dated, within two years after the execution thereof by the person by whom it was first or alone executed, or within such further time as the Commissioners may prescribe in the case of any instrument sent abroad for execution, or when from unavoidable circumstance any instrument for which another has been substituted cannot be produced within the said period;

(*b*) That in the case of an executed instrument no legal proceeding has been commenced in which the instrument could or would have been given or offered in evidence, and that the instrument is given up to be cancelled.

Allowance for misused stamps

Sec. 10. When any person has inadvertently used for an instrument liable to duty a stamp of greater value than was necessary, or has inadvertently used a stamp for an instrument not liable to any duty, the commissioners may, on application made within two years after the date of the instrument, or, if it is not dated, within two years after the execution thereof by the person by whom it was first or alone executed, and upon the instrument, if liable to duty, being stamped with the proper duty, cancel and allow as spoiled the stamp so misused.

Allowance, how to be made

Sec. 11. In any case in which allowance is made for spoiled or misused stamps the commissioners may give in lieu thereof other stamps of the same denomination and value, or, if required, and they think proper, stamps of any other denomination to the same amount in value, or in their discretion, the same value in money.

Stamps not wanted may be repurchased by commissioners

Sec. 12A.—(1) This section applies where the Commissioners are satisfied that:

(*a*) an instrument which was executed and duly stamped ("the original instrument") has been accidentally lost or spoiled; and

(*b*) in place of the original instrument, another instrument made between the same persons and for the same purpose ("the replacement instrument") has been executed; and

(*c*) an application for relief under this section is made to the Commissioners; and either

(*d*) where the original instrument has been lost, the applicant undertakes to deliver it up to the Commissioners to be cancelled if it is subsequently found; or

(*e*) where the original instrument has been spoiled;

    (i) the application is made within two years after the date of the original instrument, or if it is not dated, within two years after the time when it was executed, or within such further time as the Commissioners may allow; and

    (ii) no legal proceeding has been commenced in which the original instrument has been or could or would have been given or offered in evidence; and

    (iii) the original instrument is delivered up to the Commissioners to be cancelled.

(2) Where this section applies:

(*a*) the replacement instrument shall not be chargeable with any duty, but shall be stamped with the duty with which it would otherwise have been chargeable in accordance with the law in force at the time when it was executed, and shall be deemed for all purposes to be duly stamped; and

(*b*) if any duty, interest or penalty was paid in respect of the replacement instrument before the application was made, the Commissioners shall pay to such person as they consider appropriate an amount equal to the duty, interest or penalty so paid.

(3) For the purposes of this section the Commissioners amy require the applicant to produce such evidence by statutory declaration or otherwise as they think fit.

Notes: This section, which was inserted by Finance Act 1996, Sched. 39, Part III, has effect from . 29th April 1996.

The amendments made by this section shall not apply in relation to an instrument which has been accidentally spoiled if an application for allowance under sec. 9 of the Management Act was made before 29th April 1996.

Fees and Stamp Duties applicable to Limited Companies under the Companies Acts

There is no stamp duty chargeable on the memorandum or articles of association.

Fees to be paid to the registrar of joint stock companies by a company having a capital divided into shares

For registration of a company — a fixed fee	£20.00
For registration of an increase in share capital of a company	Nil
For re-registration of a company under the Companies Act 1985, sec. 49, etc	£20.00
For registration of a copy of an annual return (filed electronically)	£15.00
For registration of a copy of an annual return	£30.00
For entering on the register the name of a company assumed by virtue of the passing of a special resolution by virtue of Companies Act 1985, sec. 28	£10.00

Fees to be paid to the registrar of joint stock companies by a company not having a capital divided into shares

For registration of a company — a fixed fee	£20.00
For registration of an increase in the number of members	Nil
For re-registration of a company under the Companies Act 1985, sec. 49, etc	£20.00
For registration of a copy of an annual return (filed electronically)	£15.00
For registration of a copy of an annual return	£30.00
For entering on the register the name of a company assumed by virtue of the passing of a special resolution by virtue of Companies Act 1985, sec. 28	£20.00

Capital duty

Capital duty, which was imposed by Finance Act 1973, Part V, at the rate of 1% on the value of assets contributed to a company in respect of shares of the company, was abolished by Finance Act 1988, sec. 141 with effect from 22nd March 1988.

Share transactions

(a) Loan capital — *see* Note *supra.*

(b) Bearer instruments — *see* Note *supra.*

(c) Purchase by a company of its own shares: Finance Act 1986, sec. 66(2) provided that with effect from 27th October 1986, stamp duty at the rate of 0.5% will be applied where a company purchases its own shares (see Note below).

(d) Schemes of reconstruction: a new and more restricted relief was introduced for company reconstructions by Finance Act 1986, sec. 75, with effect from 25th March 1986. For the conditions of relief, see Finance Act 1986, sec. 75(1)–(5).

(e) Acquisition of undertakings: *see* Finance Act 1986, sec. 76.

(f) Acquisition of target company's share capital: *see* Finance Act 1986, sec. 77 (see Note below).

(g) Depositary receipts: duty at the rate of 1.5% *i.e.* chargeable with effect from 27th October 1986 on consideration paid when U.K. shares or other marketable securities were transferred to a nominee whose business is to issue depositary receipts (Finance Act 1986, sec. 67).

Note: Finance Act 1986, sec. 66, 67, 76 and 77 have been prospectively repealed by Finance Act 1990, sec. 132 and Sched. 19, Pt. VI. See also the provisions of Finance Act 1996, Part VI, and Finance Act 1997, Part VII for amendment to stamp duty reserve tax.

Stamp duty reserve tax

The Finance Act 1986, Part IV, as amended provides for a charge at 0.5% to be imposed on certain transactions in securities which do not attract stamp duty.

Income Tax

THIS SECTION HAS BEEN REVISED UP TO BUDGET 2008.

The main features of income tax are given in the table which reports the rates and allowances from 2002/2003. Further details are given in the notes which follow, and which are referred to in the table by number.

RATES OF INCOME TAX

	2003/04	2004/05	2005/06	2006/07	2007/8	2008/9	2009/10
Lower Rate (Note 1)							
First £1,960	10%	—	—	—	—	—	—
First £2,020	—	10%	—	—	—	—	—
First £2,090	—	—	10%	—	—	—	—
First £2,150	—	—	—	10%	—	—	—
First £2,230	—	—	—	—	10%	—	—
First £2,230	—	—	—	—	—	N/A	—
First £2,240	—	—	—	—	—	—	N/A
Basic Rate (Note 1)							
Next £28,540	22%	—	—	—	—	—	—
Next £29,380	—	22%	—	—	—	—	—
Next £30,310	—	—	22%	—	—	—	—
Next £31,149	—	—	—	22%	—	—	—
Next £32,370	—	—	—	—	22%	—	—
Next £36,000	—	—	—	—	—	20%	—
Next £37,400	—	—	—	—	—	—	20%
Higher Rates (Note 1)							
Over £30,500	40%	—	—	—	—	—	—
Over £31,400	—	40%	—	—	—	—	—
Over £32,400	—	—	40%	—	—	—	—
Over £33,300	—	—	—	40%	—	—	—
Over £34,600	—	—	—	—	40%	—	—
Over £36,000	—	—	—	—	—	40%	—
Over £37,400	—	—	—	—	—	—	40%
Higher Rates (Note 1)							
Over £150,000	—	—	—	—	—	—	50%

2009/10	Tax band:	Rate of tax
Savings rate on savings income only	£1-£2,440	10%
Basic rate	£1-£37,400	20%
Higher rate	Over £37,4800	40%

The savings rate only applies if non-savings income is covered by allowances and does not exceed the savings rate band. Savings income generally consists of interest received from bank and building society deposits. Dividends continue to be taxed at 10% within the basic rate band, or 32.5%

Allowances

	2003/04	2004/05	2005/06	2006/07	2007/08	2008/09	2009/10
Personal Allowance (Note 2)	£	£	£	£	£	£	£
(Under 65)	4,615	4,745	4,895	5,035	5,225	6,035	6,475
(65–74)	6,610	6,830	7,090	7,280	7,550	9,030	9,490
(75 and over)	6,720	6,950	7,220	7,420	7,690	9,180	9,640
Income Limit (65 and over)	18,300	18,900	19,500	20,100	20,900	21,800	22,900
Married Couple's Allowance (Note 3)							
minimum allowance	2150	2,210	2,280	2,350	2,440	2,540	2,670
(Elder spouse born before 6/4/1935)	5,565	5,725	5,905	6,065	6,285	6,535	N/A
(Elder spouse 75 and over)	5,635	5,795	5,975	6,135	6,365	6,625	6.965
Income Limit (65 and over)	18,300	18,900	19,500	20,100	20,900	21,800	22,900
Additional Personal Allowance for Children (Note 4)	—	—	—	—	—	—	—
Children's Tax Credit (Note 7)	—	—	—	—	—	—	—
Baby rate	—	—	—	—	—	—	—
Widow's Bereavement Allowance (Note 5)	—	—	—	—	—	—	—
Blind Person's Allowance (Note 6)	1,510	1,560	1,610	1,660	1,730	1,800	1,890

Notes on tables

1. Lower, basic and higher rates (1973/74 onwards)

From 6th April 1993 dividends are taxed at 20%. From 6th April 1996, income from savings and distributions are also taxed at 20%. From 6th April 1999 dividends only carry a special 10% tax credit with other savings income continuing to be taxed at 20%. Where an individual is not subject to higher rate tax, the tax credit is deemed to satisfy any liability to the basic rate. From April 2010 a rate of Income Tax of 50% will apply to income over £150,000.

2. Personal allowance

For 1990/91 *et seq.* personal allowance replaced the single person's allowance.

A higher rate of allowance is available where a person is aged 65 or over. Where the individual's total income exceeds an income limit, that higher personal allowance is reduced by one-half of the excess until the allowance is the same as the ordinary personal allowance. From April 2010 the personal allowance will be reduced for incomes over £100,000 tapering down to zero.

3. Married couple's allowance

This allowance is available from 2000/01 for a claimant who is, at any time in the year of assessment, a married man whose wife is living with him, and where at least one of them was born before 6th April 1935. From December 2005 this allowance may be claimed by registered civil partners if one partner was born before 6 April 1935, in which case it is claimed by the partner with the highest inocme for the tax year concerned.

Where the husband's (or the higher earner's) total income exceeds the income limit this allowance is reduced by one- half of the excess (less any reduction made in the claimant's personal allowance age increase) until the allowance is reduced to the minimum allowance . Income tax relief on this allowance is givne at 10%, but as a reduction in the claiment's tax liability, not as a reduction in total income.

For 1990/91 to 1999/00 this allowance was also available to claimants under the age of 65. Income tax relief on this allowance was restricted to 20% for 1994/95, 15% for 1995/96 to 1998/99 and 10% for 1999/00.

Where a claimant marries during a tax year, the allowance is reduced by one-twelfth of each fiscal month of the year ending before the date of marriage.

From 1993/94 and subsequent years, a wife may claim half the married couple's allowance or the husband and wife may jointly elect for the whole allowance to be given to the wife.

In the 2009/10 tax year all in the category of elder spouse 75 and over will become 75 and will therefore be entitled to the age 75 and over allowance.

4. Additional child allowance

For 2000/01 and subsequent tax years this allowance is no longer available.

For 1999/00 and earlier tax years this allowance could be claimed where the claimant was not entitled to the married allowance, or was married but the wife was totally physically or mentally handicapped throughout the year. The child must meet certain conditions and no other person may claim relief in respect of the child.

Income tax relief on this allowance was restricted to 20% for 1994/95, 15% for 1995/96 to 1998/99 and 10% for 1999/00.

5. Widow's bereavement allowance

Where a married man, whose wife was living with him, died before 6th April 2000, his widow was given an allowance from her total income in the year of death and for the following year provided she did not remarry before the beginning of that year.

This allowance is not available for deaths on or after 6th April 2000.

Income tax relief on this allowance was restricted to 20% for 1994/95, 15% for 1995/96 to 1998/99 and 10% for 1999/00 to 2000/01.

6. Blind person's allowance

A claimant (a single person, or either of two spouses) must be registered as blind, but HMRC will by concession allow the relief in the previous tax year if evidnece of blindness had already been obtained by the edn of that year. If both spouses are blind, the allowance applies to each. The allowance is given in addition to the personal allowance and reduces the taxpayer's total income. .

7. Children's Tax Credit

Children's Tax Credit was an income tax relief for people with children. It was introduced by the Income and Corporation Taxes Act 1988, s 257AA and began on 6th April 2001. There was an additional tax credit for families with a baby born on or after 6th April 2002 in the tax year of their child's birth.

In April 2003 the Children's Tax Credit was replaced by the Child Tax Credit, introduced by the Tax Credits Act 2002, s 1(1).

Retirement annuities and personal pension schemes

The provisions under secs. 226–229 of the Income and Corporation Taxes Act 1970 for retirement annuity contracts for the self-employed and those in non-pensionable employment are replaced with effect from 30th June 1988 by personal pension schemes (secs. 18–57 and Sched. 2, as amended by Finance Act 1988, secs. 54 and 55).

Retirement annuity schemes which are contracted before 30th June 1988 will continue to be dealt with under the existing provisions of secs. 620–629 ICTA 1988. The personal pension scheme provisions incorporate many of the features of those existing provisions.

Limits of relief

(a) Retirement annuity contracts

The following table summarises the maximum premium relief available from 1982/83 to 1986/1987.

Year of Birth	Percentage of individual's net relevant earnings
1934 or later	17½%
1916 to 1933	20
1914 or 1915	21
1912 or 1913	24
1910 or 1911	26½%
1908 or 1909	29½%
1907 or earlier	32½%

For 1987/88 and subsequent years the overall limit is $17\frac{1}{2}\%$ of net relevant earnings increased for older individuals as follows:

Age range at beginning of year of assessment	Percentage
51 to 55	20
56 to 60	$22\frac{1}{2}$
61 or more	$27\frac{1}{2}$

(b) Personal pension plans

The maximum amount for which relief is available is $17\frac{1}{2}\%$ of 'net relevant earnings', increased for older individuals as follows:

Age range at beginning of year of assessment	Percentage
36 to 45	20
46 to 50	25
51 to 55	30
56 to 60	35
61 or more	40

The permitted maximum net relevant earnings are as follows:

	£
1988/89	60,000
1989/90	60,000
1990/91	64,800
1991/92	71,400
1992/93	75,000
1993/94	75,000
1994/95	76,800
1995/96	78,600
1996/97	82,200
1997/98	84,000
1998/99	87,600
1999/00	90,600
2000/01	91,800
2001/02	95,400
2002/03	97,200
2003/04	99,000
2004/05	102,000
2005/06	105,600

From April 2006 the pension schemes earnings cap ceases. There will be two controls on an individual's savings:

	Annual Allowance.	Lifetime Allowance
2006/7	215,000	1,500,000
2007/8	225,000	1,600,000
2008/9	235,000	1,650,000
2009/10	255,000	1,750,000

Capital Gains Tax

Capital gains tax (CGT) was introduced by the Finance Act 1965 and commenced on 6th April of that year. It relates to gains in a year of assessment (*i.e.* a year ending on 5th April) accruing to individuals, personal representatives and trustees. The Capital Gains Tax Act 1979 (CGTA 1979) was re-enacted in the Taxation of Chargeable Gains Act 1992 (TCGA 1992) which contains the main current provisions in consolidated form. There are further provisions in subsequent Finance Acts.

Major changes in the scope of the tax were introduced by the Finance Act 1988. The original base date of 6th April 1965 was replaced by 31st March 1982 subject to the detailed provisions of assets held on 31st March 1982.

From 10th April 1962 to 5th April 1971 certain short-term capital gains were charged to income tax under Sched. D, Case VII. From 6th April 1971, both short- and long-term gains have been chargeable to capital gains tax. Accumulated short-term losses at 5th April 1971 are available thereafter for offset against capital gains generally (TCGA 1992, Sched. 11, para. 12).

Exemptions

The following is an abridged summary of the main exemptions or partial exemptions for capital gains tax purposes.

Private dwelling houses (where sole or main residence), private motor vehicles, savings certificates, charities, patent rights, foreign currency for personal expenditure, certain property transfers, Treasury listed government and public corporation securities (pre 2nd July 1986, exemption only if securities held for more than 12 months), tangible movable assets sold from 1989/90 onwards for £6,000 or less with marginal relief for sale proceeds exceeding £6,000. (From 1982/83 – 1988/89, limit was £3,000.)

Reference should be made to TCGA 1992 and subsequent Finance Acts for more details.

General reliefs

Reliefs are available for such matters as roll-over and hold-over relief for gifts and disposals of certain assets, roll-over relief on reinvestment in shares (entrepreneurial relief), investments in EIS companies/VCTs, etc.

Retirement relief ceased to apply in respect of disposals after 5th April 2003.

Indexation allowance

For disposals after 5th April 1982 (31st March 1982 for companies), the gain arrived at by deducting allowable expenditure from the amount realised or deemed to be realised on the disposal, is termed a "gross gain". From this "gross gain" there is to be deducted an "indexation allowance", which is the aggregate of the "indexed rise" in each item of "relevant allowable expenditure" provided the asset has been held for the "qualifying period". Qualifying period not applicable on disposals after 5th April 1985.

Special provisions apply to the calculation of the allowance in relation to disposals involving assets held on 31st March 1982 where made on or after the "1985 date" or, again, on or after 6th April 1988.

For disposals after 5th April 1985, indexation allowance can be claimed by reference to market value at 31st March 1982.

Reference should be made to Finance Act 1982 as amended by Finance Act 1985 (sec. 68 and Sched. 19) for full details relating to formula for calculating indexation allowance.

For disposals after 30th November 1994, indexation allowance cannot create or augment a capital loss. Transitional relief will be available for indexation losses arising in the period 30th November 1993 to 5th April 1995.

For disposals after 5th April 1998, indexation allowance will be available up to April 1998 but not beyond.

Re-basing to 31st March 1982

General re-basing rule is that on a disposal after 5th April 1988 of an asset held on 31st March 1982, it is to be assumed that the asset was sold on 31st March 1982 by the person making the disposal and immediately acquired by him at its market value on that date. However, if a smaller capital gain or loss would have been made by using the original cost then cost rather than 31st March 1982 value must be used in calculating the gain/loss. It was possible to make an election to have all assets rebased to their 31st March 1982 values. Reference should be made to Finance Act 1988, sec 96(1)(2).

Taper relief

Major changes in the scope of the indexation allowance were introduced by the Finance Act 1998. Companies, which pay corporation tax on chargeable gains, are not affected by these reforms.

For assets disposed of after 5th April 1998 and which were held at that date, the indexation allowance will be available up to April 1998 but not beyond. No indexation allowance will be available on disposals of assets acquired on or after 1st April 1998.

For disposals after 5th April 1998, a chargeable gain will be progressively reduced (tapered) according to the length of time the asset has been held. See the table below.

GAINS ON BUSINESS ASSETS

Number of *complete* years after 5/4/978 which asset held	Percentage of gain chargeable			Equivalent tax rates for higher rate taxpayer (2000/01 only)
	1989/99 to 1999/00	2000/01 to 2001/02	2002/03	
0	100	100	100	40
1	92.5	87.5	50	35
2	85	75	25	30
3	77.5	50	25	20
4	70	25	25	10
5	62.5	25	25	10
6	55	25	25	10
7	47.5	25	25	10
8	40	25	25	10
9	32.5	25	25	10
10 or more	25	25	25	10

For disposals in 1998/99 and 1999/00 an additional bonus holding year in respect of business assets held at 17th March 1998 was given. This no longer applies for disposals in 2000/01 and subsequent years.

GAINS ON NON-BUSINESS ASSETS

Number of *complete* years after 5/4/978 which asset held	Percentage of gain chargeable	Equivalent tax rates for higher rate taxpayer
0	100	40
1	100	40
2	100	40
3	95	38
4	90	36
5	85	34
6	80	32
7	75	30
8	70	28
9	65	26
10	60	24

For disposals of non-business assets held at 17th March 1998 an additional bonus year is given.

Reference should be made to the Finance Act 1998, secs. 119–120 for full details.

A consequence of the new taper relief rules is that the previous pooling arrangements will no longer apply to shares and securities. Disposals after 5th April 1998 will be identified with acquisitions in the following order:

—same day acquisitions;

—acquisitions within the following 30 days;

—other acquisitions after 5th April 1998 on a last in/first out basis;

—any shares in the pool at 5th April 1998;

—any shares held at 5th April 1982;

—any shares held at 6th April 1965;

—(if necessary) subsequent acquisitions.

'Bed and breakfasting'

For disposals of shares on or after 17th March 1998, 'bed and breakfasting', i.e. selling shares to realise a gain or loss and then buying them back shortly afterwards, will no longer have the desired effect for tax purposes. Any shares of the same class in the same company sold and repurchased within a 30-day period will instead be matched, so that the shares sold cannot be identified with those already held.

Rates

For 1996/97 and subsequent years capital gains will come within the new self-assessment rules. Tax will be payable by 31st January immediately after the year of assessment to which it relates.

Prior to 1996/97, tax was payable by 1st December, immediately after the year of assessment to which it related (6th July for tax relating to 1979/80 or earlier).

For 1977/78 and earlier years, the total charge was (generally) limited to additional income tax and investment income surcharge payable by an individual on one-half of net capital gains for the year, if under £5,000, or if greater, £2,500 plus the excess over £5,000. Losses could be set against gains. For 1967/71 an individual was exempt if the gains less allowable losses were not more than £50; Capital gains tax was charged on any excess.

For 1977/78 to 1979/80 the rates at which capital gains tax was charged are as follows:

Total net gains for year of assessment	Tax Chargeable
Not exceeding £1,000	Nil
£1,001–£5,000	15% on excess gains over £1,000
£5,001–£9,499	£600 + 50% on excess gains over £5,000
£9,500 or more	all gains at 30%

"Alternative charge" provisions still to apply for 1977/78 if less tax payable than under new provisions.

The rates chargeable from 1980/81 to 1987/88 are as follows:

	Total net Gains	Tax chargeable
1980/81 and 1981/82	Not exceeding £3,000	Nil
	Over £3,000	30%
1982/83	Not exceeding £5,000	Nil
	Over £5,000	30%
1983/84	Not exceeding £5,300	Nil
	Over £5,300	30%
1984/85	Not exceeding £5,600	Nil
	Over £5,600	30%
1985/86	Not exceeding £5,900	Nil
	Over 5,900	30%
1986/87	Not exceeding £6,300	Nil
	Over £6,300	30%
1987/88	Not exceeding £6,600	Nil
	Over £6,600	30%

The exemption limits and rates chargeable from 1988/89 onwards are as follows:

Annual exemption limits

	Individuals	Trusts	Chattels
1990/91	£5,000	£2,500	£6,000
1991/92	£5,500	£2,750	£6,000
1992/93	£5,800	£2,900	£6,000
1993/94	£5,800	£2,900	£6,000
1994/95	£5,800	£2,900	£6,000
1995/96	£6,000	£3,000	£6,000
1996/97	£6,300	£3,150	£6,000
1997/98	£6,500	£3,250	£6,000
1998/99	£6,800	£3,400	£6,000
1999/00	£7,100	£3,550	£6,000
2000/01	£7,200	£3,600	£6,000
2001/02	£7,500	£3,750	£6,000
2002/03	£7,700	£3,850	£6,000
2003/04	£7,900	£3,950	£6,000
2004/05	£8,200	£4,100	£6,000
2005/06	£8,500	£4,250	£6,000
2006/07	£8,800	£4,400	£6,000
2007/08	£9,200	£4,600	£6,000
2008/09	£9,600	£4,800	£6,000
2009/10	£10,100	£5,050	£6,000

Rates of Tax

	Lower rate	Basic rate	Higher rate

(*a*)Individuals: Until 1991/92 the rate of capital gains tax was equivalent to the basic rate of income tax for the fiscal year. If income tax is chargeable at the higher rate in respect of any part of an individual's income for a year of assessment, the rate of capital gains tax is equivalent to the higher rate.

For 1992/93 to 1998/99, where no income tax is chargeable at the basic rate in respect of an individual's income but the amount on which he is chargeable to capital gains tax exceeds the unused part of his lower rate band, the rate of capital gains tax on that part of the amount chargeable to capital gains tax equal to the unused part of the lower rate band is equivalent to the lower rate. If, in the same circumstances, there is no such excess, the rate of capital gains tax equivalent to the lower rate applies to all the amount chargeable to capital gains tax.

From 1999/00 individuals chargeable at lower and basic rate tax for income tax purposes will be subject to capital gains tax at 20%. The rate for higher rate taxpayers will continue to be equivalent to the higher rate.

	Lower rate	Basic rate	Higher rate
1988/89 to 1991/92		25%	40%
1992/93	20%	25%	40%
1993/94	20%	25%	40%
1994/95	20%	25%	40%
1995/96	20%	25%	40%
1996/97	20%	24%	40%
1997/98	20%	23%	40%
1998/99	20%	23%	40%
1999/00	20%	20%	40%
2000/01	10%	20%	40%
2001/02	10%	20%	40%
2002/03	10%	20%	40%
2003/04	10%	20%	40%
2004/05	10%	20%	40%
2005/06	10%	20%	40%
2006/07	10%	20%	40%
2007/08	10%	20%	40%

(b) Trusts in general

1988/89 to 1995/96	25%
1996/97	24%
1997/98	23%
1998/99 onwards	34%

(c) Accumulation and discretionary trusts

1988/89 to 1995/96	35%
1996/97 onwards	34%

(d) Chattels: If the consideration exceeds the annual exemption figure, the chargeable gain is limited to five-thirds of the excess.

Corporation Tax

Corporation tax takes the place of income tax and profits tax for companies (and other corporate bodies and unincorporated associations) and operates generally as from 1966/67. Liability will normally first arise on profits and capital gains in the business year ending in the tax year 1965/66 and not by reference to the profits of the previous year.

Profits are generally to be calculated in accordance with income tax principles and include capital gains (less losses), interest and other charges on incomes as paid under deduction of income tax, which is then accounted for. Income tax was also deductible from dividends distributed up to 1972/73 and was paid over by the company.

Partnerships are still liable for income tax. The tax is not charged on the partnership, but on the individual partners, taking into account their respective profit shares.

Corporation tax is now generally payable within nine months from the end of the accounting period, although companies which make large profits are now required to pay in instalments.

The rate of tax was 40% for financial years 1964–67, $42^1/_2$% for 1967/68, 45% for 1968/70, 40% for 1970/73.

For the financial years 1973 to 1978 inclusive, the rate was increased to 52% with a small companies' rate of 42%. For the financial years 1979 to 1981, the full rate was retained at 52%, but the small companies' rate was reduced to 40%. For the financial year 1982 the full rate was 52%, and the small companies' rate 38%. The rates for the financial years 1983 to 1999 are as follows:

Financial year	Full rate	Small Companies' rate
1984	45%	30%
1985	40%	30%
1986	35%	29%
1987	35%	27%
1988	35%	25%
1989	35%	25%
1990	34%	25%
1991	33%	25%
1992	33%	25%
1993	33%	25%
1994	33%	25%
1995	33%	25%
1996	33%	24%
1997	31%	21%
1998	31%	21%
1999	30%	20%

From the financial year 2000 onwards a new starting rate of 10% was introduced as follows:

Financial year	Full rate	Small Companies' rate	Starting rate
2000	30%	20%	10%
2001	30%	20%	10%
2002	30%	20%	10%

However, from the financial year 2003 onwards, the starting rate was reduced to nil. For the financial year 2004, however, there have been changes. The nil rate still applies, but for distributions on or after 1 April 2004, a minimum rate of 19% applies where a company whose profits are below the threshold for the small companies' rate distributes profits to a non-company shareholder.

Marginal relief — starting rate

The upper and lower limits are as follows:

Financial year	Upper limit	Lower limit	Marginal fraction
2000	£50,000	£10,000	1/40
2001	50,000	10,000	1/40
2002	50,000	10,000	19/400
2003	50,000	10,000	19/400
2004	50,000	10,000	19/400
2005	50,000	10,000	19/400
2006	50,000	10,000	19/400

Marginal relief — small companies rate

The small companies upper and lower limits are as follows:

Financial year	Upper limit	Lower limit	Marginal fraction
1975	£50,000	£30,000	3/20
1976	65,000	40,000	4/25
1977	85,000	50,000	1/7
1978	100,000	60,000	3/20
1979	130,000	70,000	7/50
1980	200,000	80,000	2/25
1981	225,000	90,000	2/25
1982	500,000	100,000	7/200
1983	500,000	100,000	1/20
1984	500,000	100,000	3/80
1985	500,000	100,000	1/40
1986	500,000	100,000	3/200
1987	500,000	100,000	1/50
1988	500,000	100,000	1/40
1989	750,000	150,000	1/40
1990	1,000,000	200,000	9/400
1991	1,250,000	250,000	1/50
1992	1,250,000	250,000	1/50
1993	1,250,000	250,000	1/50
1994	1,500,000	300,000	1/50
1995	1,500,000	300,000	1/50
1996	1,500,000	300,000	9/400
1997	1,500,000	300,000	1/40
1998	1,500,000	300,000	1/40
1999	1,500,000	300,000	1/40
2000	1,500,000	300,000	1/40
2001	1,500,000	300,000	1/40
2002	1,500,000	300,000	11/400
2003	1,500,000	300,000	11/400
2004	1,500,000	300,000	11/400
2005	1,500,000	300,000	11/400
2006	1,500.000	300,000	11/400
2007	1,500.000	300,000	11/400
2008	1,500.000	300,000	1/400
2009	1,500,000	300,000	1/400

Sec. 74 Finance Act 1987 enacts the reform of corporation tax on chargeable gains. Its effect is to remove the distinction hitherto made between income and capital profits.

Prior to 17th March 1987, companies' capital profits were taxed at 30%. From this date onwards companies' chargeable gains are included in full in taxable profits.

Advance corporation tax (ACT) was payable when dividends or distributions were made. The following is a summary of the ACT rates:

	Rates
1973/74	3/7ths
1974/75	33/67ths
1975/76	35/65ths
1967/77	35/65ths
1977/78	34/66ths
1978/79	33/67ths
1979/80	3/7ths
1980/81	3/7ths
1981/82	3/7ths
1982/83	3/7ths
1983/84	3/7ths
1984/85	3/7ths
1985/86	3/7ths
1986/87	29/71sts
1987/88	27/73rds
1988/89	1/3rd
1989/90	1/3rd
1990/91	1/3rd
1991/92	1/3rd
1992/93	1/3rd
1993/94	9/31sts
1994/95	1/4
1995/96	1/4
1996/97	1/4
1997/98	1/4
1998/99	1/4

Advance corporation tax is set against the company's total corporation tax liability. No income tax is deducted from dividends.

Advance corporation tax payments are abolished from 6th April 1999.

Inheritance Tax

Cumulative Chargeable Transfers (gross) £	Lifetime rate of tax %	Cumulative tax £	Death rate of tax %	Cumulative tax £
Commencing 17th March 1986				
Nil–£71,000	Nil	Nil	Nil	Nil
£71,001–£95,000	15	3,600	30	7,200
£95,001–£129,000	17½	9,550	35	19,100
£129,001–£164,000	20	16,550	40	33,100
£164,001–£206,000	22½	26,000	45	52,000
£206,001–£257,000	25	38,750	50	77,500
£257,001–£317,000	27½	55,250	55	110,500
Over £317,000	30		60	
After 17th March 1987				
Nil–£90,000	Nil	Nil	Nil	Nil
£90,001–£140,000	15	7,500	30	15,000
£140,001–£220,000	20	23,500	40	47,000
£220,001–£330,000	25	51,000	50	102,000
Over £330,000	30		60	
Lifetime rates do not apply to gifts between individuals				
After 14th March 1988				
Nil £110,000	Nil		Nil	
Over £110,000	20		40	
After 5th April 1989				
Nil–£118,000	Nil		Nil	
Over £118,000	20		40	
After 5th April 1990				
Nil–£128,000	Nil		Nil	
Over £128,000	20		40	
After 5th April 1991				
Nil–£140,000	Nil		Nil	
Over £140,000	20		40	
After 9th March 1992				
Nil–£150,000	Nil		Nil	
Over £150,000	20		40	
After 5th April 1995				
Nil—£154,000	Nil		Nil	
Over £154,000	20		40	
After 5th April 1996				
Nil–£200,000	Nil		Nil	
Over £200,000	20		40	

Cumulative Chargeable Transfers (gross) £	Lifetime rate of tax %	Cumulative tax £	Death rate of tax %	Cumulative tax £
After 5th April 1997				
Nil–£215,000	Nil		Nil	
Over £215,000	20		40	
After 5th April 1998				
Nil–£223,000	Nil		Nil	
Over £223,000	20		40	
After 5th April 1999				
Nil–£231,000	Nil		Nil	
Over £231,000	20		40	
After 5th April 2000				
Nil–£234,000	Nil		Nil	
Over £234,000	20		40	
After 5th April 2001				
Nil–£242,000	Nil		Nil	
Over £242,000	20		40	
After 5th April 2002				
Nil–£250,000	Nil		Nil	
Over £250,000	20		40	
After 5th April 2003				
Nil–£250,000	Nil		Nil	
Over £250,000	20		40	
After 5th April 2004				
Nil–£263,000	Nil		Nil	
Over £263,000	20		40	
After 5th April 2005				
Nil–£275,000	Nil		Nil	
Over £275,000	20		40	
After 5th April 2006				
Nil–£285,000	Nil		Nil	
Over £285,000	20		40	
After 6th April 2007				
Nil–£300,000	Nil		Nil	
Over £300,000	20		40	
After 6th April 2008				
Nil–£312,000	Nil		Nil	
Over £312,000	20		40	
After 6th April 2009				
Nil–£325,000	Nil		Nil	
Over £325,000	20		40	

Tapering relief

The value of the estate on death is taxed as the top slice of cumulative transfers in the seven years before death. Transfers on or within seven years of death are taxed on their value at the date of the gift on the death rate scale, but using the scale in force at the date of death, subject to the following taper:

No of years between gift and death	Percentage of full charge at death rates
0–3	100
3–4	80
4–5	60
5–6	40
6–7	20

List of Principal Statutory Instruments Included

.